Rigour and Reason

Essays in honour of
Hans Vilhelm Hansen

RIGOUR AND REASON

ESSAYS IN HONOUR OF HANS VILHELM HANSEN

Edited by

J. Anthony Blair & Christopher W. Tindale

Editorial and formatting assistance provided by Tamilyn Mulvaney.

Photograph on back cover of Hans V. Hansen by Madeleine Hansen, used by
permission.

ISBN 978-0-920233-92-4

WSIA

Windsor Studies
In Argumentation

CONTENTS

INTRODUCTION

Built in the centre of Copenhagen, and noted for its equestrian stairway, the Rundetaarn (Round Tower), was intended as an astronomical observatory. Part of a complex of buildings that once included a university library, it affords expansive views of the city in every direction, towering above what surrounds it. The metaphor of the towering figure, who sees what others might not, whose vantage point allows him to visualize how things fit together, and who has an earned-stature of respect and authority, fits another Danish stalwart[1], Hans Vilhelm Hansen, whose contributions to the fields of informal logic and argument theory have earned the gratitude of his colleagues, and inspired this collection of essays, written to express the appreciation of its authors and of the many, many colleagues they represent.

Hans Hansen is a man of many parts, and known for his reticence. In this introduction we limit our biographical details to a sketch of his scholarly progress. Moving from Denmark to Canada as a young boy, Hans began an engagement with his adopted country that saw him live in many parts of several provinces, settling for periods of time in both Southern and Northern Ontario, Manitoba and Newfoundland. He stopped in various places long enough to gain a first-class education as a philosopher, first a B.A. earned at Lakehead University in Thun-

---

1. The term is a variant of the now obsolete *stalworth,* which aptly (for us) combined both *stæl* '*place*' and *weorth* '*worth.*'

der Bay, Ontario ("as far north as I could get"), next an M.A. under the Churchlands at the University of Manitoba, and then outside of Canada at Wayne State University in Detroit, for another M.A., and, in 1990, his a Ph.D.

The proximity of Wayne State to the University of Windsor made for one of those strokes of serendipity that was to change both the life of the scholar in question and also the field in which he has gone on to have a substantial impact. In 1988 Hansen became the assistant to the editors of *Informal Logic*. Twelve years later, he was a co-editor of the journal, a position he held until stepping back in 2014. During the decade following the completion of his doctorate he held temporary teaching positions at Brock and McMaster Universities, and did research at the University of Amsterdam. In 2001, he accepted an appointment as an assistant professor of philosophy at the University of Windsor and there rose to the rank of Professor. He served a term as Director of Windsor's Centre for Research in Reasoning, Argumentation and Rhetoric at Windsor (2008-2010), and he became Head of Windsor's Philosophy Department in 2017.

Professor Hansen has always taken his teaching seriously and is proud to have introduced his students to the pleasure and rigours of academic work, especially in his courses in analytical philosophy, ethics, and, of course, argumentation. He gained a reputation as an entertaining but demanding professor, with a penchant for stressing details and promoting the rewards of reading texts closely in order to gain a thorough understanding of the ideas involved.

This attention to details and thoroughness characterizes the scholar and the man himself as much as it does the teacher. The range of interests that occupies Hansen's scholarship is reflected in the diversity of subjects addressed by the essays in this volume. He is a student of the history of argumentation, and he has drawn attention to ideas and figures whose importance might not otherwise be recognized in that history. His acknowledged expertise on the nature and history of fallacies is reflected in the invitation from the *Stanford Encyclopedia of Philosophy* (*SEP*) to write their entry on Fallacies. He has published significant work on the nature of informal logic, including conductive arguments and argument schemes. And he has led important research ventures on the nature of presumption and burden of proof and on rhetorical speeches, particularly those of the Canadian Métis figure Louis Riel.

More needs to be said about each of these areas lest their importance pass unappreciated.

John Locke (1632-1704), Richard Whately (1787-1863) and John Stuart Mill (1806-1873) are all figures whose writings bear directly on the historical development of argumentation studies. Locke through his observations about some of the *"ad"* fallacies, Mill through his *A System of Logic* (1843) and Whately through both his *Elements of Logic* (1826) and *Elements of Rhetoric* (1828). But Hans Hansen has distilled from these sources far more than what is commonly recognized. He sees each of them as important voices in an unfolding story of the developing relationships between logic, rhetoric and argumentation. His work on Whately and arguments involving authority (2006), for example, does more than just expose Whately's ideas to critical scrutiny; it also takes a wider perspective on his work and argues that he occupies an important developmental ground between his predecessor Locke and more contemporary views of the argument from authority.

Similarly, Hansen's varied approaches to the work of Mill address not only the quality of Mill's own proposals in *A System of Logic*, but also argue (2014) that Mill needs to be evaluated in the context of the growing interest in informal logic and argumentation theory, and he compares Mill's broad sense of logic with Blair and Johnson's version of informal logic.

Such studies, then, provide more than just historical windows onto the work of major historical figures; they reveal those figures as having contemporary value in giving early voice to issues that have subsequently grown in importance and garnered considerable attention. Hansen's larger argument is that such attention, while necessary, is incomplete without sufficient appreciation of these historical precedents.

A further strand of Hansen's research is a focus on the theory of informal logic, specifically as a logic. We see this particularly in the book-length study that is currently in progress on methods of informal logic. Here, his method is to canvas major approaches to informal logic, as seen in the work of theorists like Alec Fisher, Trudy Govier and Douglas Walton (among many others), identify the distinctive features involved in each account and weigh their strengths and weaknesses. This promises to be the first extended comparative study of such central figures, but the work is already prefigured in papers like (2010; 2011; and 2012), where accounts dealing with the *logic* of informal logic are evaluated. Also noteworthy here is the informal logic bibliography that Hansen has collected (1990) and which constitutes a concerted attempt to draw attention to an important body of related literature.

The work with which Hansen's name is most readily associated is that on the history of fallacies and fallacy theory *per se*, from papers like (1996) and (2002) and collaborations with John Woods (1997, 2001), to the seminal anthology with Robert C. Pinto (1995), and onto the equally seminal *SEP* essay published in 2015 and revised in 2019. In the latter, he draws attention to the importance of such work: "Being able to detect and avoid fallacies has been viewed as a supplement to criteria of good reasoning. The knowledge of fallacies is needed to arm us against the most enticing missteps we might take with arguments." Unsurprisingly, he enlists the agreement to this proposition of Aristotle and the early nineteenth century logicians Richard Whately and John Stuart Mill.

Readers may be less familiar with Hansen's interest in historically significant argumentative speeches. Impressed by the close attention paid to important speeches in their history by his American colleagues, he thought Canadians should follow this practice too. He undertook to lead the way through a study of Louis Riel's speeches to the jury at his trial for treason. Riel was the Canadian Métis leader of the Northwest Rebellion of 1884-85 in what was to become the province of Saskatchewan, and his trial and execution were pivotal events in the westward expansion of the Dominion of Canada. Hansen edited a volume in 2014 that grew out of an interdisciplinary conference he organized at the University of Windsor in 2010. The project involves more than a simple reflection on the work of this central Canadian figure; it also includes annotated versions of Riel's two speeches, both texts prepared by Hansen himself (2014: 25-71). The care and detail of the preparations are evident to even the cursory reader. But he also paid attention to the argumentative force of these speeches and, thus, to strategies of argumentation employed at a formative moment in Canadian history.

As important as all the preceding discussion is to a full assessment of the contributions Hans V. Hansen has made to argumentation theory and informal logic, it may be seen to pale against the role he has played as an editor: of anthologies, of books of original research, of conference proceedings, and of journals. This kind of work is often overlooked and under-appreciated, but it is difficult to imagine the state of argumentation theory as a field of study without Hansen's particular contribution, in part because of the vast amount of material involved. There are thus so many examples to illustrate our point that we run the risk of doing injustice to this accomplishment by being able to mention only a few.

His editorial work at *Informal Logic* has already been noted; it testifies to the hand Hansen has played in directing important work to the attention of the larger community. Something similar holds for the editing of a series of the proceedings from conferences of the Ontario Society for the Study of Argumentation. Recent sets of these proceedings have been guest edited, but the early sets—the first seven—all bear the mark of a person bringing his editorial skills again to the task at hand. These proceedings now live (and they are very much alive) in an online archive hosted by the University of Windsor. At time of writing, these papers have been accessed and downloaded almost 184,000 times (that is not a typographical error). Someone who sets such access in motion cannot be judged too lightly.

The anthology *Fallacies: Classical and Contemporary Readings*, co-edited with Pinto in 1995, is the go-to text for anyone working on the history and nature of the fallacies. The judicious choice of readings, particularly in the classical section, bears all the signs of the scholar whose work on the history of fallacies we discussed above. The template for this success has been repeated in *Presumptions and Burdens of Proof* (2019). While it is co-edited with three other important scholars, it is clear that Hansen has taken the lead, as is again evident from the list of classical sources and the choices involved. Collecting, collating, and editing such work can be laborious at times, but no field can flourish without both the breadth and depth of materials that such anthologies provide. The care for detail that characterized his approach to literature in his teaching is evident and even more pronounced in his editing of comparable material.

While we have stressed the historical selections in the anthologies, they also contain original works invited by the editors. Editing the work of a living author whose protective impulses naturally guard the process obviously involves skills not required for the classical material. The same holds for editing sets of selected essays by his contemporaries (Pinto, 2001; Kock 2017). The multiple duties that make up the role of the successful editor are amply displayed in these editions.

Scholar, bibliographer, editor, and, far from least, conference organizer. Of the 12 conferences of the Ontario Society for the Study of Argumentation that have taken place, including that in

2020, Hansen has been the lead organizer in all but one. More than this, he is in many senses the principal parent of these conferences, taking up the initiative at the suggestion of others and hosting the first conference at Brock University in 1995. This involved as much design as organization, deciding on the format of papers and commentators that would prove so successful in attracting scholars from around the world to return again and again. He took great care in matching appropriate commentators with authors, especially for students, and his creation of a prize for the leading student paper motivated the early work of a generation of young scholars who are now taking on leadership roles in our field. Furthermore, a crucial aspect of the organization of many of the conferences, particularly in their early instantiations, involved reaching out to cognate disciplines like Education, Rhetoric, and Computer Science, where research on similar issues was being conducted on parallel lines. Bringing those communities into fruitful conversations, many of which continue still today is a value to the field that is beyond measure. Simply put, much of the research that has been done in argumentation theory since 1995 would not exist if Hansen were taken out of the equation, and things would have developed on very different tracks, if at all.

What must not be forgotten is that so much of his contribution to our field has consisted, along with his own research, of the unselfish promotion of the work of others. For instance, the important essays of the late Robert Pinto would not be so well known had Hansen not been midwife to their assembly in a book. The editing and the conference organizing have been motivated by his utterly altruistic interest in the welfare of informal logic and argumentation.

So, the towering figure honoured in the essays that follow has earned the respect and affection that these papers convey. Here is an architect of our field who has worked tirelessly, and often invisibly, to build so much of what we cherish today: a vibrant field with a rich history and an expansive literature.

REFERENCES:

Hansen, Hans V. (2019). "Fallacies" *Stanford Encyclopaedia of Philosophy.* (1st edition, 2015).

Hansen, Hans V. (2014). *Riel's Defence: Perspectives on his Speeches.* Montreal: McGill-Queen's University Press.

Hansen, Hans V. (2014). "Mill, informal logic, and argumentation." In Anton Loizides (Ed.), *John Stuart Mill's* A System of Logic: *Critical Appraisals*, pp. 192-217. London: Routledge.

Hansen, Hans V. (2012) "An enquiry into the methods of informal logic." In Henrique Jales Ribeiro (Ed.) *Inside Arguments: Logic and the Study of Argumentation*, pp. 101-116. Newcastle upon Tyne: Cambridge Scholars Publishing.

Hansen, Hans V. (2011). "Are there methods of informal logic?" in Frank Zenker (Ed.) *Proceedings of the Argumentation: Cognition and Community conference, Windsor 2011.* Windsor, ON: CD Rom

Hansen, Hans V. (2010). "Using argument schemes as a method of informal logic." In Frans van Eemeren et al. (Eds.). *Proceedings of the 7th ISSA Conference*, pp. 738-749. Amsterdam: SicSat.

Hansen, Hans V. (2006). "Whately on arguments involving authority," *Informal Logic*, 26: 319-340.

Hansen, Hans V. (2002). "The straw thing of fallacy theory: The standard definition of 'fallacy'," *Argumentation*, 16: 133-155.

Hansen, Hans V. (1996). "Aristotle, Whately, and the taxonomy of fallacies." In Dov M. Gabbay and Hans J. Olbach (Eds.) *Practical Reasoning: International Conference on Formal and Applied Practical Reasoning*, pp. 318-330. Berlin: Springer.

Hansen, Hans V. (1990). "An informal logic bibliography," *Informal Logic*, 12: 155-184.

Hans V. Hansen, Fred Kauffeld, James B. Freeman, Lilian Bermejo-Luque (Eds.). (2019) . *Presumptions and Burdens of*

Proof: An Anthology of Argumentation and the Law. Tuscaloosa, AB: University of Alabama Press.

Hansen, Hans V. and Robert C. Pinto. (1995). *Fallacies: Classical and Contemporary Readings*. University Park: Penn State Press.

Kock, Christian. (2017). *Deliberative Rhetoric: Arguing about Doing*. Hans V. Hansen (Ed). Windsor, ON: WSIA.

Pinto, Robert C. (2001). *Argument, Inference and Dialectic*. Hans V. Hansen (Ed.). Dordrecht: Kluwer.

Woods, John and Hans V. Hansen. (2001). "The Subtleties of Aristotle on non-cause," *Logique et Analyse*, Vol 176: 395-414.

Woods, John and Hans V. Hansen. (1997). "Hintikka on Aristotle's fallacies," *Synthese*, 113: 217-239.

CHAPTER 1.

ARISTOTLE'S CONCEPTION OF A FALLACY

DAVID HITCHCOCK

ABSTRACT: Woods and Hansen (1997) showed that, contrary to Hintikka (1987), the fallacies in Aristotle's *Sophistical Refutations* are not *strongly* relative to refutation-oriented question-and-answer dialogues, but are failures to satisfy Aristotle's conditions for being a deduction. They are however *weakly* relative to them, in the sense of being the fallacies that one finds in them. Aristotle finds quite different fallacies in public speeches and in attempts at proof. Aristotle has a generic conception of mistaken reasoning, a conception that includes false assumptions as well as inferential errors (including the error of thinking that something does not follow when it does).

KEYWORDS: Aristotle, disputation, fallacies, Hans Hansen, proof, refutation, rhetoric, John Woods

Hans Hansen is the historian *par excellence* of informal logic – now re-baptized as "philosophy of argumentation".[1] Hansen's publications on Aristotle (Hansen 1996a; Woods and Hansen 1997, 2001), Locke (Hansen 1998), Whately (Hansen 1996a, 1996b, 1998, 2006a, 2015), and John Stuart Mill (Hansen 1997, 2006b, 2007, 2014) provide careful and nuanced interpretations of major contributions in the European philosophical tradition to understanding and evaluating arguments. His co-edited books on fallacies (Hansen and Pinto 1995) and on presumptions and burden of proof (Hansen et al. 2019) conveniently unite the major historical texts on these topics with a number of contemporary contributions. Collectively, these publications show that informal logic or "philosophy of argumentation" has a long and distinguished history.

A particularly significant contribution is the challenge by Hansen and John Woods to a now fashionable interpretation of the fallacies in Aristotle's *Sophistical Refutations* as violations of the rules of a question-and-answer dialogue game, rather than as logical mistakes. Charles Hamblin initiated this interpretation, as part of his project to relocate the supposedly "debased, worn-out and dogmatic" (Hamblin 1970, 12) textbook treatments of the traditional fallacies in the context of systems of rules for conversations. Aristotle's fallacies, he maintains, are analysable within such a "formal dialectic" in a way that they would not be in formal logic (254-255). Jaakko Hintikka intensified this interpretation: "Instead of being mistaken inference-types, the traditional "fallacies" were mistakes or breaches of rules in the knowledge-seeking questioning games which were practiced in Plato's Academy and later in Aristotle's Lyceum" (Hintikka 1987, 211). Hintikka's interpretation is particularly plausible with

1. See at https://wcp2018.sched.com/ the program of the 24th World Congress of Philosophy, sponsored by the Fédération Internationale des Sociétés de Philosophie (FISP), which included two sessions on philosophy of argumentation.

respect to Aristotle's fallacies of many questions and of begging the question, whose very names seem to tie them inextricably to the question-answer dialogues in which his so-called "sophistical refutations" were alleged to occur.

Woods and Hansen (1997) showed that, contrary to appearances, Aristotle did not conceive of these fallacies as violations of rules for question-and-answer conversations, but as failures of an apparent syllogism to satisfy a condition for being a syllogism or of an apparent contradiction to be a contradiction. In particular, Aristotle required that each premiss (Greek *protasis*) of a syllogism say one thing about one thing. The fallacy of many questions is to lay down a premiss (asked for by the questioner and granted by the answerer) that looks as if it says one thing about one thing but does not. One of Aristotle's examples is an argument with a premiss that Callias and Themistocles are musical, which someone might be tempted to grant if by chance Callias and Themistocles had the same name – say, Callistocles. The error involved in using as a premiss that Callistocles is musical may occur not only in question-and-answer dialogues but also in other contexts, even in solo reasoning. Thus the mistake does not consist in violating a rule for question-and-answer refutation-oriented dialogues, nor is it a mistake that can only occur in such dialogues.

The fallacy of begging the question is to get from the answerer *as a premiss* the contradictory of the answerer's thesis, i.e., the very thing that the questioner is trying to infer from what the answerer grants, or something synonymous with or equivalent to it.[2] This is a fallacy because one of the conditions for being a syllogism is that the conclusion is something other than any of

2. Aristotle also treats as forms of begging the question using a universal premiss to derive a particular conclusion that follows from it, using a particular premiss to derive the corresponding universal statement, and using two premisses as a basis for deriving their conjunction (*Topics* VIII.13.163^{b}1-8). Woods and Hansen (1997) discuss these forms of begging the question on pages 229-230.

the premisses. If one includes in the premisses from which one derives a conclusion something that amounts to the very conclusion that one derives, the argument may look like a syllogism but it is not. This mistake of deriving something from itself may occur in question-and-answer refutation-oriented dialogues, but it is not peculiar to them. Again, the fallacy is not a violation of the rules of question-and-answer refutation, nor is it a mistake that can only occur in such dialogues.[3]

Aristotle tells us (*Sophistical Refutations* 1.164ᵃ21-22) that sophistical refutations appear to be refutations but are misreasonings (*paralogismoi*), not refutations. A refutation is a deduction (*sullogismos*, traditionally translated as 'syllogism') along with a contradiction of its conclusion (1.165ᵃ2-3); in a dialectical setting, either the answerer's thesis contradicts the conclusion or a contradiction is deduced from the answerer's thesis and concessions.[4] There are thus two main ways in which something that looks like a refutation can be a "misreasoning" – by failing to be a deduction and by failing to deduce a contradiction. A deduction is an argument "from some things laid down so as to say of necessity through the things laid down something other than the things laid down" (*Sophistical Refutations* 1.165ᵃ1-2, my translation). Given the constraints that Aristotle imposes on things laid down, i.e., premisses (*protaseis*), that each must affirm or deny one thing of one thing, there are five ways in which something that looks like a syllogism can fail to be a syllogism. (1) What looks like a premiss can fail to be one, because it says more than one

---

3. (Hintikka 1997) replies to the analyses by Woods and Hansen of many questions and begging the question. The reply seems unconvincing.

4. There is a similar definition in the *Prior Analytics*: "Refutation is deduction of a contradiction" (*Prior Analytics* II.20.66ᵇ11, my translation). Aristotle's definition covers not only direct refutations (where one deduces a contradiction *of* a thesis) but also indirect refutations (where one deduces a contradiction *from* a thesis). The fallacy of treating what is not a cause as a cause (*Sophistical Refutations* 5.167ᵇ21-36) occurs in apparent indirect refutations, where the deduction is to something impossible (*eis to adunaton*, 167ᵇ23).

thing of one thing or says one thing of more than one thing or says more than one thing of more than one thing. (2) The argument can have just one premiss rather than more than one. (3) The conclusion drawn can fail to follow of necessity, for example because of exploitation of a shift of meaning or because of an implicit illicit conversion of a universal or conditional premiss. (4) A premiss can be identical with, synonymous with, or equivalent to the conclusion. (5) There can be a superfluous premiss, violating the condition that the conclusion must follow *through* the premisses. To this list we can add (6) deducing something that looks like a contradiction but is not. All 13 of the fallacies in Aristotle's *Sophistical Refutations* are failures of one of these six kinds. None of them is a violation of the rules for question-and-answer refutation dialogues; for example, none of them consists in an answerer refusing to answer a question or of a questioner using as a premiss something that the answerer has not granted. Nor can they occur only in question-and-answer refutation dialogues. As Dorion points out (Aristote 1995, 206), Aristotle's definition of a refutation as deduction of a contradiction makes no reference to a question-and-answer-context, and can be satisfied in solo reasoning by deducing a contradiction of or from a hypothesis that one is exploring. Hence sophistical refutations can also occur in solo reasoning.

The interpretation of the fallacies in Aristotle's *Sophistical Refutations* is of more than historical interest, since as Hamblin (1970) shows us in detail those fallacies have been the core of textbook treatments of logical fallacies throughout the European philosophical tradition, down to the present day. Their interpretation as specifically dialectical mistakes or rule violations reinforces a contemporary tendency to treat logical fallacies as violations of rules of a dialogue game. For example, van Eemeren and Grootendorst (1984) construct a code of conduct for rational discussants and then argue (177-192) that fallacies can be regarded as violations of this code. Walton and Krabbe (1995, 108-116) argue that the informal fallacies characteristically involve dialectical shifts, whose evaluation requires application of a normative model of reasonable dialogue. These proposals should be evaluated on their own merits, but they cannot claim Aristotle's theory of fallacies as a precedent for their approach.

In the controversy over the interpretation of the fallacies in Aristotle's *Sophistical Refutations*, not much attention has been paid to the fact that Aristotle's writings include two other lists of fallacies, one in a treatise on public speaking and the other in a treatise on scientific proof. Public speeches are monologues, not dialogues, and in his *Rhetoric* Aristotle makes no attempt to interpret them as if they were dialogues; further, he distinguishes the persuasive arguments used in public speeches, which he calls "enthymemes" (Greek *enthumêmata*), from the syllogisms of dialectical question and answer. Scientific proofs as Aristotle understands them are deductions of theorems that go back ultimately to self-evident first principles. In his *Prior Analytics*, Aristotle treats failed attempts to prove something as mistakes made by the reasoner, not as mistakes that sophists trick unwary interlocutors into making. Thus Aristotle has three different lists for three different contexts: things that appear to be refutations but are not, things that appear to be enthymemes but are not, and things that appear to be proofs but are not. The mistakes that make such *simulacra* merely apparent need not consist in an invalid inference; for example, a misconception of refutation (Greek *elenchou agnoia*, Latin *ignoratio elenchi*) can be a perfectly valid deduction of something that only seems to be a contradiction.

Woods and Hansen have shown that the fallacies in Aristotle's *Sophistical Refutations* are not *strongly* relative to the competitively oriented question-and-answer dialogues in which he found them. They are not violations of the rules for such dialogues. Nor are they mistakes peculiar to such dialogues. But they are characteristic of them. Thus they are *weakly* relative to them, in the sense that they are the kind of mistakes that tend to show up in such discourses. Public speeches have their own characteristic mistakes, which have only partial overlap with those that occur in contentious dialectical engagement. And attempts at scientific proof have yet a third set of characteristic mistakes, which overlap only partially with the mistakes characteristic of dialectical cross-examinations and public speeches. Aristotle's approach can be extended to other forms of reasoning and discourse, such as interactive policy deliberations, which presumably have their own characteristic mistakes.

Let us consider, then, Aristotle's two other lists of fallacies, starting from the types of apparent enthymemes listed in his *Rhetoric* (II.24.1400^{b}34-1402^{a}28). To understand what it is to be an apparent enthymeme, one must first understand what an enthymeme is. In contemporary English, the word 'enthymeme' is a technical term, not part of someone's vocabulary unless they have learned it from "traditional logic" or the study of rhetoric. In traditional logic, an enthymeme is described as an incomplete two-premiss Aristotelian categorical syllogism, lacking a premiss or the conclusion, and rules are given for supplying the supposedly missing component so as to produce a complete categorical syllogism – a conception that can be generalized to any argument that is not formally valid but can be made formally valid by adding a premiss or stating a conclusion. Theorists of rhetoric treat an enthymeme as an orator's argument that relies on the audience to supply some of its components. However, the concept of an enthymeme common to these two traditions (an argument with an unstated premiss or conclusion) does not come from Aristotle, but from the Hellenistic and Roman Stoics, as is attested by Epictetus (ca. 55-ca. 135 CE), who says, "The enthymeme is an incomplete syllogism" (Epictetus 1925/ca. 108 CE, p. 61 [*Discourses* I.8.3]).

Aristotle on the other hand means by an enthymeme a deduction from probabilities or signs (*Rhetoric* I.2.1357^{a}30-33; *Prior*

Analytics II.27.70[a]9-11). A probability is something that holds "for the most part" – for example, that envious people hate (*Rhetoric* I.2.1357[a]34-b1; *Prior Analytics* II.27.72[a]2-6). One thing is a sign of another thing if that other thing is found along with it (*Rhetoric* I.2.1357[b]1-21; *Prior Analytics* II.27.70[a]6-9). The other thing can be found along with its sign either universally (e.g., illness with fever) or in a particular case (e.g., justice with wisdom in Socrates) or generally (e.g., fever with breathing hard). The first kind of sign is necessary and non-defeasible (*aluton*, "unbreakable") and gives rise to a deduction. The other two kinds are defeasible (*luton*) and non-deductive (*asullogistikon*).

Rhetoric II.24 lists the following 10 rhetorical fallacies:

- *Compact and antithetical wording* of the sort used in rhetorical arguments, when there is no new conclusion (e.g., terse repetition of what has already been said)

- *Equivocation*, illegitimate trading on a shift of meaning (e.g., including in a eulogy of the dog the "Dog" in the heavens)

- *Combination and division*, saying that what is divided is combined or vice versa (e.g., that one who knows the letters of a word knows the word or that a small dose is not healthy if a large dose makes a person ill)

- *Indignant language* (e.g., exaggerating the facts of a case, with no attempt to prove guilt)

- *Sign*, when it is non-deductive (e.g., arguing that Dionysius is a thief because he is wicked – which is non-deductive, since not every wicked person is a thief)

- *Accident*, appealing to an accidental circumstance as a cause (e.g., arguing that an invitation to dinner is a great honour on the ground that Achilles was angered at not being invited to dinner – when what angered him was the insult rather than its particular form)

- *Affirming the consequent* (e.g., arguing that someone is an adulterer because he is a dandy and walks around at night, as adulterers do)

- *Non-cause as cause* (*post hoc ergo propter hoc*), arguing that something is a cause because it happened at the same time as or along with something (e.g., that Demosthenes' policy caused evils, because the war happened after it)

- *Omission of when and how* (e.g., arguing that Helen justly ran off with Paris, because her father gave her a choice of husband – when the choice he gave her was only at the time when he gave up his authority over her)

- *Dropping the qualification*, taking something as holding without qualification (*haplôs*) that does not hold without qualification (e.g., arguing that what is improbable is probable on the ground that it is probable that improbable things will happen)

These 10 rhetorical fallacies have only partial overlap with the 13 dialectical fallacies in the *Sophistical Refutations*. They make no reference to a questioner and an answerer – an understandable omission, since the forensic, deliberative and eulogistic speeches about which Aristotle is writing do not proceed by question and answer. Aristotle makes no attempt to derive them systematically or to classify them; rather, they appear to be based upon observation of the ways in which orators can appear to reason deductively or quasi-deductively from probabilities or signs when in fact they do not. In two of the cases (compact and antithetical wording, indignant language), there is no argument at all.

Aristotle identifies only two ways in which what appears to be a proof (*apodeixis*) can fail to be one: begging the question and "not because of this". Begging the question is also a way in which what appears to be a refutation (*elenchos*) can fail to be one, but Aristotle analyzes it differently when it appears in an attempt at proof. Dialectical refutations start from reputable opinions (*endoxa*), whereas proofs start ultimately from first principles (*archai*). Hence Aristotle defines begging the question in a proof-attempting context in a qualified way as "someone trying to prove through itself what is not knowable through itself" (*Prior Analytics* II.16.64^{b}36-38). This definition leaves open that one can prove through itself something that is knowable through itself, i.e., a first principle, which in Aristotle's view is known to be true once it is understood. Further, the definition makes no reference to question or answer, but envisages someone trying to prove something for themselves. According to Aristotle, a person begs the question in an attempt at proof not only by assuming immediately what is to be proved but also by using assumptions whose proof requires assuming what is to be proved. He gives the example of people who construct parallel lines by assuming things that cannot be proved unless there are parallel lines (*Prior Analytics* II.16.65^{a}4-7). The fallacy here is specific to the logic of proof as Aristotle understands it, and has nothing to do with mistakes or rule violations in question-and-answer dialogues.

"Not because of this" is Aristotle's label in the *Prior Analytics* for what he called in the *Sophistical Refutations* "non-cause as cause". The mistake is the same: in a reduction to absurdity, an assumption is rejected even though the absurdity results from the other premisses even if that assumption is rejected (*Prior Analytics* II.17.66^{a}10-11). But in a proof-attempting context, Aristotle speaks repeatedly of trying to "show" (*edeiknuto, deiknousêi, deiktikôs, deiktikois*) the thing whose contradictory was assumed – a concept missing from the treatment of this fallacy in the *Sophistical Refutations*. Further, the *Sophistical Refutations* treatment refers to questions but the *Prior Analytics* treatment does not. Thus the contexts are different. In the proof-theoretic context of the *Prior Analytics*, Aristotle describes the charge "not because of this" as one that we are often accustomed to utter in arguments (65^{a}38-39), takes pains to argue that people make

the charge in reductions to absurdity and not in direct proofs
(65^{a}39-b10), and points out that the innocent assumption that is
wrongly blamed for the absurdity can be not only a completely
irrelevant addition of the sort described in the *Sophistical Refutations* but also an assumption with a subject or predicate that
occurs in a premiss actually used to deduce the absurdity
(65^{b}13-40). Such non-obvious irrelevancies are perhaps more
likely to occur in sincere attempts at proof than in tricky and
deceptive attempts at dialectical refutation. Thus the *Prior Analytics* treatment of the fallacy is slightly different from, and more
developed than, its treatment in the *Sophistical Refutations*.

Aristotle does have a generic conception of what he calls *'paralogismos'*, a word often translated as 'fallacy', which has a cognate
verb *'paralogizesthai'* and a cognate adjective *'paralogistikos'*. He
uses one or other of these words at least 30 times, in nine different works, including not only the works where his three lists
appear but also the *Topics, Physics, On Generation and Corruption,
Metaphysics, Politics* and *Poetics*. The root *'logismos'* means calculation or reasoning, and prefixing *'para'* indicates being mistaken.
We can get a sense of what Aristotle means by these words by
transliterating them.[5]

1. In *paralogisms* nothing prevents a contradiction of the
   assumption from arising \<as a conclusion\>, for example
   if something is odd for it not to be odd. (*Prior Analytics*
   II.15.64^{b}13-15)

2. Is deduction of a falsehood deduction from opposites or a
   paralogism but a geometrical one …, as … to think that parallel lines meet is in a way geometrical but in another way

---

5. The translations that follow are my own. I omit one passage (at *Rhetoric*
I.14.1374^{b}26) where Aristotle uses *'paralogizesthai'* with the meaning of
defrauding, by means of tricky work with an abacus or similar calculating
device. Aristotle's exact contemporary Demosthenes used the word at least
twice with this meaning.

non-geometrical? (*Posterior Analytics* I.12.77ᵇ18-24)

3. In mathematics the *paralogism* does not occur in the same way, because the middle term is always the one with the double meaning. (*Posterior Analytics* I.12.77ᵇ27-29)

4. Further, besides the deductions mentioned there are the *paralogisms* that arise from things peculiar to some sciences, as has happened in geometry and kindred sciences... <The man who draws a false figure> makes his deduction from premises that are peculiar to the science but not true. (*Topics* I.1.101ª5-8, 13-15)

5. <Investigating in how many ways a thing is said> is useful for not being *paralogized* and for *paralogizing*. For by knowing in how many ways something is said we would not be *paralogized* but will know if the questioner is not asking with respect to the same meaning; and we ourselves when we are asking will be able to *paralogize* if the answerer happens not to know in how many ways something is said. This is not possible in every case, but only if some of the things said in many ways are true and others false. (*Topics* I.18.108ª26-33)

6. One must also, where possible, get the universal premiss by a definition of the term's coordinate rather than of the term itself. For they *paralogize* themselves, when the definition is gotten of the coordinate, into thinking that they are not assenting to the universal; for example, if it were necessary to get that the angry person desires vengeance for an apparent slight, one might get the admission that anger is desire for vengeance for an apparent slight. (*Topics* VIII.1.156ª27-33)

7. Let us speak about sophistical refutations, i.e., apparent refutations that are *paralogisms* and not refutations... (*Sophistical Refutations* 1.164ª20-21)

8. Therefore, just as those who are not clever at using an abacus are cheated by the experts, in the same way too in arguments those who are inexperienced in the power of names *paralogize* both when they engage in dialectic and when they listen to others. (*Sophistical Refutations* 1.165ª13-17)

9. There are seven kinds of *paralogisms* that are independent of the choice of words. (*Sophistical Refutations* 4.166ᵇ21-22)

10. The contentious person is not in every respect like the drawer of a false diagram, for the contentious person will be *paralogistic* about every genus rather than beginning from a definite genus. (*Sophistical Refutations* 11.172ᵇ1-4)

11. <Studying how to answer contentious arguments is useful> for investigations by oneself; for whoever is easily *paralogized* by someone else and does not perceive it would also often suffer this themselves by their own agency. (*Sophistical Refutations* 16.175ª9-12)

12. Melissus clearly *paralogizes*; for he thinks that he has gotten the admission, if every coming into being has a beginning, that also what has not come into being does not have a beginning. (*Physics* I.2.186ª10-13)

13. Zeno *paralogizes*; for, he says, if everything is always at rest when it is against what is equal and that which is moving is always in the now, then the moving arrow is motionless. This is false; for time, like any other magnitude, is not composed of indivisible nows. (*Physics* VI.9.239ᵇ5-9)

14. The *paralogism* is in assuming that something takes equal time to go at equal speed past a moving object and past an object at rest of equal size. This is false. (*Physics* VI.9.240ª1-4)

15. The argument that there are indivisible magnitudes *par-*

alogizes in a hidden way. (*On Generation and Corruption* I.2.317ª2)

16. We say "in virtue of what have they *paralogized* or deduced" or <equivalently> "what is the cause of the deduction or *paralogism*". (*Metaphysics* V.18.1022ª21-22)

17. It is apparent that to say 'all' is a *paralogism*, for the words 'all', 'both', 'odd' and 'even' create contentious deductions in arguments, because of their ambiguity. (*Politics* II.3.1261ᵇ27)

18. The mind is caused to *paralogize* by <small expenses>, as in the sophistical argument "if each is small, so too are all." (*Politics* V.8.1307ᵇ35-37)

19. <That the extreme is the virtue> will seem so to the many, and at the same time <identifying an extreme with a virtue> will be *paralogistic*... For someone who courts danger when it is not necessary would seem much more likely to do so when it is noble. (*Rhetoric* I.9.1367ᵇ3-5)

20. The listener *paralogizes* that he did it or did not do it, even though it has not been proved. (*Rhetoric* II.24.1401ᵇ7-9)

21. The whole line of argument <that what holds of a combination holds of its divisions, or vice versa> is *paralogistic*. (*Rhetoric* II.24.1401ª34)

22. It is always more possible to gain an advantage by means of this *paralogism* <of using a single counter-example to attack a probability> in defence than in accusation. (*Rhetoric* II.25.1402ᵇ24-26)

23. The soul *paralogizes* that the speaker tells the truth, because people speak this way in such cases, so that the audience thinks (even if things are not as the speaker says) that things are as the speaker says... (*Rhetoric* III.7.1408ª20-23)

24. Someone about whom many things are said must also be mentioned many times; so, if he is mentioned many times, many things seem to be said. So Homer has by means of this *paralogism* exaggerated the role of Niereus, even though he mentioned him once, and has created a memory, even though he never again said a word about him. (*Rhetoric* III.12.1414^{a}4-7)

25. It is also possible for a discovery to be created by a *paralogism* of the audience, as in *Odysseus the False Messenger*; for that he stretched the bow and nobody else did has been created by the poet and is an assumption, and so too that he said he would know the bow that he had not seen, but to infer from this that he would recognize it again is a *paralogism*. (*Poetics* 16.1455^{a}12-16)

26. <The way to speak falsely in poetry> is *paralogism*. For men think that if when one thing is so another thing is or occurs, then if the latter is so the former is or occurs; but this is false. (*Poetics* 24.1460^{a}20-22)

27. Because it knows that this is true, our soul *paralogizes* that its antecedent is also true. (*Poetics* 24.1460^{a}24-25)

The common thread in these 27 passages is making a mistake in reasoning. Passages 2, 4, 7, 16 contrast paralogisms with deductions or refutations; "paralogisms" are mistaken reasonings. Sometimes the mistake is a false assumption (passages 2, 4, 10, 13, 14). Otherwise the mistake is an inferential error. Aristotle mentions equivocation (3, 5, 8, 17), affirming the consequent (23, 24, 26, 27), illicit conversion (12), and combination and division (18, 21). He also mentions inferential errors that do not occur in any of his three lists: thinking that a person who faces danger unnecessarily is more likely to do so when it is noble (19), inferring, from the indignant language in which a crime is described, that the accused did it (20), using a single example to attack a probability (22), taking someone's word that they would do something because they did something else (25). It is also a "paralogism" to think that something does not follow when it actually does (6). Aristotle uses the verb 'paralogize' both transitively and intransitively. When used intransitively, it means to make a mistake in reasoning (5, 8, 12, 13, 15, 16, 20, 23, 27), and can be said either of a person who advances an argument (5, 8, 12, 13, 16) or of an argument that someone has advanced (15) or of a soul or mind that is induced to make the mistake (20, 23, 27). When used transitively, 'paralogize' means to induce someone, possibly oneself, to make a mistake in reasoning (5, 6, 11). Aristotle uses the adjective 'paralogistic' in various ways: of a person who makes deceptive mistakes in question-answer dialogues (10), of a strategy that induces an audience to make a mistake in reasoning (19), and of a kind of mistaken reasoning (21).

Thus Aristotle's conception of a fallacy transcends the contexts of contentious disputation, public speaking and scientific proof for which he develops his three lists. It covers mistaken assumptions as well as inferential errors. Further, some of the fallacies that he identifies occur in none of his three lists. And not all the things in those lists are fallacies. In particular, two kinds of apparent rhetorical proofs (compact and antithetical wording, indignant language) are not even arguments, and thus are not kinds of mistakes in reasoning; rather, they induce the audience to make a mistaken inference.

The preceding exploration of Aristotle's use of the cognate words 'paralogismos', 'parlogizesthai' and 'paralogistikon' has vindicated the rejection by Woods and Hansen (1997) of Hintikka's claim (Hintikka 1987) that the traditional fallacies were mistakes or violations of rules in the questioning games practised in Aristotle's school. Aristotle identifies some of these fallacies as occurring also in public speeches, in Eleatic treatises, and in mathematical proofs. He has a generic conception of a mistake in reasoning, a conception that covers false assumptions as well as inferential errors. The kinds of apparent refutations, apparent rhetorical proofs and apparent scientific proofs that he identifies are only weakly relative to the contexts of dialectical disputation, public speaking and scientific proof.

REFERENCES

Aristote. 1995. *Les Réfutations Sophistiques*, introduction, traduction et commentaire par Louis-André Dorion. Paris: Librairie Philosophique J. Vrin.

Aristotle. 1984. *The Complete Works of Aristotle: The Revised Oxford Translation*, 2 vols., edited by Jonathan Barnes. Princeton: Princeton University Press.

Eemeren, Frans H. van, and Rob Grootendorst. 1984. *Speech Acts in Argumentative Discussions: A Theoretical Model for the Analysis of Discussions Directed towards Solving Conflicts of Opinion*. Dordrecht: Foris.

Epictetus. 1925/ca. 108 CE. *The Discourses as Reported by Arrian, The Manual, and Fragments, with an English Translation by W. A. Oldfather*. Cambridge, MA: Harvard University Press. First published ca. 108 CE.

Hamblin, Charles L. 1971. *Fallacies*. London: Methuen.

Hansen, Hans V. 1996a. "Aristotle, Whately, and the Taxonomy of Fallacies." In *Practical Reasoning: International Conference on Formal and Applied Practical Reasoning*, edited by Dov M. Gabbay and Hans J. Ohlbach, 318-30. Berlin: Springer.

Hansen, Hans V. 1996b. "Whately on the Ad Hominem: A Liberal Exegesis." *Philosophy and Rhetoric* 24 (4): 400-15.

Hansen, Hans V. 1997. "Mill on Inference and Fallacies." In *Historical Foundations of Informal Logic*, edited by Douglas N. Walton and Alan Brinton, 125-43. Aldershot: Ashgate.

Hansen, Hans V. 1998. "Locke and Whately on the *Argumenation ad Ignorantiam*." *Philosophy and Rhetoric* 31 (1): 55-63.

Hansen, Hans V. 2006a. "Whately on Arguments Involving Authority." *Informal Logic* 26 (3): 319-40.

Hansen, Hans V. 2006b. "Mill and Pragma-Dialectics." In *Considering Pragma-Dialectics*, edited by Peter Houtlosser and Agnès van Rees, 97-107. Mahwah, NJ: Lawrence Erlbaum.

Hansen, Hans V. 2007. "Mill on Argumentation." In *Proceedings of the Sixth Conference on the International Society for the Study of Argumentation*, edited by Frans H. van Eemeren, J. Anthony Blair, Charles A. Willard, and Bart Garssen, 571-81. Amsterdam: SicSat.

Hansen, Hans V. 2014. "Mill, Informal Logic, and Argumentation." In *John Stuart Mill's* A System of Logic: *Critical Appraisals*, edited by Anton Loizides, 192-217. London: Routledge.

Hansen, Hans V. 2015. "Whately on Kinds of Arguments." *Cogency* 7 (1): 81-108.

Hansen, Hans V., and Robert C. Pinto, eds. 1995. *Fallacies: Classical and Contemporary Readings*. University Park: Pennsylvania State University Press.

Hansen, Hans V., Fred J. Kauffeld, James B. Freeman, and Lilian Bermejo-Luque. 2019. *Presumptions and Burdens of Proof: An Anthology of Argumentation and the Law*. Tuscaloosa: University of Alabama Press.

Hintikka, Jaakko. 1987. "The Fallacy of Fallacies." *Argumentation* 1 (3): 211-38.

Hintikka, Jaakko. 1997. "What Was Aristotle Doing in his Early Logic Anyway? A Reply to Woods and Hansen." *Synthese* 113 (2): 241-49.

Walton, Douglas N., and Erik C. W. Krabbe. 1995. *Commitment in Dialogue: Basic Concepts of Interpersonal Reasoning*. Albany, NY: State University of New York Press.

Woods, John, and Hans V. Hansen. 1997. "Hintikka on Aristotle's Fallacies." *Synthese* 113 (2): 217-39.

Woods, John, and Hans V. Hansen. 2001. "The Subtleties of Aristotle on Non-Cause." *Logique et Analyse* 44 (176): 395-414.

ABOUT THE AUTHOR: David Hitchcock is emeritus professor of philosophy at McMaster University in Hamilton, Canada. He is the author of *Critical Thinking: A Guide to Evaluating Information* (Methuen, 1983) and co-author with Milos Jenicek, MD, of *Evidence-Based Practice: Logic and Critical Thinking in Medicine* (AMA Press, 2005). He co-edited with Bart Verheij *Arguing on the Toulmin Model: New Essays in Argument Analysis and Evaluation* (Springer, 2007). His *On Reasoning and Argument: Essays in Informal Logic and on Critical Thinking* (Springer, 2017) brings together 25 previously published sole-authored articles, along with seven new chapters updating his views on their topics: deduction, induction and conduction; material consequence; patterns of reasoning; interpersonal discussion; evaluation of reasoning; fallacies; and informal logic and critical thinking. He is the author of the entry on critical thinking in *The Stanford Encyclopaedia of Philosophy*.

CHAPTER 2.

MILL AND THE DUTY TO ARGUE

DANIEL H. COHEN

ABSTRACT: John Stuart Mill situated "logic", in his broad sense of the term, at the confluence of empiricist epistemology, utilitarian ethics, and liberal political theory. Thus, he often commented on argumentation, especially as it appears in public forums concerning the body politic. Mill's theory of argumentation, as reconstructed by Hans V. Hansen, is not comfortably encapsulated in the "market-place of ideas" metaphor, despite the common association, but most resources of contemporary argumentation theories are already present – along with some virtues of its own. This paper uses Mill's theory to address two important but often overlooked questions: *Why should we argue, when we should?* and *Why shouldn't we argue, when we should not?*

KEYWORDS: Hansen, Mill, argumentation, argumentative virtue, argumentative utility, duty to argue

1. INTRODUCTION

Because argumentation is such a multi-faceted phenomenon, argumentation theory needs to be correspondingly multi-disciplinary. A complete accounting would have to include contributions from (at least) communications theory, linguistics, rhetoric, sociology, cognitive psychology, and, of course, philosophy. It is not enough, however, simply to mention philosophy because from out of its cacophony, logic, ethics, political philosophy, and epistemology (at least!) all need to be heard.

John Stuart Mill is among the small group of philosophers who managed to make signal contributions in each of those four areas of philosophy. Moreover, his contributions are all of a piece: his logic undergirds his epistemology, which frames his ethics, which motivates his political theory – which in turn reinforces his account of the role, nature, and critical importance of public argumentation. It should come as no surprise, then, that Mill's thought contains relevant precursors for many components of contemporary argumentation theory. But it should come as a bit of a disappointment that, for the most part, argumentation theorists have not availed themselves of the methodological tools, the conceptual resources, and the wealth of philosophical insights that he provides. The reasons for this are not hard to find. To begin, Mill's broad conception of logic was overshadowed by the groundbreaking developments in formal logic at the end of the 19th century by such figures as Boole, DeMorgan, Cantor, and Frege, before being completely eclipsed by the mathematical and philosophical agendas set by Hilbert, Russell and Whitehead, Wittgenstein, and Gödel to the point that it could even seem a bit quaint. In addition, argumentation theory is relatively young as an autonomous discipline. It has experienced incredibly rapid and exciting developments in the last half century, so its focus has been on the future to the detriment of serious historical scholarship. Furthermore, Mill may have been a victim of his own success: much of his political thought has been incorporated into western societies, so that it is now simply taken for granted.

That might explain the discipline's amnesia, but it does not to justify it.

Hans V. Hansen has been a refreshing exception to the discipline's historical blindness. He has brought the past to the present by reintroducing us to the tools they developed for dealing with the questions that occupied them, and he has then deployed them on our own question. He has also brought the present to the past by using contemporary analytic tools on historically important arguments. His work on Mill exemplifies both of those movements.

Mill understood logic in a very broad sense as, "the science of the operations of the understanding which are subservient to the estimation of evidence" (Hansen 2014, p. 192, quoting Mill 1843). Evaluating the strength of inferences from premises to conclusions is only part of it. It also includes evaluating the support for those premises. Consonant with his focus on public argumentation, Mill situated logic at the confluence of empiricist epistemology, utilitarian ethics, and liberal political theory. What Hansen effectively shows is that informal logic needs to be similarly informed by those disciplines. What Hansen performatively demonstrates, however, is that contemporary argumentation theory needs to be historically informed. Hansen's example illustrates that in the same way that we cannot fully appreciate the conclusion of an argument independent of the argumentation leading up to it, and we cannot fully comprehend the current political state of affairs in ignorance of the historical context out of which it developed, for a full understanding of contemporary informal logic and argumentation theory, we need a robust sense of how we got here.

One more thing: by highlighting the affinities between Mill's theory of logic on the one hand and contemporary informal logic and argumentation theory on the other, Hansen also highlights their differences. The juxtaposition thus exposes a curious gap in their combined coverage of argumentation. There is a blind spot of sorts in these approaches to argumentation regarding the proper occasions for arguing. The specific problem is this: most theories have the resources to provide an answer to the fundamental question "Why should we argue?"; but few theories even try to answer the question "When should we argue?"

Without that, the picture is incomplete. The problem is exacerbated because there are times when we should argue and times when we should not, so we are confronted with two subsidiary questions: "Why should we argue, when we should?" and "Why shouldn't we argue, when we shouldn't?" The obligations and prohibitions on arguers already engaged in argumentation are well-studied, but there are barely any on the prior, standing obligations and prohibitions regarding decisions to engage in argument. Borrowing some vocabulary from ethical theory, we can say that neither product-oriented 'consequentialist' theories of argumentation nor 'deontological' procedural approaches are able to answer all the questions. An examination of Mill's position shows why.

2. ARGUMENTS, BELIEFS, AND COMMITMENT

Hansen 2014 identifies several aspects of Mill's thought that anticipate prominent features of informal logic. There is, for example, Mill's strong commitment to an a posteriori methodology – and a correspondingly strong opposition to formal, analytic theories. Hansen, quoting Sparshot 1978, offers this unequivocal summation of Mill's attitude to formal logic: "He did not approve of it" (Hansen 2014, p. 195). Mill's thought also included a renewed and heightened attention to fallacies: "No one before Mill had discussed fallacies in the same detail and with the same acuteness that he did" (Hansen 2014, p. 204).[1] Predictably, given his empiricism, Mill's treatment of fallacies gives special attention to the basketful of problems associated with universal generalizations.

As an empiricist, Mill was acutely sensitive to the troublesome epistemological status of non-analytic generalizations; as a logi-

---

1. This is not to deny important earlier discussions, especially those of Richard Whateley, of which Hansen is well aware (see especially Hansen 2015 and the Introduction to Hansen and Pinto 1995); rather, it is to emphasize the sea change in the importance accorded them.

cian, he was concerned with the transmission of epistemic warrant from premises to conclusions as part of a knowledge-increasing process. He was up against the classic Greek problematic that sensation is of particulars but knowledge is of universals. His resolution was to come down hard on the side of particulars: all knowledge comes from sensation; sensation is of particulars; thus, if reasoning is a way to increase our knowledge, we must be able to make inferences from premises that are particular. But how can we infer that Socrates, who is Greek, is also mortal?

> Sticking with his thesis that all inferences are from particulars, Mill sees that there are two courses of reasoning that lie open to the inferrer: the one is a particular-to-particular pattern of inference (P-P) and the other is the "up-and-down" pattern of inference that involves generalization as an intermediate step (P-G-P). (Hansen 2014, p. 199)

The interpolation of the intermediate step has several cognitive advantages but raises the epistemological stakes: if the generalization is an implicit, pre-existing premise, the conclusion deductively follows syllogistically, which, according to Mill, would Beg the Question and thus fail to increase our knowledge; if the generalization is inferred from the prior particular, the final conclusion is easily and validly reached–but the intermediate step is not; but without something like the intermediate generalization, the reasoning prima facie violates principles of relevance.

Mill's solution distinguished two different readings of the intermediate generalization:

> … as a portion of our knowledge or as a memorandum for our guidance. Under the former or speculative aspect an affirmative general proposition is an assertion of a speculative truth, viz., that whatever has a certain attribute has a certain other attribute. Under the other aspect it is to be regarded not as a part of our knowledge but as an aid for [inference]. (Hansen 2014, p. 198, quoting Mill 1843)

Hansen notes the striking resemblances between Mill and Stephen Toulmin. The mapping of Toulmin's distinction between premises and warrants onto Mill's two readings of generalizations is striking, all the way down to use some of the same terminology.[2] Mill arrives at the distinction from an epistemological perspective; Toulmin comes from a jurisprudential model of argumentation. A third figure bears mention here: Frank Ramsey. Ramsey, whose brief career came between Mill in the mid-19th century and Toulmin in the mid-20th, hit upon a very similar position but from yet a third angle. Adding his perspective to the hopper complements the others in philosophically helpful ways.

Ramsey's career was a brilliant, meteoric flash through logic, mathematics, economics, and early analytic philosophy. For Ramsey in Cambridge, the "received view" of generalizations was that they were basically just abbreviations for the infinite conjunctions of all their instances. This was, for example, Ludwig Wittgenstein's position in the *Tractatus*, (a text that Ramsey helped translate and of which he wrote the first serious and competent review: Ramsey 1923), and Ramsey followed suit: "I adopt the view of Mr. Wittgenstein that 'For all x, fx' is to be regarded as equivalent to the logical product of all the values of 'fx', i.e., to the combination of fx_1 and fx_2 and fx_3 ..." (Ramsey 1927). Bertrand Russell had taken the same position, although in the 1918 lectures, *The Philosophy of Logical Atomism*, his internal epistemologist overcame his metaphysical spokesperson to conclude that there are irreducibly universal propositions and, thus, there must be genuinely general facts to which they correspond (Russell 1918, Lecture V). Ramsey initially adopted the infinite-conjunctions view of universal generalizations, e.g., in his 1927 "Facts and Propositions", but parted company with Russell's and

2. Hansen (2014, 202) after noting these similarities, notes without comment that Toulmin does not cite Mill.

Wittgenstein's versions of logical atomism (as did Wittgenstein[3]). In his 1929 paper, "General Propositions and Causality," Ramsey bit the bullet and rejected the assumption that universal generalizations actually expressed propositions. Rather than treating them as descriptive or fact-stating assertions, he adopted a more "instrumental" understanding of their role in language and thought (Urmson 1956, pp. 64-67).

This much of Ramsey's thought is consonant with Mill's view of universal claims as "inference licenses" but it heralded a more radical shift in his thinking towards a Peircean pragmatism. Universal sentences in our language do not correspond to discrete thoughts or beliefs in some representational "mentalese"; rather, they express our commitments to allow certain inferences and our "habits" of conceptual association (Misak 2017). Two ingredients of that claim deserve special emphasis: first, that our commitments are expressed rather than asserted and second, that they are *our* commitments, i.e., they belong to the relevant epistemic and linguistic communities, not the individual. Ramsey explicitly identified universals along with law-like statements and causal claims (cf. TLP 6.3-6.33–and especially 5.1361!), as well as some conditionals, as targets for this kind of quasi-behaviorist elimination, but it is plausible to assume that it heralded a larger move on Ramsey's part away from a representational theory of thought. Unfortunately, his untimely death within the year (before his 27th birthday) makes that more of a speculative extrapolation. Regardless, the crucial insights are already visible: (i) there is more to an individual's epistemic states than simply the aggregate of his or her believed propositions; (ii) there is more to an individual's mental life than even the sum of all of her or his propositional attitudes; and, most important, (iii) there is

---

3. Wittgenstein followed Ramsey's lead in abandoning the identification of universal propositions with infinite conjunctions, and referred to his treatment of universals as "the biggest mistake" he made in the *Tractatus*. Misak 2017, fn. 10.

more to an individual's cognitive field than just what is contained within that individual. Cognitive, social, and linguistic contexts all matter.[4]

3. THE FUNCTIONS OF ARGUMENTATION; THE RIGHTS AND DUTIES OF ARGUERS

Mill identifies two functions for argument: justification and persuasion. These more or less naturally correspond, respectively, to the internal epistemic project of testing and justifying one's own beliefs and the interpersonal rhetorical project of persuading others. It is a useful first approximation but the reality is more complicated: we also try to justify ourselves to others; on occasion we try to persuade ourselves; and very often it is unclear even to ourselves just what it is we are trying to do when we argue. It will help to augment this by thinking in terms of the effects of argumentation rather than exclusively in terms of the intentions of the arguers. The effects of argument are evident in each of the contexts just cited: cognitive, social, and linguistic. Arguments can persuade; they may demonstrate truths and generate knowledge; and, as noted, they are also capable of creating meanings for their conclusions.

It is against this backdrop that we can return to the questions posed at the beginning concerning why we argue. The concern is not the simple, general question of why we do in fact argue: that can be given an evolutionary answer of, say, the sort that Mercier and Sperber (2011) offer, and that would satisfy the strictest Positivist empiricists as well as Quinean naturalized epistemologists. Rather, the concern is the explicitly normative question, "Why

4. Although Ramsey's point is epistemological rather than semantic, a comparison to Hilary Putnam's famous claim – "Cut the pie any way you like, 'meanings' just ain't in the *head!*" – would not be inappropriate. Putnam was arguing that there is a linguistic "division of labor" in linguistic communities, and that it is entire communities, not individuals, that determine and sustain the meanings of the words that individuals use (Putnam 1973, p. 704).

should we argue?" Of course, in that explicit form, the question Begs a Question: it assumes that we should argue. There are, however, many occasions where it is obvious that we should not argue: at funerals, when threatened by inclement weather on a picnic, and tending an irritable newborn all come to mind. The fundamental question *"Why* should we argue?" has to be paired with *"When* should we argue?"

One common, tenable, plausible, but often implicit thesis is that there is a standing imperative to argue whenever there is a proposition on the table or a difference of standpoint. We can take the duty to argue as a defeasible default. Every belief should be justified and every difference resolved – unless there are "defeaters" or overriding reasons not to argue. To be sure, it is a substantial thesis and as such is in need of supporting argumentation, especially since the alternative is equally tenable and also plausible. Why not assume instead that default is not to argue unless there are compelling reasons to argue? (We can use this case, self-referentially, as an example: the existence of the first thesis would certainly qualify as a compelling reason why we would have to argue for the second.)

One of the strong points of the second option (Thou shalt not argue–unless there are reasons to do so) is that it readily explains the phenomenon of "Misbegotten Arguments" – arguments that should not have occurred and for which (at least one of) the arguers can be blamed (Cohen 2011). Even argumentation theorists who as a group are inordinately fond of argument recognize that there is such a thing as being too argumentative! Not every difference needs to be elevated into a dispute; not every occasion is appropriate for arguing; for some topics, not all would-be arguers have the relevant background knowledge, tolerance for confrontation, or proper standing to argue.

The former option (Thou shalt argue – unless there are reasons not to) has the virtue of explaining the complementary, but less common and less visible, phenomenon of "Missing Arguments"–arguments that should have occurred but did not, and for which the non-arguers are culpable, e.g., attorneys who do not defend their clients, friends who do not push back against our ill-conceived plans, and all of us who, in the absence of defeaters, do not speak up against injustice when it takes the form of casual racism, homophobic jokes, or "merely flirtatious" sexual harassment. There are usually defeaters available for those who want to use them, but probably not enough to warrant the relative dearth of argumentation when it is needed.[5]

Regardless of how we adjudicate the boundaries between these two candidates for a First Commandment of Argumentation, the fundamental questions "Why should we argue?" and "When should we argue?" have already recombined and been superseded by two more focused versions:

Why should we argue, when it is the case that we should?

Why shouldn't we argue, when it is the case that we should not?

Mill is not without resources for addressing the original questions but some problems arise when extending his thoughts to the successor questions.

Mill's two functions for argument nicely map onto the duties to argue. We have a duty to ourselves to argue because, as epistemic agents, the imperatives of rationality have traction on us, believing the truth is one of those imperatives, and arguing-to-justify, in conjunction with empiricism's respect for evidence, is arguably truth-conducive. More specifically, Mill insists that in addition to being able to provide reasons justifying our beliefs, we have a positive duty to seek out objections to our positions as well as the reasons supporting opposing opinions. While this does not guarantee that we will arrive at truth, it is at least helpful

---

5. Although the phrases "Missing Argument" and "Misbegotten Argument" were introduced as technical terms of art in Cohen 2011, the most famous missing argument – Abraham's not arguing with God when instructed to sacrifice Isaac – was described using that exact phrase in Cohen 2001.

in error detection and avoidance, and it is subjecting our beliefs to this process that gives us the "right" to judge our position better than any others (Mill 1859, Ch. II, ¶7). The duty to ourselves to argue is not the same as the duty to argue with ourselves, My duty to myself to argue is in order to insure that my beliefs are justified, which could be fulfilled by arguing about those beliefs with others. And we have duties to others to argue (again, not necessarily with those others) because the better our knowledge of the situation, the better our decisions will be, so promulgating what we sincerely take to be the truth will be to everyone's advantage, i.e., it will maximize utility both for all the enlightened individuals and, in politics like participatory democracies in which the citizenry has a voice in decision making, for the society as a whole.

To see how this might apply to the more pointed when-and-why questions, it will help to detour through the metaphor of the "marketplace of ideas" which is widely associated with Mill and argumentation. On closer inspection, however, it does not fit very comfortably, and the reasons why are revealing.

4. THE METAPHOR OF THE MARKETPLACE

Much of Mill's attention is to public argumentation. Since he comes down strongly in favor of the free exchange of ideas, and it is a commonplace now to speak in terms of the marketplace of ideas, that model is naturally and commonly ascribed to Mill (Gordon 1997 cites J. Salwyn Schapiro and Christian Bay; Hansen 2007 cites Isaiah Berlin, Alvin Goldman, and several others). For example, Woods, Irvine, and Walton 2004, write:

> What Mill is offering us, then, is a kind of free-enterprise, survival of the fittest model – and justification – of debate, one in which truth is understood to be the most important value in the free marketplace of ideas. It is in debate that truth best survives the destructive forces of opposition and criticism (Woods, et al. 2004, p. 30).

There are, however, several ways in which that metaphor is not entirely apt. In the first place, it does not appear that Mill ever explicitly used that trope (Gordon 1997, p. 235). Of much greater significance is that Mill does explicitly endorse a variety of regulations for public debate that would qualify as "market interventions" compromising an orthodox libertarian marketplace. Mill was prescient in his awareness of the ways that a free and unfettered exchange of ideas advantages establishment and majority opinions. It is never a completely level playing field. There are asymmetries that make the simplistic identification of equality with fairness, by way of complete freedom for all, both disingenuous and dangerous. Liberal participatory democracies need to provide safeguards for minority opinions and maybe even something like an affirmative action program for heterodox ideas. At the very least, there should be greater tolerance for "intemperate" arguments directed against prevailing opinions than offensive arguments in the other direction (Gordon 1997, Hansen 2007). If public debate is a market, it is not a fair one. Mill was a great champion of freedom of speech, so the metaphor of a marketplace works very well, but only up to a point (see Hansen 2007 for the key components of the metaphor).

The point at which the marketplace metaphor breaks down is when it comes to identifying what counts as argumentative success. Several distinct criteria have already been implicitly invoked and they are not easily reconciled. When doing epistemic duty for individuals, arguments are successful when they (1a) provide sufficient adequate justification for our beliefs or, in a stronger version, (1b) yield truth and knowledge. From Mill's general ethical-pragmatic perspective, the success of an argument would be measured by its "utility", understood as either (2a) its instrumental usefulness for specified purposes or, more generally, (2b) its overall pleasure- or happiness-inducing effects. Finally, in the public marketplace, the success of an argument would be measured either (3a) by its surviving, i.e., by remaining undefeated by objections or counter-arguments, or, more positively, (3b) by its thriving, i.e., by persuading others.

Mill largely glosses over the conceptual differences among truth, utility, and rational persuasion as outcomes of successful argumentation. Woods, et al., read Mill as committed to a picture in which all three converge, so that in the end they can simply be identified. It is not just that truth is what "best survives the destructive forces of opposition and criticism" (30) but that argumentation is "an effective and objective way to truth" (31). Since truth is also deemed, *the most important value* in the marketplace of ideas" (italics added), argumentation will end when everyone is sold on true ideas.

5. WHAT ARGUMENTATION CAN AND CANNOT DO

Whether or not it is actually Mill's position, it is appealing to suppose that truth, utility, and persuasion neatly coincide. It ties a lot of loose ends together into a single elegant tapestry. It weaves epistemology, ethics, and political philosophy into a tapestry that foregrounds argumentation's *telos*. It explains, justifies, motivates, and prescribes arguing.

Despite its attractive features, the picture starts to unravel once we ask the critical when-and-why questions. If truth is the most important value in the marketplace, then we are in the first option described above with respect to arguing: arguing is the proper means to a proper end, so the default would always be to argue. Every difference of opinion would be an occasion to argue because no other considerations could outweigh the highest utility that is accorded to obtaining the truth. There are no overrides to relieve us of the imperative to argue.

While this position might seem extreme, it embodies an important conceptual truth regarding truth, viz., that truth occupies a privileged position when it comes to critiquing arguments. The standard lists of fallacies can generally be partitioned into three main categories, as having unwarranted, irrelevant, or insufficient premises, depending on how they fail, say, either, Govier's "ARG" test or Blair and Johnson's "RSA" standard (Govier 1992, pp. 67ff; Johnson and Blair, 1994, pp. 55ff). Contrary to common conceptions, then, fallacies do not have to be understood as fatal flaws. The charge that a fallacy has been committed can often be taken as a request for further information in support of the premises or further refinement of the reasoning in the inferences (a point made, for pedagogical purposes, in Blair and Johnson 1977, p. 200). That is, at least some fallacies are merely weak points, places where the argument needs to be fixed, rather than irreparable failings. The charge that a premise is false is a deal-breaker: the flaw really is fatal and no amount of augmentation can fix that argumentation (Kasser and Cohen 2002). Granted, 'true' is hardly ever used purely univocally, even in relatively technical contexts, and its use here implicates an idealized, an absolute, or at least a "cautionary" sense (see, e.g., Rorty 2000, p. 57), so it arguably begs the metaphysical question – but the metaphysical question is not the one on the table. The crucial point to keep in sight here is that there are different kinds of closure to argumentation. There are different criteria we can invoke when counting an outcome as positive. Truth, in whatever sense, is only one consideration. If we conflate truth, persuasion, and utility, along with explanation, demonstration, and justification, we efface all the situational complexities that we need to do justice to argumentation's when-and-why questions.

Mill himself is more nuanced. He provides some important qualifications, two of which are particularly germane. First, the relationship between the alethic-epistemic and ethical-pragmatic outcomes of argumentation is too complex to be mere identity. He asserts that "the truth of an opinion is *part* of its utility" (Mill 1859, Ch. II, ¶10; italics added) but even that needs to be contextualized and glossed. Second, the connection between argumentation and truth is also much too complex to be adequately characterized by a simple means-ends story. Argument may have a role in discovering new truths, but it also serves other purposes, such as exposing error, providing justification, and generating consensus.

Mill's more modest claim that truth is part of the utility of an opinion does need to be questioned. From a pragmatist perspective, it can seem otiose: once all the usefulness of a belief has been taken into account, what is left to be gained by the additional assertion that it is true? That line of reasoning might be taken to recommend a deflationary account of truth but it is better taken as indicating that utility is not the only relevant criterion for explaining truth (or 'true') nor the only appropriate measure of beliefs. Since "That's true" is always a prima facie endorsement, truth cannot be an independent variable in our reckoning. By making truth merely a part of the utility of a belief, Mill appears to be opening the door to other factors. It is a doorway that many different philosophers for many different reasons have entered, ranging from general value-theoretic considerations (such as James and Nietzsche); to holistic reasons concerning the limits of empiricism (like Quine, Kuhn, and van Fraassen); and to historical or social-political forces (perhaps Derrida and Foucault fit here). That is not, however, the path that Mill wants us to follow. Rather, by including truth as an integral part of utility calculations, he was trying to highlight the compatibility of truth and utility and, even more to the point, he was de-legitimizing the idea of anything like Plato's "Noble Lie" – a claim of such great social or political importance that it becomes sacrosanct and immune from all critique, thus putting restrictions on the free exchange of ideas (Hansen 2014, 207).

Although Mill advocates the free exchange of ideas as the optimal condition for intellectual advancement, it is neither a necessary condition nor a sufficient condition for discovering truths. It cannot be a necessary condition because argumentation's role in justifying individuals' beliefs presupposes the antecedent existence of those beliefs, some of which, presumably, will be true (although perhaps not yet knowledge). Nor is it sufficient because the marketplace of ideas model would then imply that the majority opinion is the right one: the essential component of the marketplace model is that while each individual customer has the power to decide for her or himself whether to purchase or pass on the wares, the effective verdict rests with the majority. Mill, of course, does not acquiesce to the idea that the majority opinion is the right one, nor even that it is more likely to be true. History tells us otherwise, and if so, there would be no need for the "market interventions" cited earlier. Rather, the importance of a (relatively free) exchange of ideas is not that it reliably generates truth but that it allows argumentation to do what it does best: test ideas, expose errors, modify positions, and encourage the exploration of new ideas (Mill 1859, ¶¶ 7-10).

Argumentation does not always yield the truth; it is not an algorithm for producing knowledge; nevertheless, it serves positive epistemological (and social-political) purposes. In an ideal world populated by perfectly rational beings, a completely free exchange of ideas would be optimal. In this world, however, where truth is not the same as surviving public debate and public debate is not a level playing field, some interventions are called for to boost unpopular opinions and maximize our chances of arriving at truth. Mill's interventions are all on the side of encouraging and enabling argumentation. He can tell us why we should argue, when we should, but we still await an answer as to why, when we should not argue, we should not.

6. ARGUING FOR UTILITY, ARGUING FROM VIRTUE

A consequence of Mill's emphasis on the epistemological effects of argumentation and the concomitant association of truth and utility is that Mill always has ample reason to engage in argument but he needs defeaters to justify refraining from argument when that is appropriate. That is, he finds himself back at square one with respect to the when-and-why questions. Since "Is that really true?" is arguably an open question that can always be asked, argumentation can always be justified. What is needed is some way to counter the standing presumption in favor of argument. The obvious route would be to invoke Utilitarianism in order to determine what to do in specific occasions. That route can take us only so far if truth is given privileged status.

One option is simply to deny that according truth the "highest" utility means that its value is privileged or somehow qualitatively different than other considerations. Moving in that direction is consonant with the spirit of Mill's rejection of Bentham's strictly quantitative hedonism: Mill did not accede to the idea that push-pin is as good as poetry.[6] As in the general case, however, the price for recognizing qualitative differences in the utility of the effects of argumentation is having to give up the dream of a quantitative or algorithmic reckoning. Unless the myriad individual cognitive gains of argumentation and all the political benefits to public debate, as well as the personal costs to confrontation-averse individuals and all the social costs of an argumentative culture, can be quantified and put on a single scale, there can be no formula to tell us whether to argue. Thus, since an "argumentative calculus" would be no better than a hedonic calculus at accommodating qualitatively different kinds of values, it would be incomplete and inadequate as a decision procedure for when and when not to argue.

Hansen 2005 sums it up this way: "Mill's views on argumentation fit the criteria for an art, pretty much on par a par with ethics as an art." We can now add that in addition to the skills involved in knowing how to argue, there is a skill to recognizing opportunities to argue, but knowing when not to argue is an art.

---

6. There are several versions of Jeremy Bentham's oft-quoted (and misquoted) claim. An early (perhaps the first) version, from "The Rationale of Reward" in 1830 is more conditional "Prejudice apart, the game of push-pin is of equal value with the arts and sciences of music and poetry. If the game of push-pin furnish more pleasure, it is more valuable than either."

Perhaps 'art' is the wrong word because it is a positive inter-personal skill that one can deliberately set out to acquire, one that can be improved with careful nurturing, and one that can become inculcated as a habit, a standing disposition, and finally a character trait. In practice, it can be situated as the mean between the pathological extremes of over-argumentativeness, the tendency to argue about all the time about anything whatsoever, and excessive argument-avoidance, whether out of reticence, inability, disinterest, or inattentiveness. It is, in short, a virtue.[7] It is, moreover, the virtue that is characteristically on display by good citizens in the marketplace and, more generally, by rational beings at their best.

7. HISTORICIST POST-SCRIPT

Bringing in virtues answers one question for Mill's theory of argumentation but it creates two more.

First, if argumentative virtues are introduced into Mill's general framework, is their status a priori or a posteriori? If they are a priori, there is the epistemological problem of how we know them possible as well as the ethical problem that there are no guarantees that their overall net utility is positive. It would be a contingent matter, for example, whether open-mindedness, a standard example of an intellectual or argumentative virtue, is in fact a virtue. Since it exposes our existing beliefs to revision, it would have to be seen whether it results in acquiring or losing more true beliefs. On the other hand, if the virtues are a posteriori, as would be expected given Mill's thoroughgoing empiricism, then it would be a contingent and mutable matter as to which character traits count as virtues (see, e.g., Cohen 2010).

---

7. Without getting into the debates on the proper criteria for what counts as an (intellectual) virtue, I am largely following the general lead of Annas and Zagzebski, but for the specific context of argumentation, I look to the *locus classicus*, Aberdein 2010.

The second question is related to the first: what makes a virtue a virtue? That is, which comes first, utility or virtues?[8] Mill would seem committed to making utility, in an empirically testable sense, the foundational value, along with a reliabilist account of virtues determined by their consequences. That would render the virtues eliminable for theoretical purposes – but would make them unhelpful for the when-and-why questions, putting us back at square one yet again.

I would like to conclude by suggesting a line of reasoning that may answer both questions without losing the solution to the when-and-why problem. It is inspired by Hansen's extracting and reconstructing of Mill's theory of argumentation, partly by what he says but more by what he does. Hansen approaches argumentation using tools and perspectives from all of the disciplines that were cited in the opening paragraph as necessary contributors to argumentation theory: communications theory, linguistics, rhetoric, sociology, cognitive psychology, and philosophy. The list was not meant to be exhaustive but there was one very important omission: history. Hansen brings a much-needed historical perspective to bear on argumentation in two ways: as a scholar of informal logic and critical thinking, he is acutely aware of the evolution and recent growth of argumentation theory as a discipline; as a student of the history of philosophy, he is also sensitive to the evolution of the phenomenon of argumentation itself. Even if we think of arguments as more or less static or stable objects, we cannot think of argumentation that way. What counts as arguing well differs from one time and place to another.

Perhaps argumentation has not changed as dramatically as our theories have, but the practice, institutions, and significance of

8. This question is a variant of the objection raised by Godden 2016 against agent-centered, virtue theories of argumentation. The response suggested here, to abandon foundationalism in favor of a coherentist-holism, can also serve as a response to Godden.

arguments today are not what they were when Aristotle and Cicero weighed in on them. At the very least, we cannot assume at the outset that just because Mill writes in recognizable English, he was talking about the exact same thing we are. Arguing with Bertrand Russell in a Cambridge seminar differed in content, style, and goals from arguing with Aquinas in Medieval Paris – the ideal of first-order logic does not fit neatly into the *quaestio* format – and neither was the same as arguing with Socrates in the Athenian agora. And those arguments differ even more from arguments in a Canadian or American court of law, not to mention ecclesiastical or sharia courts. Could Mill have had anything like today's on-line argumentation in mind when he wrote about public debate? Do Mill's arguments for greater tolerance of intemperate arguments when they are on behalf of unpopular positions apply to the trolls infesting the internet?

The suggestion, then, is to take a more historicist approach to the phenomenon of argumentation, along with more holistic approaches to all of its constituents. Argumentation cannot be understood apart from its history and historical context. Nor can its parts be understood independent of one another: what counts as an argument, who counts as an arguer, and which traits are argumentative virtues are moving parts that have evolved together. None is the foundation for all the others. The same should be said about the telos of argumentation which explains why we bother to argue all – and the perils of argumentation which explains why sometimes we should not.

REFERENCES

Aberdein, A. 2010. "Virtue in argument." *Argumentation* 24(2), 165-179.

Annas, J. 2011. *Intelligent Virtue*. Oxford University Press.

Cohen, D.H. 2011. "On academic arguments," in F. Zenker (Ed.), *Argumentation, Cognition, and Community*: Proceedings of the

9th International Conference of the Ontario Society for the Study of Argumentation (OSSA).

Cohen, D.H. 2010. "Keeping an open mind and having a sense of proportion," *Cogency*, 1(2), 49-64.

Cohen, D.H. 2001. "Arguing with God," Ontario Society for the Study of Argumentation. Windsor, ON.

Godden, D. 2016. "On the priority of agent-based argumentative norms," *Topoi* 35(2), 354-357.

Gordon, J.P. 1997. "John Stuart Mill and the 'marketplace of ideas'," *Social Theory and Practice*, 23, 235-249.

Govier, T. 1992. *A Practical Study of Argument*, 3rd ed. Belmont CA: Wadsworth.

Hansen, H.V. 2015. "Whateley on kinds of arguments," Cogency 7, 81-108.

Hansen, H.V. 2014. "Mill, informal logic and argumentation," in Antis Loizides (Ed.), *John Stuart Mill's A System of Logic: Critical Appraisals*, pp. 192-217. London & New York: Routledge.

Hansen, H.V., 2007. "Mill on argumentation," *Proceedings of the 6th conference on the International Society for the Study of Argumentation*, pp. 71-581. Amsterdam: SicSat.

Hansen, H.V. 2006. "Mill and Pragma-Dialectics," in P. Houtlosser and A. van Rees (Eds.), *Considering Pragma-Dialectics*, pp. 97-107. Mahwah, NJ: Erlbaum.

Hansen, H.V. 2005. "Did Mill have a theory of argumentation?" Ontario Society for the Study of Argumentation. Windsor, ON.

Hansen, H.V. 1997. "Mill on inference and fallacies," in D.N. Walton and A. Brinton (Eds.), *Historical Foundations of Informal Logic*, pp. 125-143. Aldershot: Ashgate.

Hansen, H.V., 1996. "Aristotle, Whately, and the taxonomy of fallacies," in D.M. Gabbay and H.J. Ohlbach (Eds.), *Practical Reasoning: International Conference on Formal and Applied Practical Reasoning*, pp. 318-30. Berlin: Springer.

Hansen, H.V. and R.C. Pinto (Eds.). 1995. *Fallacies: Classical and Contemporary Readings.* University Park, PA: The Pennsylvania State University Press.

Johnson, R.H. and J.A. Blair. 1977. *Logical Self-Defense.* Toronto: McGraw-Hill Ryerson. (4th ed., New York: McGraw-Hill, 1994; 4th ed. reprint, New York: IDEA Press, 2006.)

Kasser, J.L. and D.H. Cohen. 2002. "Putnam, truth, and logic," *Philosophica* (Belgium) 69, 85-109.

Mercier, H. and D. Sperber. 2011. "Why do humans reason? Arguments for and argumentative theory," *Behavioral and Brain Sciences* 234, 57-111.

Mill, J.S. 1998 (1859). *On Liberty.* Penguin Books.

Mill, J.S. 2002 (1843). *A System of Logic: Ratiocinative and Inductive.* University Press of the Pacific.

Misak, C. 2017. "Ramsey's 1929 pragmatism," in C. Misak and H. Price (Eds.), *The Practical Turn: Pragmatism in Britain in the Long Twentieth Century,* pp. 11-29. Oxford: Oxford University Press.

ABOUT THE AUTHOR: Daniel H. Cohen is a professor of philosophy at Colby College in Waterville, Maine. He is the author of *Arguments and Metaphors in Philosophy* as well as numerous articles on virtue argumentation, Wittgenstein, logic and the philosophy of language. He was one of the keynote speakers at OSSA 2013 and deserves most of the blame for *The Arguer's Lexicon.*
dhcohen@colby.edu

CHAPTER 3.

RUSSELL AND ARISTOTLE ON FIRST PRINCIPLES: A SURPRISING CONCURRENCE

JOHN WOODS

ABSTRACT: Since the beginning, logic has been the canonical regulatory framework for all deductive thought. There is a particularly powerful implementation of this idea in Frege, whose purpose was to secure the foundations of mathematics by proving that all its truths lie in the demonstrative closure of the axioms of pure logic. For this to be achieved, definitions would have to be accurate and air-tight, proofs would have to be thoroughly leak-proof, and the axioms would have to be self-certifying. For a brief period, Russell had come to this view independently. When, shortly after, Russell found the contradiction in Frege's Axiom V, Frege abandoned logicism (and sets too), and Russell changed the subject in ways that aren't widely enough known. He abandoned his former quest for mathematical certainty and replaced it with a programme for its inductive justification. What he appears not to have known is that Aristotle had done the same for all of deductive science, and had done it with a greater aplomb with his use of dialectical measures.

KEYWORDS: Aristotle, axiom, demonstrative closure, dialectic, induction, mathematics, paradox, Russell, unanalyzability.

1. RUSSELL'S LOGICISMS

In *The Principles of Mathematics,* his first post-idealist book in the philosophy of mathematics, Russell described the major part of his project as advancing

> the proof that all pure mathematics deals exclusively with concepts definable in terms of a very small number of fundamental logical concepts, and that all its propositions are deducible from a very small number of fundamental logical principles. (Russell 1903, v; cf. § 434)

In its strongest and most general form, logicism asserts:

> There is a practical purely logical deductive system D such that, for every mathematical truth α, α is a theorem of D.[1]

We should note right at the start that the early logicists were operating with notions of "logical" and "logic" which aren't clearly explained. In one of its recognized senses, a logical truth is a proposition whose truth is invariant under all permutations of possible fact. It was generally conceded that, so conceived-of, logical propositions are incapable of forming existence-proofs, which are necessary for the advancement of mathematics.[2] To that end, purpose-built axioms could be added to the principles of logic. But it is deeply unclear as to how, on that account, axioms could qualify as truths of logic. For ease of reference let's call this *logic's opacity problem.* I will come back to it.

We can date the origin of Russell's logicism from his meeting with Peano in Paris at the 1900 International Congress of Philosophy, where he became aware of Peano's axiomatization of arithmetic the year before (Peano 1889). Russell would later describe

1. "Practical" here means "subject to recursive axiomatization". See Klement (2019, 165).
2. I note in passing that in his letter to Frege, Russell sounds a theme that echoes today, namely, that "foundations of mathematics and formal logic... can hardly be distinguished" (Russell 1902/1967a, 124).

this as one of the most momentous events of his philosophical life (Russell 1958, 11). For two or so years prior to the Paris Congress, Russell had been trying to free himself from Kantian and idealist distractions in the philosophy of mathematics, mainly under the influence of Moore. He had been having difficulties.[3] Paris changed all that. Russell was now a logicist. His was the logicism he saw in Peano's axiomatization.

One of the things that logicism could not be is the doctrine that Russell co-founded with Frege. Russell was too young to have co-founded logicism with anyone. He was junior to Frege by twenty-four years, and to Peano by fourteen. When the first volume of Frege's logicist masterwork *Grundgeseteze* appeared (Frege 2013), Russell was Seventh Wrangler in the Mathematics Tripos in Cambridge. When Peano advanced his axioms for number theory, Russell was seventeen. Moreover, in the run-up to his first meeting with Peano, Russell (as he reports) hadn't been aware of Frege's work on logicism.[4] Again, Russell owes his conversion to *logicism* not to Frege, but rather to Peano. Although Peano was Russell's logicist muse, it was Moore who drew him from mathematical idealism to the ways of *conceptual analysis*. Logicism was Russell's destination and Moore's conceptual analysis would be its means of arrival. Indeed, on Russell's own telling, philosophy of mathematics would have been impossible in the absence of the lessons he learned from Moore.

3. See here Griffin and Lewis (1990) and Moore (1993). Russell is not alone in having misjudged Kant's importance for the advancement of analytic philosophy. Still, this doesn't matter for what matters in the present essay. See, for example, Lapointe (2019), pages 19-27, and Heis (2019).

4. Not everyone accepts the disclaimer. Russell is said to have concealed his awareness of other breakthrough works of the period, for example that of Charles Peirce in (Peirce, 1870, 1883a, 1883b). See here Annelis (1995). In his letter to Frege, Russell says that "[f]or a year and a half I have been acquainted with your *Grundgesetze der Arithmetik...*" (Russell 1902/1967, 124). The letter is dated 16 June, 1902. Russell's acquaintance would have originated in December, 1900.

Before learning these views from him, I found myself completely unable to construct any philosophy of arithmetic, whereas their acceptance brought about an immediate liberation from a large number of difficulties which I believe to be otherwise irreparable. The doctrines just mentioned are, in my opinion quite indispensable to any even tolerably satisfactory philosophy of mathematics. (Russell 1903/1937, xviii)

We should pause to take brief note of the state that 19th century mathematics was in. It was a golden age of innovation and it was a time of methodological anxiety. New and strongly counterintuitive ideas came "fast and thick", and bold new conjectures were framed around notions with which there had been no prior acquaintance. Here is a small sample of the new ideas: Riemann's ntuply extended magnitudes, irrational, imaginary and complex numbers, complex functions, elliptical functions, progressive harmonic conjugates and Desarguesian planes. There were widely placed worries about the use of such notions in the absence of uniquely identifying definitions of them. As a broad expository expedient, we'll label the possessors of those worries as "Weierstrassian". However, there were also those who favoured putting these alien concepts into mathematical play with a view to assessing their fruitfulness in establishing independently provable results. If the record were good, a recondite term's meaning could be seen as implicitly defined. We'll say that promoters of this view were "Riemannian." I don't intend these labels in any literal way. I use them rather as labels for two different kinds of methodological sensibility. Although the labels are a loose convenience, they suffice for saying what is materially true about Russell. In his early logicism Russell was a Weierstrassian; in his later logicism he was a Riemannian.

At the heart of Weierstrassian anxiety were the three main ways in which a mathematical theory lay vulnerable to epistemic insult, that is, to the breech of its defences against inapparent error. They were (and still are) the Terrible Three:

1. False axioms.

2. Slovenly definitions.

3. Leaky proofs.

A widely shared view of how to avoid inadvertent exposure to these liabilities was to frame one's axioms as analytic truths, one's definitions as analytically rigorous and comprehensive, and one's proof rules as analyticity-preserving. The question this posed for mathematicians and philosophers alike was by what means are these safeguards effected? Let's call this *the effectuation task*.

Frege, as it happened, mismanaged the effectuation task. In *Grundlagen* (1884/1950, 4), he identifies an analytic truth of a given subject-matter as a proposition that falls in the demonstrative closure of its first principles or primitive truths. Having characterized a primitive truth as one that is neither needful nor susceptible of demonstration, it follows that no primitive truth of the subject-matter in question lies in the demonstrative closure of any of its propositions. Hence, no axiom is analytic and no axiomatic proof is analyticity-preserving. Frege did not manage to solve the effectuation task. He appears not even to have twigged to it. We might think the oversight is easily corrected. Simply retrofit the concept of analyticity to denote a subject-matter's primitive truths and all else in their demonstrative closures. It won't work. Even if we made it analytic that primitive truths are analytic, in the absence of an assured recognition-procedure for primitive truth, no given sentence S in the form "S is a primitive truth" could be known to be analytic. Frege had no recognition-procedure for analyticity and none either for primitive truth. Had he possessed one, he would have averted the embarrassment of Basic Law V. Nor was this a problem peculiar to Frege. It is an important enough matter to have a name. Let's call it the *recognizability problem* for first principles. I'll put it aside for now, and will come back to it at a more opportune moment.

What, then, are the methods that would discharge the effectuation task? For Moore they were the methods of analytical regression, the methods whereby the concepts of arithmetic are decomposed into their simpler component parts and they, in turn, are decomposed into still simpler conceptual subparts, until eventually the process of decomposition terminates in the exposure of the concept's irreducibly simple conceptual elements. These, the basic concepts, are not only indefinable, but are also intuitively grasped by the mind in ways that reveal the utter certainty of the propositions that give them expression. By this Moore means propositions for whose formulation it suffices to have an intuitive understanding of the necessary interrelations among concepts and of their links to simple concepts. Thus, from its primitive concepts do the primitive truths of arithmetic arise. The basic laws of arithmetic, we could call them. Russell summarizes the method he learned from Moore:

> [it] will therefore be one of analysis, and our problem may be called philosophical – in the sense, that it is to say, that we seek to pass from the complex to the simple, from the demonstrable to its indemonstrable premises. (Russell 1903/1937, 2)

Come back now to the opacity problem posed by the logic that logicists invoke. The truths unearthed by conceptual analysis could be (and have been) called conceptual truths. We *might* think that, like the truths of logic, a conceptual truth remains true under all permutations of possible fact. If so, a conceptual truth would have two things going for it. One is that it couldn't be false. The other is that conceptual truths are able to convey existential consequences. For example, suppose that by conceptual analysis we had it that any natural number that is the successor of no natural number is identical to zero. Then there would exist just one natural number that isn't the successor of any other. Compare this kind of case with the logical truth "$\forall x \sim (Fx \wedge \sim Fx)$". When we say that its truth is invariant under all permutations of possible fact, we mean to point out that it remains true under all uniform substitutions for its non-logical terms. Note, however, that we can't say this of "There is exactly one natural number that isn't the successor of any natural number". It is false when we substitute "first-born child" for "natural number".[5]

From its inception, logic has provided the canonical regulatory framework for all deductive thought. It would only be natural to think of each of the deductive sciences as subject to the laws of logic, which not only countervail against error but assist materially in the exposure of truth. So seen, mathematics would be a proper subtheory of logic, hence in that sense a part of it. This disposed Dedekind to say that all laws of mathematics are laws of logic (a nice lawyerly piece of wordmanship). Frege saw it the other way round. Every law of logic is a principle of mathematics. Thus does the opacity problem darken. For a valuable discussion, see Reck (2019).

Some people find Russell's tribute to Moore excessively generous and unrealistic. Russell was groping for the foundations of arithmetic, but Moore was plumbing the foundations of ethics. There is no doubt, even so, that Russell did regard Moore as fully capable of contributions to logic. In reply to his letter of 1898 concerning Moore's own Trinity Fellowship dissertation, Russell writes,

> I agree most emphatically with what you say about the several kinds of necessary relations among concepts, and I think their discovery is the true business of Logic (or Meta[physics] if you like). (Preti, 2019, 189)

On Moore's view, the primitive truths of a subject matter were self-evidently true and known to be so *à priori*. Moore also

---

5. We have here the distinction between semantically necessary and logical truths. It has widely circulated since, and before, Tarski came upon it in 1936. See Tarski (2002/1936, 186 and 188-189). A still unresolved difficulty is finding a principled way of distinguishing logical from nonlogical terms. See Tarski (1986).

thought that the definitions by which conceptual analyses were wrought were rigorous and secure, and so too the rules by which further propositions could be truth-preservingly derived from primitive truths and their *demonstrata*. That was also Peano's position and Frege's own. So, we may say that, while not of expressly logicist *intent*, Moore's tutelage of him predisposed Russell to the logicism he got from Peano and to what he later learned of Frege. So interpreted, the chief philosophical value of analytic logicism was the purport of certainty it afforded the primitive truths, definitions and proof-rules of arithmetic. In their efforts to solve the Terrible Three, Frege and the early Russell had embraced *epistemic* logicism.

Then something happened. It happened in a way that re-triggered the recognition problem for axioms. In the spring of 1901, Russell came upon the contradiction implied by *Grundgesetze*'s Basic Law V, the unrestricted comprehension axiom for sets (actually, for Frege, value-ranges of concepts and, for Russell, classes).[6] A year later, on June 16th, he communicated the discovery to Frege, and eight days after that Frege sent Russell his reply.[7] The contradiction drove Frege to abandon logicism as an irremediably lost cause. The reasons why are pondered in Woods (2019). Its impact on Russell was momentous. The year after his letter to Frege, Russell disavowed the very concept of class (set). Writing in *Principles*, he says

> I have failed to perceive *any* concept fulfilling the conditions requisite for the notion of *class*. (Russell 1903/1937, xv-xvi; emphasis in the first instance mine.)

It was a daunting concession, making it clear that Russell had come to think that the jig was up for analytical logicism. In

6. Russell appears not to have known of Zermelo's derivation of it the year before. See Hallett (1984).

7. Russell (1902/1967), in van Heijenoort (1967). Frege's reply follows at pages 127-128 (Frege, 1967).

1901-02 Russell accepted that sets or something like them were needed for modern mathematics. Given that the concept of set had now been revealed to be empty, Russell abandoned all hope that the foundations of mathematics lay within philosophy's capacity to expose. On the original understanding, sets were the instantiations of that philosophically analyzable concept. In its sadly conceded absence, it was a given that nothing whatever is a set. Although Frege forsook logicism as a lost cause, Russell retained the name and applied it to something entirely different. He found a way to make sets up. He did so by way of *mathematical definition*.

> [I]t is necessary to realize that definition, in mathematics, does not mean, as in philosophy, an analysis of the idea to be defined into constituent ideas. This notion, in any case, is only applicable to concepts, whereas in mathematics it is possible to define terms which aren't concepts. (*Ibid.*, 27)

Russell adds that

> of the three kinds of definition admitted by Peano – the nominal definition, the definition by postulates, and the definition by abstraction – I recognize only the nominal. (*Ibid.*, 112)

Russell sometimes called his new approach the method of synthesis, the method of making up new terms from bits and pieces of old ones. Henceforth his would be a *synthetic logicism,* and epistemic logicism would be a foregone dream. In short order, Russell would learn to do without certainty and settle for nonconclusive reasons to believe the logical foundations of mathematics to be true. He would try to find this justification by reducing mathematics to a nonanalytic version of logic. In effect, he had declared unsolvable the recognition problem for analyticity and first principlehood.

In *Principia Mathematica,* Whitehead and Russell introduced ramified type theory and provided for the contextual elimination of classes in favour of quantification over propositional functions. Ramified types were problematic. Some fundamental theorems of real number theory could not be proved or even expressed. Russell sought relief in the axiom of reducibility, but none of its applications managed to work. Russell finally admitted reducibility's inadequacy, and he omitted it from the second edition (Irvine 1989, 321-322). The no-class theory drew criticism from the start, and still does. The problem centres on what classes made room for. Geach (1972) found the notion of propositional function "hopelessly confused and inconsistent" (272), and years later Cartwright (2005) sounded the same bell, adding that "attempts to say what exactly a Russellian propositional function is, or is supposed to be, are bound to end in frustration" (915). However, a strong defence of Russell is advanced by Klement (2010). For all its importance to Russell scholarship, this is another of those issues that needn't over-occupy us here. It suffices to observe that the no-class manoeuvre was not part of Russell's position in the early aftermath of the paradox. We need to take care with this. Although the 1903 Russell found there to be no concept of class, he was *not* then espousing the no-class theory. He was not saying that classes could be contextually eliminated. The devices of contextual elimination were first worked out in Russell (1905) for the putative denota of definite description. It must, in truth, be said that in his disavowal of the concept of class, Russell wasn't entirely on the level. What he should have said is that he could find no concept of class that admitted of philosophical analysis.

Once again, the opacity problem has bestirred. It was commonly agreed among 19th century mathematicians that all of upper mathematics (excluding the Euclidean parts of geometry) could be re-expressed without relevant loss in number theory. This was the *arithmeticist* thesis. Logicism, in turn, was the thesis that number theory can be re-expressed without relevant loss in logic. This latter reduction, it was thought, would solve the Terrible Three problem for mathematics, since logic, as the canonical regulatory framework for all deductive thought, was itself immune from the Terrible Three. Logicism thus conceived was now at a fateful juncture. Set theory is *not* immune from the Terrible Three, and as long as it remains an undetachable part of logic, neither is logic epistemically assured. All the same, Russell is determined to proceed with the reduction of mathematics. He will proceed with it by mathematical measures that reduce mathematics to a retrofitted theory of sets that are now mathematically defined. The theory of deductive thought is fortunate in having had a single word for it – 'logic'. Had the same been true of set theory, the word would have been *setics* or some near thing.[8] If we had such a word, we'd be able to provide an accurate and non-question-begging characterization of the reductionism championed by Russell. It wouldn't be logicism. It would be *seticism*.[9] Let us note well that if setics is indeed an indispensable part of logic, then logicism is true only if seticism is. As it happens, seticism is not true.[10]

In the beginning, Russell had seen the first principles of a discipline in the way in which Moore had seen the primitive truths disclosed by conceptual analysis. Frege was similarly minded. Indeed, Frege had viewed his first principles in the way that Aristotle had viewed the first principles of any of the mature deductive sciences – as true, necessary, primary, and neither needful nor suspectible of independent demonstration. When disaster struck, Frege gave up on seticism and, believing setics to be an undetachable part of logic, he gave up on logicism too. He should, in fact, have given up on logic. Of course, that is precisely what

---

8. By analogy with *strategics,* the science of strategic reasoning.

9. The same could be said of Frege's pre-paradox reductionist programme for arithmetic. The second-order functional calculus was constructed by mathematical methods and all its major working parts had seen first light in mathematical practice – variables, variable-binding, polydic relations, functions, ω-progressions, mathematical induction, and so on.

10. Benacerraf (1965).

he didn't do.[11] As far as I know, the drastic vulnerability of the undetachability thesis hasn't been remarked on before. It is easy to see in hindsight why it would have dropped from sight about a century ago. As we have it now, logic is first-order quantification theory with identity, and set theory has gone home to mathematics where it always belonged. And what is still spoken of as logicism is, in truth, seticism and nothing more.

What concerns us here is how Russell adjusted his view of first principles or, to use the more usual term, axioms. As before a theory's theorems would be all and only those propositions in the demonstrative closure of its axioms. As before, Russell would see the axioms as instruments of logic and mathematics as wholly contained in their demonstrative closure. As before, Russell would remain faithful to the undetachability thesis, the thesis that set theory is intrinsic to logic. Even so, it is now a radically changed world for Russell. Axioms no longer go surety for irrefutable truth and the contents of their demonstrative closure have lost all claim to certainty. All the same, Russell would retain his confidence in the view that the last best hope for the rational security of mathematics lies in the embrace of a logic incapable of establishing its own foundational certitude.

Something else that Russell would retain is the regressive method. The axioms for mathematics would be disclosed by the painstaking examination of cases. Russell would search for the least class of unproved truths from which the obvious parts of mathematics ("1 + 1 = 2", e.g.) could be validly derived. Then if, in combination with some of those axioms and obvious propositions of mathematics, some further but nonobvious parts of mathematics could be derived and, by recursive repetition, still yet further ones, there would come a point at which there would be reason to believe the axioms to be true. This would mark the point at which Russell's earlier Weierstrassian sensibilities

11. For details of Frege's post-paradox work in logic see Reck and Awodey (2004). See also Woods (2019, sect. 5).

would give way to Riemannian ones. In place of the once sought-for certitude of mathematics, now abandoned as a lost cause, Russell thinks that we can make do with the lesser epistemic good afforded by reasons to believe. This plan of rescue is laid out in a lecture entitled "The regressive method of discovering the premises of mathematics", read by Russell to the Cambridge Mathematics Club in October 1907. The lecture never saw the published light of day in Russell's lifetime, first appearing three years after his death. (Russell, 1973) One wonders, why the delay?

Generalization by the examination of cases used to have the approving name of *casuistry*. Regrettably the name has now fallen out of favour, and is often taken to describe the fallacy of tendentious generalization from nonrepresentative samples. In intellectually honest form, it is standard practice in common law. It is also standard practice in the physical sciences. One examines the flow of a science's practices to see in them the recurring patterns of explanatory promise animating the data they unearth. If, over time, the patterns remain invariant over expanded data-bases, the more reasonable the inference that the principles governing those data are to be found in these patterns. This is Russell's view of how the principles of mathematics are to be discerned. He is careful to say that the inferences from data to explanatory premisses are *inductively* structured:

> The inferring of premises from consequences is the essence of induction. (*Ibid.*, 274)

They are structured in the way of inferences from observable phenomena to the laws or lawlike regularities that appear to account for them. Russell writes,

> ... the logical premises have, as a rule, many more consequences than the empirical premises, and thus lead to the discovery of many things which could not otherwise be known. The law gravitation, for example, leads to many consequences which could not be discovered merely from the apparent motion of the heavenly bodies,

which are our empirical premises. And so in arithmetic, taking the ordinary propositions of arithmetic as our empirical premises, we are led to a set of logical premises from which we can deduce Cantor's theory of the transfinite. (*Ibid.*, 275)

Thus is the measure of logic's fall from the grace of intellectual certainty to the likeliness of good reasons. On Russell's telling, it was a fall from a grace it had never actually possessed, and what it had fallen to was no wise to be considered a disgrace. Logic now enjoys the dignity of the lawlike physical sciences.

On the face of it, one might think that Russell's inductivism bears the mark of inference to the best explanation. Irvine reports a suggestion that Scott Kleiner put to him in conversation during the writing of the 1989 paper. The suggestion was that Russell's mathematical inductivism was *abductively* structured (Irvine 1989, 322, note 26). Irvine remains noncommittal, beyond remarking that "the regressive method is *similar* to Peirce's abduction." (*idem;* emphasis mine). That it isn't similar enough to matter is the burden of Woods (forthcoming) to show. I won't trifle with it here, preferring to stand moot on that question. For what presently concerns us, it suffices to highlight a fact of possibly related importance:

> *The support of mathematical practice thesis*: In its general thrust, if not in all particulars such as they may be, Russell's mathematical inductivism is discernible in mathematical practice, a practice in which axioms usually come after the benefits of employing them as working hypotheses start showing.[12]

This bears nicely on the Weierstrass-Riemann distinction. It is true that the innovative side of mathematics is heavily conjectural and Riemannian, but it is standard practice to apply Weier-

---

12. Of course, there are exceptions. *Purely* exploratory axiomatics fulfill the old Madison Avenue admonition for the thinking-up of advertising campaigns: "Let's run this one up the flag-pole and see if anyone salutes." But even these outlier ideas simply don't occur to people without experience in the fields in question.

strassian rigour to demonstrations of the validity of their fruitful consequences.

Before closing this section, it might repay us to take one more stab at the opacity of logic problem. In Britain, Germany and elsewhere there were sharp disagreements about what was logic and what was not. There were quarrels about the overall state that logic was in during the perturbations that roiled 19th century mathematics. To give some flavour of the issues in contention, here is John Cook Wilson, Oxford's Wykeham Professor of Logic, concerning what he saw as trivial encroachments on logic by "symbolic" logicians in the manner of Boole and Venn:

> [S]ymbolic logic as such consists of a solution of particular problems, which are on the same plane as the solution of geometrical or algebraic problems and, though concerned with the abstract forms of subject and predicate, as specially scientific as these mathematical processes – no more logic than they are, and related to logic precisely as they are. Incidentally there is a little elementary logic involved, but the real and serious problems of logic proper do not appear, nor is the symbolic logician able to touch them. In comparison with the serious business of logic proper, the occupations of the symbolic logician are merely trivial. (Cook Wilson 1926, 637)

Good discussions of such disputations can be found in Peckhaus, (1999) and Moktefi (2019).

Consider now an observation of Kant's which helps frame our question.

> [S]ince the time of Aristotle [formal deductive logic] has not had a single step backwards, unless we count the abolition of a few dispensable subtleties on the more distinct determination of its presentation, which improvements belong more to the elegance than to the security of that science. What is further[more] remarkable about logic is that until now it has also been unable to take a single step forward, and therefore seems to all appearance to be *finished and complete*. (Kant 1781/1787, B viii; emphasis mine)

We may take it that Kant's understanding of formal logic is, in all essentials, the logic of syllogisms in the form in which it had evolved up to his time. Kant seems not to have known that in *On Interpretation* at (17a 13, 18a 19ff, 18a 34) Aristotle makes the very strong reductionist claim that everything stateable in Greek is stateable without relevant loss in the language of categorical propositions (Aristotle 1984; Woods 2014, 31-37). The reduction claim is almost certainly false. But assuming that Aristotle didn't change his mind about it, he would have welcomed Kant's agreement with his own view that the syllogistic was the complete logic of deductive thought. It is a safe bet, however, that no one involved in the logic wars of the 19th century would have known of the reduction claim. Certainly no one would have believed it. One matter on which Aristotle and others were agreed is that the properties of interest to logicians are ascribable to linguistically expressible structures – properties such as logical consequence, logical equivalence, logical consistency, deductive validity, and the like. Others, the metalogical ones, (e.g. decidability, completeness and soundness) are definable over logistic systems. Were the reduction thesis true, the language of categorical propositions would be wholly sufficient for the regulatory control of the deductive sciences. Given that the thesis had no 19th century takers, it is easy to see the properties of logical interest instantiated by various forms of mathematics could not be intelligibly ascribable to structures expressible in the language of categorical propositions. These are, or include, properties that characterize the deductive interconnections between structures of this sort. In particular, we want a concept of generality suitable for the deductive purposes of the new mathematics. In plain words, the deductive sciences had long since outgrown the expressive powers of the syllogistic. The traditional Aristotelian inheritance had run out of steam. A new language would be needed for logic, large enough to encompass the realities of deductive enquiry.

It is beyond question that most of the 19th century innovations in the linguistic expressibility of deductive relations were made by the mathematicians who felt most need of them. It lies aside from the point I want to make here that the innovators tended to flock to wholly artificial character-systems (misleadingly called formal languages) to facilitate their growingly technical means of deductive expression. One of the motivations for turning to the artificial was economy of formulation and the perspicuity of proofs. But the point that I want to lay some stress upon is this:

> *The mathematics isn't logic thesis*: Although the general theory of deduction is distinct and separate from mathematics, it is by no means precluded that its required make-overs could be facilitated by mathematicians in the course of advancing their respective mathematical agendas by their own mathematical means.

It might help to consider this thesis entirely apart from logicistic considerations. Peirce was no logicist. But in constructing his theory of relatives, he considerably expanded the extension of the concept of deductive validity. That alone makes it a significant invitation to logic. So, too, was his invention of variable-binding. Peirce has been called the founding father of quantification theory by Putnam (1982, 298) and Quine (1995a, 259). Goldfarb (1979) is otherwise disposed. We needn't settle this matter here. What counts is that Peirce was not logistically minded, and his invention of quantification was achieved independently of Frege. In each case, mathematicians made mathematically engineered progress in finding new ways of making the *instantiations* of properties of *logical* interest linguistically expressible. It is, I think, a matter of considerable interest that Poincaré should have thought logicism to be of some slight philosophical interest, but was otherwise a distraction from progress in mathematics.

> It is time that these [logicist] exaggerations were treated as they deserve. I have no hope of convincing these logicians, for they have

lived too long in this atmosphere. Besides, when we have refuted one of their demonstrations, we are quite sure to find it cropping up several times from their ashes. Such in old times was the Lernaean hydra, with its famous heads that always grew again. Hercules was successful because his hydra had only nine heads (unless, indeed, it was eleven), but in this case there are too many, they are in England, in Germany, in Italy, and in France, and he would be forced to abandon the task. And so I appeal only to unprejudicial people of common sense." (Poincaré 1914, 145-146)

For more on Poincaré on logicism, symbolic logic and the foundations of mathematics, readers could consult Goldfarb (1988) and Detlefsen (2011-2012).

It also bears mention that in these times the word 'logic' was bandied about in loose and undefined ways,[13] evoking the difference between a Weierstrassian and Riemannian sensibility about the use and definition of terms. Of course, 'logic' was far from being a new or even recent term, but its purported denotata were indeed new and numerous. To some extent, the reformists found some advantage in basking in the reflected glory of a highly respected term, while awaiting some sure-footed measures for validating its reformist uses. That would make 'logic' a noun of convenience and self-approval. By these lights, Dedekind was a *bona fide* arithmeticist, but a logician of nominal convenience.

Logic aside, we have it now that the difference between Russell's first and second logicisms coincides perfectly with his change of mind about the nature and status of first principles, a subject to which we must now return.

2. ARISTOTLE ON FIRST PRINCIPLES

It was a great benefit to logic to have been founded by the man who perfected it. I've already touched on Aristotle's reductionist thesis, according to which everything stateable in Greek is re-

---

13. Dedekind thought that logic was mathematics and Frege thought that mathematics was logic. Russell as we see couldn't quite make up his mind.

stateable without relevant loss in the language of categorical propositions. Although Aristotle stated the claim quite clearly, he left no proof of it, and made no further mention of it in the rest of the *Organon*. When these considerations are adjoined to the thesis's utter counterintuitiveness, we have the makings of a decent case for saying that it was the subject of a brief flirtation, quickly abandoned upon more composed reflection. Still, to grasp the full majesty of Aristotle's achievement, it would repay us to grant him the brief benefit of doubting our case against him.

The heart and soul of Aristotle's logic are to be found in *Prior Analytics* and *Posterior Analytics* in that order. *Topics* and *On Sophistical Refutations* do valuable supporting work. (Aristotle 1984). One of the latter pair's most important developments were methods for refuting an opponent's thesis without either party begging the question against the other. Also important was the insertion into logic's project of the concept of fallacy, concerning which see Woods and Hansen (1997) and Hintikka (1997). The concept of fallacy is defined over syllogisms. A fallacy is an apparent syllogism which is not in fact one in reality. A syllogism is a three part sequence of categorical propositions whose terminal member follows of necessity from the two others, the premisses. In slightly different words, a syllogism is a valid premiss-conclusion argument which fulfills further conditions. One is that the premisses be two in number and that the number of its different and inequivalent general terms sum to three. Premisses may not include the syllogism's conclusion, and neither of them can directly imply it. Premisses must be both internally and collectively consistent. The result of adding a further premiss to a syllogism's three is a valid argument that is not a syllogism. So Aristotle forbids the introduction of further terms ("from the outside") that aren't "causative" of the syllogism's conclusion. Finally, conclusions of syllogisms must be single propositions only. From its very founding, Aristotle's logic was nonmonotonic, relevantist, trivially paraconsistentist, and some fair approximation to an intuitionist one. Logic entered the realm of scientific ideas in about as nonclassical a form as logic gets.

In Aristotle's approach, the concepts of validity and logical implication are theoretical primitives. They are informally defined, but aren't subject to further analyses or theoretical excavation. Implication is the converse of the relation of following of necessity from. An argument is valid just in case its premises jointly imply its conclusion. Given the utter centrality of the concept of validity to the logic of syllogisms, the absence of its theoretical development might strike one as a fateful omission, leaving the very concept of syllogism in a scientifically undeveloped state. The same, in turn, would seem to hold for the concept of fallacy. As it happens, Aristotle is well-prepared for these disappointments. It was the great and near-perfect (and repairable) achievement of *Prior Analytics* to forego the theoretical analyses of the concepts of validity in favour of a *semi-decidability proof* for it. It is a proof whereby the validity of a valid argument framed under syllogistic constraints could be made apparent to the man in the street with a practicable timeliness in a quasi-mechanical and infallible way. Once validity is a recognizable property, the concepts of syllogism and fallacy are not only fully defined, but subject in turn to effective recognizability. The details of this remarkable achievement need not detain us here. Essential reading is Corcoran (1972, 1973, 1974a, 1974b). Woods (2014) provides a running commentary.

Prior Analytics is the first breakthrough in metalogic. Should the reduction thesis have actually held water, Aristotle would have given us the first logic in which the validity of any valid argument can be made apparent, and fallacies could be entirely avoided. Aristotle frames the validity problem for the big and solves it for the small, in a way that also solves it for the big. In so doing, Aristotle's has the nose and the soul of a great logician. If, as seems a good deal more likely than not, the reduction thesis did not hold water, then Aristotle's grand programme would have suffered a demotion. He could still solve the validity and fallacy problems for all cases in which arguments meet the syllogistic conditions but not in the general case. Still, the lesson to take away from this setback is highly positive. If the reduction thesis is false, then there will be deductively significant facts to which the syllogistic cannot give expression. It is only natural to suppose that when a richer language is found, semi-decidabilty might be achieved by *modelling* the enriched theory on the methods successfully employed in *Prior Analytics*.

Prior Analytics is not, however, the centre of our present interest in Aristotle's understanding of first principles. For that we'll have to turn to the second great work of the *Organon*. We will need to examine the providence of *Posterior Analytics*. Before going there, I should say that the scholarship underlying my thumbnail sketches of *Prior Analytics* is subject to all the contentiousness and fuss-budgetry of close interpretive analyses of the extant texts. However, it will more than suffice for present purposes to point out that, on a fair and balanced reading of the canon, my sketch is a good approximation to the true-blue facts of the matter.

In turning now to *Posterior Analytics,* we have occasion to wonder what it might have been that *Prior Analytics* had left undone that *Posterior Analytics* would attempt to repair. It will assist us in our endeavours to take note of an important distinction which, to the best of my knowledge, logicians don't explicitly draw. The key concept of logic is the relation of logical consequence, the converse again of the relation of logical implication. (Hereafter I omit "logical" as understood.) There are three different and inequivalent ways in which the consequence relation manifests itself.

Consequence-having: When propositions $\alpha_1, \ldots, \alpha_n$ have β as a consequence, the α_i stand to β in a dyadic relation instantiated in *logical space.*

Consequence-spotting: When consequence-spotting occurs, some agent A rightly sees that some β is a consequence of some $α_i$. Consequence-spotting is a ternary relation defined over antecedents and consequences and cognitive agents. Consequence spotting occurs in *psychological space.*

Consequence-drawing: When consequence-drawing occurs, some agent A forms the true belief that some β is a consequence of some $α_i$ and, on that basis, adds β to his own belief-stock, making such adjustments as may be needed for consistency. Consequence-drawing is a ternary relation over antecedent and consequents and cognitive agents. Consequence-drawing occurs in *inferential* space, which can be considered a subspace of psychological space.[14]

A *full-service* logic for the consequence relation is one which *either* provides for the theoretical development of each of the three relations under present consideration *or* provides adequate compensation for any omission. Aristotle's syllogistic is a full service logic in this latter sense. It omits the theoretical development of consequence-*having*, but compensates for it with a semi-decidability proof engineered in the theoretical development of the consequence-*spotting* relation. This, again, was the principal achievement of *Prior Analytics.* It made the validity of syllogisms effectively recognizable to the man in the street – assuming effective recognizability as adequate compensation for the absence of a deep theoretical analysis of consequence-having. So far, so good, we might think. We'd be right. But there are things that *Prior Analytics* can't do. It can't adequately provide for the relation of consequence-*drawing*. For that we'll have to turn to *Posterior Analytics.*

Consider now a formal discipline such as geometry and a naturalist discipline such as physics. It was Aristotle's view that in suitably developed form, these sciences have a nomological-deductive character, in which its confirmed and/or proved

---

14. It is necessary to respect the difference between an agent's spotting devices and his drawing devices. We should also note that psychological and epistemic considerations are fully licensed parts of Aristotle's logic.

results are validated by the science's basic laws. Aristotle's task in *Posterior Analytics* is to expose the logical structure of the deductive sciences. To that end he constructed a logic of demonstration, which is ably expounded by Corcoran (2009). It is modeled as an axiom system of the same general sort essayed by Euclid. In his lectures on this subject in the UNILOG School of Logic, in the week prior to the 2015 UNILOG Congress in Istanbul, Corcoran reported that Thales has been thought to have axiomatized geometry well before Euclid.[15] Either way, Aristotle would have had the axiomatic method firmly in mind. He goes on to show how from the axioms or basic laws of a deductive science, its every truth can be made known by chains of reasoning in which by the *common rules* of proof – *reductio* proofs, modus ponens, statemental conversion, among others – syllogisms are linked to other syllogisms, eventually terminating in a now-disclosed truth of that discipline. In sum, all disciplines truths lie *transparently* in the demonstrative closure of those axioms. Moving from axioms known to be true, the chains of demonstration are not only truth-preserving but knowledge-producing as well. They are also *subject matter-preserving*, an important feature. It shows that, although he never said so explicitly, Aristotle is sensitive to the distinction between a theory's *deductive* closure and its *demonstrative* closure. To take a simple example, in Peano's system "One is a natural number" is an axiom of number theory. Because every proposition implies itself, it lies in its own deductive closure, but it does not for reasons already given, lie in *any* proposition's demonstrative closure. Axioms, after all, are indemonstrable. We also have it that "One is a natural number" implies "One is a natural number or Nice is nice in November." It lies in Peano's deductive closure but it is not a theorem of arith-

15. Corcoran also reports that Euclid was not himself a mathematician, but someone rather more in the mold of a well-informed science reporter for a good daily newspaper or for magazines for the scientifically interested general reader.

metic. So there we have it. The demonstrative closure of a set of axioms is constituted by the subject-preserving members of its deductive closure *minus* the axioms themselves. Corcoran makes a convincing case for the better than good fist that Aristotle made of the logic of demonstration. I salute it as a masterly and rather breath-taking achievement. But there is one thing that the logic of demonstration does not itself do. It does not provide a recognition-procedure for *axioms*. For that, he must look to other parts of the *Organon*. In fact, we find it elsewhere in *Post. an.*

It may surprise some readers that it was never Aristotle's position that the first principles of a deductive science are self-evident on first sight. He works out a rather complex web of conditions for making a proposition's axiomaticity accessible to someone who might be searching for it. Aristotle's account is developed in the section on *epagôgē*, whose customary translation is "induction", in which the recognition of first principleship is mediated by *noûs*, usually translated as "mind" or "intuition". Another possibility is that *noûs* is the very grasping of first principles (*Post. an.* II, 19 100b). To modern ears, the standard translations are far from helpful. But it must be said that, in the casuistry proposed by Aristotle – generalization by the examination of cases – Russell's own logical inductivism clearly echoes. Aristotle writes, "We learn by *epagôgē* and demonstration. Demonstration proceeds from universals and *epagôgē* from *kathekaston* (particulars)" (*Post. an.* I, 18 81a 40-81b 1).

Aristotle says that no science can discuss its own foundations, a task "which belongs properly, or most appropriately, to dialectic" (*Topics* 101b 2). Even the first principles of logic are the proper business of dialectic, in particular that part of it that regulates induction (*Top.* A 12), which is that mode of reasoning by which the foundations of the sciences are determined (*Post. an.* A7, 75b 12-14 and A 11 77a 26-35). Consider now refutation, itself a species of dialectical or erisitic argument. In a refutation argument one party (the questioner) attempts to refute the thesis

T of another party (the answerer). This is done by putting to T's defender a series of questions, each fully answerable by a simply and unadorned yes-or-no reply. The refutation succeeds if and only if from the answerer's own responses taken as premisses, the attacker is able to construct a syllogism whose conclusion is the contradictory of his opponent's thesis T. Because the premisses are exclusively those endorsed by the party against whom the refutation is directed, the argument cannot be a question-begging one. It is important to note that in Aristotle's rather special sense of the word, a refutation of T does not falsify it. It shows only that its promoter on that occasion has made an inconsistent defence of it. The triple constituted by T and his two conceded premisses of the syllogism against it cannot all be true. In contradicting himself he doesn't show that his *thesis* is contradictory. Aristotle is careful to say that, while a refutation of T is a proof, it is not a proof "in the full sense", though there is "a proof *ad hominem*" (*Metaphysics,* 1062a 2-3; *Pr. an.* B 27 70a 6-7, *Soph. ref.* 167b 8-9). Aristotle shows no disposition to place *ad hominem* proofs on the list of his fallacies; rightly so. This is the point at which *On Sophistical Refutations* and *Prior Analytics* hook up to make a key contribution to *Post. an.*'s attempt to elucidate our grasp of first principles. *Soph. ref.* provides the means of showing when, and under what conditions, a refutation of T succeeds. *Pr. an.* provides the means for ascertaining whether a proferred refutation is indeed a syllogism.

If a refutation succeeds on a given occasion, it mightn't on another. The parties could change and the questions and answers could be different; and rival theses could also be put to the test. An important limitation on refutations is that the theses they target must be dialectical, that is to say, opinions of all, or the many or the wise. In the present case, it is the opinions of the wise that matter – opinions advanced by the discipline's *experts*. It is they who subject the phenomena or the givens of the discipline in question to the casuistric search for candidate first principles.

Suppose that H is one of those candidates. Suppose that, no matter how varied or skillful, all efforts to refute it fail. Then H will have survived against all the expert opinion ranged against it. Suppose also that no rival candidate H* fares better than H. Then Aristotle concludes that since H solves all the current questions left open by the received wisdom and preserves as many of those expert opinions as possible (*Nichomean Ethics,* 1145b 2-7), that should tip the scales in favour of H. The last part of the inductive process is mediated by *noûs,* the faculty of mind that causes former combatants to see that H is true, necessary and primary, and causes them, in turn, to cease further refutational combat. The distinctive difference between Aristotle's and Russell's regressive approach is that, on the latter, an inductive inference to a general law is *evidentially advanced.*[16] For Aristotle a first principle is *causally grasped.* Russell's method (and Frege's too) is epistemically arrived. In the Mure translation (Aristotle, 1941), scientific principles "must be true, primary, immediate, better known than and prior to the conclusion, which is further related to them as effect to cause", thus triggering the question "in which sense of 'cause'?" (*Post. an.* 71b 21-23). The answer is *material cause* (*Physics* 195a 15-19, and *Met.* 1013b 17-21; see also Woods and Hansen, 2001; pp. 408-412).

At *Met.* 1005b 19-20, the most certain of all first principles is set out.

> It is, that the same attribute cannot at the same time belong and not belong to the same subject in the same respect; ...

Strikingly, however, in the lines immediately following, Aristotle adds that

16. I've drawn here on Woods (2019). For further discussion, readers could consult the first edition (if they can find one) of my *Aristotle's Earlier Logic* (2001), chapter 8. The book is now in a second and much revised edition (Woods, 2014). I now regret my decision to omit the original chapter 8, as the first edition is now out of print.

we must presuppose, in face of *dialectical* objections, any further qualifications which might be added. (Emphasis added)

Later, Aristotle considers the Heraclitean thesis that the Law of Non-Contradiction is false. Instead of dismissing the idea out of hand, Aristotle notes that, if true, the anti-LNC thesis is true in all respects or only in some particular respects, adding that, if not all, "the exceptions will have to be *agreed upon*" (1008a 10-11; emphasis added). We now see three senses of "dialectic" in play in Aristotle's reflections on first principles. In the first instance, candidates for consideration of first principleship, likewise those for contrary consideration, must be propositions advanced by experts, which in this case includes the Heraclitean ones. Secondly, all candidates must be subject to last-man-standing refutatory tests, subject to the rules of refutation. Thirdly, any *pro tem* agreement about a proposition's first-principles status is subject to the necessary re-negotiation when challenged by an expert. Not even LNC is immune from the dialectical provocations of expert dissent. There are, then, three important respects in which Aristotle and Russell live on the same street. Both are inductivists about how candidate-laws are thought-up. Russell's good reasons to believe are not evidentially conclusive, and Aristotle's causes to believe aren't either. Third, and foremost, the fallibilism that each subscribes to in the case of the physical sciences, is now transmitted to the foundations of logic.

That Aristotle would have taken the time to deal with the Heraclitean challenge requires some further reflection. Perhaps the first thing to notice is that although it is an imaginary representative of Heraclitus's views who challenges Aristotle's subscription to LNC, Aristotle takes it seriously. His defence of it departs markedly from the rules of procedure laid out in *Top.* and *Soph. ref.* For one thing, it is Aristotle rather than the challenger who accepts the burden of proof and, for another, the means by which he seeks to meet it was not simply by answering yes-or-no questions and hoping for the best. What we see in this is that, while it works out well on paper, the refutational apparatus is not always a readily implementable one, and there will be situations in which, for strategic reasons, it is not the optimal way to advance one's case. The *Organon* itself is the perfect example. It is replete with case-makings, both pro and contra, but only a vanishingly small percentage of them implements the procedures of *Soph. ref.* The lesson to learn from this is that Aristotle is not attempting to describe everyday case-making and case-breaking practice. The regulatory apparatus of *Soph. ref.* is a tool. And like all tools, this one is used selectively, as witness Aristotle's quite particular use of it in *Post. an.* It bears special emphasis that, as used there, yes-no refutation is never a one-shot event. Every defender will have his day as an attacker. In the attacker-defence ballet, a large corps of the wise visit and revisit one another, until the point of dialectical exhaustion is reached, when one and only one candidate is left standing. Dialectical battle is a war of attrition. Finally, that Aristotle would have taken on the Heraclitean challenge tells us (or should do) that, when he was writing *Metaphysics* the status of LNC, had not been settled. Not only was Heraclitus one of the wise – a highly regarded thinker – his outlier views were not peculiar to him only. Heraclitus was graced with some very smart fellow-travellers. He was joined in his anti-LNC endeavours by Protagoras and, in *Top* (104b 20), Aristotle himself suggests that the plausibility of [LNC] could become one of the very problems that served as a starting point for dialectical disputation ("a point of speculation") (Dutilh Novaes 2019). This should dissuade us from thinking that the Heraclitean ruckus was a radical attempt to molest the *status quo.* The LNC ball was still in the air.

This is not to say that Aristotle has been reduced to a preferential agnosticism towards LNC. Clearly, he has something to say in its defence which, while not conclusive, he thinks is nevertheless sufficiently telling to constitute a win. In *Soph. ref.,* he outlines five ways for besting one's opponent and rank orders their degrees of efficacy:

> First we must grasp the number of things entertained by those who argue as competitors and rivals to the death. These are five in number, refutation, fallacy, paradox, solecism, and finally babbling – i.e. to constrain him to repeat himself a number of times: or it is to produce the appearance of each of these things without the reality. For they choose if possible plainly to refute the other party, or as a second best to show that he is committing some fallacy, or as a third best to lead him to paradox, or fourthly to reduce him to solecism, i.e. to make the answerer, in consequence of the argument, to use an ungrammatical expression; or, as a last resort, to make him repeat himself." (3, 165b 13-22)

Very well, then, by what means might Aristotle elect to prevail against the Heraclitean menace? At *Met.* 1011b 23-29, after having written that the "most certain of all basic principles is that contradictory propositions are not true simultaneously", Aristotle says of the human reasoner at large that

> [a] principle which he must have if he is to *understand* anything is not a hypothesis; and that which one must know if he is to know anything [at all] must be in his possession for every occasion.

If this were so, a challenger could not understand the very challenge he makes against the Law. Taken at face value, Aristotle is simply mistaken. One could challenge the Law's prime certainty and one could challenge its necessity. But, as Aristotle appears to say, what he *can't* do without falling into a fugue of utter incomprehension is challenge its *truth*. In the very utterance of "LNC is false", the challenger renders himself unable to understand what he has said. We ourselves can see that what he has said is that there is at least one case in which it is possible that contradictory propositions are true simultaneously. The rest of us, however, those who acknowledge LNC, *do* understand the challenger. Dutilh Novaes (2019) picks up on this performative aspect and develops an interesting Habermasian defence of LNC, in which the utterer's challenge turns out to be performatively incoherent. If "LNC is false" is a performatively incoherent thing to utter, how could it be a performatively incoherent thing to listen to? On what basis, then, do we press our advantage against him? And what form would that advantage take? Refutation or fallacy or paradox or solecism, or babbling or *what*? Were I to be consulted on the matter, I'd propose to our Founder the following line of action:

> So, my friend, you challenge my thesis that LNC is true. Fine and dandy, nothing less than your dialectical right. Just give me a minute to refresh myself. Upon my return I'll look forward to your questions. I'll be eager to see, should you make a syllogism against me, whether you'll be able to understand its conclusion.

DEDICATION: In the mid-seventies I was graduate secretary in UVic's department of philosophy. I am told that when Hans Hansen arrived from Lakehead University to enquire about admittance to the department's very new (and very small) MA programme, I was less than inviting. Blessedly, I have no memory of this awkward event. Notwithstanding the office I held, I can only plead my disappointment in the very idea that a heaven-kissed undergraduate department would surrender its advantage to the thirst for graduate students. Some years later, Hans and I twice found ourselves together in Amsterdam, thanks to the bounty of the originators of the pragma-dialectical approach to argument, Frans van Eemeren and the now late Rob Grootendorst. The first time round, Hans and I started to organize some thoughts that would form the basis for our first co-authored paper, on Hintikka's misunderstanding of Aristotle on the fallacies. In a follow-up visit, Larry Powers had joined us and had much enlivened the scene. Hans had prevailed upon Larry to show me his manuscript of his book *Non-Contradiction*. In the aftermath of the first visit, I had been drafting a paper on Aristotle's earlier logic, prompted in large measure by my discussions with Hans about Aristotle's understanding of the fallacies. Hans had now arranged for Larry to read that draft, and meanwhile I was making my happy way through *Non-Contradiction*. In no time at all, I was aware that a better single-volume treatment of contradiction had yet to appear in English. By the end of that visit, the basis for Hans's and my paper on Aristotle's non-cause as cause had been laid, and it had become clear to me that the paper on Aristotle's earlier logic would have to be a book. It hardly needs saying that, in the absence of Hans's stimulating and instructive presence, none of this would have happened. Of the many papers I have published over the years, those co-authored with Hans remain two of my permanent favourites. And though I hadn't got it quite right even in its second and revised edition in 2014, I still cherish *Aristotle's Earlier Logic*. A last word about Larry. *Non-Contradiction* was written in the sixties and had never been submitted for publication. Larry pleaded the great size of the book, but rather unconvincingly. The likelier explanation is that Larry so much preferred the writing of things to the flogging of them, that he was reconciled to leave the volume fallow. In a later visit to Amsterdam for an ISSA meeting, Hans and I resolved to do something about this. In 2012, and with an excellent Foreword by Hans, *Non-Contradiction* appeared as volume 39 of College Publications' Studies in Logic. By the way, it was from Hans himself that I learned of the UVic unwelcome, years after it happened.

In anticipation of his pending retirement, I have the pleasure and honour of dedicating this essay to my greatly valued friend and highly prized colleague, Hans Vilhelm Hansen.

REFERENCES

Annellis, Irving H. 1995. "Peirce rustled, Russell pierced: How Charles Peirce and Bertrand Russell viewed each other's work in logic, and an assessment of Russell's accuracy and role in the historiography of logic", *Modern Logic*, 5, 270-327.

Aristotle. 1941. *Posterior Analytics*, G. R. G. Mure, (Tr.), in Richard McKeon (Ed.), *The Basic Works of Aristotle*. New York: Random House.

Aristotle. 1984. *The Complete Works of Aristotle: The Revised English Translation*, 2 volumes, Jonathan Barnes (Ed.). Princeton: Princeton University Press.

Benacerraf, Paul. 1965. "What numbers could not be", *Philosophical Review*, 74, 47-73.

Cartwright, Richard. 2005. "Remarks on propositional functions", *Mind*, 114, 915-927.

Cook Wilson, John. 1926. *Statement and Inference*, 2 volumes, Oxford: Clarendon Press.

Corcoran, John. 1972. "Completeness of an ancient logic", *Journal of Symbolic Logic*, 37, 696-702.

Corcoran, John. 1973. "A mathematical model of Aristotle's syllogistic", *Archiv für Geschicte der Philosophie*, 55, 191-219.

Corcoran, John. 1974a. (Ed.). *Ancient Logic and its Modern Interpretation*, Dordrecht: Reidel.

Corcoran, John. 1974b. "Aristotle's natural deductive system", in Corcoran (1974a), 85-132.

Corcoran, John. 2009. "Aristotle's demonstrative logic", *History and Philosophy of Logic*, 30, 1-20.

Detlefsen, Michael. 2011-12. "Poincaré versus Russell sur le role de la logique et les mathematiques", *Les Études Philosophiques*, 97, 153-178.

Dutilh Novaes, Catarina. 2019. "Aristotle's defense of the principle of non-contradiction: A performative analysis" in Gabbay et al. (2019).

Frege, Gottlob. 1884/1950. *Die Grundlagen der Arithmetik*, Breslau: Wilhelm Koebner, 1884. Translated into English as *Foundations of Arithmetic*, J. L. Austin, Oxford: Blackwell.

Frege, Gottlob. 1893-1903/2013. *Grundgesteze der Arithmetik*, Jena: Herman Pohle, 1893/1903. Translated into English as *Basic Laws of Arithmetic*, Philip A. Ebert and Marcus Rossberg, with Crispin Wright (Eds.), Oxford: Oxford University Press.

Frege, Gottlob. 1902/1967. Letter to Russell, in Jean van Heijenoort (Ed.), *From Frege to Gödel: A Source Book in Mathematical Logic*, 1879-1931, 127-128.

Gabbay, Dov M., Lorenzo Magnani, Woosuk Park and AhtiVeikko Pietarinen (Eds.). 2019. *Natural Arguments: A Tribute to John Woods*, volume 40 of the Tribute series, London: College Publications.

Geach, Peter. 1972. *Logic Matters*, Oxford: Blackwell.

Goldfarb, Warren D. 1979. "Logic in the twenties: The nature of the quantifier", *Journal of Symbolic Logic*, 44, 351-368.

Goldfarb, Warren D. 1988. "Poincaré against the logicists", in William Aspray and Philip Kitcher (Eds.), *History and Philosophy of Mathematics*, Volume XI, 61-81, Minneapolis: University of Minnesota Press

Griffin, Nicholas and Lewis, Albert C. (Eds.). 1982.. *The Collected Papers of Bertrand Russell, Volume II Philosophical Papers, 1876-1899*, 390-415, London: George Allen & Unwin.

Hallett, Michael. 1984. *Cantorian Set Theory and Limitations of Size*, Oxford: Clarendon Press.

Heis, Jeremy. 2019. "The logicians of Kant's school", in Lapointe, 28-55.

Hintikka, Jaakko. 1997. "What was Aristotle doing in his early logic, anyway? A reply to Woods and Hansen", *Synthese*, 113, 241-249.

Irvine, A. D. 1989. "Epistemic logicism and Russell's regressive method", *Philosophical Studies*, 55, 303-327.

Kant, Immanuel. 1781-1787. *Critique of Pure Reason*. Paul Guyer and Allen Wood (Tr.), Cambridge: Cambridge University Press. First edition in 1781; second edition in 1787.

Ketner, K. (Ed.). 1995. *Peirce and Contemporary Thought*, pp. 23-31. New York: Fordham University Press.

Klement, Kevin C. 2010. "The functions of Russell's no class theory", *Review of Symbolic Logic*, 3, 633-664.

Lapointe, Sandra (Ed.). 2019. *Logic From Kant to Russell: Laying the Foundations for Analytic Philosophy*, London: Routledge.

Moktefi, Amirouche. 2019. "The social shaping of modern logic", in Gabbay et al. (2019).

Moore. G. H. (Ed.). 1993. *The Collected Papers of Bertrand Russell Volume III: Toward the "Principles of Mathematics" 1900-1902*. London: Routledge.

Peano. Guiseppe. 1889/1967. "The principles of arithmetic, presented by a new method" English translation in van Heijenoort, 85-97. First published in 1889.

Peckhaus, Volker. 1999. "19th century logic between philosophy and mathematics", *Bulletin of Symbolic Logic*, 5, 433-450.

Peirce, C. S. 1870. "Description of a notation for the logic of relatives, resulting from an amplification of the conceptions of Boole's calculus of logic", *Memoirs of the American Academy*, 9, 317-378.

Peirce, C. S. 1883a. "The logic of relatives", in C. S. Peirce (Ed.), *Studies in Logic*,1870-203, Boston: Little, Brown & Co.

Peirce, C. S. 1883b. "Second intentional logic", in Peirce (1883a), 56-58.

Poincaré, Henri. 1914. *Science and Method*, London: Thomas Nelson.

Preti, Consuelo. 2019. "What Russell meant when he called Moore a logician", in Lapointe (2019), 189-205.

Putnam, Hilary. 1982. "Peirce as a logician", *Historia Mathematica*, 9, 290-301.

Quine, W. V. 1995. "Peirce's logic", in Ketner (1995), 23-31.

Reck, Erick H. 2019. "Dedekind's logicism", in Lapointe (2019), 171-188.

Reck, Erick H. and Awodey, Steve (Eds. & Trs.). 2004. *Frege's Lectures on Logic: Carnap's Student Notes* (Intr. by Gottfried Gabriel), Chicago: Open Court.

Russell, Bertrand. 1903/1937. *The Principles of Mathematics*, Cambridge: Cambridge University Press. (Second edition, London: Allen & Unwin.)

Russell, Bertrand. 1905. "On denoting", *Mind*, 14, 479-493. Reprinted in Russell 1994, 414-427.

Russell, Bertrand. 1973. "The regressive method of discovering the premises of mathematics", Douglas Lackey (Ed.), *Russell, Essays in Analysis,* London: George Allen & Unwin. (Delivered as a lecture in 1907.)

Russell, Bertrand. 1994. *The Collected Papers of Bertrand Russell, Volume 4, Foundations of Logic 1903-1905*, Urquhart, Alasdair (Ed.), London: Routledge.

Tarski, Alfred. 1986. "What are logical notions?", *History and Philosophy of Logic*, 7, 143-154.

Tarski, Alfred. 2002/1936. "On the concept of following logically", Magda Stoińska and David Hitchcock (Trs.) *History and Philosophy of Logic*, 23, 155-196. (First Polish publication in 1936, and in German the same year.)

Woods, John. 2014. *Aristotle's Earlier Logic*, 2nd ed. revised and expanded. *Studies in Logic*, Vol. 53. London: College Publications. (1st ed., Paris: Hermes Science, 2001.)

Woods, John. (Forthcoming.) "Peirce, Russell and regressive abduction", in John Shook and Sami Paavola (Eds.), *Abduction in Cognition and Action: Logical Reasoning, Scientific Inquiry, and Social Practice*, a volume in the SAPERE series, Springer.

Woods, John and Hansen, Hans V. 1997. "Hintikka on Aristotle's fallacies", *Synthese*, 113, 217-239.

Woods, John and Hansen, Hans V. 2001. "The subtleties of Aristotle on non-cause", *Logique et Analyse*, 176, 395-415.

John Woods, "What did Frege take Russell to have proved?", *Synthese*, DOI/10.10007/s11229-019-02324-4. Published online: 22 July 2019.

ABOUT THE AUTHOR: Director of the Abductive Systems Group and the University of British Columbia Honorary Professor of logic, John Woods is currently vice-President of the Charles Peirce Society. His most recent book, *Truth in Fiction: Rethinking its Logic* (2018) was the focus of an APA Book Symposium in April 2019. A further Symposium appeared in the *Journal of Applied Logic* earlier this year. Woods is a Fellow of the Royal Society of Canada, and President Emeritus of the University of Lethbridge. His present project is a naturalized logic for mathematical knowledge.

CHAPTER 4.

OPPOSITION AND POLARIZATION

TRUDY GOVIER

ABSTRACT: In this paper I explore types of logical and social opposition, and the relations that may exist between them. While logical
opposition is relevant to all inquiry and debate, social opposition
involving adversariality need not be. Opposition to a claim and
opposition to a person should be distinguished. The oft-used terms
'proponent' and 'opponent' may mislead us. In developing my
account, I critically explore Graham Priest's argument that contradictions inevitably arise in philosophy, disputing some of his key
dichotomous constructions and contending that they mistake contraries for contradictories. I also consider Hilary Putnam's comments on opposition in philosophy, in which he develops an
account of recoil and repugnance, based on simplistically construed
opposites. I seek to explain how logical and social pathologies may
buttress each other, with baneful and even fatal effects.

KEYWORDS: opposites, contradictory, contrary, opposition,
polarization, adversariality, Wittgenstein, Graham Priest, Leo
Groarke, visual arguments, missing premises, missing conclusions,
Hilary Putnam, feminism, Ralph Johnson, conflict, dichotomy.

I want to explore opposites in this paper. But before getting
started on that project, let me say how pleased I am to be con-
tributing to a volume in appreciation of Hans Hansen. It is surely

not only for his academic contributions to informal logic and other fields that Hans will be fondly remembered by his colleagues. It is for his kindness, generosity, and extraordinary energy and success in organizing conferences of the Ontario Society for the Study of Argumentation (OSSA) over several decades. His work and that of his colleagues – including notably Chris Tindale, Tony Blair, and Ralph Johnson – have made OSSA conferences enjoyable as well as academically fruitful and worthwhile. Participants have come to include scholars from Asia, Europe, and South America as well as Canada and the United States; the planning and management of the events is truly something to be emulated. My personal appreciation of Hans is not only a matter of academics. I have benefitted from his thoughtfulness and consideration, occasionally in situations of real need, and I'm sure I am not the only person who would say that. So thank you, Hans, thank you. We will think of you long and think of you well. And now – on to my theme of opposites.

Bertrand Russell once said, "what is wanted is not the will to believe, but the will to find out, which is the very opposite." Russell is known as a clear writer, but it is not obvious what he meant when he made this comment. In what sense is the will to find out the opposite, or the "very opposite" of the will to believe?

In discussion and debate, it is useful to ask whether, and in what sense, the claims people want to support are logical opposites. And if they are opposites, in what sense of logical opposition – as logical contradictories or as contraries? Do the people supporting "opposed" claims necessarily, or customarily, find themselves in opposed social roles? If so, how competitive are those roles, to what extent are they polarized, and how far does the adversariality go? Logical opposition is relevant to all inquiry and debate, but social opposition involving adversariality need not be. While all contexts in which argumentation appears should allow for reflection and criticism, not all require adversarial competition. We might call such contexts those of calm opposition or restrained partisanship in the sense understood by Wayne Brockriede (Trapp and Schuetz 2006). It is clearly possible for criticism and the consideration of objections and replies to be conducted within the bounds of calm opposition.

INEVITABLE CONTRADICTIONS IN PHILOSOPHY?

In a book entitled *Beyond the Limits of Thought* (1995), Graham Priest uses dichotomous constructions to mount an argument to the effect that contradictions inevitably emerge in philosophy. He welcomes this result, one that for many would constitute either a refutation or a paradox needing to be resolved. The standard view, that to show of any philosophical or scientific position that it leads to a contradiction constitutes a decisive refutation of it, is not accepted by Priest. As is well-known, he believes that contradictions should (presumably sometimes) be accepted; he has been a major introducer of para-consistent logic. I contend that Priest employs in his premises dichotomous constructions that are disputable.

These constructions include the following:

- Determinate/indeterminate
- Sayable/not sayable
- Expressible/inexpressible
- Intrinsic/extrinsic

A basic objection to Priest's arguments is based on the claim that they misrepresent contrary predicates as though they were contradictory. In fact, though obviously not written for that purpose, his book appears to be a prime source for this mistake.[1] Working through Priest's arguments, we often find that terms that

---

1. I am indebted to Colin Hirano for his insight into the work of Graham Priest.

should be understood as contraries and as admitting of degrees are treated as fully contradictory opposites; then paradoxes are developed from the resulting structure. For example, Priest speaks of what can be expressed in contrast to what cannot be expressed. Following Wittgenstein, Priest accepts a dichotomous opposition between what can be expressed in language and what cannot be expressed in language. In his discussion of expressibility, Wittgenstein's *Tractatus* is often quoted, as in "Propositions cannot represent logical form; it is mirrored in them;" "What finds its reflection in language, language cannot represent;" and "What can be shown cannot be said."

Priest is concerned with limits and argues that the many philosophers similarly concerned have stated contradictory views. They have wanted to say there is a limit beyond which thought or language cannot go; yet they have found themselves thinking on both sides of that supposed limit. Kant, as is well-known, argued that phenomena (within space and time and describable using the categories of pure reason) can be experienced and known, whereas noumena (not known to be within space and time, and not describable using the categories) cannot be experienced and known. Yet, contrary to the tenets of his own epistemology, Kant did make claims about noumena; he had to do that, because he would have been unable to articulate his own position within the limits he had set.

In many places, Priest's oppositions are readily interpretable as contrary opposites, and as a result his arguments fail. Priest seems insensitive to the problems that can arise when contraries are taken to be contradictories. If we represent a statement as "X is Q" and another statement that we understand as its opposite as "X is not Q", we may too easily interpret this decision as indicating that the second predicate is the contradictory opposite of the first. That is to say, an item X is either Q or it is not Q, and there is no further possibility: the 'or' is taken as exclusive. "X is Q or X is not Q" represents a true dichotomy given that the or in the statement is the exclusive 'or'. On this interpretation, the principles of non-contradiction and excluded middle both apply, and proofs erected on this dichotomous presumption need not involve a false premise. If, on the other hand, we should decide that the natural language predicates are best understood and represented as contrary predicates admitting of middles and degrees, then statements expressing their opposition should not be interpreted as contradictories and they should be formalized accordingly.

We express decisions about our pre-formal interpretation of predicates when we decide how to formally represent them. We can interpret the predicates as contraries and generate contrary propositions; we can interpret the predicates as contradictories and generate contradictory propositions. I submit that in many of Priest's arguments what should be contrary predicates are represented as contradictories, and a key premise fails for that reason. If a qualified interpretation along the lines of "X can be Q with respect to Z" and "X cannot be Q with respect to W" can be made out, then the statements "X can be Q" and "X cannot be Q" can be reconciled, and there is no contradictory opposition.

As a case in point, let us further consider the expressible and the inexpressible. One might suppose, as Priest evidently does, that something is either expressible or not, that 'expressible' and 'inexpressible' are contradictory opposite predicates and that is simply the end of the story. The presumption is that there is no "middle" here because an element either is expressible or it is NOT: if it is not expressible, then it is inexpressible. In setting up this opposition as contradictory there is no need to consider failures of exhaustiveness or exclusivity, differences of degree, borderline cases, or differential respects in which a thing might be expressible or not. No such things matter. Presuming such a dichotomous opposition, Priest constructs an argument leading to a contradictory conclusion and claims an illustration of his theory that contradictions are inevitable in philosophy when one starts to reason about the limits of knowledge and thought. I would argue that this line of reasoning is not correct, because it starts from a premise that is flawed because it is constructed on an incorrect opposition, where what should be contrary is presumed to be contradictory.

It seems to me that there are feelings and ideas that can be partially expressed. Wittgenstein famously said that if you can't say something you can't whistle it either. But the fact that this remark is well-known shouldn't isolate it from critical scrutiny. On a pleasant summer morning, a person might go for a walk and have a certain feeling of wellbeing and carefree-ness that she could not articulate in words: it would not be happiness or joy or wellbeing or gladness, let us say. Now let us suppose that this person walks along, with this sense of contentment and freedom, and begins to whistle along the way. We may say here that her feelings are inexpressible because she can't quite find a convenient word for them. But it is also fair to say that there is a sense in which her feelings are expressed, in the way she whistles as she walks along.

Nor is this the only type of example we might wish to consider. Interesting in this context are the views of Leo Groarke with regard to the feasibility of visual arguments. Groarke (2007) defends the claim that there can be such a thing as visual argument; he states categorically that a picture or item that can be seen can truly be an element of an argument. A simple example would involve the presentation of a counter-example that would refute a universal claim. Suppose you say that Elbe yoghurt will never spoil before its due date, and I on May 5, 2018 without saying a word, present you with a container of Elbe yoghurt, all moldy and spoiled, with a due date of May 10, 2018 (my example). My argument is based on my display of this item; I show you something that constitutes a refutation of the claim you made to me. We might say, I show you that your claim is false by showing you this item; seeing the item is what will, by ostensive display, demonstrate to you that you are wrong. My display is visual: you can in a fully literal sense see that there is a counter-example to your claim, even though I may not express my claim in words. What may be said in this sort of context is that even though I have said nothing, expressed nothing in words, it is reasonable to interpret me as having argued along these lines: "There exists a container of Elbe yoghurt which spoiled before its due date; therefore Elbe yoghurt can spoil before its due date."[2]

Because you can see the container of yoghurt, we can interpret my display as amounting to a visual argument, one based on ostensive display. To spell out the argument here, the instance has been described. One might say that the original argument was not expressed, meaning that it was not expressed in words, and that would be correct. If we said that the original argument was expressible in the sense that it could be captured in words, that would also seem to be correct, although one could dispute to what extent the ostensive presentation of the actual spoiled yoghurt had been captured in the words used to state the premise and conclusion of the argument. I submit that it is reasonable to conclude from this example (and many similar ones) that it makes sense to think of ideas as expressible in some sense or to some extent, and inexpressible in others.

Still clearer are cases in which arguments have premises and conclusion that are explicitly stated but are said, as well, to contain implicit material. Plausible examples are readily found. Consider:

He is Polish, so probably he is Catholic.

2. Groarke resists the idea that all arguments must be expressed, or at least expressible, in terms of claims representing premises and conclusion. See, for example, Groarke and Birdsell 2007. I do not resist this claim and am re-structuring Groarke's views according to my own assumptions, which are more standard in this regard.

The implicit premise here is "Most Polish people are Catholic." Consider as well:

> The bigger the burger, the better the burger. The burgers are bigger at Burger King.

These claims, made in an advertisement, deductively entail that the burgers are better at Burger King, which is the implicit conclusion of the argument. Although issues about implicit material in argument are large, complex, and disputed, these two cases are pretty clear and would not be contested by theorists of argument.[3] It is generally agreed that at least some arguments have implicit premises or conclusions, and these are two straightforward cases. With regard to considerations of expressibility, the case that can be made is this: if material is implicit, it is by definition not explicitly stated, but there are elements in the discourse which give us reason to claim that material as implicit.[4] Call these, for the moment, inferential elements, those elements that license the inference that such-and-such material is implicit. These inferential elements are explicit (if they are words in a text or speech) or are unstated but can be rendered in language (as when we explain the context of the burger example, saying, for example, "this is an ad"). There is a sense in which implicit elements in an argument are not spelled out and hence clearly not expressed but there is another sense in which they are made evident by what is articulated or easily made explicit. These claims are not expressed, in one sense, and yet they are (at least arguably) expressed, in another. (Compare Alston 1956) If claims can be partially expressed, it is reasonable to infer that they can be partially expressible. From that implication, we can (again) conclude

---

3. My own general approach to the problem of unstated premises and conclusion may be found in Chapter Two of *A Practical Study of Argument*, Seventh Edition (Belmont, CA: Wadsworth 2010.)

4. I include here the context. In the case of the better burgers, for instance, it is relevant to know that these claims were made in an advertisement.

that 'expressible' and 'inexpressible' are contrary predicates, not contradictory ones.

Along somewhat similar lines, we may consider "knowability" with regard to the Big Bang (the cosmic event, not the television series). Should we count this event as knowable or as unknowable? To the extent that it is known it is obviously knowable. To the extent that it is unknown, it may be unknowable given contemporary scientific resources, unknowable for the predictable future, or unknowable absolutely. It seems reasonable in this context to say that the Big Bang is knowable to some extent. Cosmologists claim to know that such an event as the Big Bang occurred and had certain characteristics but they would not (for example) claim to know what, if anything, preceded the Big Bang or what might be entailed by the view that nothing preceded it. Indeed, they might very well claim with regard to its putative precedents that such things are unknowable in the radical sense that they will never be able to be known. Now given all these considerations, it seems reasonable here to speak of what is known and hence knowable, what is knowable to some extent, what is not known and is potentially unknowable, and what is radically unknowable. To consider knowability in these terms is, in effect, to interpret 'knowable' and 'unknowable' as contrary predicates – not as contradictory ones.

REPUGNANCE AND RECOIL

In a series of lectures published under the title "Sense, Nonsense, and the Senses: An Inquiry into the Powers of the Human Mind," Hilary Putnam (1994) discusses baneful divisions in philosophy, attributing some of them to a phenomenon of recoil. Putnam claims that what happens in much philosophical debates is that two positions are defined in such a way that one is a kind of "mirror image" of the other. The positions are (in some sense) logically opposed and interpreted by their proponents as contradictorily opposed. But that is by no means the end of the matter, because the logical opposition is so often accompanied by a kind of repugnance. "One is dominated by the feeling that one must put as much distance as possible between oneself and a particular philosophical stance," Putnam says. What we find here is a pattern of recoil that causes philosophy to leap from frying pan to fire, from fire to a different frying pan, from different frying pan to a different fire, and so on, apparently without end. The response is not helpful to those seeking to develop careful and plausible philosophical accounts.

Thinking of contrary and contradictory opposites enables us to more fully understand what Putnam is alluding to as repugnance and recoil. The notion of recoil is expressed in the formula, "I don't agree with X; I support not-X, and hence Y, which is the opposite view to X." Someone reasoning this way understands two accounts as exhaustive and exclusive opposites. Because he finds one of these accounts repugnant, he recoils from it and opts for the other, presumed to be its contradictory opposite. Clearly, the logical correctness of such a move depends on the soundness of the presumption that the two accounts do indeed amount to exhaustive and exclusive alternatives. In this context, as in many others in philosophy, an "opposite" view is made in the mirror image of another presumed to constitute an exhaustive and exclusive alternative.

Consider the following as representative of simplistic opposites in philosophy:

- Relativism/Absolutism
- Feminism/Non-feminism
- Dualism/Materialism
- Analytic philosophy/continental philosophy

An illustrative case here is that of feminism. Suppose a man asserts that he is not a feminist. What could he mean? A non-feminist might be someone who simply is not a feminist in the sense that he takes little interest in the sorts of issues feminists are interested in; he can accordingly be said to be a non-feminist. (Though that description is rather vacuous and contains little information.) Another possibility is that this man might not be a feminist in the sense that he asserts claims that are denied by most feminists. He might, unlike nearly all feminists, maintain that a human embryo counts as a person from the moment of conception and has human rights fully equivalent to those of an adult woman from that moment on. Still again, he might not be a feminist in the sense of being against feminism, opposed to it in the sense of denying it and feeling some emotional involvement in doing that. He might find its disputing of social norms requiring that women defer to men objectionable theoretically and emotionally, and he might speak out strongly against such feminists, defending male privilege. Clearly, these ways of being a non-feminist are distinct from each other. Because there are many alternatives to feminism, just as there are various versions of it, the feminism/non-feminism opposition is rather simplistic; it is uninformative but misleading to say that a person is simply a feminist or not.

With philosophical "opposites" we feel ourselves in situations of dilemma, but should be suspicious of constructed opposites in the territory of antinomy. Putnam (1994) finds an antinomy in treatments of realism and anti-realism and describes himself as seeking an account that amounts neither to dogmatic realism nor to dogmatic anti-realism. After explaining recoil, he launches into a prolonged and complex discussion of debates about realism and anti-realism in twentieth century philosophy, arriving on the basis of this discussion at his own position, which he understands to be a kind of nuanced naïve realism. More briefly Putnam describes another familiar philosophical dilemma concerning materialism and consciousness. We have a sense, he claims, that we would have to either accept some version of mind/brain identity OR be committed to mind/body dualism, often assumed to be its full and only opposite. If we are repelled by dualism and presume it to be the only alternative to materialism, we may accept materialism on those grounds. In so doing we will presume a dilemma, presupposing a binary choice situation. We understand our problem as though there is an exhaustive and exclusive disjunction between accepting mind/brain identity on the one hand and accepting mind/body dualism on the other. This presumption is mistaken. The 'or' should be inclusive.

ALTERNATIVE POSITIONS

In discussing the dialectical aspects of argument and introducing the notion of a dialectical tier on which arguers respond to objections and consider positions other than the one they have defended, Ralph Johnson (2000) wrote about alternative positions.[5] Johnson acknowledged in response to criticism that it is by no means obvious just what the alternatives to a particular position are. We might think of just one: if your position is X then the alternative position is the contradictory opposite of X, namely not-X. But that is obviously over-simplified and will not do, given that there will often be many ways of denying X. There will be many possible positions contrary to X, though not contradictory to it, and some of these will qualify as opposite. In a broad sense a pro-choice view on abortion is "the opposite" of a pro-life view and as such an alternative to it. If we delve into the matter, however, we will see that there are different versions of "pro-life" and "pro-choice". Some versions of pro-life would permit abortion in a case in which a woman had been raped in time of war, or was a victim of incest, while others would not. Some versions of pro-choice would permit abortion at six months of pregnancy, while others would not. There are obviously more than two sides in such cases, which can serve as an illustration of the complications that arise when we try to explain, with regard

5. See Chapters Twelve and Thirteen of Govier 1999.

to some position X, what the alternatives to that position are. Logical alternatives are likely to be several at least, if we consider contraries as well as contradictories. Furthermore, positions that reach similar conclusions for very different reasons might be considered alternative (Govier 1988).

View 3 might be an alternative to View 1 and View 2 because it denies an assumption common to both. View 4 might account for many, but not quite all, of the phenomena dealt with by Views 1 and 2, and to some extent count as alternative to them despite its failure to handle exactly the same questions. View 5 might be a sort of compromise between Views 1 and 2, reconciling elements of each. Unless we adopt the limiting presumption that the only alternative to X is not-X, there are plural alternatives. It is highly problematic to support a view on the grounds that one is repelled by "its opposite."

LOGICAL AND SOCIAL CONFLICT

We find logic texts with duels portrayed on the cover; the roles of logical defender and logical challenger are portrayed in fighting terms. Two slightly embarrassed authors of such a book responded to feminist challenges of the representation by claiming that the illustration featuring men with swords portrayed a metaphor: they claimed that any "fight" between proponent and opponent would of course be non-literal. There is no real battle in the case, only challenge and response, where the challenge is intellectual criticism and the response is an answer to that, not by the sword but in words.

This response merits attention. We may first note that it is hard to make literal sense of the notion of being opposed to a claim; far more plausible is the idea of being opposed to a person who makes that claim. This sort of personal opposition is familiar in our daily experience. Say you are a socialist and I am a libertarian, and we enter into a discussion about politics. In our discussion I am in a role where I question and 'oppose' your position; that is the structure of our debate. The positions can be spelled out in propositions, but our actual discussion is not a set of propositions. Rather, it is a sequence of events in which you and I as persons are engaged and within which we find ourselves in "opposite" roles, you as proponent and I as your opponent. We are, by the structure of this situation, opposed. But in just what sense are we opposed? Is there a conflict between the claims we are discussing? They are opposed claims, opposed in the logical sense; they are either contradictory or contrary. Or are we ourselves, as persons, in some kind of conflict? What is the relationship here between the conflict between the claims (as contrary or contradictory) and conflict between people?

Suppose that we are arguing back and forth against each other. Now it is possible and, according to many including myself, it would be ideal, to display our opposition purely in terms of roles in a discussion, and insist that there need be no opposition between us in any sense involving alienation or hostility. But, notoriously, that is not always the case.

To the claim that there is adversariality (social opposition) in the situation, one can reply as did the authors just mentioned and say that any contest or fight in a debate or discussion is metaphorical, not real. We are not really in any sense adversaries or enemies; we merely find ourselves in opposing or opposite roles in this particular circumstance, and it is a constructed and finite circumstance from which we can easily extract ourselves. As described so far, ours is an informal discussion. In another context, we might be in a formally structured debate where as proponent and opponent we would act out opposing roles designed to facilitate the defending and challenging of claims. But even if this is the case, then adversariality should be purely role-determined and, accordingly, limited. The metaphor of a duel is just that, a metaphor about what people are doing in defending and attacking claims.

Consider here a person and her "opponent" in an argument; call them A and B. Let us say that A puts forward an argument defending claim C, and B is making a critical response to that argument. In many discussions, A is referred to as the proponent and B as the opponent. Now at this point we need to ask the "opponent or proponent of what?" Strictly speaking the answer should be that A puts forward a claim; she propounds it; she is the proponent of the claim and of an argument on its behalf. And B, in the challenging role, should be challenging either the claim C or the arguments that A has offered on its behalf. In the discussion A is the proponent of the claim, and B is the "opponent". (A and B take opposite roles.[6]) But we must ask again: of what, and in what sense, is B the opponent? Strictly speaking the only things at issue in the case are claims and arguments; there should be no people, personalities, or emotions involved.

In what sense is the opponent B against the claim C? There are many possibilities. He may accept a contrary proposition; he may accept a contradictory proposition. He may not accept any "opposite" claim but may, rather, be somewhat agnostic about C itself or the arguments that A has put forward to support it. The structuring of an argumentative discussion into one between the proponent and the opponent does not require distinctions between these different possibilities. In the discussion, B is the opponent of A, who is a proponent of claim C. As A's opponent, we may say that B is in an oppositional role in relation to A. If this is all that is involved, there need be no aspects of adversariality in the case. Clearly this oppositionality need not be adversarial nor even in any sense competitive.

However, slippage is common at this point. Often the discussion acquires a competitive overtone, as both proponent and opponent seek to dominate and "win" by showing that they are

---

6. That is a simplification because B may question various aspects of A's position; in addition, as noted earlier, B may advocate a claim either contradictory to, or contrary to, that of A.

right and the other party is wrong. People often go far beyond the calm and restrained discussion of evidence and reasons for and against opposite claims. Outside formal debates, and sometimes even within them, people engage in argumentative processes with considerable passion, experiencing strong identification with the positions they defend. The dynamic acquires a motif that some of my (male) colleagues loved to joke about: I am right and you are wrong. The message is a joking one, but the joke is not entire. The point may expand: "Ha ha, I am right and you are wrong; I am right because you are wrong, and you are wrong because I am right. Furthermore, in the fight we are having, I am victorious." The imposed assumptions are first that there are only two possibilities, right and wrong, and second that it is a competition to see which person gets to be in which position. What may have begun as an argumentative discussion involving logical conflict between claims has become a competition between people in a win/lose framework. The socialist strives to assert himself against the libertarian; the realist against the anti-realist; the monistic materialist against the dualist.

Arguing back and forth, considering claims and challenges, A and B struggle for victory. Each wants to prevail over the person understood as an opponent. Each seeks to win in the discussion or debate. Moving beyond the strict confines of intellectual discussion, competing for dominance in a game played as zero sum, A and B begin to function as opponents in a more-than-logical sense. Not to win will mean to lose and losing will be experienced as a kind of diminution to the person who has identified with the claims he is making and may even experience humiliation if he is defeated in the "battle" or battle.

PATHOLOGIES OF OPPOSITION

Conflicts between claims become conflicts between people, resulting in social opposition. Intense opposition between persons and groups, arising from disagreement about alternative positions, is expressed in a variety of ways involving competition, adversariality, ultimately even violence. Not only are there logical pathologies of opposition, social pathologies of opposition are many. Logical and social pathologies may buttress each other, with bad logical health supporting bad social health and conversely. Often people come to associate the positions they hold closely with their very identity, as when "I am a libertarian" or "I am a materialist" are taken literally. The logical opposition between claims that are contrary or contradictory becomes attached to persons who strongly identify with the claim they are defending; what could be simply a discussion of alternative positions comes to be associated with rivalry and competition. In such cases questioning a position may be understood as threatening identity, a situation underlying some unhealthy aspects of debate and facilitating such common fallacies as Straw Man, ad hominem, and guilt by association.

Rarely can differences between a pro-life position on abortion and a pro-choice position be understood purely at the level of propositional content. The pro-life supporter is likely to be opposed to the pro-choice supporter in a sense of social opposition, competition, and even animosity. The conflict has become intense to the point of murder. Socially, people may have "opponents" and be "opposed" in various ways and to various degrees. For the moment, let us define a social pathology of opposition as one in which oppositional roles have acquired extraneous and unnecessary elements of enmity and hostility. We may consider opponent roles in a variety of contexts including those of intellectual discussion and debate; competition in sports; social institutions such as court and parliament; and political conflict ranging from electioneering to outright war.

OPPOSITE SIDES?

The opponent becomes a competitor and even an enemy in a win/lose struggle – even though the role of opponent need not, in principle, include such elements of adversariality. For some competitive spirits, losing will feel costly to the point of humiliation and it will seem extraordinarily important to win. This is the kind of intellectual adversariality and struggle for dominance that feminist philosophers have strongly criticized. They deemed the adversarial and highly competitive style of much philosophy to be macho, overly-competitive, counter-productive, and alien to many women (Ayim 1988).

The common assumption that there are "two sides" to every question is incorrect (Govier 1988). Although many procedures operate along these lines, it conveys a gross over-simplification. We think of "pro" and "con" and assume that because there are only two alternatives and you are for one of them, you must therefore be against the other. A slide into pathological opposition is greatly facilitated by this sort of binary framework, as it encourages the phenomenon of recoil. We set things up so as to favour the recoil phenomenon described by Putnam (1994). Debates are typically constructed as though there are two sides, although the two positions represented distort or fail to represent relevant possibilities. Typically, the notion that there are two sides is an improvement over the notion that there is only one side, the truth, requiring no scrutiny or analysis. And yet if only two positions are considered, if people are not receptive to qualifications, considerations of borderline cases and anomalies, and the reinterpretation of constitutive terms, and if recoil is a factor, a highly partisan tone and dynamic become more likely.

Epistemically and politically the notion that discussion should be based on a consideration of two sides may have baneful consequences. It may serve to encourage the simplistic notion that objectivity is to be understood as "balance", wherein an advocacy of one "side" is accompanied by an advocacy of "the other". (It is assumed, the one other. Govier 1988.) For casual consumers of such accounts a corollary may be that there is no truth to the matter, as a position and its (single) alternative can be argued with equal force and credibility. For others, the corollary may be that the truth is to be found somewhere "in the middle." Simplified and polarized debates of this kind easily and commonly omit to display and consider interesting intermediate positions. In the context of abortion, most obviously omitted are views according to which abortion should be a matter of choice up to a certain stage in a pregnancy and restricted after that. In the context of climate change debates, those arguing against the claim that man-induced global warming is occurring have sought simply to establish that there is a debate about this matter. To the extent that they can do this, they can induce in media an obligation to portray "both sides" in the name of objectivity, and people may conclude that the truth lies somewhere "in between" or that there is no truth of the matter at all. In political contexts, including discussion of the United Kingdom election in May 2010, there is often a notion that a clear and pure campaign would involve an opposition of positions between two opponents; a situation where there are three major contenders is not only complicated in unwelcome ways, but somehow impure. In the United Kingdom and in Canada, the notion of a coalition is easily made to seem contaminated with objectionable compromises. The presumption that there is something illicit and nasty about a coalition was exploited by Canada's Stephen Harper in December 2009.

BEYOND THE ROLES: GOING TOO FAR

Many institutions and practices involve oppositional roles: courts, formal debates, and Parliament provide three important examples. In Parliament we have the government and the opposition; in law, the prosecution and defense. In debates there are those who oppose and those who support a proposition; as we have seen, theorists of debate and critical discussion use the terms proponent and opponent going so far as to portray intellectual discussions as duels between defender and challenger. In these contexts, there are important ways in which oppositional roles are useful. They are needed for the progress of discussion and investigation and, in legal contexts, for fairness and procedural justice. The accused needs a defender. These roles presuppose opposition in the sense of criticism; some persons put forward claims, and it is the role of other persons to submit those claims to scrutiny. They do not require unrestrained partisanship or adversariality. Oppositional roles have important social functions and – interestingly – require cooperation in a number of significant respects. Courts are said to be highly adversarial and are often criticized as such, for their winner/loser framework which does not easily adapt itself to compromise or the creation of new solutions to a conflict. But be this as it may, the operation of court requires rules and cooperation within the bounds of those rules. In principle and even in fact people can occupy and perform in opposing roles calmly and even noncompetitively; they need not involve one-upmanship, a quest for domination, hostility and insult, or even a spirit of competitiveness. Those who do so are often misunderstood, since expectations of battling over clearly distinguished and opposed positions are so common.

Yet as is very familiar, court, parliament, debates, and academic discussions may be conducted in a highly competitive and combative way, featuring intense rivalry and such hostile elements as name-calling and recourse to ad hominem and Straw Man fallacies. Shouting, insults, and (in some countries) even physical fighting may be involved. In 2003, the New Statesman reported that some female members of the British House of Commons, struggling to survive in the macho world of politics, were taking testosterone treatments so as to be able to participate in highly combative debates that were required for their political careers. The hormone apparently boosts competitiveness and makes people feel more confident and more powerful. A prescribing doctor defended his practice by saying that these women needed a boost to be able to compete with male colleagues in committee meetings and parliamentary debates. To many, the story was horrifying. A commentator cited the phenomenon as demonstrating that only by behaving like an alpha baboon could a person reach the top (Mallee 2003). Critics of the practice expressed concern, reminding people of the harmful side effects that turned out to result from another hormone treatment, that of female hormone replacement therapy for post menopausal women.

ADVERSARIAL EXTREMES

In some conflicts involving enmity, the idea is to win victory by the application of physical force. Opposition becomes intense to the point where it becomes a struggle to the death, resulting in war and, in the worst cases, massacre and genocide. The survival of the "us" is at stake, jeopardized by the "them", and it is presumed the "us" must eliminate the "them" in order to survive. Demonization of the enemy serves to justify the struggle. We may here think of Aryan and Jew, Serb and Croat, Tutsi and Hutu, Muslim and Hindu. Opposition is a matter of Us and Them at its most intense, expanding to the point of exterminism. If middle or outsider roles exist at all in such conflicts, they will be precarious. Sides are polarized and there is tremendous pressure to be on one side or the other. Much of the rhetoric of war can provide appalling illustrations of a slide from rhetorical opposition to enmity to demonization and de-humanization, when opposing forces are categorized in such vicious terms as 'scumbags,' 'cockroaches,' and 'vermin.' Identities may be tied to oppositional roles taken to such an extreme that survival of one side is construed as requiring the elimination of the other. We can speak here of perniciously oppositional identities.

A SEQUENCE

We can set out a sequence here, beginning with difference and proceeding to demonization and de-humanization. It goes like this:

- Difference. Things are in the world and we notice differences between them.

- Distinction. We mark those differences using words.

- Disjunction as early exclusion. (Not both, at the same time and in the same respect.) Marking those differences, we conclude that if a thing is Q, it is not at the same time P, where we have distinguished Q and P and they are contraries. (My cloth is blue; it is therefore not, at the same time, and in the same respect, green.)

- Dichotomy. We think of P and Q, which are contraries, as though they were contradictory predicates. We begin to assume that everything within our system is either P or Q, and nothing is both. We are, in effect, interpreting Q as not-P.

- Competition. People organize around the P/not-P opposition and compete. Who will win? The Ps or the not-Ps? It will be either one or the other; it cannot be both. This is a competitive struggle. At this point there are adversaries, but the adversariality is not necessary to the pursuit and is overcome when one exits the context, which is fairly easy to do.

- Polarization. Competition intensifies and is accompanied by some amount of enmity. People feel compelled to identify with one side or the other in the zero sum game that is being played. There is no middle and there will be no compromise between extremes.

- Demonization. The opponent is viewed as evil and

Satanic.

- Destruction, or Struggle to the Death. There are two hostile sides, struggling to the death. Each side thinks its well-being and survival depends on the destruction of the other

In this sequence, we must stop somewhere, presuming that we do not wish to engage in genocidal extermination. Where should we stop? That depends on the context: sometimes between distinction and dichotomy (as urged by Putnam) and sometimes between competition and polarization (as suggested when we consider violence in sports). When opposition based on logical simplifications is accompanied by adversariality and attached to one's very conception of who one is, we are definitely in a danger zone from which we have every reason to escape. Polarization is dangerous, as has been all too obvious in recent political contexts.

I don't wish to dispute the value of criticism or oppositional roles, but rather to warn against intensifying those roles so as to slide into unnecessary polarization and even further into destructive enmity and exterminism. Simplified logical opposition can support unnecessary social opposition. But the relationship almost certainly works in the other direction too. If we see others as opponents in a conflict, we are more likely to exaggerate the differences between their positions and our own, resulting in logical inaccuracies. Logically, contraries and contradictories are different opposites. Socially, people can be opponents in different senses, with different degrees and kinds of competition and hostility. The various forms of logical opposition and social opposition are related, in ways both interesting and pathological.

REFERENCES

Alston, William. 1956. "Ineffability." *Philosophical Review*, 65(4), 506-522.

Ayim, Maryann. 1988. "Violence and domination as metaphors in academic discourse." In Govier 1988, pp. 184-195.

Govier, Trudy. 1988. *Selected Issues in Logic and Communication*. Belmont CA: Wadsworth.

Govier, Trudy. 1999. *The Philosophy of Argument*. Chapters 12 and 13. Belmont CA: Wadsworth

Govier, Trudy. 2010. *A Practical Study of Argument*. Belmont CA: Wadsworth.

Groarke, Leo and David S. Birdsell. 2007. "Outlines of a theory of visual argument." *Argumentation and Advocacy*, 43 (3&4), 103-113.

Putnam, Hilary. 1994. "Sense, nonsense, and the senses: An inquiry into the powers of the human mind." *Journal of Philosophy*, 91(9): 445-517.

Trapp, Robert and Janice Schuetz (Eds.). 1990. *Perspectives on Argumentation: Essays in Honor of Wayne Brockriede*. Prospect Heights, IL: Waveland Press

Wittgenstein, Ludwig. 1922. *Tractatus Logico-Philosophicus*. Cambridge: Cambridge University Press.

ABOUT THE AUTHOR: Trudy Govier was Associate Professor of Philosophy at Trent University and later Professor of Philosophy at the University of Lethbridge. Her work has largely been in two areas: first, that of theory of argument and informal logic and secondly, that of social philosophy. For a considerable period in the 1980s and 1990s Govier was an independent scholar working in Calgary; she did extensive community work during that period. She is the author of many articles and some thirteen books, including the widely used text *A Practical Study of Argument*, and *Problems of Argument Analysis and Evaluation*, and *The Philosophy of Argument*.

CHAPTER 5.

NORMS OF ADVOCACY

JEAN GOODWIN

ABSTRACT: This essay follows Hansen in spirit, if not in letter, by defending argumentation theory as rightfully centered on argument assessment. Although advocacy is one of the paradigmatic activities within which arguments get made, many theorists have viewed it as having no norms: as being assessable only by its empirical effectiveness. But the ethical principles articulated within the advocacy professions of law and public relations show that advocates are not just out to persuade. Instead, they undertake obligations of vigor in making the case for their positions while also maintaining the integrity of the communication systems within which they operate. While not fully audience-regarding, these undertakings can benefit audiences by revealing the outer boundaries of the arguable. This account of the ordinary activity of advocating demonstrates that it is intrinsically normative, and that rhetoric conceived of as the art of advocacy has a place in a unified theory of argumentation.

KEYWORDS: Hansen, advocacy, argumentation, argument, normative pragmatics, rhetoric, norms, argument assessment, legal ethics, public relations ethics

1. INTRODUCTION

Hans Hansen closes "An Enquiry into the Methods of Informal Logic," by proposing "a new definition of 'informal logic'" as "the set of methods of non-formal illative evaluation" (2012, p. 115). Placing evaluation at the center of informal logic allows Hansen to re-vision the field; theories of argument structure and argument kind can now be seen as methods that support (or at least, ought to support) improved argument assessment.

Although Hansen focuses only on informal logic, I believe his lesson applies more broadly. Argumentation theorists should be following him in adopting assessment as the center of gravity around which will orbit the scholarship in our far-flung fields. We may be studying diverse aspects of argumentation – perhaps the arguments themselves, perhaps the argumentative activities in which arguments get made.[1] We may spend most of our time describing, cataloging or taking apart the arguments or activities we study. But at the end of all this theory-building around argumentative phenomena, we must eventually face the task of evaluating whether it is good. That is the point of argumentation theory.

There is at least one perspective on argumentation that would seem to resist this push towards normativity: a perspective that takes as irrelevant whether (e.g.) an argument is reasonable or an interaction fair, because all that really matters is whether they are successful in persuading the audience. Perhaps this perspective could allow a little normativity to sneak back in by admitting that the arguer could be aiming at noble or base ends. In that way, the Effectiveness Only argumentation theorist could say that an argument or activity was good in an extrinsic manner by asking: successful *at what?* – and then assessing the "what." But this tweak would still offer no assessment of the intrinsic merit of an

---

1. On arguments and argumentative activities as the two objects of study for any theory of argumentation, see Goodwin (2001b).

argument or its making. The standard of effectiveness would be applied equally well to arguments and hammers, to argumentative processes and procedures for repairing cell phones. "Does it work?" becomes the only question for an EO theory of argumentation.

But who in the interdisciplinary mélange of argumentation theory actually holds such a view? Ironically, it is my own field that is often considered the primary proponent of this perspective. "Rhetoric is now widely conceived" – that is, widely by theorists in *other* fields – "as the study of effective communication" (Johnson 2000, 268). A rhetorical approach to argumentation thus is supposed to focus not on normative aspects of argumentative discourse, but instead on "those properties of the argumentative discourse that play a vital role in persuading an audience" (van Eemeren et al. 2014,10).

To uphold my generalized version of Hansen's more modest claim I will need to establish the centrality of normative interests even to rhetorical perspectives on argumentation (and thus along the way the insufficiency of this view of rhetoric). While rhetoric has to maintain its long-accepted office of making a difference in the world, rhetorical approaches must (and do) also take normativity to be intrinsic to argumentation. A rhetorical theory of argumentation is both a pragmatic and a normative theory. In this paper, I thus join the tradition of insisting on an ethics of rhetoric. (And an honorable tradition it is: Johnstone, 1981; Leff, 2000; Tindale, 2004; Kock, 2007). I proceed *a fortiori*. Starting from a worst-case scenario, I show that even the most openly persuasive – that is, the most rhetorical – argumentative activity is in fact governed by intrinsic standards of good and bad. In short, I articulate the norms of advocacy.

Advocacy is often taken as oriented entirely towards persuasion – persuasion without respect for any ethical standards. In the *Oxford English Dictionary*, for example, the earliest use of *advocate* (n.) expresses just this suspicion:

1574 A. Golding tr. J. Calvin Serm. on Job (new ed.) cvi. 545/2 We shall see many, which..becomen themselues aduocates [Fr. aduocats] of vntruthes, and fall to foysting in of lies to ouerthrow the right.

A similar attitude is implicit in some informal logic textbooks. For example, Johnson and Blair in their aptly named *Logical Self-Defense* promise to arm students against such advocacy:

> Groups and individuals are incessantly vying for our support for their way of seeing things, for our acceptance of their views of what is true, important, or worth doing. The list of topics varies; the point is that we are consumers of beliefs and values as well as products. An important question thus emerges: How good are our buying habits? Some arguments are damaged goods. Buying a bad argument can, depending on the situation, do a person more harm than buying a defective CD player (1994, 1).

Here the authors distinguish their informal-logical, approach, centered as Hansen would wish on assessing the goodness of the arguments on offer, from the amoral, or immoral, art of offering them.

From this perspective, it may seem surprising that scholars of argumentation working in rhetorical traditions apparently hold a different view. The name of our leading journal is *Argumentation & Advocacy*, one of our leading textbooks is called *Advocacy and Opposition* (Rybacki & Rybacki, 2008), and many of other textbooks use the term "advocate" as a virtual synonym for "arguer," to capture the role we invite students to take. Hollihan and Baaske, for example, tell their readers that "your task as an advocate is to create the best arguments that you can" (2005, 79). We apparently think that advocacy is worthy of respect and that it is a job with responsibilities that must be met.

Both scholarly traditions recognize that advocacy is one of the paradigmatic activities within which arguments are made. One takes advocacy to be happening outside of the realm where assessment takes place. The other holds advocacy to be subject to assessment on intrinsic grounds. The rhetoricians are right. Advocacy has norms.

In this paper, I adopt an empirical approach to identify these norms. I presume that competent advocates already know what normatively good advocacy is, at least in the sense of an implicit, practical "know-how." Following Robert Craig and Karen Tracy (Craig & Tracy, 1995; Craig, 1989, 1996), I take it that one goal of theorizing is to make this implicit practical knowledge more explicit, as a first step towards putting it in order, binding it to more basic principles, critiquing its limitations, and possibly improving it. So I will look to two communities of good advocates to begin developing a clearer conception of the norms of advocacy: lawyers, and public relations professionals. Both professions (as we will see) count advocacy among their central activities. Both face suspicions from the general public – both encounter resistance to their self-assertions of normative respectability. Both therefore have engaged in significant self-reflection, articulating for themselves a variety of values, ideals, principles, rules, obligations, best practices and so on in documents that I'll lump together and call "ethics statements." These statements are a particularly reliable source for evidence of the norms of advocacy, because they have to re-assure critical public audiences of the professions' integrity while also laying out norms that advocacy professionals can in practice follow. They have to be both normatively sound and practically useful – just what we need to get clear about the norms of the ordinary activity of advocating.

In the following sections, I analyze each community's ethics statements in turn, establishing that there are norms of advocacy and detailing the fine-grained set of obligations that each community puts forward. In the final sections, I close by generalizing an account of the normative structure of the ordinary activity of advocating and by exploring the implications of this account for argumentation theory more generally.

2. NORMS OF ADVOCACY AMONG THE LAWYERS

The current American Bar Association Model Rules of Professional Conduct (2012) – the source for the code of legal ethics in most US jurisdictions – recognize advocacy as one of several roles lawyers must play. "As advocate," the Preamble explains, "a lawyer zealously asserts the client's position under the rules of the adversary system." Notice first that this principle places advocacy in the particular context of "the adversary system": paradigmatically, a trial, but by extension other processes where open disputation is expected. Notice second that this standard pulls in two directions: an advocate owes "zeal" to her client, but is also constrained by ("under") her role within the "system" in which she operates. This same tension between responsibilities to clients and to systems turns up in the other places where the Rules talk of advocacy:

> The advocate has a duty to use legal procedure for the fullest benefit of the client's cause, but also a duty not to abuse legal procedure (Rule 3.1 Comment).
>
> A lawyer acting as an advocate in an adjudicative proceeding has an obligation to present the client's case with persuasive force. Performance of that duty while maintaining confidences of the client, however, is qualified by the advocate's duty of candor to the tribunal (Rule 3.3 Comment).

These "yes, but also" statements echo the more embroidered language of the earliest set of codified provisions in the U.S., the 1908 Canons of Professional Ethics:

> Canon 15: How Far a Lawyer May Go in Supporting a Client's Cause....The lawyer owes entire devotion to the interest of the client, warm zeal in the maintenance and defense of his rights and the exertion of his utmost learning and ability, to the end that nothing be taken or be withheld from him, save by the rules of law, legally applied. No fear of judicial disfavor or public unpopularity should restrain him from the full discharge of his duty. In the judicial forum the client is entitled to the benefit of any and every rem-

edy and defense that is authorized by the law of the land, and he may expect his lawyer to assert every such remedy or defense. But it is steadfastly to be borne in the mind that the great trust of the lawyer is to be performed within and not without the bounds of the law. The office of attorney does not permit, much less does it demand of him for any client, violation of law or any manner of fraud or chicane.

The 1969 ABA Code of Professional Responsibility captured the same thought in a plainer style, stating as black letter law the principle "A Lawyer Should Represent a Client Zealously Within the Bounds of the Law" (Canon 7).

The current formulation has tried to de-emphasize zeal by taking the word out of the Rules themselves, reserving it only for less binding Comments. But as the Preamble to the Rules discusses at length, the central dilemma between an advocate's obligations of *zeal* for the client and *restraint* for the system remains. The Preamble starts with the hopeful proposition that "a lawyer's responsibilities as a representative of clients, an officer of the legal system and a public citizen are usually harmonious." Whatever boundaries one lawyer's zeal may push will be met by her opponent's equal and opposite zeal in return. But the Preamble then continues on a less optimistic note:

> In the nature of law practice, however, conflicting responsibilities are encountered. Virtually all difficult ethical problems arise from conflict between a lawyer's responsibilities to clients, to the legal system and to the lawyer's own interest in remaining an ethical person while earning a satisfactory living. The Rules of Professional Conduct often prescribe terms for resolving such conflicts. Within the framework of these Rules, however, many difficult issues of professional discretion can arise. Such issues must be resolved through the exercise of sensitive professional and moral judgment guided by the basic principles underlying the Rules. These principles include the lawyer's obligation zealously to protect and pursue a client's legitimate interests, within the bounds of the law, while maintaining a professional, courteous and civil attitude toward all persons involved in the legal system.

In the following, I examine first the lawyer's duty of zeal, and then the specific limitations placed on it by the "bounds of the law."

Most importantly, the ethics statements recognize zeal as a *responsibility* – "an obligation to present the client's case with persuasive force" (Rule 3.3 Comment), "a duty to use legal procedure for the fullest benefit of the client's cause" (Rule 3.1 Comment). Beyond this, the various legal ethics statements leave "zeal" undefined, suggesting that the background cultural understanding of a "zealous advocate" is so well established as not to need much discussion.[2] Generally, zeal is associated with activity that benefits a client, and in particular communicative activities. Thus the advocate is said to "assert [] the client's position" (Preamble) or "assert...remed[ies] or defense[s]" (Canon 15).

The limits imposed on zeal, by contrast, are treated much more explicitly. A lawyer must confine her communication to the adversary proceeding itself, and within the proceeding, to communicative methods that are appropriate. She may not communicate privately with the judge or jurors (Rule 3.5). Her rights to communicate with the public are restricted (Rule 3.6). She is barred from achieving her client's goals by illicit, non-communicative methods like bribing, intimidating or harassing any of the other key participants in the courtroom setting (Rule 3.5). As the Comment to Rule 3.6 explains, these provisions are necessary to "preserv[e] the right to a fair trial," since "if there were no such limits, the result would be the practical nullification of the protective effect of the rules of forensic decorum and the exclusionary rules of evidence." Similarly, the obligation to refrain "from abusive or obstreperous conduct" in the courtroom "is a corollary of the advocate's right to speak on behalf of litigants" there (Rule 3.5 Comment). Thus these rules oblige the lawyer not to

---

2. As pointed out by the commentator on the original version of this essay, presented at the 2013 OSSA conference, there may indeed be different and changing cultural views on what exact "zeal" requires (Cameron, 2013).

proceed in ways that would undermine the adversary system that gives her room to advocate at all.[3]

An even more detailed set of rules govern the communicative means that the lawyer is allowed to deploy within the adversary proceeding. Most stringent is an absolute prohibition against making statements known to be false, or helping others make them:

> Rule 3.3 Candor Toward The Tribunal. (a) A lawyer shall not knowingly: (1) make a false statement of fact or law to a tribunal or fail to correct a false statement of material fact or previously made to the tribunal by the lawyer;... (3) offer evidence that the lawyer knows to be false.
> Rule 3.4 Fairness to Opposing Party and Counsel: A lawyer shall not... (b) falsify evidence, [or] counsel or assist a witness to testify falsely.

The rationale given in the Comments to these Rules again stresses the lawyer's obligation "to avoid conduct that undermines the integrity of the adjudicative process" (Rule 3.3 Comment). "Destruction or concealment of evidence," for example, blocks the basic "procedure of the adversary system" which "contemplates that the evidence in a case is to be marshalled competitively by the contending parties" (Rule 3.4 Comment).

Avoiding known falsehood still leaves scope for presenting less than known truth, however. As the Comment to Rule 3.3 puts it, "The prohibition against offering false evidence only applies if the lawyer knows that the evidence is false. A lawyer's reasonable belief that evidence is false does not preclude its presentation to the trier of fact." Indeed, "a lawyer should resolve doubts about the veracity of testimony or other evidence in favor of the

3. As Cameron (2013) also pointed out, specific venues may impose additional, informal responsibilities on advocates who wish to practice there. Failure to live up to these additional responsibilities will result in the advocate losing credibility within, or even access to, the venue. Thus, as with the formal Rules, the advocate must so act as to maintain the system that gives her room to advocate.

client." Within this broad terrain of non-known-falsehood, the ethical rules require lawyers to have at least some backing for what they say. For example, a lawyer can raise any issue – including an argument for overturning current law – as long as "there is a basis in law and fact...that is not frivolous" (Rule 3.1). The Comment explains:

> Such action is not frivolous even though the lawyer believes that the client's position ultimately will not prevail. The action is frivolous, however, if the lawyer is unable either to make a good faith argument on the merits of the action taken or to support the action taken by a good faith argument for an extension, modification or reversal of existing law.

Similarly, in making arguments, "a lawyer shall not... allude to any matter... that will not be supported by admissible evidence" (Rule 3.4). Note that this Rule does not require a lawyer to actually believe the evidence ("a lawyer in an adversary proceeding is not required... to vouch for the evidence submitted in a cause," Rule 3.3 Comment); it merely requires her to base her arguments only on (non-known-to-be-false) evidence that could be admitted.

Finally, in two specific cases the lawyer is affirmatively required to present matters known to be true, even if they are adverse to her client's interests. She must disclose the law to a judge, and, if no opposing lawyer is present, must disclose all material facts (Rule 3.3). The first of these obligations is, amusingly enough, an obligation of veracity that the lawyer owes to her fellow lawyer, the judge. The Comment characterizes suppression of known legal provisions as a scandalous "dishonesty toward the tribunal." The second obligation is imposed only when in an adversarial proceeding – the presumed ordinary context of advocacy – there is no adversary present, so "there is no balance of presentation by opposing advocates." In both cases, however, the Comments stress that these are unusual situations: the exceptions which prove the rule. In general, "a lawyer is not required to make a disinterested exposition of the law," and "an advocate has [only] the limited responsibility of presenting one side of the matters that a tribunal should consider in reaching a decision" (Rule 3.3 Comment).

In sum, lawyers are obligated (a) to pursue a client's interests zealously (b) in an adversarial context, and (c) to do this exclusively by communication within the institutional setting, while ensuring that all statements made (d) are not known to be false, (e) are supportable by evidence and reasoning, and (f) in a few limited cases, are the whole truth.

3. NORMS OF ADVOCACY AMONG PUBLIC RELATIONS PROFESSIONALS

It may be surprising to some to discover that there are norms of public relations at all. The occupation seems to suffer especially in comparison to its sister profession, journalism. Both PR professionals and journalists are expected to get messages out to broader publics. But where journalists work under a well-understood set of norms including accuracy, fairness and independence, PR professionals may appear to outsiders to be subject to no such guidelines. As the Public Relations Society of America acknowledges, there are "those who refer to our craft as spin, our professionals as flacks, and our currency as misrepresentation and disinformation." But this denigration of their profession has been fiercely resisted by the PRSA and other professional associations, in part based on the "special obligation [of public relations professionals] to practice their craft ethically" (PRSA, n.d., "Communicating public relations' value"). In the following, I review the ethics codes and associated materials from these societies, to elicit the norms of advocacy in PR.

As we saw with the legal profession, PR professional associations express their central ideal as what we can recognize as a dilemma, cramming into one principle obligations to those they represent and obligations to the public. The PRSA identifies as its first value: "Advocacy. We serve the public interest by acting as responsible advocates for those we represent. We provide a voice in the marketplace of ideas, facts, and viewpoints to aid informed public debate" (PRSA Code). An earlier version of the PRSA code was explicit about the tension, insisting that PR folk maintain their integrity "while carrying out dual obligations to a client or employer and to the democratic process" (PRSA 1988 Code).

As is obvious from the above quotations, the PR community takes advocacy itself as a value. But what such advocacy requires is, as with the legal community, more assumed than specified. PRSA defines "public relations" as "a strategic communication process that builds mutually beneficial relationships between organizations and their publics" (PRSA, n.d., "About public relations"). "Strategic communication" suggests a strong goal-directedness; this emerges in another ethics statement as well, which requires professionals "to vigorously pursue their [client's] organizational goals in educating or persuading audiences that matter most to them" (PR Council). "Vigor" here parallels the lawyer's "zeal" on behalf of the client; as one case discussion put it, "PR professionals advocate – often vigorously – on behalf of those we represent. Our job is to promote a particular position or organization" (PRSA, PRSA speaks out). "Strategic communication" also puts the focus on communication – or as the PRSA Code puts it, "provid[ing] a voice in the marketplace of ideas." Finally, the context invoked in these statements is one where the PR professional must achieve his goals among multiple, relatively powerful, possibly competing voices: he is in a "marketplace of ideas, facts, and viewpoints" (PRSA Code), or "in the sphere of such complex issues as thorny policy debates, intense market competition or critical education needs in areas of public health, safety and well-being" (PR Council).

Advocacy as portrayed in these statements is thus the vigorous pursuit of a client's interests, using communication, in an environment of other communicators who do not share the same goals. What are the limits of this vigor? A first set of restrictions is imposed by the PR professional's need to preserve the system of communication which allows him room to be vigorous. Thus an earlier version of the PRSA Code echoes the Model Rules by providing that "a member shall not engage in any practice which has the purpose of corrupting the integrity of channels of communications" (PRSA 1988 Code). At times the statements speak as if what is involved is a principle of fair return: since PR advocates themselves benefit from freedom of speech and the free flow of information it allows, it is only right that they in turn respect the views and voices of others. This creates an environment where "a diversity of viewpoints and opinions" are "heard, but must compete on the merits of argument and fact" (PRSA PSA-06).

Practically speaking, however, it's hard to see how a lukewarm invocation of the Golden Rule would serve to restrain an advocate's vigor. So it is interesting that the ethics statements also put forward a second, more pointed, rationale for not "corrupting the integrity" of the communication system. PR professionals not only benefit in general from principles of free expression, they also benefit very specifically from the independence of other communicators. Producers of movies, books, software and video games for example, want independent reviewers to give them a good rating. A business wants its local newspaper and television stations to report on activities which give it a good name. But reviews and reports are only trusted by the ultimate audience if they are disinterested. Thus while it may be tempting for the PR professional to ply reviewers and reporters with gifts or threaten them with exclusion from access, when those bribes or threats are discovered the reviews and reports will then be worthless. A recorded ethics discussion of a case involving negative video game reviews analyzes this well:

> Larsen: A reviewer's credibility is on the line with their audience every time they evaluate a product – the nature of which demands

honesty, fairness and bias-free analysis. However frustrating a negative review may be, a developer's relationship with reviewers is critical in reaching the marketplace. There is a trust factor between the two that should not be inhibited or breached by threats, which ultimately invalidate the assessment...

Whalen: Absolutely. It's the independent third-party endorsement that makes public relations a valuable tool. If the client buys the review – either through actual monetary exchange or through intimidation – the reviewer has no credibility... Don't be afraid of a few negative reviews. Customers will often overlook a reviewer's comments and make up their own minds, but they have little tolerance for people who seem to be trying to manipulate them with fake reviews or intimidation (PRSA Issues in Ethics).

Thus the PRSA Code provides an explicit guideline for practice: "preserve the free flow of unprejudiced information when giving or receiving gifts by ensuring that gifts are nominal, legal, and infrequent." This injunction to avoid pay for play parallels the similar injunction in the legal setting against bribing or intimidating witnesses, jurors, judges and other courtroom actors. But the unregulated openness of the public sphere, in contrast to the institutional regularities of the courtroom, adds another layer of complexity. In fact, it is not necessarily wrong for a PR professional to give other communicators compensation or assistance. Examples which turn up in the PRSA's cases include: payments to expert and celebrity endorsers, early and free access to product reviewers, giveaways at trade shows, payments for publishing advertorials, and support for public groups who support the PR professional's client. The ethical issue that arises in these cases is instead one of openness and transparency – a very pressing issue indeed, judging from how frequently it turns up in the ethics statements. One association declares its commitments thus: "We believe that our clients and the public are best served when third party relationships with spokespeople, bloggers, partners and allies are open and transparent. Our bias in counseling clients is toward disclosure, which we believe is appropriate as a principle and effective as a communications tool" (PR Council). The

PRSA similarly warns against unattributed video news releases (PSA-13), fake online reviews and other covert uses of social media (ESA-08) and front (or astroturf) groups (PSA-06). The rationale put forward for transparency is again that it is in the "client's best interest," as one case discussion explains, "since deceiving the media and the public(s) could contribute to declining public(s) trust in the [client]… [Full disclosure of sponsorship] would preserve the integrity of processes of communication and also help the [client] (and the public relations professional/firm) maintain important relationships with… citizens, voters, media and government officials" (PRSA Public Relations Ethics Case Study #2). Or as an PRSA Ethics Standards Advisory puts it:

> If the entire weight of the PRSA Code of Ethics could be loaded into a single word, that word would be Disclosure… Disclosure is difficult, but it builds trust. Avoiding disclosure ultimately destroys trust and replaces it with fear of the unknown. From a public relations perspective, disclosure and openness are powerful tools for building relationships and encouraging progress. Whenever there is doubt, choose disclosure. Disclosure is quite simply one of the most powerful tools to enhance and ensure the well-being of everyone (PRSA ESA-19).

PR advocates are thus obligated to be open about advocacy, since in the long run that is the only way for their advocacy to be successful.

The final set of restrictions focuses not on the PR professional's relationship to other communicators, but on the commitments to veracity he is undertaking in his own communications. The ethics statements of all the organizations include inspiring language about honesty in public relations work:

> [2.] Honesty. We adhere to the highest standards of accuracy and truth in advancing the interests of those we represent and in communicating with the public (PRSA Code).

1. Tell the truth. Let the public know what's happening with honest and good intention; provide an ethically accurate picture of the enterprise's character, values, ideals and actions (Arthur Page Society).

2. We are committed to accuracy. In communicating with the public and media, Member firms will maintain total accuracy and truthfulness (PR Council).

Another association adopts a more restrained approach, including farther down on their list of principles a modest ambition:

7. Accuracy. Take all reasonable steps to ensure the truth and accuracy of all information provided;

8. Falsehood. Make every effort to not intentionally disseminate false or misleading information, exercise proper care to avoid doing so unintentionally and correct any such act promptly (IPRA).

In this version, the PR professional has a significant obligation to avoid false statements ("every effort"), a moderate obligation to make sure that what he chooses to say is true ("reasonable steps"), and apparently no obligation to say all that he knows. While some argue that complete candor is, like full disclosure, necessary in the long run to preserve trust and make continued advocacy possible, this is not the only view. As one commentator put it, "you [the PR professional] give them [news reporters] information which will benefit your client if published... You, of course, are supposed to give them accurate information and to do so as promptly as possible. But you are not obligated to tell the news media all you know" (Smith, 1972). In an advisory on "greenwashing" (advertising of products as environmentally sound), the PRSA cautions its members to "review product claims and make certain supporting marketing collateral and key messages accurately describe the product and avoid unsubstantiated claims... Product claims should be thoroughly vetted and defensible.... Ensure that your green claim is completely substantiated and that you have the evidence to back up the claim" (PRSA PSA-12). The emphasis here is on defensibility, not truth per se: on not making false claims, and on having support for the ones that do get made.

In sum: public relations professionals are obligated (a) to pursue a client's interests vigorously (b) in a context where there are other communicators with different perspectives, (c) avoiding non-communicative means like bribery and intimidation, while ensuring that all statements made (d) are not known to be false and (e) are defensible; and finally, (f') to do all this openly.

4. A GENERAL ACCOUNT OF THE NORMS OF ADVOCACY

While some aspects of legal ethics might be traced to specific features of the institutionalized practice of law, public relations ethics has been developed outside of formal institutions, and in particular in an environment that has experienced dramatic changes from traditional to new media. Despite these differences, the pictures of advocacy that have emerged from ethics statements in law and public relations appear to converge. This gives us warrant to generalize from these two special cases to an account of the ordinary communicative activity of advocating.

Lawyers and PR professionals are hired to speak for another person or organization. In general, however, an advocate does not need to formally be retained by another; she can undertake to advocate for another person or organization, for herself, for a proposal, or even for an abstract cause.[4] We have no problem understanding a headline like "thousands mobilize to advocate for an end to poverty," for example.

4. For some additional ethical complexities of advocating for a cause, see Cohen (2004). The self-appointed advocate may weigh his own vision of the future more heavily than those directly affected. Economic and identity interests in continuing the advocacy may also distort the self-appointed advocate's view.

Based on the accounts developed in law and PR, advocacy is appropriate in contexts where diverse voices, messages, positions, causes, etc. are circulating (see also Goodnight, 2009). This feature begins to differentiate advocacy from propaganda, where inequalities of power mean that only one message is being heard. It also distinguishes advocacy from the communication activities that occur against a background of agreement. To borrow an example from Roger Pielke (2007), someone who yells "get to the basement – there's a tornado coming!" would not be said to be advocating; she expects a consensus around the value of safety and the effectiveness of basements.

In the courtroom setting, the diverse voices are in direct competition – the advocates are also adversaries. While competition among advocates may also occur in non-institutionalized contexts, it is not necessary. Competition, after all, is only one strategy among others for managing diverse interests. Outside of institutionally organized adversarial contexts, advocates may find that their goals overlap, or that there are mutually beneficial ways for them to coordinate their activities while seeking different goals, or that they can simply ignore each other. Advocating may thus appropriately find a home among a broad range of ordinary interactions that are neither openly competitive nor fully collaborative.

The activity of advocating is structured around two sets of obligations: obligations undertaken to the person or cause advocated for, and obligations undertaken to the audiences and other participants in the communication setting. These two sets of obligations are often going to be in tension with each other—an unhappy situation for the advocate, who might prefer to cut through the problem by jettisoning one set of obligations. Indeed, in both legal and public relations ethics there is a long history of disputes about whether professionals should commit themselves just to persuasive effectiveness or just to public service (e.g., Andrews, 2012; L'Etang, 2004). But as Craig & Tracy

(1995) point out, "dilemmatic" goals are typical of communicative practices generally. The art of advocacy is to manage the dilemma as it arises on particular occasions.

To the person or cause she is advocating for, the advocate undertakes to communicate with zeal and vigor. She commits herself not just to diligent efforts to achieve a goal, but to "intense ardour in the pursuit of [that] end; passionate eagerness in favour of a person or cause; enthusiasm as displayed in action" (to quote the *Oxford English Dictionary's* definition of "zeal").

The advocate's obligations to others are obviously more complex. These are owed primarily to the audience, but also to other advocates, other communicators, and perhaps to the public generally. In the ethics statements in both law and PR, this set of obligations is traced back to a basic undertaking not to undermine the "integrity" of the communication "system" which makes the advocacy possible. In the case of legal ethics, the system is visible and the penalties for undermining it expressed. PR professionals work in no such institutional setting, but instead in the midst of the vast, confused and always-changing collection of communication practices we glibly name the "public sphere." So the vague idea of an obligation to a "system" needs to be made more specific, and the ethics statements do this in three ways.

First, the advocate owes it to her audience to be open about the fact that she is advocating. This obligation was not included in statements of legal ethics, likely because in the courtroom setting the lawyer is manifestly an advocate.[5] But as we saw, concerns about disclosure are prominent in PR ethics.[6] The crowded and disorderly public sphere makes it easy for an advocate to mask her dedication to her cause. But while admitting advocacy

---

5. The ABA Model Rules do provide that lawyers appearing in "nonadjudicative proceeding[s]," where communicators often speak for themselves, "shall disclose that the appearance is in a representative capacity" (Rule 3.9).

6. And in other settings; there is a literature on undisclosed "stealth" or simply inadvertent advocacy by scientists (Pielke 2007; Wilhere 2012).

can make audiences cautious, revelation of covert advocacy will destroy trust entirely. The prudent advocate will thus commit to openness from the start.

Second, the advocate owes it to other participants in the communicative situation, including her audience, to show respect for their autonomous roles. This obligation emerged in prohibitions against bribing, intimidating and harassing witnesses, reviewers, journalists, jurors and judges. As with the obligation of openness, this is not simply a responsibility to maintain a general system. The advocate needs to gain the trust of her audience, and can secure this trust only by letting other communicators remain independent.

Finally, the advocate owes her audience some obligation of veracity. Both legal and PR ethics insist that an advocate ought not say things she knows to be false. Both also agree that the advocate ought to have some non-frivolous reason(s) in support of what she said. Beyond that, it appears that the advocate's obligation of veracity is a limited one. Does she commit herself to having made a thorough investigation to back what she says, or to confirm its non-falsity? It doesn't look like it. Does she commit herself to telling the whole truth, including the bits that go against her? Not likely. Does she commit herself to sincerity—to saying only things she herself believes to be true? Definitely not. Indeed, in the courtroom setting, the legal advocate is prohibited from personally "vouching" for her client.

We can summarize this discussion with the following account of the norms of ordinary activity of advocating:

> A speaker advocates when she (a) openly commits herself (b) to the zealous, vigorous support of a person or cause (c) in the context of multiple voices or views, and to do this (c) through communication, disavowing persuasive means like bribery, intimidation and harassment, committing herself to the (d) justifiability and (e) non-known-falsity of what she says.

5. IMPLICATIONS

The account I have given demonstrates that advocacy is intrinsically normative. It is constituted of a complex of obligations the advocate undertakes towards her client or cause and towards her audience.

Advocating is not the activity of a person who simply wants to win. Indeed, some advocates representing unsavory clients may in their hearts prefer losing. Nor do we judge the advocate by her success; some of the greatest advocates know they will see no victory in their lifetimes. Instead, advocating is activity of a person who has *undertaken responsibility* for zealous support of a person, organization, proposal or cause. We criticize her not when she fails to persuade, but when she fails to be vigorous in the attempt.

However, this commitment on its own is insufficient, since as a communicative activity, advocacy needs an audience. But why should anyone consent to be the object of someone else's vigor? As a practical matter, in order to secure an audience to advocate *to*, the advocate must undertake additional, audience-regarding obligations. She commits to the veracity (although not the completeness) of what she says – a minimum guarantee that it will have informational content. She commits to the justifiability of what she says – a minimum guarantee that she won't be wasting the audience's time with matters that on inspection will be found frivolous. And finally, she commits to securing some of the conditions the audience needs in order to make good judgments. She undertakes not to distort other's communications to the audience (e.g., with bribery or intimidation), and she undertakes to be open about her own commitments.

As we saw, the advocate can feel torn between her dual and sometimes dilemmatic responsibilities. Audiences can feel a similar strain. On one hand, the advocate has openly committed herself to pursue her cause zealously. This is not an audience-regarding responsibility; she is not committing herself to saying something worth the audience's time (as in proposing, Kauffeld 1998b), or to adapting what she says to the audience's concerns (as in advising, Kauffeld 1999). She is not even committing herself to the truth of what she is saying and to having made a reasonable effort to ascertain that truth, as she would in the basic act of saying something seriously (Kauffeld 2012b). Given that the advocate has openly announced her loyalty to her cause, her audience is right to be suspicious, can subject what she tells them to heightened scrutiny, and can even discount it entirely.[7]

At the same time, even cautious audiences can find value in advocacy. An advocate holds herself out as providing the strongest possible, non-frivolous, non-known-to-be-false support for a cause. The audience can trust the advocate to do this, and presume that no stronger non-frivolous, colorable support can be given. In this way, even discounted statements have some informational value. If the advocate presents some evidence, then no better evidence for her position exists. If she ignores a topic, then that topic must not support her view. If she makes a claim, the truth may be somewhat less, but is not somewhat more, than she presents it. Recall furthermore that advocacy occurs in the context of *other* advocacy. Competing advocates can

7. It is widely recognized that audiences have to use some interpretive principles to figure out what an arguer (or indeed, any communicator) means. Trudy Govier (1997a) has proposed a universal principle of *moderate charity*, according to which the audience understands that the arguer is cooperating with them in a mutual exchange of good reasons. When faced with a patently vague statement (for example), the audience is thus licensed to presume whatever is needed to make the argument sound. The account I have given here of advocacy suggests that instead, the interpretive principles that audiences can appropriately use are context-dependent: they arise from the specific commitments that arguers have made to them. The audience of an advocate reasonably adopts a principle of *discounting*. They can presume that the zealous arguer made the strongest non-false statement possible for her claim. If the arguer is vague, the audience is licensed to think "That's the best she can do?!" and dismiss the argument. For further discussions of discounting, see Goodwin (2001a) for the context of criminal trial advocacy and Goodwin (2012, 2014) for advocacy by scientists.

be even more useful to audiences. Audiences can count on them to lay out the boundaries of what can non-falsely and non-frivolously be said on a given topic. This allows the audience to outsource some of the time-consuming and wearisome activity of reasoning to those who are obliged to be zealous about it. Cognitive misers appreciate vigorous advocates.

The codes of ethics in both law and PR envision advocacy as a specifically *communicative* activity, in contrast to bribery or intimidation. But neither profession in their ethics statements requires advocacy to be *argumentative*. Why then the longstanding association of argumentation and advocacy? The advocate does not undertake probative obligations to her audience – she does not accept a burden of proof. The obligations she does undertake, however, can often best be fulfilled by making arguments, especially when they are challenged by other advocates.[8] The advocate commits herself to the justifiability (in the weak sense of "non-frivolity") of what she says. If challenged, she can show that her advocacy is justifiable by making justifications apparent. The advocate commits herself to not saying anything she knows to be false. If challenged, she can demonstrate that she doesn't know what she is saying to be false by making manifest evidence of its truth (or at least, evidence that raises reasonable doubts of its falseness). Zealous advocacy, in short, will often take the form of making the strongest possible *case*.[9]

8. See Jackson and Jacobs' classic paper on conversational argument (1980) for a general version of this view: people make arguments when the commitments that they have undertaken in speaking get called out. In the advocacy situation, with its multiple voices, such callings out will be routine.

9. On the concept of "case" – an entire body of arguments (an "argumentation," in one meaning of that term) fulfilling an arguer's responsibilities (however conceived) – see Govier (1997b) and Kauffeld (1998a). Both Kauffeld and Govier are concerned to define the limits of an arguer's responsibility to make a case, so that she doesn't have to respond to objections *forever*. The obligation of zeal may mean that for the advocate, there are no such limits. She must continue to make her case until she succeeds, or until extrinsic cir-

To review: Advocacy has sometimes been considered a clear case of brute persuasion, unbound by considerations of goodness, lacking any intrinsic norms. Attention to the theory-in-practice articulated by competent advocates makes evident a different view. Far from being "unbound," advocates openly undertake heightened responsibilities to their cause or clients, and weaker but still significant responsibilities to their audience. These responsibilities guide both the advocate's practice and the audience's reception of it. Indeed, it is only by undertaking and fulfilling responsibilities that the advocate can earn a reception for her case; lies, specious "spin" and especially nondisclosure will lose her the basic audience trust she needs to gain hearing. The advocate thus has an investment in the "integrity" of the "system" in which she operates. To be effective, she must be ethical (Goodwin 2018).

If even advocacy has norms, then it is reasonable to infer that other, less suspicious activities where arguments tend to turn up are similarly structured. I and other argumentation theorists working in the rhetorical tradition have examined the normative constitution of proposing, accusing, advising, reporting (Kauffeld 1998b, 1999, 2012a), exhorting (Kauffeld & Innocenti 2018), and demanding (Innocenti & Kathol 2018) among other acts; and of broader activities including exercising authority (Goodwin 2010, 2011), using humor (Innocenti & Kathol 2018), appealing to emotions (Innocenti 2011) and exploiting all the affordances of language lumped generally under the term "stylistic devices" (Innocenti 2005; Kauffeld 2009a). In these studies, we fill out a rhetorical perspective on argumentation that is dedicated to accounting simultaneously for the impact and for the intrinsic norms of argumentative activities. We have dubbed this approach to argumentation theory "normative pragmatics," since we show how arguers can, practically speaking, secure or even

cumstances force her to stop (e.g., the end of the trial, or nonpayment, or death).

force an intended response from their audience by subjecting themselves to norms (for overviews, see especially Goodwin 2000, Kauffeld 2009b, Innocenti 2019).

I have thus justified hope in the Hansen-inspired vision with which I opened this essay: hope of a (loosely) unified argumentation theory centering on a core concern for assessment. Hansen ended his "Enquiry" by claiming for informal logic one large portion of territory of argumentation: "non-formal illative evaluation," i.e., assessment of the reasons given. I will close with a similar contention. Informal logic's counterpart, normative pragmatics, can cover the rest: assessment of the reason-giving.

ETHICS STATEMENTS: LAW (U.S.A.)

American Bar Association. 2012. Model Rules of Professional Conduct. Retrieved from https://www.americanbar.org/groups/professional_responsibility/publications/model_rules_of_professional_conduct/model_rules_of_professional_conduct_table_of_contents/s

American Bar Association. 1969. Model Code of Professional Responsibility. Retrieved from https://www.americanbar.org/content/dam/aba/administrative/professional_responsibility/mrpc_migrated/mcpr.pdf

American Bar Association 1908. Canons of Professional Ethics. Retrieved from https://www.americanbar.org/content/dam/aba/administrative/professional_responsibility/1908_code.pdf

Ethics Statements: Public Relations (U.S.A.)

Arthur W. Page Society. n.d. The Page Principles. Retrieved from https://page.org/site/the-page-principles

International Public Relations Association (2011). Code of Conduct. Retrieved from https://www.ipra.org/member-services/code-of-conduct/

PR Council. n.d. The PR Council code of ethics and principles. Retrieved from https://prcouncil.net/join/the-pr-council-code-of-ethics-and-principles/

Public Relations Society of America n.d. PRSA Code of Ethics. Retrieved from https://www.prsa.org/about/ethics/prsa-code-of-ethics

—— 1988. Code of Professional Standards for the Practice of Public Relations. Retrieved from http://www.paularuth.com/ethics.htm

—— 2005. Professional Standards Advisory PS-6, Disclosure by Expert Commentators and Professional Spokespersons of Payments or Financial Interests. Retrieved from https://www.prsa.org/docs/default-source/about/ethics/eas/disclosure-by-expert-commentators-and-professional-spokespersons-of-payments-or-financial-interests-(april-2005)dd1f6d652b3a4a168aaa0f726f644e88.pdf?sfvrsn=c4d09509_0

—– 2008. Public Relations Ethics Case Study #2: Representing Front Groups with Undisclosed Sponsors and Engaging in Deceptive Practices While Representing a Front Group. Retrieved from https://www.prsa.org/docs/default-source/about/ethics/ethics-case-studies/ethics-case-study-front-group.pdf?sfvrsn=83045c0_2

—— 2009. Professional Standards Advisory PSA-12, Questionable Environmental Claims and Endorsements (Greenwashing). Retrieved from https://www.prsa.org/docs/default-source/about/ethics/eas/questionable-environmental-claims-and-endorsements-(greenwashing)-(october-2009).pdf?sfvrsn=bc8be581_0

—— 2009. Professional Standards Advisory PS-13, Use of Video News Releases as a Public Relations Tool. Retrieved from https://www.prsa.org/docs/default-source/about/ethics/eas/use-of-video-news-releases-as-a-public-relations-tool-(october-2009).pdf?sfvrsn=d7a0d1f7_0

—– 2011. Issues in ethics: Rescuing reputations at risk. Retrieved from https://apps.prsa.org/Intelligence/Tactics/Articles/view/9370/1035/Issues_in_ethics_Rescuing_reputations_at_risk

—-2011. PRSA Speaks Out Against Utah Mayor's Unethical Actions.
http://prsay.prsa.org/2011/11/15/prsa-speaks-out-against-utah-mayor-unethical-communication-practices/

—– 2012. Ethical Standards Advisory ESA-08, Deceptive Online Practices and Misrepresentation of Organizations and Visuals. Retrieved from https://www.prsa.org/docs/default-source/about/ethics/eas/deceptive-online-ethical-standards-advisory.pdf?sfvrsn=806b591f_2

—– 2014. Ethical Standards Advisory ESA-19, Disclosure and Transparency in Native Advertising and Sponsored Content. Retrieved from https://www.prsa.org/docs/default-source/about/ethics/eas/ethical-standards-advisory-disclosure-and-transparency.pdf?sfvrsn=e9d89ed_2

REFERENCES

Andrews, C.R. 2012. Ethical limits on civil litigation advocacy: A historical perspective. *Case Wester Reserve Law Review, 63,* 381-439.

Lewin´ski (Eds.), *Virtues of argumentation: Proceedings of the Tenth OSSA Conference.* Windsor, ON: Ontario Society for the Study of Argumentation. Retrieved from https://scholar.uwindsor.ca/ossaarchive/OSSA10/papersandcommentaries/62/

Cohen, E.S. 2004. Advocacy and advocates: Definitions and ethical dimensions. *Generations, 28*(1), 9-16.

Craig, R.T. 1989. Communication as a practical discipline. In B. Dervin, L. Grossberg, E. Wartella & B.J. O'Keefe (Eds.), *Rethinking communication, Vol 1: Paradigm issues,* 97-122. Newbury Park, CA: Sage Publications.

Craig, R.T. 1996. Practical-theoretical argumentation. *Argumentation, 10,* 461-474.

Craig, R.T., & Tracy, K. 1995. Grounded practical theory: The case of intellectual discussion. *Communication Theory, 5*(3), 248-272.

Eemeren, F.H. van, Garssen, B., Krabbe, E.C.W., Snoeck Henkemans, A.F., Verheij, B., Wagemans, J.H.M. 2014. *Handbook of argumentation theory.* Dordrecht: Springer.

Goodnight, G.T. 2009. The duties of advocacy: Argumentation under conditions of disparity, asymmetry, and difference. In F.H. van Eemeren & B. Garssen (Eds.), *Pondering on problems of argumentation: Twenty essays on theoretical issues,* 269-286.

Goodwin, J. 2000. Comments on [Jacobs'] Rhetoric and dialectic from the standpoint of normative pragmatics. *Argumentation, 14,* 287-292.

Goodwin, J. 2001a. The noncooperative pragmatics of arguing. In E. T. Nemeth (Ed.), *Pragmatics in 2000: Selected papers from the 7th International Pragmatics Conference* (Vol. 2), 263-277. Antwerp: International Pragmatics Association.

Goodwin, J. 2001b. One question, two answers. In H. Hansen, C. W. Tindale, J. A. Blair, R. H. Johnson & R. C. Pinto (Eds.), *Argumentation and its applications.* Windsor, ON: Ontario Society for the Study of Argumentation.

Goodwin, J. 2010. Trust in experts as a principal-agent problem. In C. Reed & C.W. Tindale (Eds.), *Dialectics, dialogue and argumentation: An examination of Douglas Walton's theories of reasoning and argument,* 133-143. London: College Publications.

Goodwin, J. 2011. Accounting for the appeal to the authority of experts. *Argumentation 25*(3): 285-296.

Goodwin, J. 2012. What is "responsible advocacy" in science? Good advice. In J. Goodwin (Ed.), *Between scientists & citizens: Proceedings of a conference at Iowa State University, 1-2 June 2012,* 151-161. Ames, IA: GPSSA.

Goodwin, J. 2014. Conceptions of speech acts in the theory and practice of argumentation: A case study of a debate about advocating. *Studies in Logic, Grammar & Rhetoric, 36,* 79-98. doi:10.2478/slgr-2014-0003

Goodwin, J. 2018. Effective because ethical: Speech act theory as a framework for scientists' communication. In S. Priest, J. Goodwin, & M. Dahlstrom (Eds.) *Ethics and Practice in Science Communication,* 1-21. Chicago, IL: University of Chicago Press.

Govier, T. 1997a. A new approach to charity. In *Problems in argument analysis and evaluation,* 133-158. Dordrecht: Foris Publications.

Govier, T. 1997b. Arguing forever? Or: Two tiers of argument appraisal. In H.V. Hansen, C.W. Tindale, & A.V. Colman (Eds.), *Argumentation and Rhetoric: Proceedings of the Second OSSA Conference.* St. Catherines, ON: Brock University. Retrieved from https://scholar.uwindsor.ca/ossaarchive/OSSA2/papersand-commentaries/46

Hansen, H.V. 2012. An enquiry into the methods of informal logic. In H. J. Ribeiro (Ed.), *Inside arguments,* 101-115. Cambridge: Cambridge Scholars Publishing.

Hollihan, T.A. & Baaske, K.T. 2005. *Arguments and arguing: The products and process of human decision making* (2nd ed.). Long Grove, IL: Waveland Press.

Innocenti Manolescu, B. 2005. Norms of presentational force. *Argumentation and Advocacy, 41,* 139–151.

Innocenti, B. 2011. A normative pragmatic model of making fear appeals. *Philosophy and Rhetoric, 44*(3), 273–290.

Innocenti, B. 2019. Constructing effective arguments. In J.A. Blair (Ed.), *Studies in critical thinking* (213-224). Windsor, ON: Windsor Studies in Argumentation. Retrieved from https://windsor.scholarsportal.info/omp/index.php/wsia/catalog/view/106/106/1089-1

Innocenti, B. & Kathol, N. 2018. The persuasive force of demanding. *Philosophy and Rhetoric, 51*(1), 50–72.

Innocenti, B. & Miller, E. 2016. The persuasive force of political humor. *Journal of Communication*, 66(3), 366–385.

Jackson, S. & Jacobs, S. 1980. Structure of conversational argument: Pragmatic bases for the enthymeme. *Quarterly Journal of Speech, 66*, 251-264.

Johnson, R.H. 2000. *Manifest rationality*. Mahwah, New Jersey: Lawrence Erlbaum Associates.

Johnson, R.H. & Blair, J.A. 1994. *Logical self-defense*. New York: McGraw-Hill.

Johnstone, H.W. Jr. 1981. Towards an ethics of rhetoric. *Communication, 6*, 301-314.

Kauffeld, F.J. 1998a. The good case for practical propositions: Limits of the arguer's obligation to respond to objections. In F.H. van Eemeren, R. Grootendorst, J.A. Blair, & C.A. Willard (Eds.), *Proceedings of the Fourth International Conference of the International Society for the Study of Argumentation*, 439-444. Amsterdam: Sic Sat.

Kauffeld, F.J. 1998b. Presumptions and the distribution of argumentative burdens in acts of proposing and accusing. *Argumentation, 12*(2), 245-266.

Kauffeld, F.J. 1999. Arguments on the dialectical tier as structured by proposing and advising. In C. W. Tindale, H. V. Hansen & E. Sveda (Eds.), *Argumentation at the century's turn: Proceedings of the Third OSSA Conference*. St. Catharines, ON: OSSA.

Kauffeld, F.J. 2009a. Grice's analysis of utterance-meaning and Cicero's Catilinarian apostrophe. *Argumentation, 23*(2) 239–257.

Kauffeld, F.J. 2009b. What we are learning about the pragmatics of the arguers' obligations? In S. Jacobs (Ed.) *Concerning argument* (1–31). Washington DC: National Communication Association.

Kauffeld, F.J. 2012a. A pragmatic paradox inherent in expert reports addressed to lay citizens. In J. Goodwin (Ed.), *Between* scientists & citizens: Proceedings of a conference at Iowa State University, June 1-2, 2012, 229-240. Ames, IA: Great Plains Society for the Study of Argumentation.

Kauffeld, F.J. 2012b. Strategies for strengthening presumptions and generating ethos by manifestly ensuring accountability. In F. Zenker (Ed.), *Argument cultures: Proceedings of the 8th international conference of the Ontario Society for the Study of Argumentation (OSSA)* (1-15). Windsor, ON.

Kauffeld, F.J. & Innocenti, B. 2018. A normative pragmatic theory of exhorting. *Argumentation, 32,* 463-483.

Kock, C. 2009. Choice is not true or false: The domain of rhetorical argumentation. *Argumentation, 23*(1), 61–80.

Leff, M. 2000. Rhetoric and dialectic in the twenty-first century. *Argumentation, 14,* 241-254.

L'Etang, J. L. 2004. The myth of the 'ethical guardian': An examination of its origins, potency and illusions. *Journal of Communication Management, 8*(1), 53-67.

Pielke, R. A. 2007. *The honest broker: Making sense of science in policy and politics.* Cambridge: Cambridge University Press.

Public Relations Society of America. (n.d.). About public relations. Retrieved from https://www.prsa.org/about/all-about-pr

Public Relations Society of America. (n.d.). Communicating public relations' value: Business value and public good are essence of PR today. Retrieved from http://www.prsa.org/Intelligence/BusinessCase/ Communicating_Public_Relations'_Value

Rybacki, K.C. & Rybacki, D.J. 2008. *Advocacy and opposition: An introduction to argumentation* (6th ed.). Boston, MA: Pearson.

Smith, A.N. 1972. The principle of advocacy. *Public Relations Quarterly, 17*(1), 9-11, 23-14.

Tindale, C.W. 2004. *Rhetorical argumentation: Principles of theory and practice.* Thousand Oaks, NJ: Sage Publications. *on Biology, 26*(1), 39–46.

Wilhere, G.F. 2012. Inadvertent advocacy. *Conservation Biology*, 26(1), 39–46.

ABOUT THE AUTHOR: Jean Goodwin is SAS Institute Distinguished Professor of Rhetoric & Technical Communication at North Carolina State University. Her research has contributed to the normative pragmatic approach to argumentation, demonstrating how arguers, even those who deeply disagree, can manage to regulate their own transactions, so that arguments deserve to be, and get, heard. Working within the rhetorical tradition, her case studies have focused on civic controversies, including most recently the roles scientists can play within them.

CHAPTER 6.

JUSTIFICATION IN ETHICS

DEREK ALLEN

ABSTRACT: I begin with the question whether justification in ethics can be of the sort appropriate to knowledge and therefore epistemic. It can only if moral judgments can be true. I present a selection of metaethical views on whether there is truth in ethics and selected views on the nature of ethical justification. Ethical justification can be on-balance justification; I provide an example, using an adaptation of a schema proposed by Hansen for balance-of-considerations arguments. Next, I recommend an approach to the issue of truth in ethics for instructors of informal logic or critical thinking courses to adopt for teaching purposes. I conclude with a suggestion for a non-epistemic account of justification in ethics.

KEYWORDS: epistemic justification, cognitivism, noncognitivism, error theories, expressivism, constructivism, moral realism

INTRODUCTION

A fundamental issue raised by my topic is whether justification in ethics can be epistemic. By epistemic justification I mean what Bonjour (1985) means, namely "the species of justification appropriate to knowledge". He holds that "the goal of our distinctively cognitive endeavours is *truth*" and that "the basic role of justification is that of a *means* to truth" (7). If there can be no ethical truths, then, if there can nevertheless be justification in ethics, its role is not that of a means to truth. Nor is it epistemic justification if this is the species of justification appropriate to knowledge and if knowledge is of truths.

Audi (1988) remarks that "[t]here is ... a widespread inclination to take moral judgments to represent at best cultural assumptions with no claim to genuine truth" (124). One variant of this view "says roughly that [moral] judgments are not literally true at all; rather, they are expressions of moral attitudes – normally, attitudes rooted in the culture of the person judging – not assertions of a proposition... An attitude may be reasonable or unreasonable and may be defended with reference to what *is* true or false; but attitudes themselves are not true or false" (124). In one sense, to defend is to "attempt to justify" (NODE 1999). In this sense to defend an attitude would be to attempt to justify it, but the attempted justification would not have the role of being a means to truth; hence it would not be justification of the sort appropriate to knowledge and would therefore not be epistemic. A related point: if moral judgments are expressions of moral attitudes, not assertions of a proposition, the attitudes they express are non-propositional attitudes, not propositional (or cognitive) attitudes such as beliefs. (For a defense of the view that not all attitudes are propositional, see Grzankowski (2012).)

Some textbooks in informal logic or critical thinking endorse, at least by implication, the view that moral judgments *can* be true or false. For example:

Beardsley (1975) notes that judgments of right and wrong are sometimes construed as simple exclamations rather than as (true-or-false) statements but says that in his book he does not exclude them, or other types of value judgments, from the category of statements (9).

Churchill (1986) says that "[o]nly those sentences that could be either true or false express statements" (10; bold removed).

Later he asserts that "if it were true that moral judgments *never* expressed statements... there would be no role for logic in moral discourse. But insofar as moral judgments are incorporated in moral *reasoning*, they are used to express statements" (528). Accordingly, when moral judgments are used in moral reasoning the sentences which express them could be either true or false.

Vaughn & MacDonald (2013) say that statements or claims are either true or false (9) and that, "[a]s with other sorts of arguments, the basic building blocks of ethical arguments are claims or statements" (468). If so, then the ethical claims or statements that figure in ethical arguments are either true or false.

There are various metaethical theories which endorse the view that moral judgments can be true, and others which deny it. In this essay, I present accounts of metaethical theories of each of these kinds, including two that offer contrasting pictures of the nature of justification in ethics; given space constraints, these accounts will mostly be partial. I make some critical comments along the way, but I don't take a position on whether there are any ethical truths or adopt a particular view of how justification in ethics should be understood. My main purpose, rather, is to provide examples of some metaethical options that are available for consideration by argumentation theorists with an interest in ethical reasoning and ethical argumentation.

I proceed as follows. In section 1, I provide brief accounts of several metaethical theories: cognitivism, noncognitivism, error theories, expressivism, constructivism, and moral realism. Section 2 gives an account of John Mackie's error theory followed by a critique of that theory by Simon Blackburn, followed in turn by a critique of Blackburn's "quasi-realist" expressivism by Derek Parfit and a brief description of a hybrid theory called cognitive expressivism. I then turn to views of the moral realist Russ Shafer-Landau (2003) on moral facts and moral truths, and briefly mention similar views of the moral realist David Brink (1989). In section 3, I present views of Brink and views of Shafer-

Landau on moral justification. Section 4 is on metaethical constructivism. In section 5, I apply an adaptation of a schema proposed by Hans Hansen (2011) for balance-of-considerations (BC) arguments to a BC ethical argument with a view to deciding whether the argument's on-balance premise admits of justification. Section 6 recommends an approach that instructors of informal logic and critical thinking courses might consider taking to the issue of whether moral judgments can be true, and hence to the issue of whether justification in ethics can be a means to truth. Section 7 makes concluding remarks.

1. SOME METAETHICAL THEORIES BRIEFLY DEFINED

Cognitivism holds that

> moral judgments should be construed as assertions about the moral properties of actions… and other objects of moral assessment, that moral predicates purport to refer to properties of such objects, that moral judgments (or the propositions they express) can be true or false, and that cognizers can have the cognitive attitude of belief toward the propositions that moral judgments express. (Brink 1999, 588)

According to *noncognitivism*, moral claims do not purport to report facts in light of which they are true or false, and none are true. (Sayre-McCord 2017, n.p.)

Error theories maintain that moral claims *do* purport to report such facts, but that none are true (*ibid.*).

Expressivism holds that "moral sentences are conventional devices for expressing pro and con [noncognitive] attitudes towards their objects" (van Roojen 2018, n.p.).

Constructivism, on one account, claims that "there are moral facts and truths, but insists that these facts and truths are in some way constituted by or dependent on our moral beliefs, reactions, or attitudes" (Brink 1999, 283).

Moral realism holds that "moral claims… purport to report facts and are true if they get the facts right," and that "at least some moral claims actually are true" and others false. Some accounts of moral realism "see it as involving additional commitments, say to the independence of the moral facts from human thought and practice, or to those facts being objective in some specified way"… "[M]oral realists are united in their cognitivism and in their rejection of error theories" (Sayre-McCord, 2017 n.p.). Brink and Shafer-Landau see moral realism "as involving additional commitments". According to Brink, moral realism claims that "there are moral facts and moral properties whose existence and nature are independent of people's beliefs and attitudes about what is right or wrong" (1999, 588). On Shafer-Landau's interpretation, moral realism holds that moral judgements, "when true, are so independently of what any human being… thinks of them" (2003, 2).

2. TRUTH IN ETHICS?

Mackie's error theory

According to Mackie (1979), "ordinary moral judgments include a claim to objectivity, an assumption that there are objective values… [T]his assumption has been incorporated in the basic, conventional, meanings of moral terms" (35). For this reason, the denial of objective values cannot be put forward as the result of a linguistic or conceptual analysis of what our ordinary moral statements mean. Rather, it will have to be put forward "as an 'error theory', a theory that although most people in making moral judgments implicitly claim, among other things, to be pointing to something objectively prescriptive, these claims are all false" (35).

One argument that has been used to support an error theory is "[t]he argument from relativity" (36). This argument takes as its premise "the well-known variation in moral codes from one society to another and from one period to another, and also the differences in moral beliefs between different groups and classes within a complex community" (36). But such variations don't entail that there are no objective moral values. After all, the mere fact that two societies have different beliefs about whether polygamy, say, is a morally acceptable practice does not mean that there is not an objectively true answer to the question of whether it *is* a morally acceptable practice. So a further point needs to be made, namely that "[d]isagreement about moral codes seems to reflect people's adherence to and participation in different ways of life" (36). Mackie thinks that people who approve of monogamy, for example, do so "because they participate in a monogamous way of life"; it's not the case that "they participate in a monogamous way of life because they approve of monogamy" (36).

There is a further matter to be considered: if "the common-sense belief in the objectivity of moral values... is false," how has it "become established and is so resistant to criticisms"? (42). Mackie's answer includes the following points:

a. "[W]e can understand the supposed objectivity of moral qualities as arising from what we can call the projection or objectification of moral attitudes" (42). In other words, we project moral attitudes onto the world, but then perceive them as objective properties of the world.

b. But in moral contexts there is more than this propensity at work. Moral attitudes themselves are at least partly social in origin: socially established – and socially necessary – patterns of behaviour put pressure on individuals, and each individual tends to internalize these pressures and to join in requiring these patterns of behaviour of himself and of others. The attitudes that are objectified into moral values have indeed an external source, though not the one assigned to them by the belief in their absolute authority (42-3).

Blackburn's quasi-realism

Blackburn (1985) disagrees with Mackie's claim that there is an error in our moral language – the error of assuming that there are objective (moral) values. He thinks that we can "protect the objective appearance of morality" by endorsing what he calls "quasi-realism" (11). He also thinks, however, that "moral values are projections of sentiment" (12). He calls this view "projectivism." What he wants to do, then, is to combine projectivism with quasi-realism.

A projectivist thinks there are no moral values in the world. The world is "value-free" (12). Thus, our moral judgments are not perceptions of external moral values. Rather, they are projections of our feelings. Projectivists hold this view because they think it provides "a better explanation of moral practices" than we can give if we think that moral values exist in the world (12).

Blackburn defines quasi-realism in ethics as "the enterprise of showing how much of the apparently 'realist' appearance of ordinary moral thought is explicable and justifiable on an anti-realist picture" (4). By "the apparently 'realist' appearance of ordinary moral thought", Blackburn means the appearance that ordinary moral judgments "include an assumption that there are objective [moral] values" (1). The "anti-realist picture" Blackburn has in mind is one that he thinks "deserves to be called anti-realist because it avoids the view that when we moralize we respond to, and describe, an independent aspect of reality" (11).

But if quasi-realism avoids this view, why does it deserve to be called quasi-*realism*? What is *realist* about it? Blackburn's answer is that a quasi-realist can hold that what makes a wrong action wrong, or a right action right, is something that *is* independent of our minds (or is mainly independent of our minds). For example, she can say that what makes bear-baiting wrong is "at least mainly the effect on the bear" (6).

Blackburn thinks that projectivism, "properly protected by quasi-realism", can accommodate what he calls "the propositional grammar of ethics" (6) – i.e., the appearance that ethical judgments are either true or false. It can do so because a quasi-realist accepts the idea that if one expresses moral opposition to some practice, "one does not just express a desire that the thing should not happen, but does so while feeling that one's desires on such a matter are *right*" (5). The quasi-realist will see this "as a proper, necessary expression of an attitude to our own attitudes" (5). In other words, the quasi-realist will say that we have two attitudes: a negative attitude to the practice in question and an attitude to this attitude, namely that it is the *right* attitude for us to have to the practice.

Parfit's critique of Blackburn

Parfit (2011) classifies Blackburn as a quasi-realist expressivist, and says that moral expressivists are noncognitivists: they believe that moral claims are not intended to state facts, or that they "should not be *regarded* as intended to be true" (380); rather, moral expressivists think that moral claims express attitudes.

Parfit quotes the following passage from Blackburn: "quasi-realism is trying to earn our right to talk of moral truth, while recognizing fully the subjective sources of our judgments inside our own attitudes, needs, desires, and natures" (390; Parfit does not provide a reference for this quotation). He believes that quasi-realism cannot succeed in this endeavour, because he thinks that quasi-realism cannot be coherently combined with expressivism. He explains the problem as follows:

> Quasi-Realist Expressivists… face a dilemma. To defend their Non-Cognitivist Expressivism, these people must claim that our conative attitudes [i.e., attitudes that provide the motivation for action] cannot be correct or mistaken. To defend their Quasi-Realism, these people must claim that these attitudes *can* be correct or mistaken. These people must therefore claim that these attitudes both cannot be, and can be, correct or mistaken. Since that is impossible, no such view [as quasi-realist expressivism] could be true. (400)

Cognitive Expressivism

This is the seemingly oxymoronic name that Horgan and Timmons (2006) give to a metaethical theory they defend. The theory holds that moral judgments are truth-apt beliefs but that "their overall content is not descriptive content" (257): "there are no in-the-world moral facts that could serve as truth-makers for moral beliefs and assertions" (275). The authors' nondescriptivism about moral judgments and utterances makes their view expressivist (257), but they nevertheless argue that it is possible "to make sense of truth in ethics" (275).

Moral realism, moral facts, and moral truths

My primary focus here will be on views of Shafer-Landau's (2003). Moral realists, he says, "see moral judgments as beliefs, some of which are true, and true in virtue of correctly reporting moral facts" (17). But what are moral facts? On one view, moral facts are "a species of natural scientific facts" (3). Shafer-Landau takes this to be the view of *ethical naturalism*. He favours defining the natural "in terms of the subject matters of various disciplines" (58), and holds that "the essential feature of the natural or social sciences is their exclusion of apriori knowledge of fundamental scientific truths" (61). In contrast, he thinks it is possible to discover fundamental ethical truths in an apriori fashion.

Ethical non-naturalism, as Shafer-Landau understands it, comprises "a metaphysical claim, to the effect that moral properties are *sui generis*, and not identical to any natural properties, and a semantic claim, to the effect that moral terms cannot be given a naturalistic analysis" (66). He believes that some version of ethical non-naturalism is correct, but nevertheless argues that natural facts "exhaustively compose moral ones" (75). This is a picture that "classical naturalists", as well as non-naturalists, can endorse (75). But there is still a difference between non-naturalism as construed by Shafer-Landau and *reductive* naturalism. The difference is that "[n]on-naturalists can, and reductionists can't, allow for the possibility of a moral property's exemplification by means of some natural property other than the one whose instantiation, at a time, has in fact subserved it" (75). For example, non-naturalists can say that a person's generosity might be instantiated at a particular time by giving to certain others who need assistance, but at a different time by giving an expensive gift to a non-needy friend.

Shafer-Landau's favoured version of ethical non-naturalism holds that "a moral fact supervenes on a particular concatenation of descriptive facts just because these facts realize the moral property in question... [T]he admirability of an action or motive may be realized by different sets of descriptive facts, but on any given occasion, the moral features are fixed by the descriptive ones that compose them at that time" (77). However, an explanation is needed of "why moral properties supervene on the particular [descriptive] ones they do" (90). "Why are these [descriptive properties], and no others, invariably linked to the instantiation of a given moral property"? (93). Shafer-Landau acknowledges that this is "a hard question" (93). He believes it can be answered only by engaging in "substantive ethical investigation" (95), where this would involve participating in normative-ethical debates about "the correct standards governing our ascriptions of rightness, goodness, virtue, etc.... If non-naturalists do their job correctly, they will... [show] how our other particular and theoretical commitments mutually support the selection of just these [descriptive] base properties" (95-6). Shafer-Landau admits, however, that "[r]ealists have no explanation of what makes their favoured identities or supervenience relations true" (96). These identities or relations are expressible in fundamental moral rules, and realists will say that "there is no intelligible and plausible answer" to the question "what it is in virtue of which these fundamental moral rules are true" (96-7).

Brink's moral realism endorses a nonreductive form of ethical naturalism which, like Shafer-Landau's ethical non-naturalism, claims that "moral facts are constituted by, and so supervene on, natural facts" (1989, 191), but differs in denying that moral properties are sui generis (156). In Brink's view, "[d]etermination of just which natural facts and properties constitute which moral facts and properties is a matter of substantive moral theory" (177); hence, we may infer, it requires what Shafer-Landau calls "substantive ethical investigation".

Shafer-Landau holds that "[m]oral facts are the things in virtue of which the truth conditions of assertoric moral claims are satisfied" (2003, 15, note 2). Consider Harman's well-known cat example (1977): "you round a corner and see a group of young hoodlums pour gasoline on a cat and ignite it" (4). Assertion: what these hoodlums are doing is wrong. This assertion is true, Shafer-Landau might say, because, as a matter of moral fact, "it really is wrong to set the cat on fire" (Harman 1977, 7). Given his account of the supervenience of moral features on descriptive features, and his view that moral facts are fixed by moral standards/rules (15), Shafer-Landau might also say that this is a moral fact because setting the cat on fire violates a true moral rule to the effect that "it is wrong to cause unnecessary suffering" (Harman 1977, 8). If the objection were made that this "rule" isn't really a rule, the "best defence", in Shafer-Landau's view, would be "to do first-order ethics and to try to show the attractions of the rule vis-à-vis other warranted ethical commitments" (97).

Next, suppose you make the judgment that what the hoodlums are doing is wrong. What explains your doing so? Must it be your awareness of a moral fact, namely the fact (if it is a fact) of its being wrong to set the cat on fire? Harman doesn't think so: "an assumption about moral facts would seem to be totally irrelevant to the explanation of your making the judgment you make. It would seem that all we need assume is that you have certain more or less well articulated moral principles that are reflected in the judgments you make, based on your moral sensibility" (7).

Shafer-Landau asks the following question about moral awareness: "How are we aware of the link – the conditional that says that if these natural properties are realized, then so too are these moral ones?" (62). He calls this "the central moral epistemological problem" and says "it is equally pressing for the non-naturalist, and any naturalist who rejects an analytic equivalence between moral and descriptive terms" (62). A Harman-type rejoinder would be that there isn't a moral epistemological problem here, for there is no such conditional as Shafer-Landau formulates to be aware of; rather, whether there is a link between certain natural properties and certain moral properties is a matter of judgment based on the appraiser's moral sensibilities.

3. MORAL REALISM AND MORAL JUSTIFICATION

Brink on moral foundationalism and moral coherentism

Moral realism has an epistemological component which includes the claim that "there are methods for justifying moral beliefs" (Brink 1999, 588).

On one view, moral realism requires a foundationalist theory of justification. According to Brink (1989) "[m]oral foundationalism... holds that one's moral belief p is justified just in case p is either (a) foundational or (b) based on the appropriate kind of inference from foundational beliefs" (102). Brink notes that "[a]lmost all defenders of moral foundationalism have been intuitionists" (102); the intuitionist version of moral foundationalism says that the beliefs that are foundational for the purpose of moral justification are *moral* beliefs and that these foundational beliefs can be known to be true by intuition (rather than by inference from other beliefs).

Brink thinks that moral foundationalism is a defective theory. In his view, "there can be no genuine foundational beliefs (i.e., beliefs that are noninferentially justified)" (100). A noninferentially justified belief would be a belief that was justified in some way other than by being inferred from other beliefs. Brink thinks that if there were any noninferentially justified beliefs, they would have to be *self-justifying*, but in his view a belief *cannot* be self-justifying: a belief *p* cannot be the reason for thinking that *p* is true. This would be circular (116 ff.).

An alternative to moral foundationalism is moral coherentism. Brink believes that moral coherentism "can be defended and is compatible with [moral] realism" and that it "can be applied to the justification of our moral beliefs" (101). "Moral coherentism or a coherence theory of justification in ethics... holds that one's moral belief *p* is justified insofar as *p* is part of a coherent system of beliefs, both moral and non-moral, and *p*'s coherence at least partially explains why one holds *p*" (103). However, coherentism, like foundationalism, faces a circularity objection because it "allows justificatory chains to loop back upon themselves. One's belief *p* is justified by one's belief *q*, which is justified by one's belief *r*, which is justified ultimately, at least in part, by one's belief *p*" (105). On this model, one's belief *p* is ultimately justified, at least in part, by one's belief *p* – that is, it is ultimately justified, at least in part, by itself, and this means that the model is circular.

In response to this objection, Brink says that "[t]he coherentist needs to distinguish between two different kinds of justification: *systematic* and *contextualist*" (123). Systematic justification is *complete* justification and results from providing justification for all justifying beliefs (that is, for all beliefs which themselves justify beliefs). Contextualist justification, by contrast, is *in*complete justification, as Brink explains in the following passage:

> In the contextualist justification of some belief *p*, certain background beliefs are treated as justified that would actually have to be justified if *p* were being systematically justified. We satisfy ourselves with some degree or other of contextualist justification, both because we believe our background beliefs can be justified, and

because pursuit of systematic justification would prevent us from getting on with our inquiries. (123)

Contextualist justification need not involve justificatory chains that "loop back upon themselves" and therefore need not be circular.

Brink says that "[a] coherence theory of justification in ethics is essentially John Rawls's method of wide reflective equilibrium" (103-04), and he quotes the following description that Rawls gives of this method:

> Here the test [for justification] is that of general and wide reflective equilibrium, that is, how well the view as a whole meshes with and articulates our more firm considered convictions, at all levels of generality, after due examination, once all adjustments and revisions that seem compelling have been made. A doctrine that meets this criterion is the doctrine that, so far as we can now ascertain, is the most reasonable for us. (104; Rawls 1980, 534).

Suppose that prior to reflection we believe that it is morally wrong to break a promise. Upon reflection, however, we decide that there could be cases in which this would *not* be morally wrong. Accordingly, we might revise our belief – for example, by adding an 'other things being equal' qualifier so that the belief became 'other things being equal, it is morally wrong to break a promise'. This would be an example of revising a moral belief "after due examination."

It might be objected, however, that a coherence theory of justification in ethics (i.e., moral coherentism) isn't compatible with moral realism on Brink's objectivist account of it because, so understood, moral realism is "roughly the view that there are moral facts and true moral claims whose existence and nature are independent of our beliefs about what is right and wrong" (7), whereas for moral coherentism "the credibility of considered moral beliefs is… established by coherence with other beliefs, including other moral beliefs" (139). Consequently, "moral coherentism must fail to provide evidence of objective moral truth" (139). Coherence could provide evidence of moral truth "only if the truth of a moral belief consists in its coherence with other beliefs" (139). Hence, the objection continues, "[m]oral coherentism requires rejection of moral realism [on Brink's account of it] and acceptance of... 'constructivism in ethics'" (139), which holds that moral truths "are constituted by the evidence for them" (20). In reply, Brink says that "[c]oherence provides evidence of objective moral truth, and so is compatible with moral realism, as long as there are realist second-order beliefs about morality, which themselves form part of a coherent system of beliefs, with which our moral beliefs may cohere" (141). Furthermore, Brink claims, "there are good grounds for holding realist second-order beliefs about morality" (141). He grants that these beliefs might be mistaken but says that this possibility "threatens our claims to knowledge, not our claims to justification" (141).

Shafer-Landau on the justification of moral principles

Shafer-Landau believes that some moral propositions are self-evident. In his view, "[a] proposition p is self-evident = df. p is such that adequately understanding and attentively considering just p is sufficient to justify believing that p" (2003, 247). This is not to say that a self-evident proposition provides evidence for itself; Shafer-Landau isn't sure that this makes sense (255). Nor does he think that it is possible to prove that there are any self-evident moral propositions. All one can do is offer appealing candidates (if there are any) and reply to criticisms of the idea (247). For example, it seems to him that the following moral principle is self-evident: "other things equal, it is wrong to take pleasure in another's pain" (248). He allows, however, that self-evident propositions might be inferable from other propositions (e.g., from a more general moral principle) and hence be both "inferentially and non-inferentially justifiable" (248).

He considers several objections to self-evidence (250-65), of which I will note two. First, "if one is unable to articulate the grounds that support the content of one's belief, then one cannot be justified in believing it" (251). Shafer-Landau replies that the claim that there are self-evident beliefs cannot be undermined "just by arguing that premises must be invoked in order to *show that* one's belief is justified" (251). The objection fails to distinguish between *agent justification* and *demonstrative justification*. The former concerns whether a given believer is justified in holding a given belief, while the latter concerns whether the believer can show that the belief is plausible – for example, by persuading another person of its truth or justification (252). To condition agent justification on demonstrative justification "isn't plausible for the non-moral case, and, absent a compelling argument, it isn't plausible for the moral case, either" (252). Shafer-Landau distinguishes demonstrative justification from epistemic justification, which he takes to refer to "the conditions under which one's beliefs enjoy positive epistemic status" (96, note 8). There is an alternative view, however, which allows for the possibility of interpersonal justification whereby, under certain conditions, a speaker transmits epistemic justification to a hearer (Goldman, 1995).

A second objection claims that propositions may be self-evident for some agents but not for all (257). For example, the proposition that, other things equal, it is wrong to take pleasure in another's pain won't be self-evident for sadists, but it may be self-evident for some others. "By relativizing the property of self-evidence, we allow that a person's background beliefs or moral outlook may undermine justification of a proposition which, for others with different sensibilities, may be perfectly self-evident" (257). Shafer-Landau replies that "the only relevant basis for taking such a stand is the recognition that one's *other* beliefs bear directly on a determination of whether a belief qualifies as self-evident" (257). However, "[t]his is incompatible with the core idea of self-evidence, which makes relevantly full understanding of a proposition by itself sufficient to justify belief in it" (257).

But consider the proposition (call it q) that, other things equal, it is wrong to take pleasure in another's pain. An agent may have a relevantly full understanding of this proposition yet fail to recognize its truth (if it is true). Shafer-Landau would say that an agent's "blindness" to its truth would ordinarily be explained by reference to her "ancillary attitudes" (262); this would be "a plausible explanation of an agent's failing to see what strikes the rest of us, upon reflection, as clearly true" (263). An ancillary-attitudes explanation would presumably apply in the case of a sadist who sees nothing wrong with taking pleasure in another's pain, and therefore fails to recognize that q is true (if it is true). Ex hypothesi, this sadist has a relevantly full understanding of q, as do the rest of us, who, again ex hypothesi, see that q is clearly true. But then having a relevantly full understanding of q isn't sufficient for recognizing its truth; a fortiori, nor is it sufficient for recognizing that q is self-evidently true (if it is). Those agents who recognize q's self-evident truth differ from sadists who don't in their moral "sensibilities" or "moral outlook" (257). But this suggests that recognizing the truth of q, unlike recognizing the truth of an allegedly analytic proposition such as "all bachelors are unmarried men" (262), requires having some specifiable kind of attitude; in the case of q, it requires having a negative attitude toward the taking of pleasure in another's pain when other things are equal – an attitude expressible by saying that doing so is wrong. If so, then q could be said to be self-evidently true for those who fully understand it *and* have an attitude of the indicated kind, but not to be self-evidently true for those who fully understand it but don't have such an attitude.

According to Shafer-Landau, "self-evident propositions are precisely those that yield justification when adequately understood and believed" (279). But might it be the case that having an *adequate understanding* of a moral proposition *itself* requires having certain sensibilities, hence certain attitudes? Shafer-Landau doesn't rule out this possibility. He acknowledges that "it remains an open question as to whether or how far one can be epistemically justified in [believing a moral proposition] without correlative affective inputs (or outputs)" (279-80, note 12).

Shafer-Landau on the justification of verdictive moral beliefs

Verdictive moral beliefs, as understood by Shafer-Landau, "represent all-things-considered moral assessments of actions or agents in particular circumstances" (267). For example, a belief that, all things considered, it was wrong of Trump to break his promise to Trudeau in the circumstances concerned would be a verdictive moral belief.

In Shafer-Landau's view, verdictive moral beliefs cannot be self-evident (267, 272), nor are they inferentially justified (272). The latter claim obliges him to reject what he calls "the *standard model of ethical theory*" (268) according to which truths about the moral status of act types (e.g., promise-breaking) and act tokens (e.g., the breaking of a particular promise) are derivable from an ultimate and absolute ethical first principle. An alternative to the standard model is the particularist model. Particularists deny that there are any absolute moral principles "because they deny that any consideration is invariably and uniformly morally relevant" (269). Rather, they believe that "the salience of any given feature is dependent on context" (269). This belief also leads them to reject a second alternative to the standard model, namely the pro tanto model. An example of a pro tanto moral principle would be "whenever... one acts beneficently, then the act is *to that extent* good or admirable" (269; italics added).

Shafer-Landau is not a particularist. He thinks that there are pro tanto moral principles, but he also thinks that it needs to be explained how we can get from such principles to verdictive moral beliefs. His explanation is that "such beliefs can be epistemically warranted, provided they emerge from a reliable belief-forming process" (272). There are such processes only if there is truth in ethics (293), for "[t]o judge a process reliable is to judge that it usually yields truth" (294). However, "to make that sort of judgment, one must first have some idea of what truths there are" (294), and how can we do this without first identifying the reliable processes? A point Shafer-Landau makes in response to this difficulty is that "we don't need to *identify* the reliable processes before solving normative problems. We just need to *employ* such processes" (294). He acknowledges that "reliabilism does not guarantee that the justificatory status of a belief is accessible to the believer" but adds that "neither can its coherentist or foundationalist competitors" (295). There are other objections. One asserts that "there is no unique process that caused a given belief" (281); a second asserts that even if there is, we can't know what it is (281). In response to the second objection, Shafer-Landau says that what follows is "only" that reliabilists won't be able to defend their epistemic assessments of particular beliefs. This is a failure in demonstrative justification, but it doesn't entail a lack of *agent* justification. "It may be that our evaluative epistemic judgements are sometimes reliably formed, even if... the agent making the evaluation is unable to offer a principled basis for identifying just one candidate as the sole process responsible for generating the belief that is being evaluated" (283).

Shafer-Landau believes, however, that "there is a plausible general starting point for the identification of reliable moral processes" and that it "lies in attention to the sensitivities of moral and immoral exemplars"; the Dalai Lama is an instance of the former, Goebbels of the latter (296). But Shafer-Landau sees a problem with this procedure: "we can know which processes are reliable if we know who is and who isn't a moral exemplar. We can know whether a person is an exemplar only if we know whether her judgements are reliable. But if we knew that, then reference to the exemplars would be otiose" (297).

In response to this problem, Shafer-Landau says that "identifying moral exemplars is not claimed to be a necessary condition of identifying reliable processes" but is "one suggested way" of doing so (297). If there are no other ways, "[i]t may still be true that verdictive beliefs are defeasibly justified if and only if they emerge from a (virtuous and) reliable belief-forming process. It's just that we would be ignorant of which processes qualified" (298). But Shafer-Landau has told us that "we can know which processes are reliable if we know who is and who isn't a moral exemplar" (297). Suppose we do know this: "we identify such individuals because their behaviour comports with our settled judgements about right and wrong, good and evil" (299). Is identifying certain individuals as moral exemplars sufficient for ascertaining which processes are reliable? Surely not. We may not be able to determine what processes these people follow (or followed) in arriving at their moral judgments, nor may these people themselves. As Shafer-Landau puts it, "[g]ood people may get the right answers without identifying the processes that got them there" (294).

He thinks that "a fully worked-out version of moral reliabilism" requires, among other things, giving a "nuanced account of the processes that are genuinely reliable" and defending a specific conception of reliability. In addition, "the role of exemplars in the reliabilist theory must be elaborated or, if found unhelpful after elaboration, discarded. (The reliabilist criterion of justified verdictive belief may be true even if reliance on exemplars is not a good way to satisfy it)" (301).

4. METAETHICAL CONSTRUCTIVISM

According to Bagnoli (2017), "[m]etaethical constructivism is the view that insofar as there are normative truths, they are not fixed by normative facts that are independent of what rational agents would agree to under some specified conditions of choice" (n.p.). There are different versions of this theory, one of which (a "society-based" version) "explains the nature of moral truth in procedural terms, and thus it implies that there are no moral facts independently of the procedure". A conventionalist version holds that "moral truths are constructed by the actual agreement of some groups within specific traditions" (n.p.).

Brink takes constructivists in ethics to be opponents of moral realism (1989, 18); however, as Bagnoli (2017) notes, there are some constructivists who regard their versions of constructivism as realist theories. In Brink's view, constructivists agree with realists in holding that there are moral facts or truths but differ from realists in holding that these facts or truths are constituted by the evidence for them (20). He further claims that constructivism identifies truth and justified belief and argues that "this is the chief objection to any form of constructivism" because "[t]ruth and justification appear to be distinct properties of beliefs" (31). Shafer-Landau agrees that it is implausible to claim that "a moral judgment is true just in case, and because, the best evidence says it is," but adds that there are constructivists such as Rawls (1980) and Scanlon (1998) who "would reject the claim that moral truth is constituted by the best evidence for it, and so would reject the equivalence or identity between justification and truth that Brink attributes to constructivism" (2003, 14, note 1).

On Shafer-Landau's account, "[w]hat is common to all constructivists is the idea that moral reality is constituted by the attitudes, actions, responses, or outlooks of persons, possibly under idealized conditions" (14). He distinguishes between subjectivist and objectivist constructivisms. Subjectivist constructivisms take at least some of the "actual and uncorrected attitudes of duly selected agents as determinative of moral truths". On these views, "moral rightness is constructed from the actual agreements individuals make with one another", whereas objectivist views "require some degree of idealization for the attitudes and responses that go towards fixing truth" (39). Objectivists will require certain "corrective measures that must be met before attitudes yield moral truth"; for example, "possession of full information, vividly presented" and "freedom from errors of instrumental reasoning" (41). But there is a problem for objectivists:

> Either the initial conditions of… attitude formation are moralized or they are not. In other words, we are to envision the initial conditions as already incorporating moral constraints, or as operating free of such constraints. [In the latter case,] there is no reason to expect that the principles that emerge from such a construction process will capture our deepest ethical convictions… Alternatively, if constructivists import moral constraints… they effectively abandon constructivism, because this path acknowledges the existence of moral constraints that are conceptually and explanatorily prior to the edicts of the agents doing the construction…, and so there would be moral facts or reasons that obtain independently of constructive functions. This is realism, not constructivism. (42)

5. ON-BALANCE JUSTIFICATION

Shafer-Landau speaks of "a belief's on-balance justification" (2003, 302). A justification of this sort would present one or more reasons in support of the belief, and one or more counter-considerations – considerations that count, or are thought to count, against the belief, and so it would be a balance-of-considerations argument.

Hansen (2011) is an erudite essay on balance-of-considerations arguments. He explains that one way in which BC-arguments differ from "the general conception of argument… has to do with the role of counter-considerations. It is unclear how they can be parts of arguments" (35). One possibility is that "[c]ounter-considerations are claimed to be outweighed in an on-balance premise" (38; italics removed). BC-reasoning might then be described in general terms as follows:

> We are led to a conclusion by considering each of the independent supporting reasons and their amassed force, and by the judgment

that taken together those reasons outweigh the counter-considerations taken together... The general schema for BC-arguments would then look something like this (with 'CC' abbreviating 'counter-consideration'):

P_1:   Independent reason$_1$ (for conclusion K)
                  ....
P_n: Independent reason$_n$ (for conclusion K)
P_{n+1}:   The reasons in P_1 to P_n taken together
                  outweigh the independent counter-
                  considerations to K, CC_1 to CC_n taken
                  together (value judgment)
Conclusion: *K even though CC_1 & ... & CC_n*
                  (inference to 'even though')
Premise: *K even though CC_1 & ... & CC_n*
Conclusion: K (simplification) (38-9)

In a subsequent table, Hansen compares the role of 'even' (**"even a has P"**) and 'even though' (**"p even though q"**) and describes the "[j]ustification" role of 'even though' thus: "by using '*p* even though *q*' in a context in which there is doubt about *p*, the speaker implies that s/he has a good reason for *p*" (47). But we may wonder whether the speaker also has a good reason for the "*outweigh*" value judgment represented in the above schema by P_{n+1}. Hansen argues, contra Possin (2010), that "the inclusion of the on-balance premise as part of the structure of BC-arguments does not open the gate to an infinite series of more on-balance premises" (42). Even if this is so, we may ask whether the "*outweigh*"/"*outweighs*" value judgment in a BC-argument standardized in accordance with Hansen's schema admits, or may admit, of justification.

The relevant case for our purposes is that of *ethical* BC-arguments, and here I will consider a thought-experiment in Kagan (1998, 71).

[T]here are five patients, each of whom will soon die unless they receive an appropriate transplanted organ... Unfortunately, due to tissue incompatibilities, none of the five can act as donor for the others. But here is Chuck [an innocent person], who is in hospital for some fairly routine tests… [and] his tissue is completely compatible with [that of] the five patients. You are a surgeon, and it now occurs to you that you could chop up Chuck and use his organs to save the five others [all of whom are also innocent]. What should you do?

The structure of the following BC-argument is an adaptation of Hansen's schema.

Argument 1

Premise 1:	Chuck is an innocent person.
CC:	If you chop up Chuck this will enable five other innocent persons to be saved.
Premise 2:	The fact that Chuck is an innocent person outweighs the fact that if you chop him up this will enable five other innocent persons to be saved.
Thus,	
Conclusion:	It would be morally wrong for you to chop up Chuck even though if you chop him up this will enable five other innocent persons to be saved.
Thus,	
Conclusion:	It would be morally wrong for you to chop up Chuck.
Thus,	
Conclusion:	You should not chop up Chuck.

Premise 2 is an on-balance premise by Hansen's criterion, for it claims that the indicated counter-consideration is outweighed (by premise 1). Our question is whether it admits of justification. Kagan remarks: "Intuitively, at least, most of us have little doubt that it is morally forbidden to chop up an innocent person, even if this is the only way to save five other innocent people from death" (71). Those who think that there are moral truths, as Kagan does, might, depending on their moral sensibilities, take premise 2 to be self-evidently true. However, it may nevertheless not only admit of justification but require justification. After all, "[f]rom the utilitarian standpoint the results certainly seem to be better if you chop up Chuck... Obviously, it is a horrible result that Chuck will end up dead; but it would be an even worse result if *five* people end up dead. So the right thing to do – according to utilitarianism – is to kill Chuck" (71). Not so fast, say deontologists, understood per Kagan as "those who believe in additional normative factors that generate constraints" (73) – that is, factors that generate constraints on bringing about the best results. If performing a certain type of act (in this case, doing harm) "is necessary to bring about the best results overall" (72) then it is forbidden to perform acts of that type, according to a deontology that "recognizes a *constraint* against doing harm" (72). Premise 2 admits of a deontological justification along these lines, given that to chop up Chuck would be to harm him. For example:

Argument 2

(1) It is morally wrong to harm an innocent person, even if doing so would produce the best results.
(2) Chopping up Chuck would produce the best results by enabling five innocent persons to be saved, but would harm an innocent person (Chuck).

Thus,

(3) It would be morally wrong for you to chop up Chuck even though this would enable five innocent persons to be saved.

Thus,

(4) The fact that Chuck is an innocent person [per (2)] outweighs the fact that if you chop him up this will enable five other innocent persons to be saved. (Premise 2 in Argument 1)

6. PEDAGOGY

Whether moral judgments can be true is a contested issue in metaethics, and this fact presents a problem for instructors of informal logic or critical thinking courses when it comes to the analysis and evaluation of ethical arguments. One option would be to assign students background reading that treats the relevant issues at an introductory level. Another would be to devote a class to a synopsis of relevant metaethical standpoints and arguments, again at an introductory level. But these options, useful though they might be, would still leave the instructor with the question of what stance to adopt on the issue of truth in ethics for teaching purposes, in particular for the purpose of interpreting and appraising ethical reasoning. My recommendation would be to adopt Brink's approach and treat moral realism as a tacit presupposition of "commonsense moral thinking", a viewpoint to be abandoned only if shown to be untenable by antirealist argumentation.

Brink says: "We begin as (tacit)… realists about ethics" and are "*led to* some form of antirealism (if we are) only because we come to regard the moral realist's commitments as untenable, say, because of the apparently occult nature of moral facts or because of the apparent lack of a well developed and respectable methodology in ethics" (1989, 23). For this reason, "[m]oral realism should be our metaethical starting point, and we should give it up only if it does involve unacceptable metaphysical and epistemological commitments" (24).

Brink thinks that moral realism and other cognitivist theories derive support from "the form and content of our moral judgments" (25):

a. "[M]oral discourse is typically declarative or assertive in form." For example: "'The government's tax plan is unfair'" (25).

b. Moral judgments often make reference to moral facts or moral knowledge; for example, "one should not be held responsible for actions one could not have *known were wrong*" (25).

c. "If we reject moral realism (or any other antinoncognitivist and antirelativist metaethical view), it seems we must regard the form of our moral judgments as misleading and inappropriate" and we must treat sentences that seem to be assertions of moral fact, such as 'lying is wrong,' as "disguised expressions of the appraiser's disapproval of [lying] or as disguised prescriptions to avoid [lying]" (26).

"Commonsense moral thinking also supports moral realism insofar as we act as if there are moral facts" (29; cf. Nosich 1982, 236). For example: (a) "We often *recognize* the existence of moral requirements that constrain our conduct in certain ways." (b) "[W]e often *deliberate* as if there were a right answer to the issue before us" (29) – for example, the issue of whether animals have rights.

"Moral argument and deliberation presuppose not only correct answers to moral questions but also answers whose correctness is independent of our moral beliefs. In moral deliberation and argument we try and hope to *arrive* at the correct answer, that is, at the answer that is correct prior to, and independently of, our coming upon it" (31). Brink adds that "the burden of proof is on the antirealist to explain why the apparent realist presuppositions of commonsense morality are mistaken" (36; cf. Sayre-McCord 2017, final two sentences).

This approach makes a prima facie case for moral realism while signalling that our (alleged) initial tacit endorsement of realism should be considered provisional given the possibility of successful antirealist criticism. For this reason, I think it is an attractive pedagogical approach for informal logic/critical thinking courses, at least at the introductory level.

7. CONCLUDING REMARKS

Moral-realist theories and constructivist theories, unlike noncognitivist and error theories, hold that moral judgments can be true. Consequently, they can treat justification in ethics as a means to truth and hence as epistemic. However, a moral skeptic might argue that the realist theories of Brink and Shafer-Landau fail to make a convincing case for the existence of objective (mind-independent) moral facts. To judge, perhaps with the aid of ethical theories or ethical investigation, that certain natural facts jointly constitute some moral fact is simply to project an attitude of approval or disapproval toward those natural facts; at any rate, a skeptic might claim, the realist theories of Brink and Shafer-Landau do not prove otherwise.

I noted Audi's point that although (non-propositional) attitudes are not true or false they may be defended with reference to what *is* true or false, and I said that in one sense to defend an attitude would be to attempt to justify it. A person who disapproves of bear-baiting (to take Blackburn's example) might attempt to justify this attitude with reference to the fact that bear-baiting causes the bear to suffer; she might think that the effect of bear-baiting on the bear gives her a reason to disapprove of bear-baiting and that she is therefore *justified* in disapproving of it. This example suggests the possibility of a noncognitivist attitudinal account of non-epistemic justification in ethics. At the core of such an account would be the idea of there being agent-relative reasons for non-propositional attitudes expressible in sentences with moral predicates, as in "bear-baiting is wrong".

REFERENCES

Audi, Robert. 1988. *Belief, Justification, and Knowledge: An Introduction to Epistemology.* Belmont, California: Wadsworth Publishing Company.

Bagnoli, Carla. 2017. Constructivism in Metaethics. *The Stanford Encyclopedia of Philosophy* (Winter 2017 Edition), Edward N. Zalta (ed.), URL = https://plato.stanford.edu/archives/win2017/entries/constructivism-metaethics/

Beardsley, Monroe C. 1975. *Thinking Straight: Principles of Reasoning for Readers and Writers*. Englewood Cliffs, New Jersey: Prentice-Hall, Inc.

Blackburn, Simon. 1985. Errors and the Phenomenology of Value. In Ted Honderich (ed.) *Morality and Objectivity: A Tribute to J. L. Mackie,* 1-22. London: Routledge & Kegan Paul.

Bonjour, Laurence. 1985. *The Structure of Empirical Knowledge*. Cambridge, Mass. and London, England: Harvard University Press.

Brink, David. 1989. *Moral Realism and The Foundations of Ethics*. Cambridge: Cambridge University Press.

Brink, David, 1999. Moral Realism. In Robert Audi (ed.) *The Cambridge Dictionary of Philosophy*. Cambridge: Cambridge University Press.

Churchill, Robert Paul. 1986. *Becoming Logical: An Introduction to Logic*. New York: St. Martin's Press, Inc.

Goldman, Alvin I. 1995. Argumentation and interpersonal justification. In Frans H. van Eemeren, Rob Grootendorst, Charles A. Willard (eds.), *Proceedings of the third conference of the International Society for the Study of Argumentation,* Vol. 1, 53-61. Amsterdam: SicSat.

Grzankowski, Alex. 2012. Not All Attitudes Are Propositional. *European Journal of Philosophy*: 1-18. Wiley Online Library: doi/10.1111/j.1468-0378.2012.00534.x.

Hansen, Hans. 2011. Notes on Balance-of-Considerations Arguments. In J. Anthony Blair & Ralph Johnson (eds.), *Conductive Argument: An Overlooked Type of Defeasible Reasoning,* 31-51. Milton Keynes, UK: College Publications.

Harman, Gilbert. 1977. *The Nature of Morality: An Introduction to Ethics*. New York: Oxford University Press.

Horgan, Terry, and Mark Timmons. 2006. Cognitive Expressivism. In Terry Horgan & Mark Timmons (Eds.), *Metaethics after Moore*. Oxford: Clarendon Press.

Kagan, Shelly. 1998. *Normative Ethics*. Boulder, Colo.: Westview Press.

Mackie, John L. 1979. *Ethics: Inventing Right and Wrong*. Harmondsworth; New York: Penguin.

NODE. 1999. *The New Oxford Dictionary of English*. Oxford: Oxford University Press.

Nosich, Gerald M. 1982. *Reasons and Arguments*. Belmont, California: Wadsworth Publishing Company.

Parfit, Derek. 2011. *On What Matters*, Volume Two. Oxford: Oxford University Press.

Possin, Kevin. 2010. What the Tortoise Said to Hans. Session of the Association for Informal Logic and Critical Thinking, Central Division of the American Philosophical Association Meetings, Chicago, February.

Rawls, John. 1980. Kantian Constructivism in Moral Theory. *Journal of Philosophy* 77: 515-72.

Sayre-McCord, Geoff. 2017. Moral Realism. *The Stanford Encyclopedia of Philosophy* (Fall 2017 Edition), Edward N. Zalta (ed.), URL = https://plato.stanford.edu/archives/fall2017/entries/moral-realism/

Scanlon, Thomas, 1998. *What We Owe to Each Other*. Cambridge, Mass.: Harvard University Press.

Shafer-Landau, Russ. 2003. *Moral Realism: A Defence*. Oxford: Clarendon Press.

van Roojen, Mark. 2018. Moral Cognitivism vs. Non-Cognitivism. *The Stanford Encyclopedia of Philosophy* (Fall 2018 Edition). Edward N. Zalta (ed.), URL = https://plato.stanford.edu/archives/fall2018/entries/moral-cognitivism/

Vaughn, Lewis, and Chris MacDonald. 2013. *The Power of Critical Thinking*. Don Mills, Ontario: Oxford University Press Canada.

ABOUT THE AUTHOR: Derek Allen is Professor Emeritus of Philosophy at the University of Toronto and an Honorary Fellow of Trinity College, University of Toronto. He has written a number of conference papers and commentaries in argumentation studies and has published journal and anthology articles in informal logic. He and three co-authors (Sharon Bailin, Mark Battersby, James Freeman) have written an invited article on critical thinking for a forthcoming Oxford University Press research encyclopedia. He is a member of the editorial board of the journal *Informal Logic* and a past-president of the Association for Informal Logic and Critical Thinking (AILACT).

derekallen@trinity.utoronto.ca

CHAPTER 7.

JUST FOLLOWING THE RULES: COLLAPSE/ INCOHERENCE PROBLEMS IN ETHICS, EPISTEMOLOGY, AND ARGUMENTATION THEORY

PATRICK BONDY

ABSTRACT: This essay addresses the collapse/incoherence problem for normative frameworks that contain both fundamental values and rules for promoting those values. The problem is that in some cases, we would bring about more of the fundamental value by violating the framework's rules than by following them. In such cases, if the framework requires us to follow the rules anyway, then it appears to be incoherent; but if it allows us to make exceptions to the rules, then the framework "collapses" into one that doesn't make use of rules in the first place. The chapter begins with an examination of happiness and truth as fundamental values in Mill's work, which lead into parallel versions of the collapse/ incoherence problem in ethics and epistemology. It then sets out the collapse problem for rule-consequentialist approaches in ethics, truth-directed accounts of justification in epistemology, and epistemological approaches to argument cogency. The chapter closes with discussion of two potential solutions to the problem.

KEYWORDS: consequentialism; utilitarianism; rule-consequentialism; collapse problem; epistemic justification; argumentation; Mill; Hooker; cogency

1. INTRODUCTION

This essay addresses a difficult problem that arises when we are working with normative frameworks containing fundamental values or goals, and rules or criteria aimed at promoting those values. The problem is that rules that appear to embody entirely sensible recommendations for the purpose of promoting the achievement of the fundamental value in a domain can in some cases inhibit the achievement of that very value. For example: we post speed limits in order to promote human well-being, by minimizing the risk of accidents – but, in exceptional cases, driving the posted speed limit can be detrimental to a person's well-being. (Imagine keeping within the posted speed limit, while driving a seriously injured person to hospital, and every second counts. That seems like a poor way to promote your passenger's well-being!) Although following the rule of driving no more than the posted speed limit generally promotes people's well-being, in some cases following that rule would have the opposite effect.

Cases like these pose both practical and theoretical problems. From a practical perspective, it's not always clear how to proceed when faced with them. Should we follow the rule because it's the rule, or should we violate the rule in order to produce better consequences in the case at hand? From a theoretical perspective, cases like these put pressure on the idea that the fundamental values ostensibly justifying the rules in question really do justify those rules.

This problem threatens rule-based consequentialist accounts in ethics and in other domains. Perhaps the most familiar version of this problem is the "collapse/incoherence" problem for rule consequentialism in ethics, but the problem arises in other domains too, such as epistemology and argumentation theory. This essay addresses the problem as it arises in these three domains.

Collapse and incoherence are of course not the same thing. But the collapse/incoherence problem is really just one problem: it is the problem that either a rule-based consequentialist theory "collapses" into a type of theory that the rule-based theory was constructed to avoid, or else the theory ends up being incoherent. The collapse/incoherence problem will become clearer as we go.

It is worth noting that the "paradox of deontology" poses a similar problem for deontologists: if there is a deontological prohibition on acts of a certain type, then it seems like we should minimize acts of that type, and so it should be permissible to commit one act of the forbidden type if it will prevent many other occurrences of acts of that type. Deontological theories, however, do not permit such "preventive rule-violations." (See Foot (1985) and Scheffler (1985) for useful discussion.) But the problem for the justification of rules that produce sub-optimal outcomes in specific cases is even starker in a consequentialist framework than in a deontological one. For consequentialists are committed to viewing moral statuses as depending on consequences, and it seems like they *should* want to minimize bad consequences. Deontological theories do not in principle contain a commitment to minimizing bad outcomes, or minimizing tokens of forbidden act-types.

The chapter begins in section 2 with a brief examination of the role of the fundamental values of truth and happiness in Mill's ethical and epistemological views. As we'll see, Mill lays the groundwork for a kind of consequentialist approach in these domains that appears to open the door to collapse problems. Section 3 then sets out the act/rule utilitarianism distinction in ethics, and the collapse/incoherence problem for rule utilitarianism. Section 4 explains the analogous problem in epistemology, as Maitzen (1995) employs it against consequentialist accounts of epistemic justification. Section 5 discusses the problem in the context of argumentation theory, showing that if there is a collapse/incoherence problem for accounts of epistemic justification, then that problem will carry over to epistemic accounts of argument cogency. Fortunately, however, epistemologists and epistemologically-minded argumentation theorists need not worry, because the collapse/incoherence problem for accounts of epistemic justification can be handled. Section 6 explains Hooker's (2000; 2007; 2016) defense of rule-consequentialism in ethics, and explains how his solution to the collapse problem might be applied in the context of epistemic justification. It also presents a different solution to the problem, which is perhaps preferable to Hooker's approach, at least in the context of accounts of epistemic justification.

2. MILL'S FUNDAMENTAL VALUES: TRUTH AND HAPPINESS

Mill's ethical and political work is a useful and familiar place to look for a developed, unified normative framework containing explicit fundamental values, rules for promoting those values, and applications of those values. Mill provides a subtle articulation of happiness as the central ethical value, makes use of that value in addressing specific social issues, and suggests that there are various rules we should follow in order to promote people's general happiness. Regarding the fundamental ethical value, he writes:

> The creed which accepts as the foundation of morals, Utility, or the Greatest Happiness Principle, holds that actions are right in proportion as they tend to promote happiness, wrong as they tend to produce the reverse of happiness. By happiness is intended pleasure, and the absence of pain; by unhappiness, pain, and the privation of pleasure. ... pleasure, and freedom from pain, are the only things desirable as ends... (1861, p. 210)

And on the subject of rules, Mill writes:

> To inform a traveller respecting the place of his ultimate destination, is not to forbid the use of landmarks and direction-posts on the way... (1861, p. 224)

> Whatever we adopt as the fundamental principle of morality, we require subordinate principles to apply it by... (1861, p. 225)

The idea is that bringing about overall happiness is the ultimate goal, but we need to take intermediate steps in working toward that goal, applying general moral rules derived from our experience of their effects on people's happiness. These are the rules of common morality (don't lie, don't cheat, and so on), which Mill thinks can be and ought to be refined, but which are nevertheless good general ethical guides.

In light of passages like the ones cited above, Urmson (1953) urged that Mill should be read as a rule-utilitarian. However, Mill is arguably an act-utilitarian; he just thinks that following the common rules of morality is the best way to promote general happiness in most cases – as long as we don't have information indicating that following the common moral rules will bring about less happiness in the case at hand than violating them would do. (See Brown (1974) and Cupples (1972) on the interpretation of Mill as an act-utilitarian.)

Interestingly, however, happiness is arguably not the only fundamental value Mill acknowledges. For truth plays a similarly fundamental role in Mill's treatment of ethical and political problems. In *On Liberty*, for example, he writes that

> Complete liberty of contradicting and disproving our opinion, is the very condition which justifies us in assuming its truth for purposes of action; and on no other terms can a being with human faculties have any rational assurance of being right. (1859, p. 231)

Mill's point here is that we can only be confident enough in the truth of a proposition for us to be justified in acting on it, if we allow and seek out objections and dissenting opinions. Justified action depends on justified confidence in the truth of the beliefs that prompt action.

So it seems that there are two fundamental normative principles in Mill's work. There is the utilitarian principle, which is a principle about what makes actions right or wrong. And then there is a principle of truth-seeking, which involves a commitment to encouraging free speech and to actively seeking objections to our views. The latter principle tells us what we ought to believe and what beliefs we are justified in acting on.

These principles are meant to go together, of course. If the principles were to come apart – if false beliefs can sometimes bring about greater happiness for the greater number than corresponding true beliefs would – then it's not clear whether the utilitarian or the truth-seeking principle would take precedence. But, as Hansen notes (2014, p. 207), Mill is not worried about that, because he sees these two principles as linked. For one thing, in *Utilitarianism*, Mill provides a lengthy, dialectically engaged argument in defense of the truth of the utilitarian principle. Mill argues at length that the Utilitarian principle is true, and therefore to be believed. And, in arguing for its truth, he displays his view of justified belief as depending on the satisfaction of very stringent dialectical obligations, in the service of arriving at the truth.[1]

For another thing, Mill writes in *On Liberty*:

> The truth of an opinion is part of its utility. If we would know whether or not it is desirable that a proposition should be believed, is it possible to exclude the consideration of whether or not it is true? In the opinion, not of bad men, but of the best men, no belief which is contrary to truth can be really useful: and can you prevent such men from urging that plea, when they are charged with culpability for denying some doctrine which they are told is useful, but which they believe to be false? (1859, pp. 233-4)

In other words, the best people reject popular opinions if they take the opinions to be false; and when they are told that we *must* believe a particular proposition because it is harmful for anyone

---

1. See Hansen (2006; 2014) for extended discussion and reconstruction of Mill's (partly implicit, partly explicit) dialectical and epistemic theory of argument.

not to believe it, the best people reply that the opinion is *not* useful precisely when, and precisely *because*, it is false.

The passage continues:

> Those who are on the side of received opinions, never fail to take all possible advantage of this plea; you do not find *them* handling the question of utility as if it could be completely abstracted from that of truth: on the contrary, it is, above all, because their doctrine is "the truth," that the knowledge or the belief of it is held to be so indispensable. (1859, p. 234, italics in original)

The claim here is that even people who hold that it is *harmful* to lack certain beliefs (and who therefore advocate the suppression of contrary opinions) only hold that it is harmful to lack these beliefs *because* they think that these are *true* beliefs about important matters. So, Mill thinks, everyone already acknowledges that truth is essential to the utility of belief.

Still, one wonders what Mill would recommend in cases where truth and utility come apart, if it turns out that such cases are possible. Indeed, many recent epistemologists have thought that there are clear cases where true belief is unimportant, or is no better than false belief, or is even positively bad to have. Of course, some epistemologists think that true beliefs are always good to have at least to some extent (see Foley 1993, chapter 1, and Lynch 2004, for example). But even if it's *usually* the case that true beliefs are to some extent useful, there do appear to be at least some cases where it's better to have a false belief. For example, Heil (1992) describes a case where a subject's marriage is so important to him that even if his spouse were unfaithful to him, he'd rather not know, for fear that the knowledge would cause him to behave in such a way that the marriage will end. Kelly (2003) suggests that it's better to lack a true belief about how a movie will end, before going to see it. Klein (2008) argues that there are false beliefs that are epistemically good because they lead to further knowledge. And Elgin (2007; 2009) argues that some false beliefs are epistemically good because they are essential to scientific understanding.[2]

Still, Mill is likely correct in thinking that social policy is better – both in the sense that it aims at better goals, and that it proceeds in ways that are more likely to achieve its goals – when it is based on true beliefs. And we will be likelier to arrive at the truth on important matters if we allow and encourage arguments in defense of any opinions.

The point to take away here is that there appear to be two distinct fundamental values in Mill's normative framework: one for action (happiness) and one for belief (truth). The point isn't to try to decide which of these (if any) is more fundamental, or to decide how to resolve potential conflicts between them. Rather, the point is to set the groundwork for the collapse problem in ethics, epistemology, and argumentation theory. The two fundamental values in Mill's work naturally lead into parallel versions of the problem in these domains. In Section 3, we'll see the problem as it arises in ethics, as a problem for rule-utilitarianism (or more generally, rule-consequentialism). Section 4 will then illustrate the problem as it arises in epistemology, as a problem for accounts of justification that are aimed at truth. Section 5 will address the problem as it arises for some goal-oriented approaches in argumentation theory, such as a truth-directed epistemic approach, and Section 6 will show how the problem can be resolved.

3. COLLAPSE PROBLEMS IN ETHICS

A familiar complaint about classical utilitarianism is that it seems to permit, or even require, serious injustices in some cases. For example, if the net happiness of the majority requires us to capture and sacrifice a few innocent, unwilling individuals—well then, it seems that that's just what utilitarianism requires us to

2. See Bondy (2018, ch. 6) for further discussion of these sorts of cases.

do! But that result seems unacceptable. Surely, we can't be ethically permitted or required to sacrifice innocent, unwilling people in order to bring about great happiness for everyone else.

Another complaint is that it's not psychologically plausible that people should be required to perform utilitarian calculations, determining the course of action that is most likely to bring about the greatest happiness for the greatest number, before undertaking any actions. That's just far too complex a task to expect people to undertake, say, before crossing a street, or buying a sandwich, and so on. But the utilitarian principle applies to all human actions: they are right only if they bring about the greatest happiness for the greatest number.

One way to respond to these complaints is to stick to the fundamental framework of act-utilitarianism (AU), and to try to show that it does not have the unacceptable consequences. Norcross (1997; 2011), for example, responds to these kinds of problems for utilitarianism, without opting for the rule-utilitarian approach. The focus of this chapter, however, is on the alternative solution of opting for rule-utilitarianism (RU) instead of AU. Whereas AU holds that actions are right or wrong depending on whether they bring about the greatest happiness for the greatest number, RU holds that actions are right or wrong depending on whether they accord with *rules* that would bring about the greatest happiness for the greatest number, if everyone or overwhelmingly many people were to follow or accept them. RU seems to handle the first complaint about classical utilitarianism, because rules permitting the sacrifice of innocents for the happiness of others would not bring about the greatest happiness if everyone followed them. And RU appears to handle the second complaint, because it only requires that people act according to relatively simple moral rules, rather than requiring people to always calculate which of the available actions will have the best consequences.

So far so good: RU appears to handle those initial worries for AU well enough. But once we move away from an act-based utilitarian framework and toward a rule-based one (or, toward a rule-based consequentialist framework more generally), the *collapse/incoherence* objection will rear its head. This is the objection that either RU collapses into AU, yielding the same results about what is right and wrong in every case, or else RU must conflict with its own fundamental rationale. On the first horn, RU is no different from AU, and it is vulnerable to the same problems; on the second, RU seems incoherent.

The argument goes as follows. Suppose that RU is not just AU under a different name. Then the two must yield different results regarding what is right and wrong in some cases. But AU holds that actions are morally right when they bring about the greatest amount of net happiness. So, in a case, C, where RU and AU yield conflicting results, RU tells us to follow a rule, R, that will result in a lower amount of net happiness than if we were to not follow R in C. A different rule, R', just like R except that it allows an exception in C, would bring about a greater amount of net happiness than R does overall. R' is therefore the superior rule from the utilitarian standpoint; clinging to R in C even though it yields less net happiness seems to result in an incoherent form of utilitarianism.

The trouble now is that if we *do* build an exception into R for case C, then it seems like we are committed to building exceptions into the rules for *all* cases where AU and RU diverge. And if we do build in exceptions in every case in which AU and RU diverge, then RU just becomes a much more complicated formulation of AU, yielding the same moral requirements as AU in every case. Surely, then, it is better just to stick with AU. That is the *collapse* problem.

On the other hand, if we do *not* build exceptions into the rules for every case in which AU and RU diverge, then we'll be embracing rules that conflict with the underlying rationale of utilitarianism, because they will fail to maximize net happiness. Then RU conflicts with its own underlying rationale, and appears to be incoherent. That is the *incoherence* problem. The upshot is that the best version of utilitarianism is AU, because at least AU is coherent with its own underlying rationale.

Lyons (1965) famously pressed this line of argument against rule-utilitarianism. Hooker (2000; 2016) has argued that rule-consequentialism can handle the collapse/incoherence objection. Card (2007) presses the objection against Hooker, and Hooker (2007) responds. We'll come to Hooker's way of responding to the problem below, in Section 6. (See also Wiland (2010) for a generalization of the objection, and a way to try to handle it. The responses discussed below do not make use of Wiland's strategy.)

4. COLLAPSE PROBLEMS IN EPISTEMOLOGY

We've seen that Mill's account of justified belief – or at least, his account of belief that is justified strongly enough to act on responsibly – is truth-directed, and it entails an openness to listening to arguments and objections from people who think that our beliefs are mistaken. The idea was that we can only have sufficient justified confidence in the truth of a proposition if we find and respond to the strongest objections anyone can raise against it.

Contemporary epistemologists by and large do not require people to meet the high standard of seeking out all objections and responding to them, in order to have justified confidence in the truth of a proposition. But the view that justification is truth-directed remains very popular. Different epistemologists cash out the truth-directedness of justification in different ways, of course. One popular approach to epistemic justification, reliabilism, holds roughly that beliefs are justified just in case they are produced reliably. Another popular view of justification, evidentialism, holds roughly that beliefs are epistemically justified just in case they are properly held on the basis of good evidence. Both of these approaches are truth-directed in an important sense. Reliabilism is truth-directed in the sense that a process's reliability is defined by its true- to false-belief output ratio. Evidentialism is truth-directed in the sense that evidence is what bears on the truth-value or the probability of the truth of a target proposition.

Both of these generic views of epistemic justification have a kind of truth-directedness built into them – but, importantly, they do not typically require justified beliefs to be infallible; they normally allow the possibility of justified false beliefs. Reliabilists typically allow that false beliefs can be justified, when they are produced by highly reliable processes; reliabilists don't require infallible causal histories as a necessary condition for a belief's being justified, because that would lead to a kind of skepticism (after all, we have few if any infallibly produced beliefs). Evidentialists also typically allow that there can be justified false beliefs, when they are held on the basis of good but misleading evidence.

To illustrate: Martha sits in her favourite chair in her living room, in the early afternoon of a sunny Tuesday, and she closes her eyes for a brief nap. Then, waking up and feeling refreshed (if a bit stiff), she turns on the television to watch her favourite Tuesday afternoon program, but she can't seem to find it. She checks the program guide, and finds that it's now Wednesday! Somehow, she has managed to sleep for an entire day.

Post-nap Martha believed that it was still Tuesday. Her belief was held on the basis of good evidence (Martha normally doesn't sleep an entire day; the sun is shining as it was when she went to sleep; etc.), and the belief had a reliable causal history. So, her belief appears to have been well justified, up until she turned on the television guide program and obtained evidence indicating that it was now Wednesday.

The point is that there is an intuitive sense in which beliefs seem to be capable of being justified even if they turn out to be mistaken, and there is also an intuitive sense in which beliefs can be unjustified, even if they turn out to be true. Most, though not all, popular theories of epistemic justification yield these results. Some epistemologists have argued that only true beliefs can be justified, while false beliefs can be at best excused (see Sutton 2007; Littlejohn 2012; Boult 2017). Still, these epistemologists hold that there can be *un*justified true beliefs. And the possibility of unjustified true beliefs, just as much as the possibility of justified false beliefs, is threatened by the collapse objection. In what follows, for the most part, I'll mostly set aside references to unjustified true beliefs, and talk only about justified false beliefs, for simplicity.

Maitzen (1995) has argued that a collapse/incoherence problem faces theories of justification that aim at the truth, but which allow that there can be justified false beliefs and unjustified true beliefs. The argument proceeds just as in the case of rule-utilitarianism in ethics. Typical truth-directed accounts of justification take some version of a truth-goal – say, the goal of acquiring true beliefs and avoiding false beliefs, or the goal of improving one's ratio of true to false beliefs, or another goal along these lines – and articulate a set of criteria or rules for beliefs to count as epistemically justified in light of that goal. So, we can take any arbitrary case of a false belief that satisfies the conditions on some analysis of justification – say, Martha's post-nap belief that today is Tuesday. If the criteria in an account of justification are supposed to be truth-directed, then to the extent that the account of justification counts Martha's false belief as justified, those criteria must fail to achieve their goal. A different account of justification, which excludes Martha's belief, would to that extent be more appropriately truth-directed.

In other words, if a belief is false, it can't help but make a person's body of beliefs worse, from the point of view that is concerned with acquiring true beliefs and avoiding false ones. Plausibly, a truth-goal such as that one is precisely what epistemic justification aims at: beliefs are epistemically justified in virtue of their being appropriately directed toward promoting some suitable version of the goal of acquiring true beliefs and avoiding false ones. Because false beliefs must detract from the achievement of that goal, false beliefs should not count as justified. Or, if we want to continue counting some false beliefs as justified, then Maitzen argues that we should acknowledge that the epistemic point of view is after all not properly characterized as concerned with the goal of achieving true beliefs and avoiding false ones.

There are some more moves Maitzen makes in the paper by way of replying to objections, but that is the key to the argument. One objection Maitzen responds to is that false beliefs can be justified because they can *tend* to promote the acquisition of true beliefs. Maitzen replies that false beliefs can't help but tend to lower the truth-falsity ratio of a set of beliefs. A false belief's *causal history* might tend to promote the acquisition of mostly true beliefs, but false beliefs *themselves* tend to inhibit the acquisition of mostly true beliefs, even if they are produced by reliable processes.

Maitzen's discussion is mostly conducted in terms of whether an arbitrary true belief held at a time t can run contrary to the goal of having true beliefs at t, or whether an arbitrary false belief held at t can help achieve the truth-goal at t. But he concedes (pp.872-3) that one might make the case that, in some few instances, there can be particular true beliefs that *tend in the long run* to run contrary to the goal of achieving true beliefs and avoiding false ones. Similarly, some few false beliefs might run contrary to the truth-goal in the long run. (Perhaps such a false belief might be: "the more true beliefs I form and hold, the richer I will become.") Nevertheless, such beliefs are very exceptional; most intuitively justified false beliefs, and unjustified true beliefs, will not promote a long-run truth-goal. So, appealing to long-run truth-goals does not save the spirit of views that allow justified false beliefs and unjustified true beliefs.[3]

The collapse problem, then, is that in searching for an adequate theory of epistemic justification, we are pushed toward an account that will exclude any false beliefs, because false beliefs must always run contrary to the goal of acquiring true beliefs and avoiding false beliefs. Similarly, we are pushed toward an account that will include all true beliefs, because true beliefs always contribute to achieving the goal of acquiring true beliefs and avoiding false ones. And so, we are pushed toward a theory of justification according to which all and only true beliefs are justified (that is, justified belief "collapses into" true belief.)

That is a counterintuitive result, to be sure. So perhaps we will want to resist this collapse of justified belief and true belief, and cling to an account of justification that allows for justified false beliefs and/or unjustified true beliefs. If so, then Maitzen argues that we will face the incoherence problem: our account of justification will seem to conflict with its own underlying truth-directed rationale. We want an account of epistemic justification, surely, because we want an account of a property or a set of properties that make people well-placed to have true beliefs and avoid false ones. If we knowingly cling to an account of justification that does worse at that job than a rival account of justification does, then it looks like our account of justification is incoherent.[4]

3. Thanks to Dan Coren for pressing me to consider what Maitzen would say about long-run truth-goals in this context.

4. A close cousin to the collapse problem in epistemology is the recently much-discussed *swamping problem*. This is a problem for accounts according to which epistemic justification is only *instrumentally valuable*, as a means for the achievement of true beliefs. The problem is that the instrumental value of the means doesn't appear to transfer to their product, or to the belief that is produced via those means. After all, true beliefs are not made any truer in virtue of their being justified. The same goes for false beliefs: being justified does not make them any truer. The epistemic value of a belief's actual truth or falsity "swamps," or overwhelms, or screens off, the instrumental value of its justification. We can set aside the swamping problem and focus just on

To sum up the collapse/incoherence problem in epistemology: this problem appears to arise when we have an epistemic goal, such as the goal of achieving true beliefs and avoiding false ones, and we have rules or criteria for beliefs articulated in light of that goal, such that beliefs satisfying those criteria will be more likely to achieve the goal. The problem is that we want to maintain both (i) that the criteria of epistemically justified belief are such that having justified beliefs will contribute to maximizing one's stock of true beliefs and minimizing one's stock of false beliefs (or some other similar truth-goal), and (ii) that the criteria of epistemically justified belief allow that there are some justified false beliefs, and some unjustified true beliefs. Maitzen's argument is that (i) and (ii) each appears to entail the denial of the other. If we embrace (i), then we have the *collapse problem*: all and only true beliefs must be justified, because unjustified true beliefs promote the truth-goal just as much as justified ones do, and justified false beliefs run counter to the truth goal just as much as unjustified false ones do. So we must deny (ii). If instead we embrace (ii), then we have the *incoherence problem*: we will be embracing criteria of justification that do worse in light of the truth-goal than an alternative set of criteria would do (namely, the set consisting of the sole criterion that a belief is justified iff it is true.) So we must deny (i).

In the next section, we'll see how the collapse/incoherence problem bears on some consequentialist approaches in argumentation theory, especially epistemic approaches. Then in section 6, we'll see that there is a plausible general solution to the collapse/incoherence problems in ethics, epistemology, and argumentation theory.

the collapse problem here, in order to keep this chapter focused. For further discussion of problems relating to the value of true belief, justification, and knowledge, see Kvanvig (2003), Zagzebski (2003), Carter and Jarvis (2012), Pritchard, Turri, and Carter (2018), and Bondy (2018, ch. 7).

5. COLLAPSE PROBLEMS IN ARGUMENTATION THEORY

One of the central goals of argumentation theory is to identify conditions under which argumentation counts as cogent, taking "cogency" in a broad sense to mean "argumentation that satisfies the applicable norms," whatever those norms might be. One common approach to giving an account of cogency is to proceed by identifying a set of goals at which argumentation characteristically aims, and then articulating norms or rules that promote the achievement of those goals. Cogent argumentation will be argumentation that satisfies those norms.

Just as in ethics and epistemology, the collapse/incoherence problem also looms for this kind of consequentialist approach to argumentation theory. In particular, the problem applies straightforwardly to standard epistemic accounts of argument cogency. Typically, epistemic approaches hold that good or cogent arguments are those that yield or can yield epistemically justified belief in their conclusions for the participants in the argumentative situation.[5] On an evidentialist account of epistemic justification, for example, the goal of generating justified belief in the conclusion of an argument can only be met if the argument's premises constitute good evidence for the truth of its conclusion.

The worry for this kind of consequentialist epistemic approach to argumentation theory is that if our accounts of epistemic justification cannot handle the collapse problem, then it

5. Goldman (1999) and Lumer (2005a, 2005b) offer useful elaboration and defense of epistemic approaches to argumentation. Note that epistemic approaches to argumentation can be developed in broader ways than one might expect. For example, Bermejo-Luque (2010) contains a clear treatment of how the rhetorical aspects of argumentation can be incorporated within a truth-directed, justificatory framework for argumentation, and Bondy (2019) argues that epistemic approaches to inference and argument can incorporate non-epistemic reasons for belief.

turns out that there are no justified false beliefs, and no unjustified true beliefs—justified belief collapses into true belief. But if all and only true beliefs are epistemically justified, then all and only arguments capable of generating true beliefs in their conclusions will satisfy the epistemic standard of argument cogency. And if epistemic approaches to argument cogency are saddled with that result, then that is bad news for such approaches. For surely there are at least *some* good arguments for false conclusions, and at least some bad arguments for true conclusions.

The collapse problem in argumentation theory is especially clear for the kind of epistemic approach just sketched, but keep in mind that it also threatens to arise for any account of cogency according to which (i) there is a characteristic goal of argumentation, G, and norms of argumentation that aim at the achievement of G, but (ii) in some instances, bad arguments can achieve G, or cogent arguments can fail to achieve G. If the problem cannot be handled, then that gives us a reason to abandon goal-oriented accounts of cogency.

6. WITHSTANDING COLLAPSE WITHOUT INCOHERENCE

The goal in this section is to show that goal-oriented approaches in ethics, epistemology, and argumentation theory can handle the collapse problem after all.

There are two broad responses to the collapse problem available. One response is to hold that consequentialist approaches need not be committed to maximizing the goal or value that the theory posits. The second response is to distinguish the goals or values explaining why we *care* about having justification, and the goals or values that are themselves *built in* as constitutive elements of justification. Both responses can work, but I will suggest that the second is better motivated than the first.

Hooker (2000; 2007; 2016) defends rule-consequentialism (RC) in ethics against the collapse objection.[6] He begins his defense by arguing that we should not select rules that would produce the most good if most people *complied* with them; we should instead select rules in light of the consequences that would follow if most people were to *accept* or internalize them. There are costs associated with learning and accepting very complex rules that have very many exceptions built into them, in terms of wasted cognitive resources and time lost trying to apply the rules, as well as in terms of lost opportunities for people to form trusting relationships with each other. (E.g., people will trust each other more if they know that most other people follow the simple rule "don't steal" instead of a complex rule with many exception clauses built in.) So, Hooker argues, the best rules are relatively simple. And so his kind of RC does not collapse into act-consequentialism (AC) after all.

Now the other horn of the dilemma looms: if RC doesn't collapse into AC, then mustn't RC be incoherent? After all, the response to the collapse objection just offered was that we should select rules that will produce sub-optimal consequences in specific cases, and it can even be *known* ahead of time that the rules will have those results. And isn't the fundamental motivation for any plausible form of consequentialism the idea that we *ought* to maximize the good?

In response to this worry, Hooker argues that it's perfectly coherent for rule-consequentialists not to be committed to maximizing the good. One *could* argue for RC in the first place by appealing to the basic idea that we should maximize the good, and so we should select rules that will do that. If that were the motivation for Hooker's rule-consequentialism, then his rule-

6. RC, of course, is just like RU except that it allows a more ecumenical take on the kinds of consequences that matter. Utilitarians are consequentialists who think that happiness or perhaps well-being is the kind of consequence that matters for ethics, but other consequentialists are free to invoke other kinds of consequences as the ethically important ones.

consequentialism would indeed seem to be incoherent with its own underlying rationale. But Hooker (2007) makes his rejection of that argument for RC quite clear. Instead, Hooker claims that we should accept RC – and specifically, a version of RC with relatively simple rules – simply because that is the way to achieve reflective equilibrium at the theoretical level regarding our firmly held moral convictions. Positing moral rules that generate good consequences in general but produce sub-optimal results in some cases is the best way to make sense of our various moral convictions. We don't need to have a commitment to maximizing the good built into either the rule-consequentialist theory or the moral psychology of rule-consequentialist agents.

Applying Hooker's move to the case of epistemic justification, we would reject the idea that the rules or criteria for epistemically justified belief are grounded in the fact that those criteria maximize true belief and minimize false belief. Instead, we would see the criteria for justified belief as grounded in the fact that the criteria best explain and organize our firmly held intuitions and principles about epistemically justified beliefs.[7] In this way, we can avoid the collapse of justified belief into true belief. We can view the criteria of epistemically justified belief as grounded not in the fact that certain criteria will in fact maximize true belief and minimize false belief, but instead, in the fact that certain criteria will likely maximize true belief and minimize false belief, from the limited perspective of the agents in question. That is, criteria for epistemically justified belief should be selected by reference to a goal as well as a set of other constraints, including especially the available cognitive resources.[8]

7. This move is similar to the explanation of why epistemic reasons are evidential offered in Bondy (2018), chapters 2 and 7.

8. Foley's (1993) articulation of an instrumentalist account of epistemic rationality makes this perspectival character of the criteria and of our judgments of epistemic rationality clear.

A second response to the collapse problem, offered by David (2001),[9] is to notice that there are two different levels at which we might invoke goals in our theories of epistemic justification, and the collapse argument only works on one of them. On the one hand, we might invoke the goal of true belief as part of what *constitutes* epistemic justification – i.e., we might hold that epistemic justification is constituted by features that must in fact contribute to the goal of achieving true beliefs. Call that *level 1*. On the other hand, we might invoke the goal of true belief not as part of what constitutes epistemically justified beliefs, but instead simply as the goal for the purpose of which we *care* about having epistemically justified beliefs. Call that *level 2*. To illustrate, consider an analogy offered by David (2001). Suppose you have a dog, who keeps away the nosy neighbours, and suppose that you only care about the dog because you care about keeping away the neighbours. Then there is a goal that you have, and that goal is the only reason you care about having the dog. But the dog itself is not constituted, not even a little bit, by your goal of keeping away the neighbours.

In that analogy, the goal of keeping away the neighbours is not invoked at level 1, as part of what constitutes the dog; it is invoked only at level 2, as the reason why you care about having the dog. Similarly, we might give an account of epistemic justification according to which the goal of true beliefs is not part of what *constitutes* epistemic justification, but according to which we only care about having justified beliefs because we care about having true beliefs. For example, we might say that epistemic justification is determined strictly by the quality of the evidence on the basis of which beliefs are held; and we care about having justified beliefs because having justified beliefs is, from the perspec-

9. I am following David in this narrow response to Maitzen's argument, but note that David goes on to articulate an account of justification according to which a version of the truth-goal is built into the concept of justification. The discussion offered here does not follow David down that road.

tive of cognitively limited creatures like us, the best way to try to achieve the further goal of getting true beliefs.

Maitzen's collapse argument begins with the observation that, according to many epistemologists at least, the only reason we really *care* about having justified beliefs (level 2) is as a means to having true beliefs. But his argument only works if it follows from invoking true belief as a goal at level 2, that we must also invoke it at level 1, as part of what grounds the criteria of epistemic justification themselves. And that just doesn't follow.

Because we humans are cognitively limited, in the sense that we are rarely if ever able to directly intuit the truth of empirical propositions,[10] it follows that when we want to have true beliefs and avoid false ones, we must very often take certain indirect means to achieving that goal. In particular, we must seek out good evidence, and we must hold our beliefs on the basis thereof. Taking these steps is often very fast (e.g., I look in the cupboard, have a visual impression as of coffee remaining in the jar, and I form the belief that there remains coffee in the jar, without reflecting on it explicitly), but we do take them.

Taking the appropriate steps to achieve our goals is what makes us justified in a consequentialist sense with respect to those goals. For a godlike being, who is capable of directly and infallibly intuiting truths about the world, the appropriate thing to do in order to achieve the goal of getting true beliefs is just to go ahead and form the beliefs that it intuits. For such a being, there is no distinction between justified belief and true belief. Maybe the concept of justified belief does not even make sense as applied to an infallible being. But for us, the appropriate steps to take for the purpose of achieving the truth-goal involve forming beliefs on the basis of good evidence. And because evidence

10. Indeed, the point applies to most a priori knowable or justifiable beliefs too. Is 253 + 4290 equal to 4543? If we can know that to be so, we will normally know it only indirectly, by way of performing the calculation, or by way of trusting the report of a person or a calculator.

can sometimes be misleading, for us there can be well supported but false beliefs. So for fallible and limited being like us, there remains a distinction between justified belief and true belief.

Let me close with two final thoughts about these two responses to the collapse problem, which seem to favour embracing the second response rather than the first, if not in the domain of ethics then at least in epistemology. First: Hooker's response to the collapse problem is that his version of RC does not involve a commitment to maximizing the good. But for consequentialists in ethics who remain committed to the view that we *should* maximize the good, it looks like Hooker's strategy for defending RC will be unavailable. Similarly, for consequentialists in epistemology, who think that we should always or at least in most cases aim to maximize our stock of true beliefs, or our true-to-false-belief-ratio, Hooker's strategy might be unavailable. For there are cases where a person *wants* to acquire true beliefs, and where it's *important* that she do so. And in such cases, the subject might acquire good but misleading evidence, in which case she can form a justified but false belief. In cases like that, we can't respond to the collapse problem by pulling back from the commitment to maximizing the (epistemic) good, because that commitment is built into the description of the case.

Now, maybe subjects are just *wrong* when they want to maximize their stock of true beliefs; that's a commitment they shouldn't have. If it's a commitment that people shouldn't have, then the Hooker-style response to the collapse problem in epistemology becomes available again. But if it is alright for people to remain committed to maximizing the epistemic good of true beliefs, then these problematic cases will come up, and Hooker's move won't solve them.

The second and final thought about the two responses to the collapse/incoherence problem is that there is an important disanalogy between the ethical and the epistemic cases, which seems to support the second response over the first in the context of the collapse problem for accounts of epistemic justification.

In the ethical case, the collapse problem arises because we can see that following a rule in a given case will yield a bad or suboptimal outcome – and that result can be known or at least rationally expected ahead of time. That is why clinging to the rule in cases like this seems incoherent with the fundamental motivation for RC, if that motivation is that we care about maximizing the good.

In the epistemic case, however, the subject *cannot* know ahead of time in a particular case that following the rule of forming beliefs only when there is adequate evidential support will lead to an epistemically bad outcome (i.e., a false belief). For suppose that we have a proposition, p, which is well supported by a body of evidence, E. And then we get some new information, indicating that p is false and E is misleading. Importantly, this new information is not telling us that belief in p is both evidentially supported and false. Rather, the new information is new evidence, which we ought to take into account, and which renders p no longer evidentially well-supported. So, following the rule of believing only what is evidentially well-supported, because we care about getting a true belief and avoiding a false one regarding p, we will end up not believing p.

To be a bit more precise: it *is* possible to know, of a given proposition that is (now) evidentially well-supported, that belief in it (once formed) will be false. That happens when we have self-undermining beliefs, such that the subject knows that immediately upon forming a belief, she will possess new evidence indicating that the belief is false. But even when it comes to self-undermining beliefs, we know ahead of time that we cannot at the same time believe the proposition and possess good evidence supporting it. So we should read the rule of believing only what the evidence supports as really a prohibition on forming beliefs for which one will lack adequate evidence while one holds them.

Because it can be known ahead of time that following an ethical rule will produce sub-optimal consequences, while it cannot be known ahead of time that believing what the evidence supports will lead to a false belief, one can at the same time have a commitment to a truth-goal (such as the goal of maximizing one's stock of true beliefs and minimizing one's false beliefs) as part of one's motivations, while at the same time remaining committed to following the rule of believing only what the evidence supports even in cases where the evidence is misleading – and all of that, without being involved in incoherence. We therefore don't need to make Hooker's kind of move in epistemology: we don't need to drop anyone's commitment to maximizing the epistemic good in particular cases, in order to avoid collapse. That's not to say that everyone always does want to acquire true beliefs and avoid false ones; sometimes people just don't care about having true beliefs on a given topic. But people do care very much about getting true beliefs in many cases, and it's important that our response to the collapse problem for justification be consistent with people's desire to maximize their true beliefs in those cases.

7. CONCLUSION

The main goal of this chapter has been to show how collapse/incoherence problems can arise for consequentialists in ethics, epistemology, and argumentation theory, and to show how these problems can be handled. In particular, it has explained Hooker's response on behalf of rule-consequentialism in ethics, and it has shown how that kind of response might be applied to the collapse problem for epistemic justification. But it has also explained a second response, that we can care about acquiring true beliefs, and care about justification only as a means to truth, while at the same time viewing justification as not at all constituted by the aim of achieving true beliefs. This second response also handles the collapse problem in epistemology, and is perhaps the preferable solution to the problem in that domain. And, importantly, whichever solution to the collapse problem in epistemology we opt for, we'll be able to use that solution to block the collapse problem for epistemic approaches to argument cogency, too.

ACKNOWLEDGEMENTS: Many thanks to Daniel Coren and J. Anthony Blair for valuable feedback on previous drafts of this chapter.

REFERENCES

Bermejo-Luque, Lilian (2010). Intrinsic versus instrumenta values of argumentation: The rhetorical dimension of argumentation. *Argumentation* 2, 453–474.

Bondy, Patrick (2018). *Epistemic Rationality and Epistemic Normativity*. New York: Routledge.

Bondy, Patrick (2019). The epistemic norm of inference and non-epistemic reasons for belief. *Synthese*, Online first, https://doi.org/10.1007/s11229-019-02163-3.

Boult, Cameron (2017). Epistemic normativity and the justification-excuse distinction. *Synthese* 194 (10), 4065–4081

Brown, D. G. (1974). Mill's act-utilitarianism. *The Philosophical Quarterly* 24 (94), 67–68.

Card, Robert (2007). Inconsistency and the theoretical commitments of Hooker's rule-consequentialism. *Utilitas* 19 (2), 243–258.

Carter, Adam, and Benjamin Jarvis (2012). Against swamping. *Analysis* 72 (4), 690–699.

Cupples, Brian (1972). A defense of the received interpretation of J. S. Mill. *Australasian Journal of Philosophy* 50 (2), 131–137.

David, Marian (2001). Truth as the epistemic goal. In Matthias Steup (Ed.), *Knowledge, Truth, and Duty: Essays on Epistemic Justification*, pp. 151–169. New York and Oxford: Oxford University Press.

Elgin, Catherine (2007). Understanding and the facts. *Philosophical Studies* 132 (1), 33–42.

Elgin, Catherine (2009). Is understanding factive? In Adrian Haddock, Allan Millar, and Duncan Pritchard (Eds.), *Epistemic Value*, pp. 322–330. Oxford: Oxford University Press.

Foley, Richard (1993). *Working without a net: A study of egocentric Rationality*. New York and Oxford: Oxford University Press.

Foot, Philippa (1985). Utilitarianism and the virtues. *Mind* 94 (374), 196–209.

Goldman, Alvin (1999). *Knowledge in a Social World*. Oxford: Oxford University Press.

Hansen, Hans (2006). Mill and Pragma-Dialectics. In P. Houtlosser and A. van Rees (Eds.), *Considering Pragma-Dialectics*, pp. 97–107. Mahwah, NJ: Erlbaum.

Hansen, Hans (2014). Mill, informal logic, and argumentation. In Anton Loizides (Ed.), *John Stuart Mill's A System of Logic: Critical Appraisals*, pp. 192–217 London: Routledge.

Heil, John (1992). Believing reasonably. *Noûs* 26 (1), 47–62.

Hooker, Brad (2000). *Ideal Code, Real World: A Rule-consequentialist Theory of Morality*. Oxford: Oxford University Press.

Hooker, Brad (2007). Rule-consequentialism and internal consistency: A reply to Card. *Utilitas* 19 (4), 514–9.

Hooker, Brad (2016). Rule consequentialism. *The Stanford Encyclopedia of Philosophy* (Winter 2016 Edition), Edward N. Zalta (ed.), URL = <https://plato.stanford.edu/archives/win2016/entries/consequentialism-rule/>.

Kelly, Thomas (2003). Epistemic rationality as instrumental rationality: A critique. *Philosophy and Phenomenological Research* 66 (3), 612–640.

Klein, Peter (2008). Useful false beliefs. In Quentin Smith (Ed.), *Epistemology: New Essays*, pp. 25–63. Oxford University Press.

Kvanvig, Jonathan (2003). *The Value of Knowledge and the Pursuit of Understanding*. Cambridge: Cambridge University Press.

Littlejohn, Clayton (2012). *Justification and the Truth-Connection*. Cambridge: Cambridge University Press.

Lumer, Christoph (2005a). Introduction: The epistemological approach to argumentation – A map. *Informal Logic* 25 (3), 189–212.

Lumer, Christoph (2005b). The epistemological theory of argument – how and why? *Informal Logic* 25 (3), 213–243.

Lynch, Michael (2004). *True to Life: Why truth* Matters. Cambridge, Mass: MIT Press.

Maitzen, Stephen. (1995). Our errant epistemic aim. *Philosophy and Phenomenological Research* 55 (4), 869–876.

Mill, J. S. (1859). *On Liberty*, in vol. XVIII (1977) of Mill (1963–1991).

Mill, J. S. (1861). *Utilitarianism*, in vol. X (1969) of Mill (1963–1991).

Mill, J. S. (1963–1991). *Collected Works of John Stuart Mill*, F.E.L. Priestly (Gen. Ed.) and subsequently J. M. Robson (Ed.), 33 vols. (London/ Toronto: Routledge and Kegan Paul/University of Toronto Press).

Norcross, Alastair (2007). Consequentialism and commitment. *Pacific Philosophical Quarterly* 78, 380–403.

Norcross, Alastair (2011). Act-utilitarianism and promissory obligation. In Hannoch Sheinman (ed.), *Promises and Agreements: Philosophical Essays*, pp. 217–236. Oxford: Oxford University Press.

Pritchard, Duncan, John Turri, and J. Adam Carter (2018). The value of knowledge. *The Stanford Encyclopedia of Philosophy* (Spring 2018 Edition), Edward N. Zalta (ed.), URL = <https://plato.stanford.edu/archives/spr2018/entries/knowledge-value/>.

Scheffler, Samuel (1985). Agent-centered restrictions, rationality, and the virtues. *Mind* 94 (375), 409–419.

Sutton, Jonathan (2007). *Without Justification*. Cambridge, MA: MIT Press.

Urmson, J. O. (1953). The interpretation of the moral philosophy of J. S. Mill. *The Philosophical Quarterly* 3 (10), 33–39.

Wiland, Eric (2010). The incoherence objection in moral theory. *Acta Analytica* 25, 279–284.

Zagzebski, Linda (2003). The search for the source of epistemic good. *Metaphilosophy* 34 (1/2), 12–28.

ABOUT THE AUTHOR: Patrick Bondy is an Assistant Professor in the Department of Philosophy at Wichita State University. His publications include *Epistemic Rationality and Epistemic Normativity* (2018, Routledge), as well as articles on various topics related to knowledge, justification, inference, and argument.
patrick.bondy@wichita.edu

CHAPTER 8.

FLEW ON THE PRESUMPTION OF ATHEISM AND HIS CASE FOR DEISM: A PERSPECTIVE FROM ARGUMENTATION THEORY

JAMES B. FREEMAN

ABSTRACT: We first present Flew's understanding of the presumption of atheism, his case that the concept of God is incoherent, and his reply to the free-will defense. We then argue that Flew has not shown that every concept of God is incoherent, but at most the concept in classical theism. By contrast, neither in process theism nor in deism is the concept of God incoherent. We next present Flew's case for deism, critically assess his argument, and argue that he has successfully shifted the burden of proof to the atheist.
KEYWORDS: positive versus negative presumption, negative atheism, incoherence of theism, free will, classical theism, process theism, Divine omnipotence, compatibility with free will, teleology

1. THE PRESUMPTION OF ATHEISM

Flew distinguishes positive from negative atheism. Suppose I perceive a tree in full green leaf outside my office window. My sense perception vouches for the proposition "There is a tree in full green leaf outside my office window." There is a presumption for sense perception. That is, if my sense perception vouches for a statement, there is a positive presumption for the statement from my point of view. I may categorically assert it. By contrast, suppose I claimed that there were exactly 1,768 leaves on the tree. Does my sense perception vouch for that? A challenger could ask me for proof and might phrase her question this way: "For all you have shown, the number of leaves on the tree is not 1,768. Please show that it is." The challenger would be making a challenge or cautious denial (compare Rescher 1977, p. 9). She is not making a categorical assertion that 1,768 is wrong, but that I must show it is right. That is, she is recognizing a negative presumption for my claim. Presumptions may be determined on many grounds, law being a paradigm case. At the beginning of a criminal trial, the burden of proof is on the prosecution to establish guilt. The presumption of innocence then is a negative presumption.

Flew understands the presumption of atheism as a negative presumption. The burden is on the theist to show God is, not on the atheist to produce a body of reasons sufficient to show that God is not. Flew calls his view "negative atheism." The presumption of atheism is exactly analogous to the presumption of innocence. It is an instance of what Rescher (1977) calls "the probative burden of an initiating assertion." "Whichever side initiates the assertion of a thesis within the dialectical situation has the burden of supporting it in argument" (1977, p. 27). However, Flew insists that the theist's claim will always be the initial assertion in a disputation with an atheist. How does Flew defend assigning the initiating burden of proof always to the theist? What value analogous to avoiding punishing the innocent in a criminal case is preserved by assigning the initiating burden of proof to the theist? Flew asserts that it is knowledge. Flew virtually subscribes to the understanding of knowledge as justified true belief. To know, Flew asserts, the believer must "be in a position to know" (1984, p. 22). This means that the believer must "have 'grounds sufficient' to warrant the claim" (p. 22). This is the key to understanding why the initiating presumption lies with theism. "If it is to be established that there is a God, then we have to have good grounds for believing that this is indeed so" (p. 22). Flew sees discharging the burden of giving good grounds for theism involving two parts, first to give a coherent concept of "God" and second to give sufficient reason to show that this concept is satisfied.

Why could not an atheist accept an initiating burden of proof for atheism and argue from there to advocate positive atheism? This grants more than what the negative atheist will allow. It presupposes that the atheist has a coherent concept of God. Flew objects that the theist's very concept of God needs to be defended first (1984, p. 15). In particular the theist must show that the concept is coherent, to "ensure that the word 'God' is provided with a meaning such that it is theoretically possible for an actual being to be so described" (1984, p. 16). Whatever else one might mean by saying that a set of statements is incoherent, if that set is logically inconsistent it is incoherent. If one shows that a set ostensibly yields a contradiction, one shows that the set is ostensibly incoherent. A set ostensibly yields a contradiction if either the set together with one or more additional plausible statements yields a contradiction or, where universal generalizations are used in deriving the contradiction, they are acceptable only when interpreted as *ceteris paribus* universals. Flew specifically indicts the concept of God with ostensible incoherence in the last paragraphs of "The presumption of atheism." He refers "to the ostensible incoherence … between the concept of a flawless Creator and the notion of His creatures flawed by their sins" (1984, p. 30). How can a flawless Creator create flawed creatures? The concept seems incoherent, i.e., *is* ostensibly incoherent. Flew's argument adapts the familiar argument from evil against the existence of the Deity. If God is all-powerful, he can remove all evils. If God is all-good, he seeks to remove all evils. Yet evil exists. So, God cannot be both all-powerful and all good. So, an all-powerful and all good Deity does not exist.

The theist has a rejoinder, The Free Will Defense. Flew states the argument succinctly in "Divine omnipotence and human freedom" (1955, pp. 144-69).

1. That God cannot do what is logically impossible in no way compromises his omnipotence.

2. God gave humans free-will which implies the possibility of their choosing to do evil.

3. Certain goods, e.g. the virtues, logically presuppose either the ability to freely reject evils or the actual occurrence of certain evils (e.g. there could be no compassion without the evil of suffering). Therefore

4. The goods of moral virtues logically presuppose the possibility of certain evils and in some cases the actuality of certain evils.

5. God could not have created a world with such goods without allowing at least for the possibility and in some cases the actuality of certain evils. But

6. Humans have freely chosen to do what is wrong on some occasions. But

7. The Deity is not responsible for their bad choices. Therefore,

8. The presence of evil in the world does not imply that God cannot be both all-powerful and all-good.

To the objection that the Deity could have created the universe so that everyone both always acted freely and always chose the right, Flew responds that the Free Will Defense holds that such a suggestion is contradictory.

If the Free Will Defense is a rebuttal to the argument for the presumption of atheism, how can this rebuttal in turn be countered? Flew proceeds. It appears that a universe created so that humans always choose what is right would be one in which human choices are always determined – at least when it comes to choosing between right and wrong, and thus not free. It is precisely this disjunction, no free will, i.e., determinism *or* at least the possibility of evil freely chosen, that Flew wants to question. Is it exclusive disjunction or are both Free Will and Determinism possible together? As Flew puts it, is it "Free will *and* determinism *or* free will *or* determinism?" (1984, p. 83, italics added). The former is the Compatibility Thesis, the latter the Incompatibility Thesis (p. 84). Flew replies that answering this question requires distinguishing two senses of free will, a technical philosophical sense and an ordinary sense. On the technical notion, also called libertarian free will, an action is free just in case it is completely uncaused (and thus unpredictable). By contrast, on the non-technical notion, actions can be either freely chosen or done under constraint (p. 84). To say that an action was chosen freely means that the agent could have done otherwise. On the technical philosophical sense, the claim of universal causal determinism rules out any free will. But this consequence does not follow for the non-technical concept (p. 84). Having drawn this distinction, Flew turns to the question of whether the Deity's creating a world in which human beings were free but always did what is right is somehow contradictory. For a libertarian incompatibilist, the answer to the question is yes. A free action is either uncaused or has a causal ancestor which is uncaused. So free actions are not determined; *a fortiori* is not possible that all actions are free yet determined to go right.

Flew now thrusts his main point. Is the libertarian notion of free will coherent with the core theist notion that "All created beings ... are always utterly dependent upon God as their sustaining cause" (p. 88). Flew asks "Just how is the idea of God as the sustaining cause of all creation to be reconciled with the insistence that this creation includes uncaused causes" (p. 88)? Reconciling these two notions seems impossible. Can the compatibilist show that there is no contradiction in claiming that God can create a world in which humans are free in the compatibilist sense but will always chose to do right? The compatibilists' argument encounters a similar problem as the libertarians'. Both run up against Divine omnipotence. Consider an action we regard as free in the compatibilist sense. Flew comments, "It is surely not inconsistent to say that God is the ultimate sufficient condition of all [voluntary movements]" (p. 93). What Aquinas and Luther said can be applied to actions free in the compatibilist sense. Aquinas says that "We receive from God not only the power of willing but its employment also." Upon introspection, a human may recognize no cause compelling an action he regards as free (could have done otherwise) but God is still its sufficient condition. But what does "sufficient condition" mean in this context? Flew holds that it is not the relation of deterministic cause to effect seen in the natural world. God is not a puppeteer and a creature a puppet whose action is bound to happen. This would mean that a person's recognition that he could have acted otherwise is illusory. Nor is the relation one of receiving a compelling motive to perform some action. One could chose to do differently but given the motive would not, perhaps for moral reasons. But, Flew maintains, we are aware of no such causing by the Deity.

Rather, Flew holds, that the relation of Creator to creature involves causing in the way an agent "might, by direct physiological manipulations, ensure that someone [else] performs whatever actions [the agent] determines, and that the actions of this creature would nevertheless be genuine actions, such that it could always be truly said that in the fundamental sense he could have done otherwise than he did" (p. 99). One can only wish that Flew had given us one or more examples of the physiological manipulation he had in mind. Perhaps mythology can give us an example. Brangone gave Tristan a love potion. Upon taking it, Tristan developed a strong passion for Isolde, which led him to act improperly with her. Taking the potion did not mech-anistically or deterministically cause him to act as he did. His loyalty to King Mark may have given him a strong motive to resist his passion. The love potion provided the physiological motivation to behave improperly with Isolde. But if the Deity causes human actions in this way, is it fair to say that the Deity has no responsibility for human actions of wrongdoing? In this sense, the Deity is still the Great Manipulator. Flew comments, "It would be absurd, even monstrous, to suggest that the person who is in this third way caused to decide thus rather than thus, instead of the [agent] who caused him to decide, ought to be called to account, perhaps to eternal account, for the sense of the decision" (p. 99).

In the light of this third sense, what may we say about the cogency of the Free-will Defense? To the question of why the Deity could not create free humans who *always* and not just sometimes do what is right, the Free-will defender responded that the question presupposes an inconsistency. But in this third sense of cause, the Deity could manipulate humans always to do what is right, yet still be open to doing otherwise than what they actually did. One who handed over his money to an armed rob-ber could do otherwise, even though it meant being shot. But as Flew puts it, if the Deity as sustainer of the universe causes all human actions in this sense of cause, can humans be justly held culpable for these actions when they do wrong? Is it fair to say that the Deity has no responsibility for human actions of wrong-doing? The Free-will defender cannot maintain that in this third sense it is contradictory to say that God could have created free agents who always did what is right. However, in light of the evil in the world it is impossible to say on this interpretation that God is all good. Either the Free Will Defense denies God's universal sovereignty – incompatible with theism – or makes God a responsible partner in evil – again incompatible with the-ism. The Free-will Defense does not work and the incoherence of maintaining that the Deity is all powerful and all good still stands. That is, the presumption for atheism still stands.

2. A CRITICAL QUESTION FOR FLEW'S CASE THAT THEISM IS INCOHERENT

In asserting that there is a presumption for atheism, Flew is understanding theism as classical theism – God is omnipotent, omniscient, and all good. But is classical theism the only form of theism? If there are theistic alternatives to classical theism, are they all incoherent simply because they are theistic? Flew's phrase "the presumption of atheism" suggests theism *per se* is incoherent. But there are alternative conceptions of the Deity, and one cannot dismiss them all as incoherent just by showing that one is incoherent. To counter Flew's argument, it is sufficient to find just one coherent alternative. We shall consider the concept of God as Creative-Responsive Love as characterized by Cobb and Griffin (1976), and deriving from the process theism of Whitehead and Hartshorne. Characterizing the Deity as responsive already marks a distinct break from classical theism which ascribes immutability to the Deity as a corollary of omnipotence. *Prima facie*, immutability suggests that the Deity does not change at all. If so, the Deity would also be impassible, immune to being affected by any outside factor. But then the Deity would be non-responsive. By contraposition, then, responsiveness implies passibility and thus mutability. But, we may agree, if the Deity is passible, then the Deity is not omnipotent, at least in the way classical theism understands omnipotence. Why? Perhaps we can get a clue through Mill's referring to infinite power in discussing "the impossible problem of reconciling infinite benevolence with infinite power in the Creator of such a world as this" (*Three Essays on Religion*, quoted in Flew and MacIntyre 1955, p. 144). How may we understand "infinite power"? Let us suggest "overwhelming power." Could a being of overwhelming power be affected by anything external to that being? It would seem only if the being "let his guard down," i.e., only by giving up some of his power, at least for the moment, and thus being less than omnipotent. But if the Deity is immutable, this is just nonsense. So omnipotence together with immutability implies non-responsiveness. The Deity of Creative-Responsive Love is not omnipotent. But what then of Flew's charge that the concept of God is ostensibly incoherent?

This charge is dissolved. There is no inconsistency in saying that the Deity of Creative-Responsive Love is all-benevolent. We would expect this true of the Deity. But if the Deity is not omnipotent in the sense of being able to bring about any non-contradictory state of affairs, there is no contradiction in saying that there are some things the Deity cannot do such as eliminate all evil. Unless one can sustain a charge of incoherence on other grounds, the concept of God as Creative-Responsive Love is coherent. Giving up omnipotence allows making further points in a case for the coherence of process theism.

Excluding omnipotence from the Deity's attributes does not mean that the Deity has no influence. Rather, the influence is persuasion. Cobb and Griffin, following Whitehead, characterize Divine persuasion as the Deity's giving not only each person but each actuality in the world an "impulse" to actualize the best possibility open to it, given its concrete situation" (Peterson *et al.* 1996, p. 140). The actuality is under no compulsion or other determination to actualize this impulse and is free to actualize alternative possibilities. Because the impulse is the best possibility and the actuality is free to actualize alternative possibilities, the impulse is a means of persuasion, not of determination.

We may press another question for the coherence of process theism. Is granting actualities the freedom to realize less than optimal possibilities for themselves consistent with perfect benevolence? Surely, we can expect the Deity to foresee the *possibility* that those beings would go wrong and indeed the extent and degree this would bring about. Why should a perfectly good

Deity risk that possibility? We can offer three responses. First, if we pay heed to our own moral sense, we may recognize that freedom has a very high value. The loss of freedom is not to be outweighed by a plurality of other goods. Besides the testimony of our own moral sense, you have the corroboration of countless others who place a very high value on freedom.

Secondly, as Cobb and Griffin point out, "We can gain both from psychologists and from our own experience, that if we truly love others we do not seek to control them" (1996, p. 140). Is this true of the Deity likewise? Finally, if the Deity's risking the freedom of creatures has led to evils, is it logically impossible to say that the Deity lacks the power to outweigh or overcome those evils? Consider what Philo and Demea say at the end of the discussion of evil in Hume's *Dialogues on Natural Religion.* "This world is but a point in comparison of the universe; this life but a moment in comparison of eternity. The present evil phenomena, therefore, are rectified in other regions, and in some future period of existence. And the eyes of men, being then opened to larger views of things, see the whole connection of general laws, and trace, with adoration, the benevolence and rectitude of the Deity through all the mazes and intricacies of his providence" (reprinted in Peterson *et al.* 1996, pp. 240-41).

Process theism, by giving up omnipotence as an attribute of the Deity, allows for a concept of God consistent with the existence of evil and is not incoherent. Hence there is not a presumption for atheism in general but at best a presumption against classical theism. As is well known, towards the end of his life, Flew rejected atheism for deism, which is neither a form of classical or process theism, What is his argument then in defense of an alternative form of theism?

3. FLEW TAKES UP THE BURDEN OF PROOF FOR THEISM

In *There Is A God* (2007), Flew explicitly identifies three facts about the world as evidence for a "presumption for theism." These are "the laws of nature, life with its teleological organization and the existence of the universe" (2007, p. 155). His argument is a convergence of three inference to best explanation arguments. He states explicitly that these three facts "can only be explained in the light of an Intelligence that explains both its own existence and that of the world" (p. 155). Flew asks first "Who wrote the laws of nature?" His answer constitutes a version of the design argument. Flew answers that the origin of this order of regularity or symmetry in nature" (p. 96) is the Mind of God" (p. 96). To defend this assertion, he assembles quotes from a number of prominent scientific authorities including Einstein, Plank, Heisenberg, Schrodinger, Dirac, and Hawking from the twentieth century, and Darwin from the nineteenth. For Einstein, God has manifested himself in the laws of nature as their transcendent source, indeed the source of rationality in nature, "reason incarnate in existence" (1973, p. 49; quoted in (2007), p. 102). Einstein did not simply give intellectual assent to this view. For him it was akin to a religious conviction. Dirac asserted that "God is a mathematician of a very high order and He used advanced mathematics in constructing the universe" (1963; quoted in Flew 2007, pp. 105-106). Darwin held that it was impossible to look at the universe as a product of "blind chance or necessity," but rather of an intelligent First Cause, whose intelligence is analogous to the intelligence of man (1958, pp. 92-93; see Flew 2007, p. 106). Again, Flew cites the contemporary expositor of science, Paul Davies, who asks "How is it that we have a set of laws that drive featureless gases to life, consciousness, and intelligence? (1995, quoted in Flew, 2007, p. 108). We cannot take all this as brute fact. There is a deeper meaning behind it (p. 108).

Flew holds that Intelligence or Spirit is not only the best explanation for the laws ordering nature, but also for a discernable direction in the development or evolution of the natural world. Nature appears ordered to the emergence of rational, reflective conscious life. Flew puts the question this way: "Did the universe know we were coming?" The positive answer affirms the anthropic principle. It is well known that if the value of any of at least twenty constants had differed ever so slightly, the emergence of life, in some cases the emergence of the world as we know it, would have been impossible. There are two possible explanations of this fact – either the universe is the work of Intelligence or the cosmos is a multiverse, a plurality of causally independent universes governed by different natural laws. We just happen to live in a universe conducive to the emergence of intelligent life. That there are many universes, that the dice have been thrown many times, perhaps infinitely many times, raises the probability that intelligent life will emerge in at least one universe.

What may we say to the hypothesis that our universe is one of the lucky ones, hospitable to life? Let us take the claim of the plurality of universes in its most extreme form: If a universe is logically possible, it exists and thus is included in the multiverse. Although it follows that every possible universe will be in the multiverse, including our universe, as Flew points out, this explains nothing. We just have all these universes around. Why? The question is unanswerable. "If we are trying to understand why the universe is bio-friendly, we are not helped by being told that all universes exist" (2007, p. 118). Could the multiverse operate by laws which determine which laws govern particular universes? But this simply pushes the question up one level. Who wrote the laws of the multiverse? At the deepest level, the attempt to give a purely naturalistic explanation of the laws of nature appealing to no Intelligence seems forced to concede that there is no explanation. The universe or the multiverse is simply a brute fact. Flew concludes, "Multiverse or not, we still have to come to terms with the origin of the laws of nature. And the only viable explanation here is the divine Mind" (p. 121). We add that if any hypothesis is *ad hoc*, the multiverse hypothesis is. No causal connection holds between any of the universes within the multiverse. Hence we do not, indeed cannot, have any evidence even of their existence. If there is no causal connection between any of these universes, how could our universe receive any information from any of them?

Besides the universe's having laws, there is a further fact requiring explanation. Why did life develop in the universe? Flew's answer presents his second inference to best explanation. Flew argues that what is characteristic of living organisms is teleology. Organisms and their parts display functions. By contrast, non-living matter has no ends. So how did end or goal-oriented organisms, including having the goal of self-replication, rise from non-goal-oriented matter? Flew sees two hypotheses presenting themselves – a completely naturalistic, materialist explanation or the agency of some Intelligence. As of Flew's writing in 2007, there was no naturalistic explanation for the first emergence of self-reproducing life forms. An additional related fact calling for explanation is the emergence of biological information. In Flew's words, what is the origin "of the coding and information processing that is central to all life-forms"? (p. 126). Can this be explained in a way that makes no reference to facts about codes, languages, or communication? How does coded chemistry arise from totally uncoded matter? Referring to Paul Davies, Flew points out that "A gene is nothing but a set of coded instructions.... These genetic instructions are not the kind of information you find in thermodynamics and statistical mechanics; rather they constitute *semantic* information.... They have a specific *meaning*" (pp. 128-29, italics added). How then did semantic information arise from mindless molecules?

As with the question of why the universe manifests physical laws, Flew quotes a number of scientists who have pondered the origin of life and its genetic coding. These scientists affirm that we have no current understanding of the emergence of life from non-life. Flew concludes, "The only satisfactory explanation for the origin of such "end-directed, self-replicating life as we see on earth is an infinitely intelligent Mind" (p. 132).

Beyond the teleological questions of order in the universe and the emergence of life, the cosmological question asks why is there a universe at all? Flew admits that in *The Presumption of Atheism* (1972) he regarded the existence of the world as a brute fact. There is no explanation for it. It just *is*. His argument was that any attempt at explanation was futile. "I did not see how anything within our universe can be either known or reasonably conjectured to be pointing to some transcendent reality behind, above, or beyond. So why not take the universe and its most fundamental features as the ultimate fact?" (2007, p. 135). A major scientific development, however, led him to reconsider – the advent of big bang cosmology. This theory suggests that the universe had a beginning. It was not something which was eternally there as a brute fact. But if the universe had a beginning, what caused it? Flew remarks that a statement made by Stephen Hawking casts doubt on a purely physical explanation. "One may say that time had a beginning at the big bang, in the sense that earlier times simply would not be defined" (1988, p. 9; quoted in 2007, p. 138). If so, and the cause of an event temporally precedes the event, the question of a cause of the big bang would be meaningless.

Some scientists have speculated that the big bang was not the radical beginning of the universe, a coming into being from absolute nothing, but rather that the universe came from empty space. Flew points out that "'Empty space is not nothing, but rather an 'identifiable particular,' a something that is already there" (p. 141). But such an explanation raises further questions.

Did empty space give rise to the universe in a law-like way or was the rising simply a brute fact? If law-like, then whence come those laws and whence is that empty space? Other physical questions do not answer the cosmological question either. If the universe arose from nothing understood to be "a fluctuation in the vacuum of larger space" or "a chaotic space-time foam with fantastically high energy density" (p. 142), the cosmological question still has not been answered. The mere fact of laws and events does not rule out asking for their explanation.

If the big bang is not the absolute beginning, could one postulate that there is an infinite regression of states, each state being preceded by an "earlier" state, its cause? Each state, then, would have an explanation. Is there a need to look for an explanation of the whole series? In a very different scientific context, David Hume pressed that there was no such need. If each member of the series is explained by the previous member, what more is there to explain? Why should one think that we need an explanation for the entire series as a whole? Flew cites Swinburne who points out that the picture of an infinite regression of contingent causes leaves the infinite series a brute fact. Why is there this infinite series? Here again, the hypothesis of a Divine Intelligence gives an explanation.

We have now reviewed Flew's three arguments for the conclusion that the best explanation for why the universe has laws, why life has emerged, and why there is a universe at all is the agency of a Divine Intelligence. Two questions arise at this point, Are each of the three explanations best explanations? Has Flew discharged his burden of proof to show that the best explanation of the universe is an Intelligence? We address these questions in the next section.

4. CRITICAL EVALUATION OF FLEW'S ARGUMENT FOR A DIVINE INTELLIGENCE

4.1 The argument from the laws of nature and their fine tuning for life

This particular argument raises two questions of its own. First, Flew quotes a number of scientists to support his conclusion. But the scientists are physicists. The conclusion is a proposition in metaphysics. Is this a fallacious appeal to authority? Second, is an Intelligence the best explanation for why nature is governed by laws, in particular, laws which have furnished a universe satisfying the necessary conditions for the emergence of life? First, following Coady in (1992), we may distinguish two types of authority-conferring fields – formal and informal. Typically, a branch of knowledge, such as an empirical science, counts as a formal field. The field has a set subject matter and specified criteria for certifying an expert in the field. By contrast, a skilled practical craft or an area involving appraisal may constitute an informal field. I submit that the scientists whom Flew quotes are experts in both formal and informal fields. No doubt physics is a formal field and the authorities Flew quotes are certified authorities in physics. But as research scientists do they not also have a personal acquaintance with their fields analogous to the acquaintance artisans or appraisers have with theirs? Consider Einstein's statement: "Everyone who is seriously engaged in the pursuit of science becomes convinced that the laws of nature manifest the existence of a spirit vastly superior to that of men, and one in the face of which we with our modest powers must feel humble" (Jammer 1999, p. 193; quoted in Flew 2007, p. 102). Do not those "seriously engaged in the pursuit of science" become not only authorities in their formal fields but also in the informal field constituting their practice of that science and its wider implications? Is Einstein's view that these laws of nature are "reason incarnate" any less an expression of informal expertise than a jeweler's appraisal of a gem? Can a challenger maintain that

Einstein's approach is simply his subjective opinion when a consensus of physicists from Newton to Heisenberg have become convinced that the laws of nature express "the Mind of God" (p. 96)?

Is Flew's argument a cogent inference to best explanation? As presented in textbooks such as Copi and Cohen's (2005) and Govier's (2014), the scheme of an inference to best explanation has three premises and one conclusion:

1. A surprising event or condition E has occurred.

2. If hypothesis H holds, then E should hold as a matter of course.

3. H is the best explanation of E.
   Therefore

4. H is true.

Does Flew's argument from natural laws and anthropic coincidences satisfy (1), (2), and (3)? First, who will dispute that nature has regularities and deeper investigations of nature arouse for many admiration for the natural order. This order is surprising. It calls for an explanation. The first premise is obviously acceptable. Secondly, if this universe were designed by an Intelligence, we would expect it to display order. Intelligence expresses itself in order and purpose. Again, if I find that a number of conditions have been satisfied, each with a low probability of occurring but together assuring that the necessary conditions for some complex configuration will come about, would not the hypothesis that this result was intended by an intelligence with purpose explain this configuration?

Thirdly, how may one justify that a given explanation is the best and does Flew's argument here qualify? There are three specific criteria for evaluating explanations: simplicity, uniformity (i.e., compatibility with confirmed results) and explanatory scope. Relevance and testability are preliminary criteria. That

Intelligence explains order shows that the hypothesis of an Intelligence is relevant to explaining order. But is the explanation testable? If the divine Intelligence is outside the natural order, how can there be any observation and any test? However, do we need to observe the divine Intelligence to test this hypothesis? If we had a criterion for identifying via observation when intelligence was involved in causing some event, process, or condition, we would have a way of testing the hypothesis that an intelligence of some order was involved. Dembski in (Dembski and Kushiner, 2001) presents an argument that the presence of intelligence can be scientifically identified. Identifying design involves the complexity-specification criterion. There are three components to the criterion: contingency – the existence of the designed object does not violate natural law, but natural law does not require it to come about; complexity – the object is not so simple that it could have occurred by chance; and specification – "the object exhibits the type of pattern characteristic of intelligence" (Dembski in Dembski and Kushiner 2001; reprinted in Pojman and Rea 2008, p. 450). What do these components involve? Suppose someone thoroughly shuffled the diamonds in a set of playing cards and then, without seeing the cards drawn, lined up the thirteen cards face down. Clearly this sequence of cards is contingent. No natural regularity or directive purpose had anything to do with it. The sequence is also complex. The probability that someone by chance would identify the first card is $1/13$, the first three in order $1/2{,}197$, and the first seven $1/62{,}748{,}517$. Clearly, the more cards in the sequence, the greater its complexity. As the length of the sequence increases, the probability that one could by chance identify the cards in order decreases dramatically. If anyone correctly identified the first seven, we would have little doubt that he had insider "intelligence." To warrant an inference of design by intelligence, an event requires sufficiently high complexity. But high complexity is not sufficient. The sequence of the first seven cards drawn might exhibit no pattern. But ace, two, three, four, five, six, seven is detachable (p. 452). "Given an event (whose design is in question) and a pattern describing it, would we be able to construct that pattern if we had no knowledge of which event occurred? ... If so, the pattern is detachable from the event" (p. 452).

How does the complexity-specification criterion warrant an inference to design? Intelligent agency involves choice between or among various possibilities. What justifies claiming that an intelligent agent has made a choice in a given case? The case must be sufficiently complex to rule out that the choice was made by chance. If the case exhibits a pattern which is one among a number which could be specified in advance, then an agent has made a choice or the case was designed (p. 455). "In general, to recognize intelligent agency we must observe an actualization of one among several competing possibilities, note which possibilities were ruled out, and then be able to specify the possibility that was actualized" (p. 456). Dembski's discussion implies that an hypothesis of intelligent agency is testable by asking a series of questions open to empirically based answers. We observe an event (or condition or state of affairs). Given our knowledge of natural laws, was this event necessitated by antecedent events? If no, did the event have a low probability of occurring? If yes, could one have antecedently specified the pattern of the event?

How well does the hypothesis that the laws of nature and the anthropic coincidences are the result of Divine Intelligence satisfy the explanatory conditions of simplicity, uniformity, and explanatory scope? Govier (2014) reminds us that in answering these questions our goal should be to identify the best available hypothesis, not necessarily the best conceivable hypothesis. In judging whether an explanation is the best available, then, we should look at the hypothesis together with its rivals which are actually on the table. Flew entertains alternative hypotheses concerning the laws of nature. First, they are human constructs, not objectively true of nature. Secondly, they are brute facts having no explanation. Thirdly, they are the laws of one in a multiverse of universes. The human construction hypothesis may be discounted for its lack of acceptance by practicing physicists. Students of science point this out. Paul Davies has said that "Physicists will not believe that Newton's inverse law of gravitation is a cultural creation" (Flew 2007, p. 107). Saying that the laws of nature are brute facts is resigning from giving an explanation. Any hypothesis which affords some explanation is more plausible on the ground of explanatory scope. The multiverse hypothesis likewise in the end offers no explanation. *Why* is our universe one of the lucky ones? Just saying that the universe is lucky explains nothing. As with the brute fact hypothesis, the multiverse hypothesis fails to give an explanation. Since there is no evidence for these alternative universes, the multiverse hypothesis may also be discounted on the uniformity criterion.

Finally, we can pose a dilemma to the multiverse hypothesis. Either all logically possible universes are included in the multiverse – there are infinitely many – or only some of the logically possible universes are included. But if there is no empirical evidence of other universes in a possibly finite multiverse, *a fortiori* there is no evidence for an infinity of them. If less than all the logically possible universes are included in the multiverse, why were just these universes included?

Are there any other hypotheses which deserve to be put on the table? Why speak of *the* divine Mind? Does Flew's argument justify that the divine Mind is unique? As is well known, Aristotle at one point postulated fifty-five unmoved movers. We can argue that Flew is justified in hypothesizing just one on simplicity grounds. Certainly, one divine Mind is a much simpler hypothesis than fifty-five. Unless there were evidence for a plurality of divine Minds, the hypothesis of one divine Mind is more plausible. Hence, the divine Mind hypothesis seems the best available explanation of the fact that the universe is ordered by laws and has an anthropic orientation.

4.2 The argument from the emergence of life

What may we say of Flew's argument that an infinitely intelligent Mind is the best explanation for the emergence of life from non-living matter? Again, we find that any charge that Flew's argument involves a fallacious appeal to authority without merit. The scientists Flew cites are authorities about the current limitations of their disciplines to explain the origin of teleological, self-reproducing, code interpreting life. Scientists do not have an account of the quantum leap from non-life to life. Hence, there is no accepted alternative naturalistic explanation on the table to compete with the divine Mind hypothesis.

How successfully does this hypothesis satisfy the three criteria for best explanation? Is it consistent with previous explanations? Our answer basically repeats points made with the previous argument. We know that intelligent agents may produce objects exhibiting design, system, purpose. So the hypothesized agency of the Divine Mind is consistent with how intelligent agents behave.

Flew briefly mentions that some scientists have proposed naturalistic theories of the origin of life. "Protobiologists are now well able to produce theories of the evolution of the first living matter and that several of these theories are consistent with all the so-far-confirmed scientific evidence" (2007, pp. 123-24). But this response is all he says of these protobiological theories, except that "The present physicists' view of the age of the universe gives too little time for these theories of abiogenesis to get the job done" (p. 124). Here Flew gives us not an argument but a report that an argument can be made. There is one point to note, however. Should an argument successfully show that an intelligent Mind is the best explanation for the origin of life, these considerations would increase the explanatory scope of the Divine Mind hypothesis. Not only may it be invoked to explain why there are laws for inanimate matter but also the emergence of life.

4.3 The argument from the existence of the universe as a whole

To show that a Divine Intelligence is the best available explanation for the universe as a whole requires a case for why the universe is neither eternal nor the product of purely natural forces. In this connection, Flew considers three hypotheses proposed by scientists and argues against each of them, the multiverse, endless series of vacuum fluctuations, and self-contained universe hypothesis. We have already discussed shortcomings of the multiverse hypothesis. Regarding the endless series of vacuum fluctuations hypothesis, Flew's argument needs to be constructed from one of his quotes from Stephen Hawking. "One may say that time had a beginning in the big bang, in the sense that earlier times would not be defined" (Hawking 1988, p. 9; quoted in Flew 2007, p. 138). (Thus, to talk about what caused the big bang and thus temporally preceded it would be meaningless.) Hence there could not be a naturalistic causal explanation of the big bang. *A fortiori* what sense could we make of an infinite series of universes each launched by a big bang, assuming the fluctuations involved big bangs. If these considerations be sound, the successive universe – quantum fluctuation hypothesis does not furnish an explanation. At best, we could say that the hypothesis renders this series a brute fact.

Thirdly, what of Stephen Hawking's proposal of a self-contained universe? Flew quotes Hawking, "If the universe is really self-contained. having no boundary or edge, it would have neither beginning nor end, it would simply be. What place, then, for a creator?" (Hawking, 1988. quoted in Flew 2007, pp. 137-38) But what may we say of causal sequences in this self-contained universe? That a self-contained universe has no beginning (nor end) does not rule out causal sequences within the self-contained universe. Do these sequences have explanations? At this point, Flew considers Hume's critique of the cosmological argument. To those who argued that an infinitely receding sequence still requires an explanation of the sequence itself, Hume replies that this requirement is wrong headed. If each member of a causal sequence is preceded by a cause, each element in the sequence has an explanation and there is no need to seek further causes.

Flew responds that such an infinite chain, even if it were the entire universe, would be a brute fact, not an explanation. But Flew is unwilling to leave the argument there. Quoting Swinburne, Flew says "It is very unlikely that a universe would exist uncaused" (Swinburne, p. 102; quoted in Flew, pp. 144-45). But why should we accept Swinburne's assertion here? Flew presents it without argument.

Finding a reason for Swinburne's claim leads us to the Principle of Sufficient Reason, PSR for short. As formulated by Rowe in (1978, p. 20) it states "There must be an explanation (a) of the existence of any being, and (b) of any positive fact whatever." How does PSR support Flew's claim that the universe is caused by a self-existent being? If a being has a cause, it is either self-caused or caused by another. PSR does not rule out infinitely regressing causal sequences but, should there be such a sequence, it requires an explanation. Why are there all these dependent beings, the elements of the sequence? Each being in the series might be explained by its predecessor in the series, but what is the explanation of the positive fact that there is this chain?

But why should one accept PSR? Rowe finds two proposed answers wanting. Is the statement intuitively true? If so, one would expect near universal acceptance from those who sufficiently considered the principle. But no such consensus holds. The other proposed answer holds that although PSR "is not known to be true, it is nevertheless a presupposition of reason, a basic assumption that rational people make, whether or not they reflect sufficiently to become aware of the assumption" (1978, p. 27). But, as Rowe points out, just because PSR is presupposed and assumed does not imply that it is true. We do not know PSR to be true, hence we cannot argue from it that a self-existent being exists.

Argumentation theory provides an additional way to understand the Principle of Sufficient Reason. We need to specify first the difference between a presupposition and a presumption. Walton in (2019) illustrates presuppositions through complex questions. "Why have you registered to vote as an Independent?" A presupposition is retrospective, referring back to a statement already accepted or conceded. By contrast, a presumption is prospective. A proponent may use it as a premise, unless or until it is challenged. We have to go further. As Rescher puts it, presumptions possess "significant probative weight" (1977, p. 31). They stand until "being overthrown by significantly weighty countervailing considerations" (p. 31).

Presumption bears directly on Rowe's rejection of the Principle of Sufficient Reason on the grounds that we do not have reason to accept it. "Why, after all, should we accept the idea that every being and every positive fact must have an explanation?" (Rowe 2001, pp. 26-27). If we do not know that the Principle of Sufficient Reason is true, we do not know that Swinburne's claim that an uncaused universe is very unlikely to be true. But do we have to *know* that fact to recognize a presumption for the Principle of Sufficient Reason? Is there a *presumption* for PSR? In light of Rescher's discussion of the relation between plausibility and presumption in (1977), the argument is straightforward. First, "Presumption favors the most *plausible* of rival alternatives – when indeed there is one" (1977, p. 38). Various principles indicate the most plausible alternatives in different contexts. We may appeal to the Uniformity Principle here: "In the absence of explicit counterindications, a thesis about unscrutinized cases which conforms to a patterned uniformity obtaining among the data at our disposal with respect to scrutinized cases – a uniformity that is in fact present throughout these data – is more plausible than any of its regularity-discordant contraries" (1977, p. 40). Contrast the following with the Principle of Sufficient Reason: "There is at least one being or at least one fact for which there is no explanation." Given the Uniformity Principle, which thesis is more plausible? Clearly, it is the Principle of Sufficient Reason. Hence, there is a presumption for Swinburne's claim that the universe is caused. Hence, there is a presumption for the conclusion of Flew's argument "that the existence of the universe … can only be explained in light of an Intelligence that explains both its own existence and that of the world" (2007, p. 155). Insofar as Flew's argument rests on the Principle of Sufficient Reason, that principle is more plausible than its negation and thus there is a presumption for it. So both on the grounds of the laws of nature and the existence of the universe, Flew has shown that the theistic explanation is the best available explanation.

5. HAS FLEW SUCCESSFULLY SHIFTED THE BURDEN OF PROOF TO THE ATHEIST?

Flew has not shifted the burden of proof to the atheist who simply denies that the God of classical theism exists. He makes almost no reference to the Deity's being omnibenevolent or even good. He regards this question as independent of the question of the existence of the Intelligence he wishes to call the Deity. Flew is in no way affirming the God of classical theism, which he found to be incoherent. He speaks of the ultimate Reality as "a self-existent, immutable, immaterial, omnipotent, and omniscient Being" (2007, p. 155). Do Flew's inference to best explanation arguments show even this? To be the source of the laws of nature, teleologically oriented life, and even the universe as a whole, does this Intelligence have to be both omnipotent and omniscient, or be immutable and immaterial?

What then of shifting the burden of proof to the atheist who asserts that there is no God at all? May Flew's Intelligence be regarded as the Deity? Although omnipotence, omniscience, and omnibenevolence may be the "big three" divine attributes, there are many more. Possession of one of these attributes is a sign of Deity. They suggest how one may personally relate to what one apprehends as the presence of the Deity. Consider infinity, understood as predicating that God cannot be measured (Macquarrie, 1966, p. 205). Measuring is a first step in mastering. Can any sense be associated with mastering the Intelligence which is the source of order in the universe? The very thought is redolent with hubris. Consider Einstein's words: "The laws of nature manifest the existence of a spirit vastly superior to that of men, and one in the face of which we with our modest powers must feel humble" (Jammer 1999, p. 93; reprinted in Flew 2007, p. 102). How can one feel humble toward what one would master? The features of the universe such as its operating according to laws, which Flew seeks to explain as the activity of the Intelligence, do not suggest a development which is willy-nilly, but rather of constancy to a purpose. This constancy can be characterized by immutability, another traditional Divine attribute. A further attribute is not being constrained by any external factors. What sense can be associated with saying that the Intelligence is or has been constrained in constructing the universe? In authoring the laws of nature, what was there to constrain the Intelligence? But if the Intelligence possesses these attributes. and they can be apprehended to signify Deity, is the burden of proof then on the atheist either to rebut Flew's argument to an Intelligence or to show that these attributes are *not* signs of Deity? If so, then Flew has shifted the burden of proof to the atheist to show that there is no God.

REFERENCES

Coady, C. A. J. 1992. *Testimony: A Philosophical Study*. Oxford: Clarendon Press.

Copi, Inving M. and Cohen, Carl. 2005. *Introduction to Logic*, 12th ed. Upper Saddle River, NJ: Pearson Prentice Hall.

Cobb, John B. and Griffin, David Ray. 1976. "God is Creative-Responsive Love." in Peterson et al., 1996, pp. 134-40.

Darwin, Charles. 1958. *The Autobiography of Charles Darwin*. London: Collins.

Davies, Paul. 1995. Templeton Prize Address. http://aca.mq.edu.au/PaulDavies/prize_address.htm.

Dembski, William and Kushiner, James (eds.). 2001. *Signs of Intelligence: Understanding Intellignt Design*. Grand Rapids: MI: Brazos Press.

Dirac, Paul A. M. 1963. "The Evolution of the Physicist's Picture of Nature." *Scientific American* 208.

Einstein, Albert. *Ideas and Opinions*. 1973. New York: Dell.

Flew, Antony. 1972. "The Presumption of Atheism." *Canadian Journal of Philosophy* 22, 29-46. Reprinted in Flew, 1984, pp. 13-30.

Flew, Antony. 1984. *God, Freedom, and Immortality: A Critical Analysis*. Amherst, NY: Prometheus Books.

Flew, Antony. 2007. *There is a God: How the World's Most Notorious Atheist Changed His Mind*. New York: Harper Collins Publishers.

Flew, Antony. 1955. "Divine Omnipotence and Human Freedom." in Flew and MacIntyre, 1955, pp. 144-69.

Flew, Antony and MacIntyre, Alasdair, 1955. *New Essays in Philosophical Theology*. London: SCM Press Ltd.

Govier, Trudy. 2014. *A Practical Study of Argument*, enhanced edition, 7th ed. Boston: Cengage Learning.

Hansen, Hans V., Kauffeld, Fred, Freeman, James B., and Bermejo-Luque, Lilian (eds.). 2019. *Presumptions and Burdens of Proof*. Tuscaloosa, AL: The University of Alabama Press.

Hawking, Stephen. 1988. *A Brief History of Time*. Boston: Bantam.

Jammer, Max. 1999. *Einstein and Religion*. Princeton, NJ: Princeton University Press.

Macquarrie, John. 1966. *Principles of Christian Theology* 2nd ed. New York: Charles Scribner's Sons.

Peterson, Michael, Hasker, William, Reichenbach, Bruce, and Basinger, David (eds.). 1996. *Philosophy of Religion: Selected Readings*. New York: Oxford University Press.

Pojman, Louis P. and Rea, Michael. 2008. *Philosophy of Religion: An Anthology*, 5th ed. Belmont, CA: Thomson Wadsworth.

Rescher, Nicholas. 1977. *Dialectics: A Controversy-Oriented Approach to the Theory of Knowledge*. Albany: State University of New York Press.

Rowe, William L. 1978. *Philosophy of Religion: An Introduction*, 3rd ed. Belmont, CA: Wadsworth/Thomson Learning.

Walton, Douglas. 2019. "The Speech Act of Presumption by Reversal of Burden of Proof." in Hansen et al, 2019, pp. 221-23.

ABOUT THE AUTHOR: James B. Freeman is Professor of Philosophy Emeritus at Hunter College, City University of New York. His research has centered on logic and argumentation theory. His books include *Acceptable Premises: An Epistemic Approach to an Informal Logic Problem* and *Argument Structure: Representation and Theory*, along with many papers. He is co-editor, with Hans V. Hansen, Lilian Bermejo-Luque, and the late Fred Kauffeld of *Presumptions and Burdens of Proof*.

CHAPTER 9.

HOW TO DEFINE AN INFORMAL LOGIC

LEO GROARKE

ABSTRACT: In its mature form, formal logic is understood as a discipline which is the study of not one, but many, formal logics (and, more broadly, families of formal logics). I argue that it is time to understand informal logic in a similar way, recognizing it as the study of not one, but many, informal logics. Building on Hansen's work on the methods of informal logic, I propose a systematic account of the field which allows us to define, identify and compare many distinct informal logics. These logics include many logics developed in both teaching and research. Approaching the field in this way allows us to better understand the structure of informal logic as a discipline, and the differences that distinguish the various logics that it studies.

KEYWORDS: informal logic, informal logics, methods of informal logic, formal logic, BLAST definition

1. INTRODUCTION

Half a century after its beginnings, informal logic remains a young discipline. In its early years, its development was motivated by the belief that the analysis and assessment of real life arguments requires a logic other than classical formal logic (or, more generally, what Johnson labeled "FDL": Formal Deductive

Logic). Its continued evolution is less dramatically opposed to formal logic, but it still consists of attempts to create a logic which can be used to analyze, assess and model the kinds of argument one finds in public discourse, interpersonal exchange, and non-technical discussions of law, science, medicine, and other fields.

Hansen's "Are there methods of informal logic?" (2019) is a poignant attempt to clarify the nature of informal logic and the ways in which it differs from (and is similar to) its formal cousin. In this essay I focus my attention on his suggestion that the field is characterized by different methods of analysis and assessment that need to be distinguished. My own view can be summarized as the claim that these different methods show that we should stop talking about informal logic as though it were a field devoted to the development of *a* logic designed to analyze and evaluate real life arguments. In the case of formal logic, logicians understand it as the study of many logics that approach key elements of reasoning (conditionals, predication, proofs, modalities, etc.) in a variety of ways. In the case of informal logic, we should similarly recognize it as a field which studies not one, but a multitude of logics which incorporate different (and sometimes contrary) approaches to the study of real life arguments.

Needless to say, the thesis that there are many different informal logics invites the question whether one or more of them is an effective way to model, analyze, and evaluate real life argument (or particular kinds of argument). Hansen provides criteria that can be used in attempts to answer questions of this sort (by considering whether a particular informal logic is reliable; is efficient; has a broad or narrow scope; is an effective teaching tool; etc.), but I will not pursue them in this essay. Here I want to focus my attention on the more preliminary question whether and how we can define and distinguish different informal logics. My goal is a systematic definition (which I will label "BLAST") that will allow us to understand informal logic, like formal logic, as a field that is constituted of a collection of different logics.

2. HOW CAN WE DISTINGUISH DIFFERENT INFORMAL LOGICS?

I take the ultimate aim of informal logic to be the evaluation of real life arguments. For the most part, it understands arguments as logic traditionally understands them: as attempts to provide reasons (premises) in support of some conclusion. So understood, the simplest way to test the strength of an argument is by asking two questions: (i) whether it contains premises which should be accepted (because they are true, correct, reliable, trustworthy, etc.); and (ii) whether it proposes a conclusion that follows from them in some way (deductively, inductively, abductively, defeasibly, etc., etc.). I will say that those arguments that satisfy the first of these criteria have *acceptable* premises; and that those that satisfy the second contain a *valid* inference from premises to conclusion (understanding "validity" as a broad notion which encompasses more than deductive validity). Considered from this point of view, we can describe a logically successful (cogent, strong, good) argument as one that provides acceptable premises that provide valid reasons for accepting the conclusion it proposes.

This general account of argument strength (and how we can test for it) is, in a number of ways, open ended. For the moment, it will suffice to say that premise acceptability and validity can be understood in a variety of ways, and that this is one of the key differences that distinguishes different informal logics. I will more formally describe this situation by saying that a central part of the definition of a particular informal logic, **I**, is the way in which it tests the strength of arguments (**T**), and that this incorporates two elements: (i) some way of evaluating the acceptability of an argument's premises (**P**); and (ii) some way of evaluating the strength of the inference from the argument's premises to its conclusion (**V**).

Considered from this point of view, we can provisionally define a particular informal logic by understanding it as **I = T**, where:

> **T** is its criteria for testing arguments; and
> **T** = {**P, V**}, where:
> **P** is its account of premise acceptability, and
> **V** is its account of inference validity.

To take one example, the informal logic developed in the 1977 edition of Johnson and Blair's popular textbook, *Logical Self-Defense*, can be provisionally understood as **I = T**, where **P** is its account of premise acceptability and **V** is its account of inference strength (what this consists of in practice is discussed below). Going one step further, we can distinguish between different informal logics, $I_1, I_2, I_3...$, by recognizing their testing methods, $T_1, T_2, T_3...$, where: $T_1 = \{P_1, V_1\}$, $T_2 = \{P_2, V_2\}$, $T_3 = \{P_3, V_3\}$, and so on.

3. AN OBJECTION: WHERE DOES PREMISE ACCEPTABILITY FIT IN?

One might contrast this way of defining informal logics with Hansen's account of informal logic methods, which focuses on "illative evaluation." As he puts it: "I use the term *illative evaluation* to refer to the evaluation of the premiss-conclusion relationship in an argument or inference. The general problem that concerns us ... is how to determine the *illative strength* of arguments, and how to justify our illative judgments." According to this account, questions about premise acceptability lie outside of informal logic, and accounts of it should focus (exclusively) on premise-conclusion relations – what I have termed "validity."

Hansen's claim that premise acceptability is a topic that lies outside of informal logic is founded on his suggestion that the attempt to include it undermines the attempt to make informal logic an independent discipline with its own area of expertise.

> For any questions of premiss acceptability that reach beyond the very familiar, or common sense, must be shared with colleagues in particular disciplines such as history, politics, economics, biology, statistics, etc. as well as those in more general fields such as epistemology, philosophy of science, rhetoric and dialectical studies. People with special training in field F will, in general, be in a much better position to say whether a statement belonging to F is acceptable than a logician would be... Judgments about premises in field F must ultimately be made by experts in field F or by informal logicians who happen to be experts in field F... Conversely, the experts about premiss acceptability in special fields do not make a study of how to evaluate illative relationships. I do not mean that they are not discriminating in their illative judgments. They work with the standards implicit in their fields, but they make no specialty of the study of illative goodness or the practical problem of how to determine it. (2019, pp. 133-134)

If one insists, as I have, that the business of informal logic includes the assessment of premise acceptability, then Hansen says that the only way to avoid this problem is by limiting the arguments it deals with in a way that does not make them arguments with premises which are best judged by experts in other areas. But in that case:

> ...informal logic ... is an instrument for evaluating arguments that includes the evaluation of premises, then it must limit itself to a very narrow range of arguments – those whose premises belong to common sense, or are "everyday", or require no special training or knowledge at all. Perhaps there is such a domain of knowledge. However, if informal logic is to be circumscribed by being restrained to deal only with arguments whose premises are of this kind, then the scope of informal logic will be so restricted that it can be neither of great interest nor of great value. (2019, p. 134)

Hansen concludes that informal logic is best conceived of as a discipline which is exclusively focused on the study and assessment of premise-conclusion relations in an argument.

In sorting out what is right and wrong with Hansen's argument, it will help to distinguish between "pure" and "applied" informal logic. In the former case, informal logic can be understood as a purely theoretical endeavour which aims to construct a system of logic which models real life arguments well (by capturing its nature and the normative standards that should be used to judge it). It is important to note that this is a different endeavour than the attempt to *apply* a system of informal logic and the tools that it provides to real life instances of argument (about abortion, the exploration of space, international affairs, and so on) – an endeavour I will call "applied" informal logic. Pure informal logic is an attempt to get our logic right. Applied informal logic is an attempt to apply a system of logic to arguing about moral, political, economic, legal, scientific, etc. issues. In the former case, an informal logic is a theoretical end in itself. In the latter case, it is a means to a practical end.

As it is studied and taught today, informal logic is a pure and applied pursuit. In theoretical discussions, the emphasis continues to be theoretical – focused on the attempt to develop a logic that successfully models real life reasoning (something which is not easily accomplished). In contrast, the teaching of informal logic tends to focus on, and be motivated by, the attempt to use the tools that it provides in the analysis and evaluation of real life arguments. These theoretical and applied endeavours are not wholly separate given that a decision whether a "pure" informal logic is successful must be made by considering the extent to which it provides a plausible account of instances of real life argument. Considered from this point of view, informal logic aims at a "reflective equilibrium" which judges systems of informal logic by considering their applied success. One might compare attempts to judge ethical and political theories by considering the extent to which they successfully answer the questions raised by real life ethical and political issues.

In a context in which the scholarly discussion of informal logic continues to emphasize theoretical questions, it is important to recognize applied informal logic as a valuable endeavour. Partly because it informs theoretical pursuits, but more importantly because it embodies the core values that motivated the development of informal logic in the first place – i.e., the desire to improve public discourse by providing tools and standards that inform it. It is hard to overstate the ultimate importance of this goal, which aims to substitute a model of cogent argument for the many more problematic ways in which public issues and disputes may be resolved: in the worst cases, via a resort to fallacious reasoning, prejudice, acrimony, and anger and incivility in a way that may include, at its extreme end, violence and war. One might compare informal logic to the critical thinking movement in this regard, for both aim to replace these ways of settling disputes with careful argument, something that requires that its norms be integrated into the practice of real life discussion and debate.

In the attempt to judge real arguments, premise acceptability must obviously play a role. But even if we ignore this applied pursuit, premise acceptability has a role to play in the theory of informal logic, for an informal logic needs an account of it that answers important theoretical questions like the following.

- Is there a standard procedure that can be used to determine whether the premises of an argument are acceptable?

- To what extent is premise acceptability reducible to truth?

- How should an informal logic deal with acceptability when premises are complicated by issues of vagueness and inconsistency?

- In real life arguments, when is consensus the proper arbiter of acceptability?

- How should we decide acceptability in moral, political and aesthetic contexts?

- Is acceptability relative to an audience ("universal" or particular)?

- What role do emotion and intuition play in determining acceptability?

- Are there "deep disagreements" which make some questions of acceptability unresolvable?

- When are appeals to authority and expertise a reasonable way to judge issues of acceptability?

Answers to questions of this sort are properly located within informal logic and cannot be easily assigned to other domains of knowledge. The account of premise acceptability included within a particular informal logic can be understood as a response to the issues that they raise.

I conclude that questions of premise acceptability have a role to play within pure and applied informal logic. In the assessment of real life arguments, premise acceptability is in many cases easy to assess – because the truth or acceptability (or falsity or unacceptability) of a premise is obvious or probable, easily established, or widely acknowledged. As Hansen points out, the evaluation of premise acceptability is a more complex endeavour when we deal with arguments within specialized fields (say, eighteenth century Chinese history, genetic screening, astrophysics, etc.). In many cases, this does require expertise in the field in question. In such cases it can be said that the application of an informal logic, I, depends on $I + D$, where D is knowledge of that domain. This implies that applied informal logic does at times require the combining of two kinds of knowledge: of informal logic and of some other domain. Such combining can be compared to the combining of knowledge required in other applied disciplines – as when we apply statistical analysis to the study of a social problem; a theory of international relations to a particular political situation; and so on.

McPeck (1982) adds another wrinkle to this story. He argues that different domains of knowledge require different standards of reasoning, something which suggests that there may be a series of informal logics: I_1, I_2, I_3, etc. which incorporate the standards that apply to these different domains. For reasons discussed in Govier (2018, pp. 20-55), such views are no longer popular. Here it will suffice to say that any distinction between general standards of reasoning and domain specific knowledge suggests that we should distinguish between a logic, **I**, and specific knowledge of the domain, **D**, that it applies to, and that the application of the logic will require **I + D**.

4. WHAT ELSE DEFINES AN INFORMAL LOGIC?

So far, I have extended Hansen's account of informal logic so that it incorporates premise acceptability as well as illative strength (in the form of inference validity) as a defining element of an informal logic. Insofar as the aim of an informal logic is the development of tools that can be used to test the strength of real life arguments, these two elements might be said to be its most important features. That said, there are other important ways in which informal logics may differ from each other. The following four are worthy of note.

(i) Theoretical background

Every informal logic is built upon an explicit or implicit theoretical account of the ways in which arguments should be understood, analyzed, and evaluated. In this way, an informal logic is rooted in a broader point of view that it assumes. This broader point of view may be a particular view of human interaction or communication; an account of the contexts in which arguments occur; or a particular epistemology. When we explain an informal logic, it may be this theoretical background which explains why it is shaped the way it is.

(ii) Language

Formal logics are founded on formal languages which are expressly designed to represent arguments and their contents in a way that highlights key logical properties. This makes the sentences that are premises and conclusions in formal arguments "wffs" – well-formed formulae which must obey strict syntactical requirements. Because informal logic is an attempt to understand real life arguments, most informal logics adopt "natural" language as the language of choice when it comes to representing, analyzing and evaluating arguments. This does not mean that informal logics all assume the same account of language, for even when they do so, natural language can be understood in different ways that have important logical implications (for we may understand and interpret arguments differently, depending on how we understand the speech acts that constitute natural language communication).

One important difference that characterizes alternative accounts of natural language is the extent to which one understands language in a way that incorporates non-verbal speech acts. We can capture this distinction by distinguishing between L and L+, where L is language narrowly understood (as a means of communication that consists exclusively of words and verbal claims) and L+, where L+ ("language plus") combines L and non-verbal means of communication that may play a key role in arguments (which may use visual, auditory, and emotional displays to provide evidence in favour of some conclusion). In defining particular informal logics, we may go one step further and distinguish between different variants of L and L+. We can, for example, distinguish between an L+ which adds visual elements (photographs, videos, illustrations, virtual reality, etc.) to words, and one which goes further and adds visual and auditory elements (non-verbal natural sounds, music, prosodic elements, and so on).

(iii) A Definition of argument

Another foundational element an informal logic assumes is the definition of argument it adopts. In most cases, informal logics borrow from philosophy and the logic tradition, understanding an argument as a three part entity made up of premises, a conclusion, and an inference from the former to the latter. The definition of an argument may still vary, because different logics propose different accounts of premises and conclusions (that turn on the question whether they are propositions, necessarily verbal, etc.) or, more radically, because some informal logicians have broadened the standard account of argument to include any attempt to overcome disagreement. The latter move is influenced by rhetorical accounts of argument. Other definitions may emphasize rhetorical or dialectical aspects of arguing.

(iv) Standardizing methods

The application of an informal logic depends on some standard way of organizing and presenting arguments, especially when one is subjecting them to analysis and assessment. This is a first step in analysis which clarifies the content and the inferences in an argument. It is an important step because real life arguments are (in contrast with formal arguments) "unrefined" and unclear, and in this sense, not well formed. In many cases, standardization must eliminate redundant repetitions, digressions and asides; resolve potential inconsistencies; and recognize unstated premises, conclusions, and assumptions. Woods (1995) helpfully compares the standardizing of arguments to the work of a butcher, because it takes arguments "on the hoof" (as they naturally occur, as a butcher takes unslaughtered animals) and "dresses" them in a way that displays their key components and the relationships that connect them. Depending on the form of standardizing used, it may include some form of argument diagramming which depicts the key components of an argument and the ways in which they are connected (as linked or convergent premises, as parts of an overarching inference, etc.). Different diagramming techniques may be used.

5. HOW TO DEFINE AN INFORMAL LOGIC

Having identified the different parts of informal logic, we can formally define a particular informal logic, I, as:

> $I = \{B, L, A, S, T\}$, where:
> B is the theoretical background that informs the logic;
> L is the account of language it depends on (typically, some variant of L or $L+$);
> A is a definition of argument;
> S is a way of standardizing arguments;
> T is a set of tools used to test the strength of arguments; where $T = \{P, V\}$, P is an account of premise acceptability, and V is an account of validity (i.e. illative strength).

We can extend this definition further by understanding the application of an informal logic to a particular domain of knowledge as $I + D$, where I is the logic and D is the domain.

The "BLAST" definition of an informal logic can be used to provide a precise and systematic account of a range of informal logics. Doing so allows us to understand the discipline of informal logic as one which consists of a diverse collection of logics which share the general structure the definition outlines. In situations in which informal logicians do not explicitly define all the elements of the BLAST definition, the attempt to refine their accounts by doing so is a useful exercise. Once defined, different informal logics can be compared, contrasted, evaluated and applied to different instances of real life reasoning.

I cannot undertake a comprehensive attempt to define a range of informal logics in this preliminary essay, but an example which illustrates how the BLAST definition works may be helpful. In attempts to find an alternative to formal logic that can better account for real life reasoning, many informal logicians have turned to fallacy theory as a way to create an alternative basis for argument evaluation. Variants of this approach continue to be popular, some of them listing hundreds of fallacies that can be used to critique particular kinds of argument – straw man reasoning, hasty generalizations, slippery slope reasoning, and so on (see, e.g., Bennett 2018). Approaches of this sort develop informal logics which can be defined as:

$I = \{B, L, A, S, T\}$, where:
B is the theory of fallacies (as found in Hamblin, etc.);
L is ordinary language (**L**);
A understands an argument as a collection of premises and a conclusion;
S consists of common standardization and diagramming practices; and
$T = F$, where:
F is a set of fallacies used for judging premise acceptability (**P**) or validity (**V**).

In this example, the proposed BLAST definition outlines a family of informal logics committed to fallacies as a preferred way to test argument strength. We can distinguish between different members of this family by distinguishing the different sets of fallacies (F_1, F_2, F_3...) they employ in this regard. The "One Fallacy Theory" advocated by Powers 1996, confines the set **F** to exactly one member (the fallacy of equivocation). Other variants of "fallacy logic" are more expansive, incorporating a set **F** which includes many other fallacies. In other cases, informal logicians extend such logics by combining some set of fallacies, **F**, with other tools for judging premise acceptability and inference strength (e.g. argument schemes).

In other cases, the BLAST definition allows us to distinguish between different informal logics by recognizing the different ways in which they instantiate the six variables it proposes (**B**, **L**, **A**, **S**, **T** – where **T** incorporates the two variables **P** and **V**). The following examples show what this implies in each case.

(i) B: Theoretical background

Many informal logics are notable for their roots in broader theoretical inquiries. Johnson (2000) builds a logic which is ultimately based on an account of rationality; Hamblin (1970) develops a logic which is rooted in his review (and criticism) of the fallacy tradition; and Walton (1998) proposes a logic based on his account of different kinds of dialogues and the standards of arguing they incorporate. In cases such as these, one of the defining features of an informal logic is the theoretical background it assumes.

(ii) L: Language (L and L+)

Even when informal logics endorse (or assume) some variant of **L**, different logics can be distinguished. In most cases, informal logics assume an account of **L** which allows for implicit speech acts which may, in the case of arguments, mean implicit premises and conclusions. But Hitchcock (2019) rejects implicit premises and conclusions, restricting the ways in which arguments can be interpreted and analyzed.

In their textbook, Groarke & Tindale (2015) move in the opposite direction, developing a variant of **L+** which is based on the pragma-dialectical principles of communication elaborated by van Eemeren and Grootendorst, (2004). This allows an expanded account of implicit speech acts which lets images function as implicit premises and conclusions in arguments. The result is an informal logic which has a broad scope which includes visual arguments. Groarke (2015) goes even further, broadening his account of arguments to include other kinds of non-verbal phenomena (natural sounds, music, smells, tastes, etc.).

In a different way, Gilbert (1997) develops an L+ which is founded on a broad account of communication which dramatically expands what traditionally counts as argument. In his case, L+ may include emotional responses, intuitions, and physical actions which he recognizes as key elements of argument (elements which affect the strength and success of many arguments).

(iii) A: A Definition of argument

Most informal logics understand an argument as a set of premises, an inference, and a conclusion. Gilbert (1997) is notable for his much broader account, which understands an argument as an attempt to overcome disagreement (to bring about "coalescence"). In a number of ways, arguments in this broad sense may not conform to traditional notions of argument, though they often function as effective ways to overcome disagreement. Johnson (2019) expands the notion of argument in another direction in his account of the "dialectical tier," claiming that arguments are intrinsically dialectical and need to be analyzed and assessed accordingly. As he puts it, "Arguments in the paradigmatic sense require a dialectical tier in which the arguer discharges his or her dialectical obligations: i.e., anticipates objections, deals with alternative positions, etc." (p. 178).

(iv) S: Standardizing

In its simplest form, the standardization of an argument is accomplished by listing its premises and conclusions. More sophisticated forms of standardization combine such a list with a diagram that illustrates the inferences in the argument. In a rudimentary way, standardization of this sort is employed in Whately's *Elements of Logic* (1855) in the middle of the nineteenth century. The standard approach to argument diagrams today can be traced to Beardsley (1950) and to Thomas (1973) and Scriven (1976), who refine his approach. Toulmin adds another wrinkle by adding warrants to his diagrams. Today "Logical Argument

Mapping" in a variety of forms is a key tool used in the analysis of real life arguing (see Hoffman 2011). Groarke (2019) has developed a standardizing method that constructs "KC tables" tailored to **L** arguments that employ non-verbal components, allowing one to recognize them as key components of an argument (as non-verbal premises and conclusions) that can be recognized and represented in a standard argument diagram.

(v) P: Premise acceptability

Within an informal logic, some account of premise acceptability provides one way in which we can test the strength of an argument. Criteria for acceptability may invoke fallacies (like begging the question and equivocation), issues like inconsistency, and appeals to expert or public consensus. Traditional accounts of argument (like those embedded in classical formal logic) equate premise acceptability and truth, understanding an acceptable premise to be one that is true. For a variety of reasons, this is a problematic view in the contexts which characterize real life arguments, for:

- they are often characterized by conditions of great uncertainty (where it is difficult to determine what is true);

- they are tied to moral, political, aesthetic and emotional dispositions which are not easily classified as true or false;

- theoretical accounts of truth are, in general, controversial and difficult; and

- there are many circumstances in which the views of one's intended audience, not a broader account of truth, determines an argument's success.

Tindale (2015) has defended the latter point of view, advocating a rapprochement between informal logic and rhetoric, making audience acceptability an essential element of premise acceptability.

(vi) V: Validity

As Hansen emphasizes, the testing of validity – of inference strength (the extent to which a set of premises warrants an inference to a proposed conclusion) – is a defining element of a logic, formal or informal. Validity for a logic (what we might call "metavalidity") is defined by the criteria it uses to determine whether particular arguments are valid. An argument is valid according to this logic when it satisfies these criteria.

In the case of formal logic, proof procedures and rules of inference typically determine inference strength. In the case of informal logic, a variety of other tools have been proposed. Johnson and Blair (1977) use selected fallacies and their "ARS" criteria ("Acceptability, Relevance, and Sufficiency") to test inference strength. Variants of the ARS criteria have been adopted by Govier (2014) and many other authors.

Argument schemes are another important way to test validity. They understand valid arguments of a specified kind (causal, by analogy, by authority, etc.) to be arguments which answer an associated set of "critical questions." Walton et. al. (2008) provide one standard catalogue of schemes. Metavalidity for a particular informal logic is often defined (in whole or in part) by specifying a set of schemes it utilizes in assessments of validity.

6. BEYOND INFORMAL LOGICS

The proposed approach to informal logics defines a logic in terms of the constituent parts I have identified. In some cases the BLAST definition requires that we make explicit some aspects of a logic which are ordinarily assumed and not explicitly specified. In other cases, the attempt to define a logic shows that the received account of it is incomplete – and can, in such situations, be completed in a variety of ways (by interpreting the incomplete variables in different ways). When generally applied, the BLAST definition allows us to compare and contrast the content of different informal logics and proactively develop new logics in a more systematic way than that which has characterized informal logic in the past. Most importantly, the BLAST definition is a tool that precisely summarizes an informal logic, and in this way allows us to assess its success (or lack of success) modeling real life reasoning.

I have argued that we should understand the field of informal logic as a collection of informal logics – and the application of these logics to real life arguing. Like Hansen's account of informal logic as a discipline, this approach usefully clarifies why informal logic is properly characterized as a *logic*, but it is not intended as a way to isolate the development of such logics from other ways of studying real life reasoning. Battersby and Bailin (2019) have, to take one example, developed an "inquiry" approach to critical thinking which pointedly emphasizes, not the evaluation of individual arguments, but the much broader practices and attitudes (the comparison of contending positions, historical context, etc.) that inform them. The BLAST account of informal logics complements, and in making room for broader theoretical inquiries, can be easily and productively combined with this and similar approaches to critical thinking.

Another example that can illustrate how the BLAST approach combines with broader developments in argumentation theory is the study of dialogues. Walton is, in particular, notable for an account of dialogues which suggests that the normative standards that apply to arguments change when they are embedded in different kinds of dialogue. To take an extreme example, an eristic dialogue is a verbal fight (a quarrel) which is characterized by an "anarchy in rules" (Walton and Macagno 2008, 105) that permits fallacious arguments in an attempt to vanquish one's opponent (often, in a way that aims to embarrass them). In contrast, fallacies are forbidden and strict standards of acceptability and validity apply to the arguments used in an inquiry or deliberation dialogue. This is a theoretical perspective that suggests that we need to develop, not one, but a family of informal logics which can be applied to different kinds of dialogue. The BLAST definition can be used to define the different logics this implies.

Examples of this sort show how the study of real life reasoning encompasses more than the development of individual informal logics, but in a way that suggests that this development is a complementary and theoretically conjoined endeavour. So long as the evaluation of individual arguments plays a role in the study of real life reasoning, the BLAST definition has a role to play defining the logics which can guide this assessment.

REFERENCES

Battersby, Mark and Sharon Bailin. 2019. *Inquiry: A New Paradigm for Critical Thinking.* Windsor, ON: Windsor Studies in Argumentation.

Beardsley, Monroe C. 1950. *Practical logic.* New York: Prentice-Hall.

Bennett, Bo. 2018. *Logically Fallacious: The Ultimate Collection of Over 300 Fallacies.* Sudbury, MA: Archieboy Holdings.

Eemeren, Frans. H. van, and Rob Grootendorst. 2004. *A systematic theory of argumentation: The pragma-dialectical approach.* Cambridge: Cambridge University Press.

Gilbert, Michael. 1997. *Coalescent Argumentation.* Mahwah, NJ: Lawrence Erlbaum Associates.

Govier, Trudy. 2018. *Problems in Argument Analysis and Evaluation.* Windsor: Windsor, ON: Studies in Argumentation.

Govier, Trudy. 2014. *A Practical Study of Argument.* 7th ed. Boston: Wadsworth.

Groarke, Leo. 2019. "Depicting visual arguments: An ART approach." In Puppo (Ed.), Pp. 330-371.

Groarke, Leo. 2018. "Going multimodal: What is a mode of arguing and why does it matter?" *Argumentation* 29(2), 133-155.

Groarke, Leo A. and Christopher W. Tindale. 2013. *Good Reasoning Matters!* 5th ed. Toronto: Oxford University Press.

Hamblin, Charles, L. 1970. *Fallacies*. London: Methuen.

Hitchcock, David. 2019. "The problem of missing premises." In Puppo (Ed.), pp. 103-128.\

Hoffmann, Michael H. G. 2011. Analyzing framing processes in conflicts and communication by means of logical argument mapping. In W. A. Donohue, R. G. Rogan and S. Kaufman, (Eds.), *Framing Matters: Perspectives on Negotiation Research and Practice in Communication* , pp. 136-164. New York: Peter Lang.

Johnson, Ralph H. and J. Anthony Blair. 1977. *Logical Self-Defense*. Toronto : McGraw-Hill Ryerson.

Johnson, Ralph H. 2000. *Manifest Rationality: A Pragmatic Theory of Argument*. Mahwah, NJ: Lawrence Erlbaum.

Johnson, Ralph H. 2019. The dialectical tier revisited. In Puppo (Ed.), pp. 175-195.

McPeck, John E. 1982, *Critical Thinking and Education*. Oxford: Martin Robertson.

Powers, Lawrence H. 1995. "The one fallacy theory." *Informal Logic* 17(2), 303-314.

Puppo, Federico, (Ed.), 2019. *Informal Logic: A "Canadian" Approach to Argument*. Windsor, ON: Windsor Studies in Argumentation.

Scriven, Michael. 1976. *Reasoning*. New York: McGraw-Hill.

Thomas, Stephen N. 1973. *Practical Reasoning In Natural Language*. Englewood Cliffs, NJ: Prentice-Hall.

Toulmin, Stephen. 1958. *The Uses of Argument*. Cambridge: Cambridge University Press.

Tindale, Christopher W. 2015. *Philosophy of Argument and Audience Reception*. Cambridge: Cambridge University Press.

Walton, Douglas N. 1998. *The New Dialectic: Conversational Contexts of Argument*. Toronto: University of Toronto Press.

Walton, Douglas N. and Fabrizio Macagno. 2007. "Types of dialogue, dialectical relevance and textual congruity," *Anthropology & Philosophy* 8(1-2), 100-119.

Walton, Douglas N., Chris Reed and Fabrizio Macagno. 2008. *Argumentation Schemes*. Cambridge: Cambridge University Press.

Whately, Richard. 1855. *Elements of Logic*. 12th ed. Boston and Cambridge: James Munro and Company.

Woods, John. 1995. "Fearful symmetry," in H.V. Hansen and R.C. Pinto (Eds.), *Fallacies: Classical and Contemporary Readings*, University Park, PA: Pennsylvania State University Press.

ABOUT THE AUTHOR: Leo Groarke is President and Professor of Philosophy at Trent University. He has contributed to informal logic for many years, through articles, books and conference presentations. His areas of interest include the history and development of the field, visual and multimodal argument, pedagogy, and the criteria that can be used to evaluate real life argument. He is, with Christopher Tindale, the author of the popular textbook, *Good Reasoning Matters!* (5th ed. Oxford) and an Editor in Chief of the series Windsor Studies in Argumentation (WSIA).

CHAPTER 10.

ARGUMENTATION SCHEMES AND AUDIENCES: WHAT RHETORIC CAN BRING TO SCHEME THEORY

CHRISTOPHER W. TINDALE

ABSTRACT: In discussing what a rhetorical perspective on argumentation offers to the study of schemes (and thus contributes further to informal logic), I focus on three aspects of scheme theory: the use of the method of critical questions for evaluation; the structure of various taxonomies; and the central concept of "defeasibility". Drawing on insights from Robert C. Pinto and Michael C. Leff, and reviewing some of the recent suggestions of Hans V. Hansen, I look to show ways in which rhetorical features are relevant to some of the ongoing discussions in scheme theory.

KEYWORDS: Defeasibility, Pinto, rhetoric, schemes, taxonomies, Walton

1. THE NATURE OF SCHEME STUDIES

In his *Rhetoric*, Aristotle (2018) famously defines his central term as an ability (or capacity) to see the available means of persuasion in any particular case (1355^b26). So, what kinds of things present themselves as "available," as per the "available means of persuasion"? Among the many relevant answers to this question, the one device or item that I will devote attention to here is the argumentation scheme, or argument scheme. Schemes may have their conceptual ground in Aristotle's theory of *topoi*, but they certainly fall among those matters that lie within the skills of the arguer (*entechnic*).

Scheme studies is developing as an important sub-area of argumentation studies (Wagemans 2019; Groarke 2018; Blair 2012a: 137-46; Blair 2012b: 147-169; Hitchcock 2010: 157-66; Prakken 2010: 167-85; Walton 1996).[1] This is in part due to the significance that has been extended to argumentation schemes in the development of informal logic. Arguably, they have become a principal focus, replacing the previous attention on fallacy theory and continuing the concern to develop adequate tools to evaluate and assess everyday argumentation. In this respect, it is interesting to see a scholar like Hans V. Hansen, who made important contributions to fallacy theory, shifting his attention to scheme theory (Hansen forthcoming).

2. WHAT IS AN ARGUMENTATION SCHEME?

I begin by reviewing some of the central and most-cited definitions of argumentation (or argument) schemes.

A prominent figure in scheme theory is Douglas Walton (1996; and Walton *et al.* 2008), who defines the "argumentation scheme" quite loosely: "argumentation schemes, such as argument from expert opinion… represent commonly used types of arguments that are defeasible… Schemes identify patterns of reasoning linking premises to a conclusion that can be challenged by raising critical questions" (2013, p.6). Several ideas are gathered here: that schemes are patterns of reason that have a common usage

---

1. In an account that has distinctive value in setting out the problems confronting any general theory of schemes, Blair 2012b shifts terminology from 'argument' scheme to 'reasoning' scheme. I will stay with the language that has received most common adoption.

and that are defeasible.[2] They also have sets of critical questions associated with them, although it seems unwise to include this feature in the definition of a scheme.

A tighter definition is offered by David Hitchcock: "An argumentation scheme is a pattern of argument, a sequence of sentential forms with variables, with the last sentential form introduced by a conclusion indicator like 'so' or 'therefore'. The scheme becomes an argument when each variable is replaced uniformly in all its occurrences with a constant of the sort over which the variable ranges" (2010, p.157). The added detail here involves the identification of variables.

More recently, Hans V. Hansen (forthcoming) has explored the nature of argumentation schemes, distinguishing syntactic and normative aspects and producing the following definition:

> A BASIC ARGUMENT SCHEME is (i) a pattern of argument, (ii) made of a sequence of sentential forms with variables, of which (iii) at least one of the sentential forms contains a use of a schematic constant or a schematic quantifier, and (iv) the last sentential form is introduced by a conclusion indicator like 'so' or 'therefore' (p.6).

This advances the previous definitions in one important way, captured in the third point: "at least one of the sentential forms contains a use of a schematic constant or a schematic quantifier." This point marks the difference between schematic logic and formal logic. "All argument schemes will have at least one schematic constant or one scheme quantifier" (ibid.). Logical forms are argument patterns with neither. By way of explaining what he means by a "schematic constant," Hansen offers an example: "The sentence form "X said that p" uses the schematic constant "...said that"..."

In a major theoretical treatment of schemes, Walton, Reed and Macagno (2008) identify sixty varieties, along with subtypes for a number of them. While they understand traditional deduc-

---

2. This is an important term that will be discussed in detail below.

tively valid and inductively strong forms of argument as argument schemes, what they are principally interested in are schemes for presumptive reasoning. Walton believes that a major aim of arguments is to shift the burden of proof between people, and schemes do this by creating a presumption in favour of a conclusion. If there is such a presumption, then the burden of proof is on an opponent to challenge it, rather than on the arguer to further support it.

As a preliminary example to illustrate argumentation schemes I will take Walton, Reed and Macagno's scheme for "Emotional Plea: Argument from need for help":

P1: For all x and y, y ought to help x, if x is in a situation where x needs help, and y can give help, and y's giving help would not be too costly for y.
P2: x is in a situation where some action A by y would help x.
P3: y can carry out A.
P4: y's carrying out A would not be too costly for y – that is, the negative side effects would not be too great, as y sees it.
C: Therefore, y ought to carry out A. (2008, p.109).

The adoption of various letters like x and y represents the variables mentioned in the Hitchcock and Hansen definitions. This is one of the schemes associated with practical reasoning, intended to help an agent think through a situation and come to a decision on which an action can be made. I set aside here the larger question of the relation between emotion and reason and the reasonableness of treating emotion in argumentation. That has been thoroughly addressed in the work of people like Michael Gilbert (1997; 2014).

Like other schemes, the conclusion of "Emotional Plea: Argument from need for help" is defeasible in the sense that it is not guaranteed and can be revisited in light of new evidence. Our everyday arguments can have the characteristic that they are strong given the evidence available at the time, but other (or later) evidence may emerge that can (or should) lead us to rethink the conclusion.

Many examples could be suggested that would fit the scheme of this argument. For example, consider treating A as "providing aid to Syrian refugees", with x represented by those refugees, and y represented by Canadians and their respective levels of government. This is an issue that has been argued in various media in Canada and elsewhere in ways that essentially reflect this scheme.

A second scheme to consider is "Argument from Expert Opinion":

Major Premise: Source E is an expert in subject domain S containing proposition A.
Minor Premise: E asserts that proposition A is true (false).
Conclusion: A is true (false) (Walton, Reed & Macagno 2008:91).

Textbooks routinely treat the "Argument from Expert Opinion" (sometimes they refer to authority, but I would treat this as a separate scheme involving a person's status). The scheme captures the pattern of reasoning involved when appeals are made to some person or source that has specific knowledge that gives them expertise.

This is also a good scheme with which to consider how argumentation schemes are evaluated. The tool used is a set of critical questions for each argumentation scheme. Pinto (2001: 111) has argued that the very value of identifying argument schemes lies with the critical questions associated with them, and I will return to his argument below. The critical questions are aids for the critic in evaluating arguments (as well as for inventing them), facilitating the focus on the right things. They tell us the kinds of things we should be looking for with respect to each argument. For the "Argument from Expert Opinion" we have, as might be expected, questions on the nature of the expert as a source of expertise (credibility); on the field in which the expert operates (relevance of expert); on the assertion that the expert actually made; on the trustworthiness of the expert; on the level of agreement among experts on the issue; and on the evidence from which the expert draws. We have six questions in total, with a number of sub-questions under each of these.

To illustrate the use and value of the questions for evaluating schemes, consider the following example:

> P1: Fish may not audibly scream when they are impaled on hooks, but their behaviour provides evidence that they do suffer.
> P2: Neurobiologists have long recognized fish have nervous systems that respond to trauma.
> P3: Researchers have found more than 20 such receptors in the mouth and head of fish, and
> P4: Researchers at the University of Guelph concluded that fish feel fear when they are chased.
> Sub-C: No doubt the two-hour ordeal the white sturgeon went through caused pain and fear.
> Main C: People need to think seriously about the ethics of catch-and-release fishing for entertainment and competition.

Actually, this argument can be approached using both the scheme for "Argument from Expert Opinion" and also Walton's scheme for "Emotional Plea: Argument from need for help", since both are present here. The latter would be reconstructed from P1 and the sub-conclusion (Fish may not audibly scream when they are impaled on hooks, but their behaviour provides evidence that they do suffer, therefore no doubt the two-hour ordeal the white sturgeon went through caused pain and fear). Recast in the wording of the scheme we get:

> x is [fish are] in a situation where some action A [people thinking seriously about the ethics involved] by y [people/society] would help x.
> y can carry out A.
> y's carrying out A would not be too costly for y – that is, the negative side effects would not be too great, as y sees it.
> Therefore, y ought to carry out A. [people ought to think seriously about the ethics involved].

The set of critical questions attached to a scheme don't tell us whether an argument is good. What they do is aid our judgment by identifying the kinds of things that we should be looking for with respect to each scheme. In many cases they reveal a societal norm or value at the heart of the scheme, as in the value of expertise, or a principle of fairness, or altruism (as in the "Argument from need for help" scheme).

The questions for the argument from need for help focus on specific things relevant to the kinds of situations the scheme covers. They comprise:

CQ1: Would the proposed action A really help x?
CQ2: Is it possible for x to carry out A?
CQ3: Would there be negative side effects of carrying out A that would be too great?

Would a review of the ethics involved help the case of fish? Well, it likely wouldn't hurt, although the response might not be so obvious or immediate as the writer may think. Is it possible for the victim here (fish) to help themselves? Obviously not. Would the side effects of doing the proposed action be negative? It would likely put the sports fishing industry at some risk, which is a consequence that would needed to be considered, along with a weighing of the different values involved. But, on balance, we have a useful piece of reasoning. It will still be subject to further debate on what values to prioritize, but it makes its case in a reasonable fashion.

Turning to the "Argument from Expert Opinion", we might see that it arises several times in this piece of reasoning: each of premises 2-4 provide such potential evidence for the sub-claim, appealing in turn to neurobiologists; researchers; and researchers at the University of Guelph. I will consider the weakest and the strongest of these:

P3: Researchers have found more than 20 receptors typically associated with pain in the mouth and head of fish,

Sub-C: No doubt the two-hour ordeal the white sturgeon went through caused pain and fear.

P4: Researchers at the University of Guelph concluded that fish feel fear when they are chased.

Sub-C: No doubt the two-hour ordeal the white sturgeon went through caused pain and fear.

The questions for the "Argument from Expert Opinion" reveal some problems when they are applied to this argument. The first question, for example, asks how credible the expert is as an expert source, and we can see the difficulty that would be involved in answering this question when the experts are unnamed, as in Premise 3, compared to when they are better identified, as in Premise 4. We have the prospect of exploring what researchers at the University of Guelph have said, we can uncover their expertise in the relevant field of research. But this is not possible with Premise 3. Moreover, knowing the source of the experts allows us to make reasonable judgments with respect to other questions, like the trustworthiness question and the field question.

Now, on balance, looking at the two schemes involved, there are identifiable strengths to the argumentation. And where weaknesses are apparent, the critical questions that expose them also point the way to how they could be remedied and the argument strengthened. This where Pinto's insight into the value of critical questions becomes clear and where the rhetorical dimension involved starts to become apparent. Pinto is insistent that the normative force of an argument is not to be found in its exemplification of an argument scheme, but in contextual considerations that bear on rhetorical factors specific to a case: "considerations that would justify the use of *this* sort of evidence in *this* sort of context to settle *this* sort of question" (Pinto 2001: 111). It can't be the scheme itself that provides the validation of presumptive reasoning, because the use of the scheme on any occasion itself requires validation. In fact, even this talk of a *sort of* evidence, context, or question betrays the particularity of the case that mitigates the easy use of logical criteria with a reliance on patterns and forms, a point we will see Michael Leff argue below.

Justifying the use of a scheme in any particular case is the first step in assessment, and to this end the first critical question in a set should be one of identification, ensuring that the argument under review meets the conditions of the scheme and is thus open to evaluation using the subsequent questions.

That Pinto shares Leff's reticence for the abstractness of some approaches to schemes is to be seen in his disagreement with Walton on the role of critical questions. As we will recall, Walton uses them to shift the burden of proof back and forth between proponent and respondent; Pinto claims otherwise, and illustrates his position with examples that show critical questions that demand too much of a respondent. By contrast, he argues, the "proper function" of critical questions is to direct people to possible overriding or undermining evidence, to the central issue of (potential) refutation, which, as we will again see, is the principal criterion of evaluation in rhetorical argumentation.[3]

3. TAXONOMIES

The feasibility of the various categories suggested for argumentation schemes depends to some degree on how many such schemes there are. The Pragma-dialectical model of argumentation, for example, identifies only three types of scheme, although we might prefer to call these categories. Walton and his co-authors, on the other hand, identify at least 60 schemes, with a number of variants of many of those schemes.

While earlier taxonomies of schemes are found (or suggested) in the work of theorists like Perelman and Olbrechts-Tyteca (1958/1969), I will focus on the two more recent taxonomies

---

3. At least with respect to the evaluation criteria put forward by Chaim Perelman and Lucie Olbrechts-Tyteca.

mentioned, those proposed by pragma-dialectician Frans van Eemeren and those by Douglas Walton before offering some suggestions of my own.

In a recent paper on argumentative style, Frans van Eemeren (2019) reminds us of the pragma-dialectical approach to argument schemes:

> Various types of argumentation can be advanced to enhance the acceptability of a standpoint, each of them characterized by the employment of a specific argument scheme. The argument schemes of "symptomatic", "comparison" and "causal" argumentation distinguished in pragma-dialectics have a pragmatic basis in the arguers' human experience regarding the justificatory principles appealed upon in legitimizing the transfer of acceptance from the arguments constituting the argumentation to the standpoints that are defended. In symptomatic argumentation the argument scheme is used to establish a relation of concomitance between the argument concerned and the standpoint that is supported, in comparison argumentation to establish a relation of comparability, and in causal argumentation to establish a relation of causality (2019: 156).

This recalls the more elaborate discussion provided in van Eemeren & Grootendorst (1992: 94-102). For the Dutch authors, an argumentation scheme is a conventional way that the relation between what is stated in the argument and what is stated in the standpoint [conclusion] is represented. The principle behind the *symptomatic* categorization is that there is "a relation of *concomitance*" between the argument and the standpoint. That is, the argumentation is given as if it is an expression, phenomenon or sign *of* what is stated in the standpoint. The principle behind the comparison category is that there is a relationship of analogy between what is stated in the argument and the standpoint. The third category involved instrumentality and expresses relationships of causality between the argument and the standpoint (van Eemeren and Grootendorst 1992: 97).

Now, these theorists point out that there are many sub-types of the three basic categories, while, perhaps wisely, declining to suggest just how many there may be. Still, as with other attempts to corral schemes into related categories, problems have been identified with the account. Hitchcock and Wagemans (2011) have difficulty determining, for example, the ordering principle between each main type and its sub-types. They also raise more important concerns about the ability of the account to be exhaustive with respect to all schemes and for the categories to be mutually exclusive: the "addition of variants and sub-types to the original three main types raises a doubt about the mutual exclusiveness of symptomatic argumentation and causal argumentation," for example (2011: 193-5). While they proceed to offer remedies for these problems, it remains that the theory is susceptible to such concerns. Similarly, Christoph Lumer (2010), approaching the matter from an epistemological point of view (which challenges the kind of consensualism promoted in the pragma-dialectical theory), asserts that the pragma-dialectical account of argument schemes lacks a rational (i.e. epistemic) foundation for its validity criteria (2010: 66). And he laments the mix of deduction, induction and abduction within the main types of scheme. This results in what he believes is a largely unsystematic arrangement, which is obviously not the intent behind the account.

While the pragma-dialecticians resist suggesting how many sub-types there are, no such reticence restricts Douglas Walton. The initial taxonomy he provides (Walton 2005), and which is adopted in Walton *et al.* (2008), also consists of three main categories: reasoning arguments; source-based arguments; and arguments applying rules to cases. And again, each of these categories has sub-categories to which the individual schemes are assigned. This taxonomy suffered from limitations[4] that led to a revision in Walton and Macagno (2016). Under this proposal the principal

---

4. It failed to identify common characteristics within the schemes each embraced by several categories (Walton and Macagno 2016: 21).

division is between (i)[5] source-based arguments and (ii) non-source-based arguments. Source-based arguments are further divided into (ia) epistemic and (ib) practical, and the former are then further divided into those that involve (iai) applying rules to cases, and (iaii) discovery arguments. Individual schemes are then distributed under these categories (see Figure 1).[6]

The complexity involved in this taxonomy is not surprising given the number of argument schemes that Walton and his colleagues have identified, all of which need to find a place. And while this is the most complete system yet devised (assuming the sixty-plus number of schemes) is still requires work, as the authors themselves note. The principal criterion behind the taxonomy is based on the structure of each argument and the nature of the generalization involved. Other classifications could be introduced based on a different criterion "more adequate for specific purposes" (Walton and Macagno 2016: 24). Moreover, an entire sub-category of linguistic arguments (including arguments from verbal classification and so forth) has yet to be included.

The impetus behind each of these taxonomies is an attempt to identify the principal ways in which schemes are either structured (Walton and Macagno) or evaluated (van Eemeren and Grootendorst). This leaves me to observe something that became apparent in the discussion of critical questions: some schemes lend themselves more to a rhetorical evaluation than do others. That is, some schemes directly implicate the audience in their evaluation. The sub-category of schemes involving practical reasoning is most apparent here.

---

5. The numbering scheme is my own, adopted to make sense of the discussion.

6. Figure 1 indicates some slight variants from my discussion, which is based on their discussion in the text, but the thrust of the relationships is apparent.

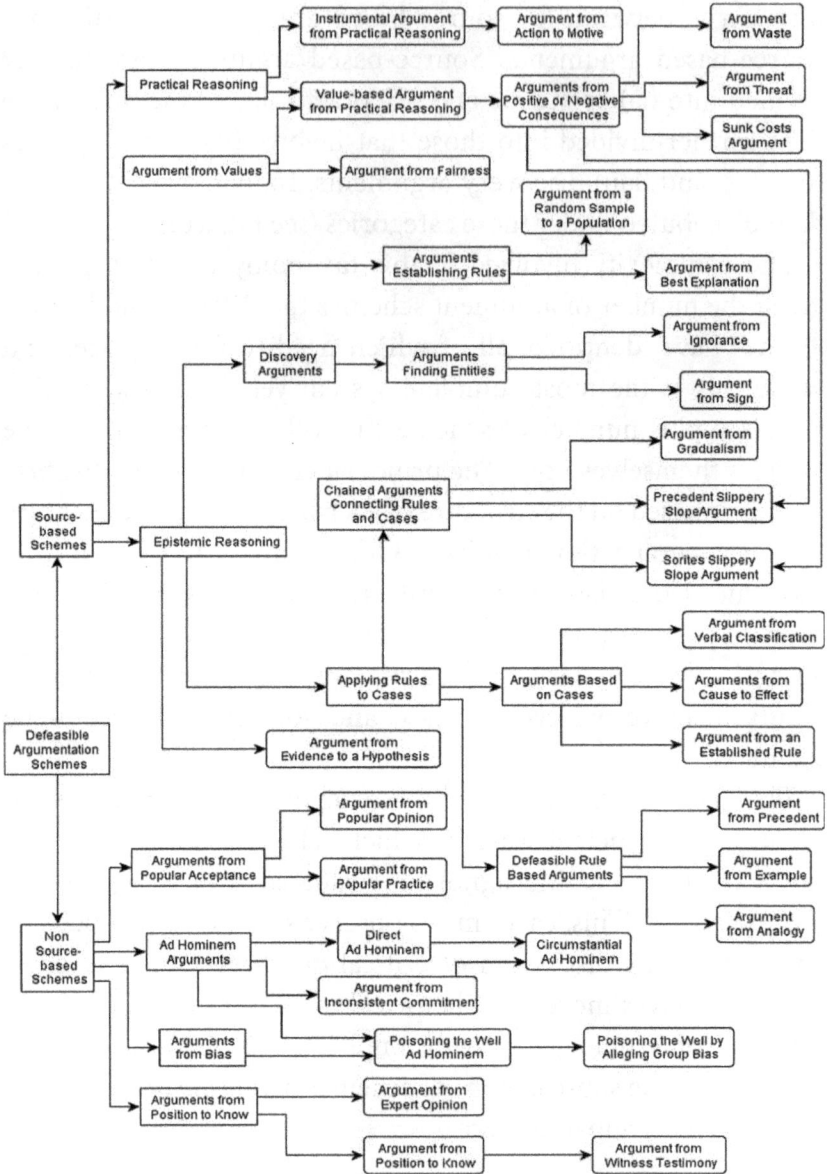

Figure 1 (From Walton and Macagno 2016:23)

For example, we have the prudential inference in the 'Argument from Negative Consequences' that must rank among the more important of those particular schemes in which an audience – an individual or group – is addressed.[7]

P1. You were considering not doing *A*
P2: But not doing *A* will result in an extremely dire consequence.
C: Therefore, it is prudent to reconsider and do *A*.

Without even turning to the set of critical questions that have been provided by Walton and his co-authors, we can see that any evaluation will require consideration of the values and intentions of those at whom the argument is directed. What counts as a dire consequence, a negative outcome, may well vary among persons (or groups). The contextual details of the argumentation will provide the thickness we need to appreciate the dimensions involved: how important is not doing or doing A? What risks or disadvantage is someone (or group) prepared to assume in this situation? Indeed, are the alleged consequences indeed negative when weighed against the possible benefits of doing A? These are not questions to be answered in the abstract, or for which responses can be transferred from one instance of the scheme to another. And there is a range of argument schemes where this would be the case, where an audience is directly addressed (with a threat, a benefit, a plea). This reinforces the importance that the critical questions (however they are sourced) lend to the value of identifying schemes. In such cases, the abstract is brought down to the level of the personal, *humanizing* the conclusion to be supported. Whatever may be asserted in propositions, *showing* those same things has more force in achieving adherence and with the right kind of relevance.

This is not a place to suggest a taxonomy of my own, given the complexity we can see that any system of categorization

---

7. Along with others like, for example, the "Argument from Commitment", or Walton's scheme for 'Practical Reasoning'. Adapted from Walton, *et al.* (2008: 332).

must involve. But there is the prospect of looking at schemes in terms of the type of audiences they address and, following Pinto, the kinds of contexts involved. Perelman and Olbrechts-Tyteca's proposal for distinguishing audiences that involve the self, a single interlocutor, and a larger ("universal") collective could be a place to start.

4. RHETORICAL OPENNESS AND DEFEASIBILITY

In his study of the nature of argument schemes, Henry Prakken (2010) argues that:

> Argument schemes are essentially logical constructs, so that a procedure for evaluating arguments primarily takes the form of a logic. More specifically, I shall argue that most argument schemes are defeasible inference rules and that their critical questions are pointers to counterarguments, so that the logic governing the use of argument schemes should be a logic for nonmonotonic or defeasible reasoning (2010: 167).

Prakken largely delivers on this argument, stressing the fundamental logical nature of the schemes in contrast to the position of Douglas Walton, who views them as dialogical devices. There are several important points here to note – that the evaluation of schemes is primarily a logical one,[8] for example – but the most valuable for our purposes is the stress laid on defeasibility and the role that this plays in evaluation.

For John Pollock (1995), reasoning that is "defeasible" is "reasoning that can lead not only to the adoption of new beliefs but also to the retraction of previously held beliefs" (85). He identifies two types of reasons, those that are conclusive, and those that are prima facie. The latter create a presumption in favour of their conclusion, but they can be defeated. It is this sense of vul-

---

8. Recall, in this respect, Hansen's discussion that distinguishes logical form from schemes: argument schemes are argument patterns that have at least one schematic constant or schematic quantifier, whereas logical forms are argument patterns with none (Hansen, forthcoming).

nerability or openness to revision that has characterized the use of "defeasibility" in scheme studies. Pinto (2009) recognizes two types of defeaters, undermining or overriding, roughly equivalent to what Pollock had termed undercutting and rebutting defeaters. Undercutters attack the connection between the reason and the conclusion rather than the conclusion itself; a reason is a rebutter if it denies the conclusion (Pollock 1995: 40-41).

In the terms used in the passage from Prakken, the counter-arguments that may emerge from the use of critical questions are those that rebut, or undermine, the conclusion, attacking the presumption that was in its favour. Thus, this is one way that "defeasibility" should inform our discussions. But it is also possible to apply the critical questions to an argument and find it reasonable on their terms and at that time. It is only subsequently that further evidence comes to light that undermines the conclusion, either by raising direct doubts about it, or by weakening the link in the relationships between the reason and conclusion of the original argument. This kind of case indicates the greater importance of "defeasibility." The same argument is involved that might have been rebutted when first evaluated. But that it lost its initial appearance of strength speaks to the essential "openness to revision" that characterizes much of the presumptive reasoning in scheme studies. From this perspective, defeasibility (or openness) is a significant feature that a schemes approach brings to light.

For Michael Leff, rhetoric, as it is applied to communication and argumentation, is also an open-ended matter (Leff 2016) in a sense that bears resemblance to the informal logicians' talk of defeasibility. There may be moments of pause, times when an action must be taken on the basis of the evidence available, but things are not decisively determined in the sense that decisions cannot be revised, judgments cannot be further challenged, and debates cannot be revisited. This is the nature of the domain involved. The same domain that Aristotle in his *Rhetoric* identified as that which is characterized by uncertainty, and which Perelman and Olbrechts-Tyteca set in opposition to demonstration.

Leff is struck by the problems that come to light when people try to determine in advance criteria of dialectical adequacy. There is an abstractness involved in the reliance on patterns and forms. By contrast:

> The rhetorical sensibility cuts through this cycle of frustration by offering a grounded judgment about the case at hand and thus providing a provisional, local closure. Such judgment is, of course, imperfect, but it is also corrigible. One arguer's point of closure can become the ground for another's alternative position, and the choice between the two, once they are embodied, is open to rational argument. (Leff 2000: 11).

Of note here is Leff's reference to the "provisional, local closure" deriving from the grounded judgment that a rhetorical view provides to the case. While closure has been achieved, the conclusion remains open to revision. For Leff, this openness is a quality of rhetoric itself, in opposition to the technical, precise language of dialectic and logic. He sees the three perspectives as cooperative, and it is this cooperation that we might see as an important feature of some argumentation schemes.[9]

Let's begin with a consideration of counterargument and rebuttal as they are approached in rhetorical argumentation, considered now as types of defeaters. Here, we need to look no further than Perelman and Olbrechts-Tyteca.

In the later pages of *The New Rhetoric*, Chaim Perelman and Lucie Olbrechts-Tyteca approach the "confused, but apparently essential, concept, that of *strength [or force] of the arguments*" (1969: 461, their italics). To this end, they continue:

9. I would not, at this stage, want to offer more than this weaker claim. As I suggested at the close of the previous section, some schemes are primarily logical in nature (as Prakken insists), but others seem primarily dialectical or rhetorical.

This notion is certainly connected both with the intensity of the hearer's *adherence* to the premises (including the connecting links used) and with the *relevance* of the arguments in the particular discussion. But intensity of adherence as well as relevance are at the mercy of argumentation directed against them. Thus, the strength of an argument shows itself as much by the *difficulty there is in refuting* it as by its inherent qualities (461, the italics are mine).[10]

The italicized terms refer to the core criteria for assessing the strength of rhetorical arguments. My concern here is with the last of them: the ability to resist refutation.[11] It's to be noted that this criterion is singled out for its importance. Both adherence and relevance "are at the mercy of" arguments that might be brought against them, that might combat them. As expressed in the *New Rhetoric*: "the strength of an argument shows itself as much by the *difficulty there is in refuting* it as by its inherent qualities." As strong as an argument appears, it remains to be asked how difficult it is to develop counter-arguments against it.[12]

We will be reminded here not just of the importance of defeaters in scheme theory but of the role that rebuttal plays in Toulmin's model of argument, where he includes "conditions of rebuttal (R) indicating circumstances in which the general authority of the warrant would have to be set aside" (1958: 94). Thus, a conclusion follows from data (D) with the support of a warrant (W), unless there is a rebuttal (R). Again, the rebuttal has prominence, acting as a kind of veto and at least qualifying the force of the conclusion that might be drawn.

10. "Celle-ci est certainement liée d'une part, à l'intensité d'adhésion de l'auditeur aux prémisses, y compris les liaisons utilisées, d'autre part, à la relevance des arguments dans le débat en cours. Mais l'intensité d'adhésion, et aussi la relevance, sont à la merci d'une argumentation qui viendrait les combattre. Aussi la force d'un argument se manifeste tout autant par la difficulté qu'il y aurait à le refuter que par ses qualities propres" (1958/1970: 611).

11. The same criterion is included among the set provided in Perelman (1982).

12. Thanks to J. Anthony Blair for pointing out the similarity between this view and that which Carl Wellman espouses in *Challenge and Response* (1971).

In Toulmin's discussion of rebuttal he explicitly refers to the conditions that pertain in law, where exceptions and qualifications may undermine the considerations of a case (1958: 93). And, given the background of the principal researcher, it is not difficult to imagine the same source having influenced the stress that Perelman and Olbrechts-Tyteca place on refutation. Such a context helps us to understand the contextual nature of what is being required. Of course, we are not expected to consider all possible refutations; that would have the result of delaying conclusions, sometimes indefinitely. Refutability is relevant to an argument in its contexts, just as the exceptions and qualifications to an application of law depend on the details of the case to which the application is being considered. And it is this focus we should expect critical questions to provide. Refutability is a condition of the realm of argumentation. Stronger arguments will resist it, but they remain open to it as a case evolves and new details come to light or become relevant to it.

In Toulmin's terms, rebuttals affect the "degree of force" which the evidence confers on a claim, thus requiring a qualifier such as "probably" or "presumably." There is no reason not to read a similar understanding into the way in which force is understood in the rhetorical criteria. To resist refutation in a context is to successfully preclude exceptions and qualifications that diminish the force of the conclusion for now.

5. CONCLUSIONS

What I have attempted in the preceding is to read the literature on scheme theory through the lens of a rhetorical perspective of argumentation in order to consider whether relevant contributions can be made to that theory or whether avenues of research have been missed. While it has not been a central concern in scheme theory, beneath the core of that work run threads that connect schemes to contexts and raise questions of normativity that involve issues usefully, if not better, dealt with in rhetorical theory.

How schemes gain their normative force has been an important issue in scheme theory (Blair 2012b; Hitchcock 2010). I have said little about the normativity of schemes, even though some of the foregoing has relevance to this issue. Rather than seeking a single standard of reasonableness, Hansen (forthcoming) traces the normativity of schemes to three sources: the *evidential* (a class of arguments all of which "provide some kind of reasons or evidence for why a conclusion could be true"), the *interactional* (a class where the reasons given involve an interlocutor rather than evidence for a proposition), and the *inferential* (a class of arguments, like arguments from analogy and sign, that don't provide kinds of reasons but rather transfer evidence to conclusions) (pp.8-9). There is clearly the start of an interesting taxonomy at work here. Ultimately, Hansen tracks the normativity of schemes to the prescriptive standards of various areas of value theory, thus putting the matter, strictly speaking, beyond the business of scheme theorists. But his classification does support a more bottom-up rather than top-down approach to normativity. Reasonableness is always reflected in the practices of communities of arguers and those communities will largely determine whether schemes and the questions associated with them are descriptive of ordinary language communication, which is the domain that informal logic has always looked to illuminate. Thus, scheme theory as an area of informal logic might find value in the focus on the interactions, inference patterns and types of evidence adopted by reasoners in situ. This would have the further advantage of developing a theory that promises application across cultures.

Leff's insights into the provisional, local closure advised by rhetorical evaluation forms an important bridge to the parallel discussions of defeasibility. But the contributions should work in both directions, and as much as Leff remains skeptical of a dependence on patterns and forms, theorists are not likely to be satisfied by a purely case-by-case treatment that his "rhetorical sensibility" might be seen to advocate. Applied sensitively with the contexts determining the validity of its application, as Pinto recommends, a scheme and its associated critical questions can serve as important tools to unpack the reasoning in a case and assist in its evaluation. I will leave Pinto with the final word: "The articulation and elaboration of standards for the appraisal of arguments and inferences is in no sense a *fait accompli*; rather it is an on-going process that is also an intrinsic and essential component of arguing and reasoning" (2001: 140). Indeed, like the subjects of its attention there is much in scheme theory that remains open to revision.

REFERENCES

Aristotle. (2018) *The Art of Rhetoric*, R. Waterfield (Tr.). Oxford: Oxford University Press.

Blair, J. Anthony. (2012a) "Walton's Argumentation Schemes for Presumptive Reasoning: A Critique and Development," in *Groundwork in the Theory of Argumentation: Selected Papers of J. Anthony Blair*. Dordrecht: Springer: 137-146.

Blair, J. Anthony. (2012b) "A Theory of normative reasoning schemes," in *Groundwork in the Theory of Argumentation: Selected Papers of J. Anthony Blair*, pp.147-169. Dordrecht: Springer.

Eemeren, Frans H. van. (2019). "Argumentative Style: A Complex Notion," *Argumentation*, 33(2),153-171.

Eemeren, Frans H. van and Rob Grootendorst. (1992). *Argumentation, Communication, and Fallacies. A Pragma-dialectical Perspective*. Hillsdale, NJ: Lawrence Erlbaum.

Gilbert, Michael A. (2014) *Arguing with People*. Peterborough, ON: Broadview Press.

Gilbert, Michael A. (1997) *Coalescent Argumentation*. Mahwah, NJ.: Lawrence Erlbaum Associates.

Groarke, Leo A. (2018). "Matching schemes of argument: Verbal, visual, multimodal," *Proceedings of the 9th International Conference on Argumentation*, pp. 443-457. Amsterdam: SicSat.

Hansen, Hans V. (Forthcoming) "Scheme theory," paper read at the 3rd European Conference on Argument, Groningen, June, 2019.

Hitchcock, David. (2010). "The generation of argumentation schemes," in C. Reed and C. W. Tindale (Eds.), *Dialectics, Dialogue and Argumentation*, pp.157-166. London: College Publications.

Hitchcock, David and Jean Wagemans. (2011). "The Pragma-dialectical account of argumentation schemes," in Eveline T. Feteris, *et al.* (Eds.) *Keeping in Touch with Pragma-dialectics: In Honor of Frans H. van Eemeren*, pp. 185-206. Amsterdam: John Benjamins Publishers.

Leff, Michael C. (2016). *Rethinking rhetorical theory, criticism, and pedagogy: The living art of Michael C. Leff*. Antonio de Velasco, John Angus Campbell, and David Henry (Eds.), East Lansing, Michigan: Michigan State University Press.

Leff, Michael C. (2000). "Rhetoric and dialectic in the twenty first century," Windsor, ON: OSSA.

Lumer, Christoph. (2010). "Pragma-dialectics and the function of Argument," *Argumentation* 24, 41-69.

Perelman, Chaim. (1982). *The Realm of Rhetoric*. Notre Dame, IN: University of Notre Dame Press.

Perelman, Chaim and Lucie Olbrechts-Tyteca. (1958). *Traité de l'argumentation: La nouvelle rhétorique*. Paris: Presses Universitaires de France. English translation (1969), *The New Rhetoric: A Treatise on Argumentation*. J. Wilkinson and P. Weaver (Trans.) Notre Dame, IN: University of Notre Dame Press.

Pinto, Robert C. (2001). *Argument, Inference and Dialectic: Collected Papers on Informal Logic*. Dordrecht: Kluwer Academic Publishers.

Pollock, John. (1995). *Cognitive Carpentry: A Blueprint on how to Build a Person*. Cambridge, MA: MIT Press.

Prakken, Henry. (2010). "On the Nature of Argument Schemes," in C. Reed and C. W. Tindale (Eds.) *Dialectics, Dialogue and Argumentation*, pp. 167-185. London: College Publications.

Todd, Peter M. and Gerd Gigerenzer. (2000). "Précis of simple heuristics that make us smart," *Behavioral and Brain Sciences* 23, 727–780.

Toulmin, Stephen. (1958). *The Uses of Argument*. Cambridge: Cambridge University Press.

Wagemans, Jean H.M. (2019) "Four Basic Argument Forms," *Research in Language*, 17 (1), 57-69.

Walton, Douglas (2013) *Methods of Argumentation*. Cambridge: Cambridge University Press.

Walton, Douglas (2005) *Argumentation Methods for Artificial Intelligence and Law*. Berlin: Springer.

Walton, Douglas (1996) *Argumentation Schemes for Presumptive Reasoning*. Mahwah, N.J., Lawrence Erlbaum Associates.

Walton, Douglas and Fabrizio Macagno (2016) "A classification system for argumentation schemes," *Argument and Computation*. http://dx.doi.org/10.1080/19462166.2015.1123772

Walton, Douglas, *et al.* (2008) *Argumentation Schemes*. Cambridge: Cambridge University Press.

Wellman, Carl. (1971). *Challenge and Response: Justification in Ethics*. Carbondale, IL: Southern Illinois University Press.

ABOUT THE AUTHOR: Christopher W. Tindale is Director of the Centre of Research in Reasoning, Argumentation, and Rhetoric and Professor of Philosophy at the University of Windsor, where he is also co-editor of *Informal Logic* and the book series Windsor Studies in Argumentation. His textbook authorship includes *Good Reasoning Matters* (with Groarke, 5th edition, Oxford 2013) and *Fallacies and Argument Appraisal* (Cambridge 2007). He is the author of many papers in argumentation theory, and his most recent books include *Reason's Dark* Champions (USC Press 2010), *The Philosophy of Argument and Audience Reception* (Cambridge 2015), and a series of essays in Spanish, *Retórica y teoría de la argumentación contemporáneas: ensayos escogidos de Christopher Tindale* (EAFIT 2017).

CHAPTER 11.

THE STRAW MAN AND ITS BABY SEMANTICS

MARCIN LEWIŃSKI

ABSTRACT: In this essay, inspired by Hansen's analysis of the concept of fallacy (Hansen 2002; Hansen and Pinto 1995), I examine what it can possibly mean that the straw man fallacy attacks something else than the "real argument" or the "actual meaning" of one's argumentative opponent. The results are not exactly uplifting for argumentation theory, which seems to employ a textbook-level baby semantics to exemplify and identify the fallacy. I draw on a recent philosophical work on meaning underdetermination and metalinguistic disagreements (Ludlow 2014; Plunkett 2015; Plunkett and Sundell 2013, 2019), to show that "the real arguments" or "meanings" used in the definitions of the straw man are folk concepts that do not stand up to any serious scrutiny. I offer some ways out of the predicament, by arguing that: (1) in certain contexts the identification of the straw man is possible based on contextual parameters for meaning attribution, and that (2) dialectical discussions are often partly, or even primarily, conceptual discussions, where what seem to be attempted straw men and what are typical straw man accusations ("Don't twist my words around!") are part and parcel of a healthy process of conceptual refinement (see Davidson 1994).

KEYWORDS: dialectic, fallacies, Hans V. Hansen, meaning underdetermination, metalinguistic disagreements, semantics of arguments, the straw man fallacy, verbal disputes

1. INTRODUCTION

Hans Hansen has always been a vivid presence in the argumentation community: through his stimulating publications and presentations, thought-provoking comments, probing questions, and, of course, organizational achievements (every OSSA conference I attended since 2009 was Hans's doing). But two of his qualities unquestionably stand out. The first is Hans's erudite insight into the history of the discipline, and its key concepts such as fallacies (Hansen & Pinto 1995) and presumptions (Hansen, Kauffeld, Freeman and Bermejo-Luque 2019). This competence, alongside sheer analytic skills, made his dialectical engagements with other argumentation scholars both helpful and sharp at the same time. The second quality is, then, his persistent and even provocative – but, in the end, always friendly – Socratic questioning of others' work, both in the oral context of presentations and seminars and in written commentaries. This questioning so well epitomizes the dialectical tier in the informal logic school!

These two, I trust, are collectively acknowledged qualities of Hans. But they are also the two qualities I'd like to make a theoretical point of. I will do so while discussing the straw man fallacy, the fallacy of misrepresenting one's opponent's position with the aim of easily refuting this position. The first point regards the connection of the straw man fallacy to the broader intellectual context of argumentation theory, philosophy, and linguistics. Frankly, is there anything *scholarly* to be said about the straw man? It is a term commonly used in ordinary English, it is about argumentation, it is, arguably, a fallacy, and so argumentation scholars are surely supposed to say something about it. But can they say something *substantive* that goes beyond the ordinary treatment? Perhaps I will spoil the fun now, but my argument, while critical, will end with the conclusion that they can, and even should. Only then will I be able to move to my second point, that of the dialectical background of the straw man, namely, of the extent to which hard dialectical questioning can be seen as strawmanning one's opponent. Does being a sharp and relentless critic – a dialectical virtue recognized since Socratic *elenchus* – not violate another dialectical virtue, that of being charitable to one's opponent? And even if it doesn't, how can we distinguish between harsh and even uncomfortable, but altogether reasonable, argumentative interrogation from irrelevant nit-picking, quibbling, or "just playing with words," to use a common expression for dialectical exasperation?

While I am not aware of Hansen's published studies on the straw man fallacy, my analysis will benefit, both in content and method, from his published work on fallacies in general, especially his examination of the very concept of 'fallacy' (Hansen, 2002) and the discussion of fallacies in Hansen and Pinto (1995).

2. IS STRAW MAN A STRAW CONCEPT?

My digital *Oxford English Dictionary* tells me under the 'straw man' entry that it is "an intentionally misrepresented proposition that is set up because it is easier to defeat than an opponent's real argument." Surely, a lot can be said about this definition. In the spirit of Hansen's analysis of the definition of fallacies in general (Hansen 2002), let me be as analytically critical as it gets here. First, this definition is replete with complicated words, such as "intentionally," "proposition," and "because." Is straw man committed *exclusively* when one advances a fishy "proposition" "because" of one's "intention" to easier defeat an opponent's argument? I don't think so – see below for details. Second, it is replete with *very* complicated words, such as "real argument" and "misrepresented." I think we all get the point here. There are some things we say or at least convey in our arguments – and other things we don't convey, let alone explicitly say. Examples abound, and these are the examples typically given in textbooks on fallacies. Many of them are good, intelligent, even realistic examples. But often things are not so simple. Especially, claiming that there are things such as "real arguments" or "words which mean what they mean" – while possibly useful for introductory pedagogical or encyclopedic purposes – is either oblivious to or iconoclastic of the entire tradition of semantics and pragmatics. It is, then, surely something to be investigated – and, indeed, below I will focus on just that.

However, a third notable feature of the *Oxford English Dictionary* definition needs to be noted first: no mention of 'fallacy' is included there, although it can perhaps be easily inferred as an offense against the "real argument." Fallacies are, in an important sense, simply bad arguments which are also characteristically treacherous, in that they hide their own badness (Lewiński and Oswald 2013; Oswald and Lewiński 2014). As such, their treatment is, perhaps necessarily so, parasitic on the treatment of good arguments and can never stand on its own: "There *is* no such thing as a classification of the ways in which men may arrive at an error: it is much to be doubted whether there ever *can be*" (De Morgan 1847, 237; as cited in Hansen 2002,147; see also Hamblin 1970, 13). Whether the fallacy theory as an error theory of sorts can be conceived of or not, the link between fallaciousness and argumentative "goodness" (deductive validity, inductive cogency, dialectical appropriateness) cannot be easily undercut. This is clear in Hansen's definition of a fallacy as *"an argument that appears to be a better argument of its kind than it really is"* (Hansen 2002, 152, italics in original). *OED's* definition of the straw man as a "misrepresented real argument that is easier to defeat" fits in nicely here. Only that it makes the task of understanding what a "misrepresented real argument" is ever more urgent.

Before I take up this task, one final clarification is in place. Is the straw man fallacy an "argument" in the first place? I have discussed this issue earlier (see Lewiński 2011), and I still think the fair solution is this: Committing the straw man fallacy can be seen as (at least) a two-step process consisting of: (1) "setting up a straw man," i.e., unjustifiably representing the opponent's conclusion or premises and (2) "attacking a straw man," i.e., attacking the misrepresentation as if it were the actual conclusion or premises of the opponent. (1) does not necessarily involve an argument. It can be a critical question, such as "How many times did you have a sexual intercourse with Miss Lewiński?", to which a proponent can respond, "I did not have sexual relations with that woman, Miss Lewiński; I only said I had improper physical relationship with her. Please don't twist my words around!" Under proper contextual circumstances, the first question – "How many times did you..." – can be seen as a straw man that is already "set up," but is not yet used. (2) would likely involve a complete argument (something consisting of a conclusion and premises) in which either the conclusion or one of the premises relied on the misrepresentation set up in (1). In particular, if the conclusion is misrepresented and then refuted as if it were the actual conclusion of the proponent, then we can see the straw man as an important subtype of *ignoratio elenchi*: the classic Aristotelian fallacy of ignoring the proper refutation (*elenchus*). An opponent may even construct a sound (true and valid) argument, just not against the conclusion the proponent defended (see Hamblin 1970, 31-32, 87-88; Hansen 2002, 144-145).

In any case, rather than being a strictly "logical" fallacy, the straw man is clearly a dialectical fallacy occurring in argumentative discussions where something is done to the words (meanings? thoughts?) of one's dialectical opponent (Lewiński 2011, 2012; Lewiński and Oswald 2013; Oswald and Lewiński 2014; de Saussure 2018).

3. THE SEMANTICS OF THE STRAW MAN: IN SEARCH OF "THE REAL ARGUMENT"

The fact that the *OED's* definition of the straw man uses the notion of "an opponent's real argument" in the *explanans* of the term might be explained away as a necessary encyclopedic simplification which resorts to folk terminology in order to be understood by folks. But the argumentation scholars' habitual use of expressions such as "the real argument" or "the real position" when discussing the straw man (see Walton 1996, Tindale 2007, 19ff.) deserves some additional critical scrutiny. When working on the issue of the charity of interpretation in argumentative exchanges (Lewiński 2012), I was urged by one of the two peer reviewers for *Informal Logic* to similarly treat as a basis for any discussion of complex, even suspicious, cases, "the real position" of an arguer, explained as what "the arguer really just means," or "what the arguer's argument really is." I never quite understood these comments, even though I still think one can discern a mis-representation inherent in the straw man fallacy from some re-representation that might just be fine (see also Aikin and Casey 2011).

Consider the following examples, due to Schumann, Zufferey and Oswald (2019, 10-11). In these cases, Barbara supports a social policy change (*It is crucial to better support young parents*) resorting to a prudential, economic argument (*because having a child means a lot of financial charges*). Four possible reformulations of Barbara's position put in the mouth of Alexandre have then been analyzed by the authors:

(1)

> Barbara: *It is crucial to better support young parents because having a child means a lot of financial charges.*
>
> (1a) Alexandre: *Let's raise the family allowance since having a child means financial ruin.*
>
> (1b) Alexandre: *Let's raise the family allowance since it only is about the money.*
>
> (1c) Alexandre: *Let's raise the family allowance since having a child can be a financial weight.*
>
> (1d) Alexandre: *Let's raise the family allowance since parents are under economic pressure.*

Two things are noteworthy here. First, none of Alexandre's response uses precisely the expressions Barbara originally uttered. Yet, one can quickly see that while (1c) and (1d) are more or less acceptable paraphrases of Barbara's utterance, (1a) and (1b) are some kind of misrepresentations, and thus very strong straw man candidates. More specifically, (1a) involves an *explicit* misrepresentation by means of a lexical exaggeration of the noun phrase ("financial ruin" instead of "financial charges"), while (1b) an *implicit* misrepresentation by virtue of drawing a contextually illicit pragmatic inference from her argument (a possible gloss by Alexandre: "if you exclusively mention financial charges, that implies it's only about the money") (see Schumann, Zufferey and Oswald 2019, 10-11). Second, I would say – speaking exclusively for myself, not the authors of the said study – that one can arrive at this judgment without quite knowing what Barbara "really just meant." Let's even assume that in some private moment of utter sincerity, she once said off-record that "the way things are now, it's really just about money, young people are so much afraid of the financial burden that they don't have kids anymore. We need to raise the family allowance or we'll be a childless, aging society on its way to extinction." Given the public context of the debate one could argue that, confronted with Alexandre's attack on (1b), she would still have the perfect right to object: "Don't twist my words around! I primarily care about the emotional well-being of our families and the future of our country, but I cannot deny that one problem that can be solved here and now are financial incentives." What is her "real position" now?

Perhaps I am just strawmanning the concept of a straw man; or rather, the concept of "the real man," the "actually meant real argument" of one's opponent. So let me go carefully through the argument, resorting to another example. Consider the following exchange between an external candidate for a head of department at a university (A), and a search committee member (B):

(2)

    A: I think I am the right candidate for the job,
       I have written a number of books on the topic.

    B: Excuse me, sir, but so far as I can see you
       have only one book published on the topic
       with you as the single or first author.

    A: Well, with all due respect, please don't twist
       my words around, I never said all these books
       were published with me as the sole or first
       author. I often write with two of my colleagues.
       Besides, another book is written, submitted, and
       accepted for publication, but not out yet (it will
       be early next year). Finally, my last individual
       monograph is actually written, and about to be
       submitted for evaluation to a very prestigious
       university press.

    B: Why would you even mention in this context a
       manuscript that is not even submitted?! We're
       evaluating people based on their actual results,
       not imagined plans…

Again, was A's "real argument" or "real position" that he should get a job (conclusion) because he has "written a number of books on the topic" (premise), this including books published with him as a second or third author, books written but not published yet, perhaps even books "written" but waiting quietly on his hard disk for better times? Or maybe he "just meant" *published, real books*, including those merely co-authored by him, but excluding edited volumes, books written but not published yet, short eBooks etc. Did A have any "real position" that a reasonable dialectical opponent could and even should "interpret […] as carefully and accurately as possible" (rule 10 of pragma-dialectics, see van Eemeren & Grootendorst 1992, 196)? In general, can we "decide what an arguer's real position actually is" (Tindale 2007, 26), perhaps based on the idea that "words mean what they mean" and, as such, have some kind of an "original meaning," as some legal scholars would claim (see Ludlow 2014, 64ff.)?

Well, an irreverent response could be that "here as elsewhere it doesn't make much sense to divine what the words originally meant – the authors may not have given it any thought" (Ludlow

2014, 59). Do professors writing books have a crystal-clear grasp of what books "really are"? It would seem not. Do institutions employing book writers—such as universities—have a crystal-clear grasp of what books "really are"? It would seem not. Some of them might be favorable to your promotion or tenure if you "have a book" in the sense of a prestigious edited volume. Some not. Some would flatly dismiss an eBook openly accessible via your library's depository. Some would count it in. Etcetera.

Note, these are not primarily empirical arguments, although to an extent they can be. In particular, the example above is not an empirically observed and transcribed conversation. Instead, it is a made-up case that I invented ripping off Ludlow's (2014) opening example of how underdetermined the very concept of a 'book' is. 'Book' is such a basic word in English, and many other languages, but still, as Ludlow observes, "even after a millennium of shared usage the meaning is quite open-ended" (2014, 1). Because of this, in the case reported by Ludlow, his position as a writer himself can be that he has "written two or three or six or ten books" (2014, 1) without *any* change to the facts on the ground.

This, of course, has serious consequences for how argumentative exchanges—such as the one during a somewhat fraught job interview—develop and, indeed, what they are about. One of the things that happen in argumentative discussions is that both speakers legitimately and quite ordinarily modulate an underdetermined meaning—and they do so in a strategically advantageous manner (Lewiński 2011, 2012). Think of the book argument advanced by the aspiring department chair. Unsurprisingly, his opponent (the bitchy committee member) would likely endorse the most stringent meaning of a 'book' as a substantive text, written exclusively or primarily by a specific author, and published by an esteemed international press. The proponent, the job candidate, could possibly stretch the meaning to the other extreme: why not include a collection of essays edited by me and a colleague that is still to be sent to the publisher, and will be freely available as an eBook in our university's digital library? Depending on the purported meaning, the argument of the candidate could be numerically glossed as, "hire me, I have *eight* books on the topic," while the critique of the committee member as, "I don't think you're a strong candidate, just *one* book..." None of them would likely intentionally misrepresent some "real position" grounded in some "real meaning" of the concept of 'book'—just because, so the underdetermination of meaning argument goes, there is no such real meaning.

But would not all this take down the *real* dialectic, where arguers discuss substantive issues, the facts on the ground, off its pedestal and into the realm of semantic quibbles and merely verbal disputes (see Chalmers 2011, Krabbe and van Laar 2019)? Isn't there simply a real book, on whose meaning the arguers should settle before getting down to the real business of discussing serious issues at hand such as tenures and promotions, rather than mere words, words, words? A real and ideal book in the Platonic sense, perhaps?

> I agree that Plato is elucidating a number of important concepts and they are getting more and more precise, but I don't agree that this is because we are getting closer to the concepts themselves as they rest in Plato's heaven. I would argue that we are merely coming up with better and better modulations—or if you prefer, we are constructing better and better concepts. What makes them better is not that they are closer to some perfect target, but rather that [...] we are coming up with progressively more serviceable modulations via a normatively constrained process of argumentation. (Ludlow 2014, 111)

This, admittedly, is an argument well-known since Quine's thesis of the indeterminacy of meaning and his critique of "the myth of the museum":

> Uncritical semantics is the myth of a museum in which the exhibits are meanings and the words are labels. [...] Seen according to the

museum myth, the words and sentences of a language have their determinate meanings. To discover the meanings of the native's words we may have to observe his behavior, but still the meanings of the words are supposed to be determinate in the native's mind, his mental museum, even in cases where behavioral criteria are powerless to discover them for us. When on the other hand we recognize with Dewey that "meaning ... is primarily a property of behavior," we recognize that there are no meanings, nor likenesses nor distinctions of meaning, beyond what are implicit in people's dispositions to overt behavior. (Quine 1968, 186-187)

What emerges from Quine's critique of the "uncritical semantics" where words and sentences are attached to *fixed* and *determined* meanings is, then, semantics which instead acknowledges an intrinsic relationship between the way we use our words and our concepts. Our conversational interactions – and argumentative interactions in particular – are where our *dynamic* and *underdetermined* meanings are put to the critical test and, hopefully, become somewhat sharper. Some kind of a conceptual clarification and resulting mutual understanding of what the other means are thus likely the results of – not the prerequisites for – reasonable, "normatively constrained" argumentative discussions.

Of course, critics of the strong indeterminacy thesis (Quine: there is no fact of the matter regarding real meanings) and the weaker underdetermination thesis (Davidson, Ludlow: meanings can be sharpened and mutually agreed on) point to the fact that communication typically *is* successful, that speakers often impart their mental contents to others without great effort (Pagin 2008). This, of course, has not escaped the attention of Quine (1960, 1968) and those after him. The crucial point here is that our theories of meaning need to be sensitive to the possibility of entirely legitimate processes of argumentation over meaning, recently described in some detail under the terms of *meaning negotiations, meaning litigation, metalinguistic disputes,* or *conceptual engineering* (Cappelen 2018, Ludlow 2014, Plunkett 2015, Plunkett and Sundell 2013, 2019). Once this weaker argument is recognized, not everything that looks, walks, and talks like a straw man turns out to be a straw man.

All the same, argumentation theorists dedicated to the study of fallacies are often bound to the Aristotelian tradition of analyzing abuses of argumentation (see Hamblin 1970, Hansen 2002, Hansen and Pinto 1995). This is not surprising, given Aristotle's foundational contributions to the study of argumentation and his historical prominence. One enduring idea is to divide fallacies into those dependent on language (*in dictione*) and those outside of language (*extra dictionem*) (Aristotle, *Sophistical Refutations*; Hamblin 1970, Chs. 2-3). Aristotle indeed provided a very powerful catalogue of what can go wrong with the use of language in argumentative discourse, this including the problems of ambiguity and equivocation, the cornerstone of the theories of semantic underdetermination. Some even claim this is all there is to fallacies. Powers (1995) proposes his "One Fallacy Theory" departing from precisely this assumption:

> [One Fallacy Theory] insists that there is no fallacy unless there is a clearly specifiable appearance of validity (or goodness of whatever kind). Since I believe there is no clear way to make an argument appear to have a goodness it really lacks except by playing with ambiguities, every real fallacy will turn out to be a fallacy of equivocation. (Powers 1995, 290)

Indeed, attention to the linguistic treacherousness of fallacies, and especially the clearly language-based fallacies such as the straw man, is a *sine qua non* condition in any comprehensive treatment of fallacies (see our arguments in Lewiński and Oswald 2013 and Oswald and Lewiński 2014). As repeatedly noted, however (Tindale 2007, Walton 1996), the straw man – its Ancient Greek structural or functional equivalent, that is – has not been among the fallacies recognized by Aristotle. Moreover, as already mentioned, the nearest possible classical counterpart would be *ignoratio elenchi*, curiously, a fallacy *not* based in language. As a result, Powers, who avowedly follows Aristotle in his treatment of fallacies dependent on language, has nothing to say about the straw man. Instead, he propounds his theory based on the following semantics of ambiguity:

> All the fallacies involve playing with ambiguities. So we divide the different types of ambiguity. A sentence is built out of words or word-parts or phrases to which meanings are conventionally assigned. The meanings of the ultimate meaningful parts are said to be *lexically* assigned. Thus in "rented" a meaning is assigned to "rent" and one to the part "ed." The phrase "fell off the wagon" may be understood literally in terms of its parts "fell," "off," "the," and "wagon," or lexically as a whole receive the meaning "went back to drinking." The lexically meaningful parts are then put together grammatically to make up the sentence.

If a lexical part has more than one meaning, we have a *lexical* ambiguity. (Sometimes "equivocation" is used in a narrower sense than mine to cover only lexical equivocations.) If the lexical parts are unambiguous, but it is ambiguous how the parts are grammatically put together, we have a grammatical ambiguity, also called an *amphiboly*. (Powers 1995, 291)

What is the "conventionally assigned" meaning of a 'book'? If there isn't one, perhaps we are constantly committing the fallacy of equivocation whenever mentioning a "book"? We can even make this point more precise: while the notion of 'book' is perhaps not *ambiguous*, whereby two or more determinate meanings are "conventionally assigned" to the same word (like in 'bank' or 'runs'), it is nonetheless *vague*, in the sense that we don't have a determinate concept in the first place, as discussed above. Even in this case, however, it would fall under the "One Fallacy Theory" (Powers 1995, 297-298). If we follow the arguments of the semantic underdeterminists, we would then have a systemic implosion of the fallacy of equivocation in any use of language – and the corresponding shrinking of the straw man fallacy to only most blatant abuses (for then the "error" would lie in the vague expression in the first place, not in the attacker's misrepresentation).

How can this *reductio ad absurdum* be averted? One famous response is to abandon natural language as inherently vague, and turn instead to formal logic as a proper area of inquiry into inference and argument (see Grice 1989, for a well-known exposition and criticism of this argument). Another, noted in passing by Powers, is to resort to semantic conventionalism (for a recent account, see Lepore and Stone 2015): there are socially recognized conventions that might quite precisely determine the meaning of a given term in a specific context of use. There might even be some kind of institutional ontology around a concept such as a 'book' (see Searle 2010), an ontology that would define what *counts as* a book in a given context (e.g., "a (co-authored), peer-reviewed scientific text of 50.000 words or more, published as an individual volume at one of the commercial or university presses officially indexed in the Web of Science"). Conventionalism, however, cannot account for many phenomena of rational linguistic communication, as argued by intentionalists (e.g., Strawson 1964; Grice 1989; Sperber and Wilson 1995): much of what is communicated is grounded in what speakers intend to convey, over and above the literal, explicit meanings, via the process of pragmatic inference, notably implicatures. Finally, one might want to resort to semantic minimalism and claim that at bottom there *is* a minimal, fixed meaning, grounded in the literal meaning of non-indexical expressions, or to semantic contextualism that would instead insist that the meaning of propositions is always contextually-variant, open to contextually-relevant pragmatic enrichment, especially in the case of indexicals (see Cappelen and Lepore 2005, for a discussion).

Now, I am mentioning these obvious facts only in an encyclopedically simplified form. But even in this form they allow me to sketch two conclusions, both of which are almost grim for argumentation theory. First, the discipline, in its attempts to define what rational argumentative interaction is, is bound by the principle requiring arguers to have clear and distinct definitions of concepts ready prior to any meaningful dispute. If the speakers do not mutually agree on the meanings and definitions of terms, they are in effect talking past each other, sinking ever deeper in their futile misunderstandings rather than resolving worthwhile disagreements. In many practical contexts this is, of course, a reasonable requirement: colloquially speaking, "we need to know what we're talking about," so as to avoid a *merely* verbal dispute and instead produce some fruitful dialectic.

However, this colloquial idea does not easily pass muster of critical scrutiny. Geach, in his analysis of Plato's first Socratic dialogue, *Euthyphro*, calls it a *Socratic fallacy* and insists on the following:

> Let us be clear that this *is* a fallacy, and nothing better. It has stimulated philosophical enquiry, but still it is a fallacy. We know heaps of things without being able to define the terms in which we express our knowledge. Formal definitions are only one way of elucidating terms; a set of examples may in a given case be more useful than a formal definition. (Geach 1966, 371)

This criticism has not lost its currency today. Quite the contrary, as already discussed above, it fuels recent discussions of meaning underdetermination and the value of metalinguistic disputes. Among others, Plunkett and Sundell argue that "the assumption that sameness of meaning is necessary for the expression of genuine disagreement is what leads so many theorists to ascribe meanings to speakers that systematically diverge from those speakers' usage and first-order intuitions" (Plunkett and Sundell 2019, 18).

That is to say, in its allegiance to the Ancient Greek principles, such as the priority of definitions and determination of meanings, the discipline might be committing a fallacy itself. This brings me to the second grim point: even assuming that these principles *are* defensible – in many ordinary contexts they perhaps even are – argumentation theory has not produced its clear position on how the allegedly fixed and definable meanings can actually be fixed: by linguistic conventions alone, by speakers' intentions, by contextual features, by the circumstances of evaluation, etc., etc. As a result, when discussing the straw man and other fallacies of language, the discipline resorts to textbook quality explanations and folk concepts such as "what the arguer really just means." In this way – involuntarily, one would hope – it produces its baby semantics for absolute beginners. This conclusion is, I think, very much in the spirit of Hansen's investigations of the discipline, both historical and conceptual. One of their chief result is that argumentation theory is not a *biblia pauperum* of sorts, a largely pedagogical discipline meant to translate the complexities of logic and the philosophy of language to "dummies" interested in everyday argumentation. Instead, it is a rich discipline with its own canon of works, original concepts, and self-aware critical responses to its nearest cousins such as formal logic.

Now, in all fairness, when it comes to the straw man fallacy argumentation scholars are aware of the fact that concepts such as "the real argument," "the real position," or "the standpoint actually advanced" are idealizations that might not necessarily work well in actual discussions.[1] However, for ease of exposition

---

1. To give but two, but prominent and quite representative, examples:"In practice, the differences between the attacked standpoint and the original standpoint will often be quite subtle. By design, the opponent's words are so twisted that it becomes at the same time easy for the distorter to tackle and difficult for an outsider to tell whether justice is being done to the original standpoint." (van Eemeren & Grootendorst 1992, 127–128)."Because of the various kinds of problems and trickiness in determining what an arguer's position really is in a given case, it can be easy to get this wrong, and to mistake an arguer's real position for something else that is not her real position, but only appears to be. This is the essence of the deception or error inherent in the straw man fallacy as a distinctive type of sophistical tactic. [...] It is important to realize that the job of determining what an arguer's commit-

(that's my best guess), they still discuss the puzzles involved parenthetically – and, in any case, treat them as *practical* problems of implementation rather than *theoretical* issues in semantics that need to be, one way or another, addressed.

One final remark before getting out of the dark: here, I focus exclusively on the *semantics* of the straw man fallacy, while, together with Steve Oswald, I treated its *pragmatics* in other work (esp. Lewiński 2011; Lewiński and Oswald 2013; Oswald and Lewiński 2014). Thanks in part to the pragmatic theories of argumentation, such as pragma-dialectics (see esp. van Eemeren, Grootendorst, Jackson and Jacobs 1993), the pragmatic phenomena of argumentative exchanges have received closer attention. This attention has recently turned into a serious empirical program of investigating the linguistic and pragmatic details of various forms of possible straw man (see de Saussure 2018; Schumann, Zufferey and Oswald 2019; Mu̇ller forthcoming).

4. THE DIALECTIC OF THE STRAW MAN

The discussion in the previous section lets me also formulate the guiding principle for this section, namely: playing on the meaning of words or phrases is *not* necessarily a straw man. It might instead be a necessary, indeed valuable, contribution to a collective conceptual refinement of vague, ambiguous, unclear, or otherwise underdetermined terms.

Above, I already suggested what the possible relation between the concept of open-ended, underdetermined meanings and an argumentative discussion can be. Part and parcel of an argumentative exchange in natural language would not only be an argumentative contest over the "facts on the ground" but also a dispute over the meaning of the words used. These two aspects – traditionally dichotomized into, respectively, substantive and

ments really are, or may fairly be taken to be, in a real case, is by no means trivial" (Walton 1996, 125-126).

verbal disputes – have intricate relations that are yet to be fully appreciated (see Balcerak Jackson 2014; Chalmers 2011; Plunkett 2015; Plunkett and Sundell 2013, 2019; Rott 2015; Vermeulen 2018; for some of the recent contributions to the debate). The meaning is, of course, consequential for how a given position can be defended and objected to – it would be utterly surprising, then, if arguers were not attentive to this element in their discussions. How can this process be grasped in terms of argumentation?

To start with, I will assume an adversarial view on argumentative discussions, not unlike the classic Socratic elenchus referred to above, or its contemporary rendering in pragma-dialectics (see Lewiński 2011, 2012, 2017 for a detailed defense). Arguers are out to defend their position on an issue and have it accepted by their critics. To this end, they go through an agonistic process of advancing arguments, asking critical questions, providing counterarguments, etc. This process, while agonistic and thus likely strategic, is also inherently cooperative: for the whole process to be reasonable and simply meaningful, arguers need to follow some basic rules, such as those defining relevant types of speech acts, acceptable inferences (formal and informal), possible responses to an opponent's contributions, and commitments that arguers are bound to undertake or retract, as needed (see Hamblin 1970). It is, shortly, both a normative and a strategic endeavor (see van Eemeren 2010).

Now, whenever some term, such as 'book', is underdetermined it will characteristically have various plausible interpretations ("modulations", in Ludlow's 2014, parlance), some of them benefitting one arguer, and others her opponent. Let's return to our job interview and the book argument. As already described, the job candidate would most likely stretch the concept of 'book' to its widest possible extension, including edited books, eBooks, and written manuscripts, even those still under review. By contrast, the uncharitable committee member would likely say something like, "Let's be professional about it, this is a profes-sional context, right? For me a 'book' is, I quote, 'a (co-)authored, peer-reviewed scientific text of 50.000 words or more, published as an individual volume at one of the commercial or university presses officially indexed in the Web of Science.' You have merely *one* of those, and I hope I'll die in a ditch before we have a depart-ment chair like that." The job candidate can then respond, "That's just like, your opinion, man... I quote from the APA's recent rule-book where a book means 'a substantive text written or edited by a scholar, and published through traditional or digital chan-nels, or considered for such publication'. I have *eight* of those, you won't get a better hire!" Importantly, throughout this process, neither of them is misrepresenting the (real?) concept of 'book', but rather modulating it to his or her own dialectical advantage. And, as long as their arguments are reasonable – those above probably are – they are not only *not* committing a straw man (nor any other fallacy of language described by Powers 1995), but rather engaging in a strategically understandable and, poten-tially, conceptually fruitful *elenchus* over the meaning in ques-tion.[2]

Yet, one cannot deny that straw men do happen. My argument so far has been limited to *underdetermined* terms; but many would argue this pertains to virtually all our vocabulary ("What exactly does '3 o'clock' mean?"; see Ludlow 2014), or at least to the

2. However, there is a difference between attributing to the protagonist a meaning that patently misrepresents the meaning he intended, and signaled as intended, and advancing a reasonable metalinguistic argument. Compare the committee member's retort, "Well, if any written text is a 'book' to you, I have written about 237 of them!", with, "I see what you're trying to say, but at our university 'books' are only *published* books, period." While in both cases the protagonist (the job candidate) can claim to "own" the meaning or at least have some meaning precedence, only in the former case could he justifiably issue a straw man accusation ("Don't twist my words around!"). As a conse-quence, assuming both retorts of the committee member are *metalinguistic* arguments, meaning disputes can still include moves which commit a straw man fallacy. (Thank you to Steve Oswald for pointing this out!)

most important part of it ("Is waterboarding 'torture'?"; see Plunkett and Sundell 2013, 2019), or least to the most esteemed and famous part of the most important part ("Is our will 'free'?"; see Chalmers 2011). Still, let's bar meaning underdetermination for a second as a philosophers' gibberish. Here's a semantic straw man:

(3)

> A: I won't go there again. The food was pretty
> bland, and expensive for that.

> B: Well, no, I myself didn't find it inedible.
> And the company paid, so what's the problem?

'Bland' and 'inedible' cannot easily be modulated so as to be one and the same concept – all the troubles regarding the predicates of personal taste notwithstanding (see Stojanovic, 2007). So we clearly have a straw man here. But real examples – I again invented this one – are hardly ever so simple. Meticulous analyses of actual cases (see Lewiński 2011; Lewiński and Oswald 2013; Oswald and Lewiński 2014) reveal that much of the difficulty rests in the pragmatic aspect of natural language: strawmanners may astutely manipulate various types of pragmatic inference in order to cover up and get away with the abuse. Here, as already mentioned, I limit myself to the semantic issues – all the troubles regarding the semantics-pragmatics distinction notwithstanding, again (see Plunkett and Sundell 2019, for a discussion in the context of metalinguistic negotiations).

In any case, the dialectical discussion over meanings should be governed by "a normatively constrained process of argumentation" (Ludlow 2014, 111). For Ludlow, this process is primarily grounded in analogical argumentation: one would argue analogically from undisputed, canonical cases, thus tracking the important properties of the term as applied in the new context of the current dispute. Importantly, much has to do with the contextual conditions of the debate: the question of whether a "fetus" is a "person" can lead to a very different answer in the strictly legal, strictly medical, or strictly religious context. That is, different arguments from analogy would be deemed reasonable in various context of an argumentative discussion over meanings.

In my earlier work (see Lewiński 2011; 2012; Lewiński and Oswald 2013), I have advocated similar contextual conditions for what I have called an *intersubjective interpretation procedure*. When in dispute over the meaning of their expressions – which can be triggered by the straw man attempts or straw man accusations – arguers need to abide by two crisscrossing criteria of interpretation: the precision required by the context at hand and the charity of interpretation. The resulting simple matrix of four options is presented in Table 1.

	Precise interpretation	Loose interpretation
Highly critical (uncharitable)	Criminal trial, blind academic review, job interview?	Political debates
Constructive (charitable)	Doctor-patient consultation, classroom discussion, conference presentation?	Small friendly talk, family dinner table

Table 1. Contextual precision and charity of interpretation

In the first place, various forms of institutionalized activities offer precise rules of interpretation of discourse. Legal discourse is a paradigmatic example here, but so is any specialized context, including perhaps a job interview at a university, where a 'book' can mean a specific type of scholarly publication, rather than just any longer written text. Other contexts in the private or public sphere may allow for more laxity in meaning, thereby making a meaning dispute ever more likely and the straw man ever more unlikely. In the second place, one can distinguish between charitable (constructive) and uncharitable (critical) argumentative contexts. A certain expectation of constructive or critical engagement affects the contextually appropriate level of meaning nit-pickiness. Compare an argument over an experiment in a high-school chemistry class with cross-examination in a criminal trial: while similar levels of precision might be required in both contexts, the classroom discussion calls for the interpretive benefit of the doubt, when necessary, at least on the part of the teacher. As a result, in the classroom context the attacks on interpretations which are plausible, but less than charitable, can be seen as attacks on straw men, whereas they would be seen as tough but overall reasonable criticisms in the legal context. As for our job interview: there doesn't seem to exist any firm convention regarding the levels of necessary charity, but an interrogative, even bitchy, critical attitude of the committee members seem to be one recognizable option for a job interview. Similarly for the precision of rules of interpretation: there might be institutional regulations defining what counts as a 'book', or 'an academic publication' at large, and in this case arguers should in principle be bound by them. Only "in principle," however, because *descriptive* metalinguistic disputes, with arguments resorting to how a term actually *is* used by some authority, institution, or by custom, do not preclude *normative* metalinguistic disputes, where arguments turn on how a term *ought to* be used, even despite the currently accepted, prevalent, or even mandated meaning (Plunkett and Sundell 2013, 2019).

To sum up, arguers should conduct their argumentative discussions with these general rules in mind. Depending on the contextual conditions, meaning disputes will be more or less open to arguers' modulating the meaning of the words, and, respectively, less or more rigid when it comes to the straw man identification.

5. CONCLUSION: TOWARD MEANING ARGUMENTATIVISM

Before reaching an optimistic conclusion, let me first summarize the argument of the entire chapter in three sentences. In order to identify the straw man fallacy, we need to have some idea of how to adjudicate between the meaning of the original arguments and the meanings attributed in the alleged straw man attack. There are various ways of solving this semantic predicament: we can rely on the intention of the original arguer ("No, no, don't twist my words around, I meant..."), on some governing convention ("At our university 'x' means "x""), on mutual agreement between speakers ("For the current purposes, let us define 'x' as "x""), etc. And while none of these solutions is fully satisfactory – by virtue of each of them being unreflectively tied to spurious assumptions regarding the determination of meaning – one possible idea is to resort to the contextual criteria of precision and constructiveness of linguistic usage and vary our fallacy judgements accordingly.

The optimistic conclusion is that whereas argumentation theory has not been capable of producing or even resorting to some defensible theory of meaning, it can find a solution in its own midst. The varied contextual criteria proposed above allow us to undermine the dubious assumptions about meaning and come up with a less-than-grim solution. I will call this solution *meaning argumentativism*. In a sense, it has been argued for all along this essay through my critical arguments and the analyses of examples; yet, I surely haven't been able to express it in as few words as Donald Davidson when he spoke about "the cooperative reworking of verbal usage that occurs in dialectical exchange" (1994, 435). Analyzing Plato's *Euthyphro*—the exact same dialogue that led Geach to identify the *Socratic fallacy*—Davidson declares the he sees "the Socratic elenchus as a crucible in which some of our most important words, and the concepts they express, are tested, melted down, reshaped, and given a new edge" (1994, 435):

> As they try to understand each other, people in open discussion use the same words, but whether they mean the same things by those words, or mean anything clear at all, only the process of question and answer can reveal. [...] If it attains its purpose, an elenctic discussion is an event in which the meanings of words, the concepts entertained by the speakers, evolve and are clarified. In this respect

it is a model of every successful attempt at communication. (Davidson 1994, 432)

This is more than little praise for the role of argumentation in our communication. But it's also an indictment and a challenge to abandon the baby semantics of "the real argument" and engage in serious reconsideration of the functions of argumentative discussions. Instead of being a *sine qua non* condition for meaningful argumentative discussions, semantic clarification and refinement is their result, and often a precious one (for recent arguments, see Cappelen 2018; Ludlow 2014; Plunkett and Sundell 2013, 2019). As I have argued, the analysis of one single fallacy, the straw man, can be a good point of entry into such reconsideration. Yes, it will likely make the straw man a concept more obscure than our students need, but it can also lead us to a better understanding of what argumentation, and argumentation theory, is about.

REFERENCES

Aikin, S. J. and Casey, J. 2011. Straw men, weak men, and hollow men. *Argumentation, 25*(1), 87-105.

Aristotle. 1984. *The complete works of Aristotle.* Ed. by J. Barnes. Princeton, NJ: Princeton University Press.

Balcerak Jackson, B. 2014. Verbal disputes and substantiveness. *Erkenntnis, 79*(S1), 31–54.

Cappelen, H. and Lepore, E. 2005. *Insensitive semantics. A defense of semantic minimalism and speech act pluralism.* Oxford: Blackwell.

Chalmers, D. J. 2011. Verbal disputes. *Philosophical Review, 120*(4), 515-566.

Davidson, D. 1994. Dialectic and dialogue. In G. Preyer, F. Siebelt and A. Ulfig (eds.), *Language, Mind and Epistemology, Synthese Library, Vol. 241* (429-437). Dordrecht: Springer.

Eemeren, F.H. van. 2010. *Strategic maneuvering in argumentative discourse: Extending the pragma-dialectical theory of argumentation*. Amsterdam: John Benjamins.

Eemeren, F. H. van and Grootendorst, R. 1992. *Argumentation, communication, and fallacies: A pragma-dialectical perspective*. Hillsdale, NJ: Lawrence Erlbaum.

Eemeren, F.H. van, Grootendorst, R., Jackson, S. and Jacobs, S. 1993. *Reconstructing argumentative discourse*. Tuscaloosa, AL: University of Alabama Press.

Geach, P. T. 1966. Plato's "Euthyphro": An analysis and commentary. *The Monist, 50*(3), 369-382.

Grice, P. 1989. *Studies in the way of words*. Cambridge, MA: Harvard University Press.

Hamblin, C. L. 1970. *Fallacies*. London: Methuen.

Hansen, H. V. 2002. The straw thing of fallacy theory: The standard definition of 'fallacy'. *Argumentation, 16*(2), 133–155.

Hansen, H. V., Kauffeld, F. J., Freeman, J. B. and Bermejo-Luque, L. (Eds.). 2019. *Presumptions and burdens of proof: An anthology of argumentation and the law*. Tuscaloosa, AL: University of Alabama Press.

Hansen, H. V. and Pinto, R. C. 1995. *Fallacies: Classical and contemporary readings*. University Park, PA: The Pennsylvania State University Press.

Krabbe, E. C. W. and van Laar, J. A. 2019. In the quagmire of quibbles: A dialectical exploration. *Synthese*, DOI: 10.1007/s11229-019-02289-4.

Lepore, E. and Stone, M. 2015. *Imagination and convention: Distinguishing grammar and inference in language*. Oxford: Oxford University Press.

Lewiński, M. 2011. Towards a critique-friendly approach to the straw man fallacy evaluation. *Argumentation, 25*(4), 469–497.

Lewiński, M. 2012. The paradox of charity. *Informal Logic, 32*(4), 403-439.

Lewiński, M. 2017. Practical argumentation as reasoned advocacy. *Informal Logic, 37*(2), 85-113.

Lewiński, M. and Oswald, S. 2013. When and how do we deal with straw men? A normative and cognitive pragmatic account. *Journal of Pragmatics, 59,* 164-177.

Ludlow, P. 2014. *Living words: Meaning underdetermination and the dynamic lexicon.* Oxford: Oxford University Press.

Müller, M. L. forthcoming. Non-propositional meanings and commitment attribution: More arguments in favor of a cognitive approach. Forthcoming in the *Journal of Argumentation in Context, 9*(1).

Oswald, S, and Lewin´ski, M. 2014. Pragmatics, cognitive heuristics and the straw man fallacy. In T. Herman and S. Oswald (eds.), *Rhetoric and cognition: Theoretical perspectives and persuasive strategies* (313-343). Bern: Peter Lang.

Pagin, P. 2008. What is communicative success? *Canadian Journal of Philosophy, 38*(1), 85-115.

Plunkett, D. 2015. Which concepts should we use? Metalinguistic negotiations and the methodology of philosophy. *Inquiry, 58* (7-8), 828–874.

Plunkett, D. and Sundell, T. 2013. Disagreement and the semantics of normative and evaluative terms. *Philosophers' Imprint, 13* (23), 1–37.

Plunkett, D. and Sundell, T. 2019. Metalinguistic negotiation and speaker error. *Inquiry,*
DOI: 10.1080/0020174X.2019.1610055.

Powers, L. H. 1995. Equivocation. In H. V. Hansen and R. C. Pinto (eds.), *Fallacies: Classical and contemporary readings* (287-301). University Park, PA: The Pennsylvania State University Press.

Quine, W.V.O. 1960. *Word and object.* Cambridge, MA: MIT Press.

Quine, W.V.O. 1968. Ontological relativity. *The Journal of Philosophy, 65*(7), 185-212.

Rott, H. 2015. A puzzle about disputes and disagreements. *Erkenntnis, 80*(S1), 167–189.

Saussure, L. de. 2018. The straw man fallacy as a prestige-gaining device. In S. Oswald, T. Herman and J. Jacquin (eds.), *Argumentation and language. Linguistic, cognitive and discursive explorations* (171-190). Cham: Springer.

Schumann, J., Zufferey, S. and Oswald, S. 2019. What makes a straw man acceptable? Three experiments assessing linguistic factors. *Journal of Pragmatics, 141,* 1-15.

Searle, J. R. 2010. *Making the social world: The structure of human civilization.* Oxford: Oxford University Press.

Sperber, D. and Wilson, D. 1995. *Relevance: Communication and cognition* (2nd ed.). Malden, MA: Blackwell.

Stojanovic, I. 2007. Talking about taste: Disagreement, implicit arguments, and relative truth. *Linguistics and Philosophy, 30,* 691–706.

Strawson, P. F. 1964. Intention and convention in speech acts. *The Philosophical Review, 73*(4), 439-460.

Tindale, C. W. 2007. *Fallacies and argument appraisal.* Cambridge: Cambridge University Press.

Vermeulen, I. 2018. Verbal disputes and the varieties of verbalness. *Erkenntnis, 83*(2), 331–348.

Walton, D. N. (1996). The straw man fallacy. In J. van Benthem, F.H. van Eemeren, R. Grootendorst, & F. Veltman (eds.), Logic and argumentation (pp. 115–128). Amsterdam: Royal Netherlands Academy of Arts and Sciences.

ABOUT THE AUTHOR: Marcin Lewiński is assistant professor and the coordinator of the Reasoning and Argumentation Lab (ArgLab) at the Nova Institute of Philosophy (IFILNOVA), Nova University of Lisbon, Portugal. He is the Main Proposer and Chair of the COST Action CA17132: *European Network for Argumentation and Public Policy Analysis (APPLY),* funded by the Horizon 2020 Programme of the European Commission. In his work, Marcin uses concepts from argumentation theory, the philosophy of language, and discourse analysis to shed light on the complexity of today's public discourse and the resulting challenges to the rationality of argumentation, especially in deliberative contexts. He has published widely on these topics and is currently consolidating his research in the Polylogue Framework.

CHAPTER 12.

HANSEN ON THE STRUCTURE OF BALANCE-OF-CONSIDERATIONS ARGUMENTS

YUN XIE

ABSTRACT: This paper is a critical examination of Hans Hansen's structural account of balance-of-considerations arguments. On the one hand, it shows that Hansen has developed an innovative structure for balance-of-considerations arguments in terms of an infer-ence to 'even though', and further defended it with a linguistic foundation. On the other hand, it argues that Hansen has over-interpreted the contrastive import of 'even though' to be an effect of unequal strength, and in that way failed to offer sufficient justi-fication for the element of on-balance premise in his novel struc-ture. However, it is further indicated that Hansen's insights about the rhetorical meaning of 'even though' can be developed to validate the presence of the on-balance premise in his own account.

KEYWORDS: balance-of-considerations argument, counter-consideration, even-though relation, the on-balance premise

1. INTRODUCTION

Since its introduction into the argumentation scholarly commu-nity in 1980s, the notion of conductive arguments has received much attention (Govier 1979, 1987, 1999; Blair 2011; Possin

2012; Hitchcock 1981, 2013). Over the last decade, based on a variety of views, as well as controversies, about the mechanism of justification in conduction and its resulting argument structure, different approaches have been developed to its analysis and evaluation (Blair & Johnson 2011; Wohlrapp 2011; Adler 2013; van Laar 2014; Blair 2016; Possin 2016; Xie 2017; Juthe 2019; Yu & Zenker 2019; Bermejo-Luque 2019). During the course of such a development in theorizing conductive arguments, undoubtedly Hans Hansen has made very important contributions. He not only provides a unique account for understanding the structure of conductive arguments, but also probes into the most fundamental issues, with deep insights, pertaining to the nature of conduction (Hansen 2010, 2011).

This paper aims to provide an analysis and a critical examination of Hansen's structural account of balance-of-considerations arguments, i.e., the third-pattern conductive arguments. On the one hand, it shows that Hansen has developed an innovative structure for balance-of-considerations arguments, and also laid for it a linguistic foundation through a thorough analysis of the 'even-though' relation. On the other hand, it argues that Hansen has over-interpreted the contrastive import of 'even though' and failed to offer a sufficient justification for a core element in his own account. In section 2, I first sketch Hansen's structural account of balance-of-considerations arguments that is built on an intermediate inference to "even though". Then I discuss in section 3 Hansen's critical scrutiny of different possible roles of counter-considerations, with a special focus on its relation to the development of his own structural model. And in section 4 I review Hansen's study of linguistic counter-consideration indicators and explain how he has tried to substantiate his novel structure in terms of the "even-though" relation. After that, in sections 5 and 6, I offer a criticism of his linguistic analysis of "even though", and then consider a proposal that could fulfill the potential of his linguistic study of 'even though' to defend his structure of balance-of-considerations arguments. In Section 7, I provide some concluding remarks.

2. A NOVEL STRUCTURE OF BALANCE-OF-CONSIDERATIONS ARGUMENTS

As far as I can trace it back, Hansen started to be interested in studying conductive arguments since 2008. He has discussed different topics related to conduction on several occasions, for example the meeting of the NCA Annual Convention, the Group Session at the Central Division of American Philosophical Association Meetings, and the Windsor Symposium on Conductive Arguments. Later on, his main ideas on conductive arguments have been presented in a more comprehensive way in a paper published in 2011, "Notes on balance-of-considerations arguments". In that paper, Hansen offered insightful discussions on different aspects of balance-of-considerations arguments, including the historical antecedents of Wellman's notion of conduction, the defining characteristics of conductive arguments, the role of counter-considerations, the problems related to the on-balance premises, and the "even-though" relation. On that basis, notably, Hansen has developed a brand-new account for understanding the logical structure of balance-of-considerations arguments, according to which the general schema for balance-of-considerations arguments would be like this (with 'CC' abbreviating 'counter-consideration'):

P_1: Independent reason$_1$ (for conclusion K)

...

P_n: Independent reason$_n$ (for conclusion K)

P_{n+1}: The reasons in P_1 to P_n taken together *outweigh* the independent counter-considerations to K, CC_1 to CC_n taken together

C: *K even though* CC_1 *&...&* CC_n (inference to 'even though')

P: *K even though* CC_1 *&...&* CC_n

C: *K* (simplification) (Hansen 2011, p. 39)[1]

This way of structuring balance-of-considerations arguments is then diagrammed as the following (p. 40):

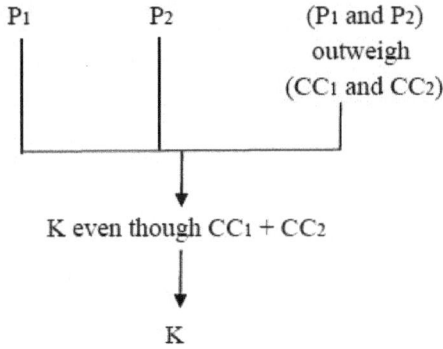

It is easy to see that here Hansen is proposing a sub-argument structure for balance-of-considerations arguments, a structure that is indeed more complicated than the general model proposed by many others (Govier 2010; Blair 2016; see Jin 2011 for an overview). For instance, Blair once offered a structure for conductive arguments which is in a much simpler form (2016, p. 124):

1.1 a, b, c, ... , support p.
1.2 w, x, y, ... , support not-p.
1.3 a, b, c, ... outweigh w, x, y, ... (or conversely).
So,
1 p (or not-p).

Apparently, unlike the others who envisage only one conclusion being drawn in a balance-of-considerations argument, Hansen conceives of it as including two sub-arguments one of which argues for an intermediate claim in order to reach the final conclusion. As he has clarified, the first part of a balance-of-con-

1. Since in this chapter all my quotations of Hansen's words are from Hansen (2011), so in the remainder of the chapter I will only specify them by page numbers.

siderations argument is "an argument that goes from the observation that one set of considerations outweighs a second set – the counter-considerations – to the conclusion that some claim is reasonable even though the counter-considerations are true, or acceptable. It is an inference from *p outweighs q* to *p even though q*",[2] and then "a second inference must follow", resulting in the second part of a balance-of-considerations argument as "a matter of simplification from a sentence of the form '*p even though q*' to *p*" (p. 39). This unique way of structuring balance-of-considerations arguments, as it turns out, is well received as a promising proposal that is "on the right track" (Blair 2016, p. 123), and is regarded as "the most reasonable and plausible account of pro/con argumentation from an argument-as-a-product perspective" (Juthe 2019, p. 427, note 27).[3]

3. THE ROLE OF COUNTER-CONSIDERATIONS IN BALANCE-OF-CONSIDERATIONS ARGUMENTS

The distinctive feature of Hansen's structural model of balance-of-considerations arguments, as is indicated above, is the intermediate inference to "even though". The invention of such an idea, however, is not made by imagination, but on a proper understanding of the role of counter-considerations in balance-of-considerations arguments. In his paper (2011), Hansen provided a detailed discussion of six different possibilities in regard to the role of counter-considerations, and assessed their adequacy in light of the defining characteristics of conductive arguments. Accordingly, the idea of an intermediate inference to

---

2. I suspect that what Hansen really means here is not an inference from "*p outweighs q*" to "*p even though q*", but an inference from "*p outweighs q*" to "*k even though q*", where *p* and *q* are, respectively, pro and con considerations to *k*.

3. There are also dissenters from Hansen's account, for example, Govier (2011, p. 272) is not fully content with Hansen's model for it makes the convergence of premises disappeared. See also a criticism in Xie (2019).

"even though" is developed step by step from his critical scrutiny of these different possible roles.

The first possibility, which simply takes counter-considerations to be the premises of balance-of-considerations arguments, Hansen deems to be incorrect because "anything that is negatively relevant to the conclusion could not function as a premise" in a premise-conclusion kind of argument (p. 36), for they are not put forward by the arguer as supporting the conclusion. The second possibility, which regards counter-considerations as background knowledge, Hansen rejects on the ground that relegating counter-considerations to a background role "fails to allow for their impact in balance-of-considerations arguments", because they are "not just latently present but explicitly acknowledged" (p. 36).

The third possibility considered by Hansen is to take counter-considerations as expressions of reservation about the conclusion, and this proposal is discounted for two reasons. For the first, in balance-of-considerations arguments "we reason *from* the premises and counter-considerations taken together, not *towards* the counter-considerations" (p. 37, italics original). Second, as Hansen has explained, assigning to counter-considerations a role of qualification about the conclusion just amounts to a mechanism of balance-of-considerations arguments in the form of "P_1, P_2, therefore, K even though CC_1+CC_2". However, as Hansen suggests, the linguistic indicator "even though" could indeed be taken as a conjunctive operator serving the function that "sentences of the form 'p even though q' imply, by simplification, 'p' and 'q'" (p. 37). Therefore, the counter-considerations in balance-of-considerations arguments, if taken as part of the conclusion (i.e., as conjuncts in the conclusion, CC_1, CC_2), would receive no support at all from the premises (i.e., P_1 and P_2), hence the argument itself would have to be rendered a very bad one, "much worse than we think it should have turned out" (p. 37).

Here it is important to note that, in those remarks, we have encountered the prototype of the inference to "even though" that has later to become the core element in Hansen's novel structural model for balance-of-considerations arguments. Obviously, with such a prototype in mind, Hansen has already found the second part of his model, namely "K even though CC_1+CC_2" implies, by simplification, "K". Nevertheless, as is indicated by his criticism of the third possible role of counter-considerations, Hansen is also fully aware that such an inference by implication will also cause a problem. That is, "K even though CC_1+CC_2" will at the same time imply "CC_1+CC_2", hence having the result that some components of the conclusion will appear to have no connection, either in propositional content or in inferential support, to all the given premises. As a result, their being part of the conclusion, thus part of the argument, becomes clearly questionable and quite problematic. However, Hansen does not take this to be a problem of the inference to "even though" *per se*, for such an idea of structuring balance-of-considerations arguments, so he claims, does have the potential of overcoming the difficulties with the other two previous proposals (p. 37). Therefore, despite the fact that the proposal of assigning to counter-considerations a role of qualification turns out to be flawed, the idea of an inference to "even though" remains to be a possible way of considering balance-of-considerations arguments, as long as the oddness of counter-considerations' being part of the conclusion can be explained away in some other way. As we shall see soon, a solution just comes out in Hansen's examinations on the next two possible ways of understanding the role of counter-considerations.

The fourth possibility discussed in Hansen's paper is to take counter-considerations as the premises of a counter-argument, a proposal which seems to be quite plausible in light of the work on argument defeasibility by scholars like Pollock (2008). However, Hansen rejects it by pointing out that it amounts to an understanding of balance-of-considerations arguments as consisting of two opposing arguments, but "to have two opposing arguments is not to have a single argument with one conclusion, which is, what a balance-of-considerations argument is" (p. 37). Moreover, a balance-of-considerations argument "moves beyond mere recognition of the opposition, deciding, if possible, which of the two sets of considerations to favour. Therefore, there must be something in the argument that gives expression to the view that the disagreement presented by the two opposing arguments has been overcome" (p. 38). In other words, here Hansen is contending that the concept of balance-of-considerations arguments captures something more than the opposing of two arguments, because there is always only one conclusion reached, hence meaning that there must be a verdict already made in overcoming the opposition. As a result, in his later discussions such a verdict is further taken by Hansen to be a unique feature of balance-of-considerations arguments.

The fifth possibility under Hansen's scrutiny is to treat counter-considerations as independent elements juxtaposed with all the premises in the argument, as is represented in Govier's diagramming of balance-of-considerations arguments. While admitting that Govier's diagram does help in conveying the information that the premises have outweighed the counter-considerations, or vice versa, Hansen still believes that it remains unsatisfactory, for it "does not show the *reasoning* that is *unique* to balance-of-considerations arguments because that the premises have been judged to outweigh the counter-considerations is left *implicit* in this way of picturing balance-of-considerations arguments" (p. 38, italics added). This shows that Hansen first agrees with Govier in interpreting the unique feature of balance-of-considerations arguments in terms of an outweighing-relation, that is, the already made verdict in overcoming the opposition is now specified as a judgment made about the relative strengths between opposing considerations. But he is not fully content with Govier's view because it fails to represent this feature in a clearer way and to accommodate it in a particular form of reasoning. Accordingly, in order to make explicit and fully account for such a unique feature that is of special significance, Hansen brings in the sixth possibility, which suggests that counter-considerations are claimed to be outweighed in an on-balance premise. An on-balance premise represents exactly the outweighing-relation between the premises and the counter-considerations, embodying it into a judgment "that taken together those reasons outweigh the counter-considerations taken together" (p. 39). Together with the other premises, an on-balance premise constitutes a premise set from which an even-though conclusion is to be inferred, thereby a unique form of reasoning, i.e., an inference to "even though", comes into being. Hansen believes that this is the proper way to understand the role of counter-considerations, and as we have seen in section 2, his model for structuring balance-of-considerations arguments is then based exactly on this proposal.

Indeed, picturing balance-of-considerations arguments with a sub-argument structure built on an intermediate inference to "even though" is really a sophisticated invention. On the one hand, with the inference from the premises and the on-balance premise to an even-though conclusion including counter-considerations as its conjuncts, it retains all the counter-considerations as legitimate components of the argument, but meanwhile prevents them in a delicate way from being premises on their own. On the other hand, the inference by simplification from the even-though conclusion to the final conclusion also adapts the model to the reality that when balance-of-considerations arguments are put to use it is always only one simple claim without even-though clause that is concluded. Therefore, an intermediate inference to "even though" is of great advantage to structure balance-of-considerations arguments. In Hansen's own words, it overcomes the shortcomings of the other possibilities we looked at. (i) The counter-considerations are not presented as parts of the argument for the conclusion but they still find their way into the argument as subject of the on-balance premise; (ii) they are not mixed in with other background knowledge, but neither are they stated on their own as premises; (iii) they are not given the role of qualifying the conclusion, yet they have a place that shows they are relevant to the conclusion; (iv) although they are not placed in the role of being premises in a counter-argument, they are recognized as being negatively relevant to the conclusion; and (v) the counter-considerations are not just stated without resolution along with the reasons for the conclusion. The inclusion of the implicit on-balance premise acknowledges the weighing of premises and counter-considerations as an essential part of balance-of-considerations argument (pp. 39-40).

4. THE ON-BALANCE PREMISE AND THE "EVEN-THOUGH" RELATION

Through the above analysis, it is worth noting that the notion of an on-balance premise has played a very crucial role in Hansen's formulation of a structural model for balance-of-considerations arguments. In particular, the inclusion of such a premise, by making explicit a working outweighing-relation between premises and counter-considerations, perfectly solves the remaining problem caused by the inference to "even though" that we have mentioned before, namely the oddness of counter-considerations as being part of the conclusion. It is easy to see that now having "CC_1+CC_2" as part of the conclusion is no longer questionable or problematic, because the adding of the on-balance premise establishes their relevance to the premise set, both in propositional content and in inferential link. In Hansen's own words, "with the on-balance premises included in balance-of-considerations arguments a certain problem is solved (that of the relating the premises to the counter-considerations)" (p. 42). Thus, it can be seen that the presence of an on-balance premise indeed *validates* the feasibility of an inference to "even though", which, in turn, is taken by Hansen as the unique reasoning in balance-of-considerations arguments and the core of his structural account. As he himself has also affirmed, "the presence of the on-balance premise is needed to allow the reasoning to go forward to the even-though conclusion, an intermediate step *en route* to the final conclusion" (p. 41).

Nevertheless, if the on-balance premise comes into existence *solely* for the purpose of making an inference to "even though" possible or viable as a way to structuring balance-of-considerations arguments, it could easily be charged as an *ad hoc* strategy in theorizing. I think Hansen is fully aware of this concern, for he has devoted considerable effort to finding some other way to justify the presence of on-balance premise in balance-of-considerations arguments. In general, Hansen resorts to Govier's comment that "a person who explicitly acknowledges counter-considerations and nevertheless still claims that her conclusion is supported by positively relevant premises is committed to the judgment that the positively relevant premises outweigh the counter-considerations" (Govier 2005, p. 397). Here Govier is suggesting that the on-balance premise is in fact a commitment of the arguer, therefore it would be reasonable for us to confirm its existence and to supplement it in our reconstruction of balance-of-considerations arguments. Moreover, the reason why the arguer is to be taken as committed to such a premise is her reaching a conclusion while acknowledging its counter-considerations at the same time, as indicated by the arguer's use of some particular words to introduce counter-considerations, such as *even though, although, notwithstanding*, etc. Hansen calls these words *"linguistic counter-consideration indicators"* (p. 42), and further undertakes a very insightful analysis of their function in balance-of-considerations arguments.

Basically, Hansen submits that all these linguistic counter-consideration indicators have "a similar functional role and meaning in argumentative contexts" (p. 42), and then his discussion is focused on examining the "even-though" relation, as expressed by using *'even though'* or *'although'* to introduce a counter-consideration. He starts from the observations made by logicians on conjunctive operators. After a brief review on the thoughts of Quine, Goldfarb, Rubin and Young, Hansen finds out that, unlike the standard conjunctive operators like *'and'*, the expressions of 'even though' or 'although' have some non-truth-functional, communicational implications. On the one hand, the use of 'even though' or 'although' just "signals that there are 'obstacles or opposing conditions' taken into consideration", which, according to Hansen, represents exactly "a unique character of balance-of-considerations arguments: (a) they explicitly acknowledge the existence of counter-considerations, and (b) they do not dismiss them or attempt to refute them, but (c) take them into consideration in the reasoning towards their conclusions" (p. 44). On the other hand, the use of 'even though' or 'although' as a conjunctive operator has, more importantly, a distinguishing effect that "the conjunct following it is downplayed in importance while the other conjunct is emphasized" (p. 44). In other words, Hansen contends that the two conjuncts are thus joined in a rhetorically unequal way by the linguistic indicators of "even though" and "although".

Then, by extending the linguistic insights offered by Ducrot on the connective *'but'*, Hansen gives a further analysis on the conjunctions made by 'even though'. As Ducrot has observed, while the conjunctive operator 'but' always connects two propositions that have opposite orientations, the overall direction of implication in a but-conjunction will turn out to be that implied by the proposition introduced by 'but'. According to Hansen, in a similar manner 'even though' could also be analyzed as connecting statements with opposite orientations, but "in even-though-conjunctions the overall direction of implication is opposite to that implied by the proposition in the scope of 'even though'" (p. 45). Consequently, as Hansen continues to contend, "in the formula *'p* even though q', p and q have opposite orientations and q, which is nested in the scope of *even though*, is represented as weaker than p. Thus, the argument schema 'k even though q, because p' implies (i) that k is a conclusion and q is a set of reasons oriented against, or away from k, and (ii) that p is a set of reasons oriented toward k, and (iii) that p is a stronger consideration than q." (p. 45) Here it is easy to see the emergence of the on-balance premise, as the third part of the implication. That is to say, up to now Hansen seems to have found a possible justification for the on-balance premise on the basis of his linguistic analysis on even-though-conjunctions: it is implied by the argument scheme that is built on an even-though-conjunction. Clearly, this way of justifying the presence of on-balance premise is in line with Govier's general suggestion that on-balance premise is a commitment of the arguer, but Hansen has substantially enhanced Govier's view by laying for it a linguistic groundwork.

However, notably, Hansen did not stop there. Agreeing with Adler (1992, p. 25) that the understanding of 'even though' presupposes the understanding of 'even', he continues to consolidate his analysis of the even-though relation by a comparative study between 'even' and 'even though'. Adler (1992) once made a careful analysis of "even" and "even-arguments", from which Hansen correctly believes that an extension to "even though" is quite plausible. As he claims, "the insights regarding 'even' are easily adapted to 'even though' and they fill in our understanding of the latter expressions"(p. 48). Therefore, based on Adler's observations about 'even', Hansen has tried to offer a clarification of the semantic and rhetorical meanings of 'even though', as summarized in the following table (p. 47).

even ('even *a* has *P*')	even though ('*p* even though *q*')
a used to modify a term (a subject). [*Syntactical role*]	a sentential connective. [*Syntactical role*]
b not relevant to this comparison.	'*p* even though *q*' is true just in case *p* and *q* are both true. [*Semantic role 1*]
c not relevant to this comparison.	*Orientation*: *p* and *q* have opposite orientations. [*Semantic role 2*]
d 'even *a* has *P*' is a weightier reason than '*a* has *P*' [*Semantic role*]	*p* is represented as stronger than *q*. [*Semantic role 3*]
e *Doubt*: by using 'even *a* has *P*' a speaker acknowledges that there are some reasons to think '*a* has *P*' is false; it is thus a context in which doubt exists. [*Rhetorical role 1*]	*Doubt*: by using '*p* even though *q*' the speaker acknowledges to her audience that there are reasons opposed to *p*; it is thus a context in which doubt about *p* exists. [*Rhetorical role 1*]
f *Unexpectedness*: use of 'even' implies that it is contrary-to-expectation that the subject *a* would have the property *P* predicated of it. [*Rhetorical role 2*]	*Unexpectedness*: use of '*p* even though *q*' implies that *p* is surprising or unexpected in light of the fact that *q* is true; (perhaps because there is a presumption for *q*). [*Rhetorical role 2*]
g *Justification*: by using 'even *a* has *P*' in a context in which doubt exists, the speaker claims to be able to ally the reasons for doubting '*a* has *P*'. [*Rhetorical role 3*]	*Justification*: by using '*p* even though *q*' in a context in which there is doubt about *p*, the speaker implies that s/he has a good reason for *p*. [*Rhetorical role 3*]

With all his detailed discussions regarding the above different roles, Hansen has indeed offered a general account of the "even-though" relation. Furthermore, as is shown by his case study on the "notwithstanding clause" of the Canadian Charter of Rights and Freedoms (pp. 48-51), Hansen believes that such an account is quite plausible and also useful in our understanding of balance-of-considerations arguments. Specifically, it not only helps in justifying his structural model based on an inference to "even though", but also contributes to our knowledge about how a balance-of-considerations argument is generated. As he has explained it (pp. 46-48), any use of the expression '*p* even though *q*' will first indicate an explicit recognition of the fact that there are reasons, as represented by q, to doubt that p is the case. As a result, then, given the presence of q it will be surprising to assert p, and asserting p, consequently, "is to put ourselves in a position of having to defend the claim with reasons. Thus sentences of the form 'p even though q' that merely appear to make a claim will implicitly imply an argument of the form 'p because r, even though q', where p holds the place of the conclusion, q the presumptive reason against the conclusion, and r holds the place of the reasons for the conclusion" (p. 48). It could be seen from this that the balance-of-considerations arguments are indeed formulated for defending a claim, p, in a context where an "even-though" relation, "p even though q", already exists. Accordingly, given such an understanding about the genesis of balance-of-considerations arguments, it will also turn out to be correct for us to unpack their logical structure in terms of the "even-though" relation, just as Hansen has done with his novel structural account: a balance-of-considerations argument will always take a "p even though q" claim as its intermediate conclusion. Thus, it can be said that here, by developing a deep analysis of 'even though' expressions in argumentative contexts, Hansen is in fact trying to offer a further defense of his own view from a linguistic perspective.

5. THE CONCESSIVE MEANING OF 'EVEN THOUGH'

In general, I think Hansen is definitely on the right track when trying to legitimatize his own structural model through an analysis of the linguistic counter-consideration indicators, for the distinctiveness of balance-of-considerations arguments lies apparently in the arguer's intentional mention of counter-considerations in a particular way, and it is explicable only in the light of the linguistic devices that are used to present them. As we have seen, Hansen has focused in particular on the indicator 'even though', and explored its linguistic peculiarities in a systematic and deliberate way. For the first, he highlights the contrast between "even though" and the standard logical conjunctive operator "*and*", hence pointing out their difference in the rhetorical aspects of language. Then, he makes a comparison with the connective "*but*", thereby clarifying the concessive meaning of "even though" that, for the most part, is associated with "*though*". And last, he absorbs the pragmatic insights about "*even*" into his understanding of "even though", thus uncovering its communicative nuances that are contributed by the "even" part. While admitting that Hansen has offered a very thorough analysis, and with many deep insights, on the meaning of 'even though', I also find myself unconvinced about his way of filling these insights in his own understanding of balance-of-considerations arguments. In a word, I suspect that Hansen has over-interpreted the contrastive import of 'even though', and therefore failed in his attempt to lay a solid linguistic foundation for a core element of his model, namely the on-balance premise.

More specifically, I think Hansen has overstated the concessive meaning of 'though' in his analysis of even-though expressions. As is indicated, in view of Rubin and Young's (1989, p. 93) observation that the indicator of 'although' would have the effect of "*deemphasizing* the point" introduced by it, Hansen also contends that "although" or "even though" differs from "and" in that it would conjoin two propositions in a rhetorically unequal way. As he clarifies, "what is distinguished for the role of 'although' is that the conjunct following it (or 'even though') is *downplayed in importance* while the other conjunct is emphasized" (p. 44, italics added). This characterization, as far as I understand it, well captures the basic concessive meaning of 'although' or 'even though'. As a conjunctive operator, 'although' or 'even though' conjoins two statements. But more importantly, as a concessive connective, "although" or "even though" forms a dramatic contrast, by introducing a subordinate clause which concedes the truth of some proposition, or the existence of something, that will make the proposition expressed in the main clause appear to be surprising or unexpected. However, since the proposition in the main clause remains to be asserted, then the concession introduced by 'although' or 'even though' just turns out to be some background information for that assertion, therefore in this way it is deemphasized, or is downplayed in importance. But, as we have discussed in last section, Hansen only takes this basic meaning as a point of departure. By extending Ducrot's analysis of 'but' to 'even though', he has tried to further interpret the contrastive import of the latter in terms of "orientation". As a result, he reached the conclusion that 'even though' is "like 'but' and 'however' in that it connects statements with opposite orientations and represents them as being of *unequal strength*" (p. 44, italics added). Specifically, as he explains, for a conjunction in the form of "*p* even though *q*", it is indicated that "*q*, which is nested in the scope of 'even though', is represented as *weaker* than *p*" (p. 45, italics added).

Within the above analysis, it is noteworthy that Hansen has actually changed the notion of unbalanced importance, as revealed by logicians to be a rhetorical effect, into an idea of unequal strength, as understood to be stronger or weaker in force in reaching a conclusion. And as is indicated above, such a transformation is made possible via Ducrot's notion of *orientation*, which means particularly "a direction of implication suggested by the conventional meaning of a word that will lead us to *infer one conclusion rather than another*" (p. 44, italics added). This notion of orientation, in line with Ducrot's Radical Argumentativism theory, presumes that all sentences are inherently argumentative (van Eemeren *et al.*, 2014, p. 492), therefore any proposition would be taken as a consideration (or a reason) from which we are able to draw a particular conclusion. Accordingly, when two propositions with opposite orientations are conjoined by 'even though' with an effect of being unbalanced in their importance, it would certainly be understood as that they have unequal strength in leading us to their own direction of inferring, or in other words, they have unequal argumentative force in reaching their own conclusions. In this connection, when endorsing such an idea of unequal strength, Hansen will also have to inherit its underlying radical Argumentativist assumption, an assumption that will in turn make his own account for 'even though' become constrained, and to some extent also radical. As we shall see soon, because of an undue stress on the argumentative dimension of language, some of his analysis simply appears to be unnatural, and sometimes it even seems to be problematic.

If we take a close look at Hansen's efforts in extending Ducrot's insights about 'but' to his own examination of 'even though', it can be seen that the analyzing framework based on orientation does not really lend itself to his purpose. In Ducrot's theory, a proposition's orientation towards a direction just means that we are led to make an inference from that proposition to a certain conclusion. As in his example of the utterance "The weather is beautiful but I am tired" in response to the suggestion to take a walk, "the segment 'the weather is beautiful' is oriented towards agreeing to the walk and the segment 'but I'm tired' is oriented towards declining the invitation" (p. 44), it is perfectly clear that here both conjuncts are taken as reasons for drawing, respectively, two other different conclusions, "I agree to take a walk" and "I do not agree to take a walk". However, this would not be the case when we are concerning a compound proposition in the form of 'p even though q'. For instance, in a response like "I agree to take a walk even though I am tired", it is easy to see that the above analysis does not fit in the conjunct of "I agree to take a walk", because that conjunct itself is the final end of a direction (or the conclusion to be inferred) in the sentence. As a result, it would be unnatural to understand that conjunct as being further oriented towards somewhere else, and it would also be unreasonable if we take it to be leading us to draw a circular inference whose conclusion is the same as its premise.

Consequently, such a kind of inapplicability becomes the cause of a defect in Hansen's account, particularly in his discussions about the unequal strength in even-though conjunctions. As we have discussed, in Ducrot's analysis of but-conjunctions, since their conjuncts are indeed competing considerations that incline us towards inferring two opposing conclusions, it would follow plausibly that their overall direction of implication, as indicated by the use of 'but', signals an unequal strength between the two conjuncts in supporting their own conclusions, i.e., the conjunct in the scope of 'but' is stronger than the other in determining the overall final conclusion. In line with this analysis, Hansen has also come to the claim that the expressions in the form of 'p even though q' also represent p and q as being of unequal strength, namely "q is represented as weaker than p" (p. 45). However, just recall our above analysis of the example "I agree to take a walk even though I am tired". It is not so clear why the conjunct "I'm tired", being a consideration oriented towards drawing the conclusion "I do not agree to take a walk", would be weaker in strength than the conjunct "I agree to take a walk", which is exactly the opposite of its intended conclusion. In other words, where Ducrot is comparing the strength of two reasons in his discussion of but-conjunctions, Hansen is comparing the strength between a reason and a conclusion, an endeavor that seems obviously odd and questionable.

Nevertheless, as we have seen, Hansen has not noticed that as a problem, for he continues to extend this discussion of orientation and unequal strength about even-though relation to his analysis of balance-of-considerations arguments: "Thus, the argument schema 'k even though q, because p' implies (i) that k is a conclusion and q is a set of reasons oriented against, or away from k, and (ii) that p is a set of reasons oriented toward k, and (iii) that p is a *stronger* consideration than q" (p. 45, italics added). Here again we find something that appears to be odd, for in reaching this conclusion Hansen has simply jumped from a comparison of strength within the even-though conjunction (i.e., k is stronger than q) to another one that goes beyond the conjunction (i.e., p is stronger than q). It is not clear how the former could be used to establish the latter. Although in such an argument schema it is obvious that p and q do have opposite orientations, they do not form an even-though conjunction in any way, thus their unequal strength remains unknown, or still needs to be uncovered by some other linguistic clues.

However, as is indicated in last section, the unequal strength between p and q in this argument schema relates exactly to the content of the on-balance premise, a core element in Hansen's structural model for balance-of-considerations. Hence, here I suspect that by taking such an inferential leap Hansen is attempting to offer a justification for the presence of an on-balance premise: it is implied by the argument scheme that is built on an even-though-conjunction. If that is really the case, then I believe it is now easy to see that such a justification is unsuccessful. As we have revealed above, Hansen's interpretation on the contrastive import of 'even though' in terms of unequal strength is still questionable, and even if such an interpretation is correct, a justificatory link from it to the presence of on-balance premise will still need to be created, or at least better clarified.

6. THE RHETORICAL MEANING OF "EVEN"

Nevertheless, if close attention is paid to Hansen's comparative study made between "even" and "even though", we may find that he has also pointed out another possible way of legitimizing the presence of the on-balance premise. Although Hansen did not articulate it in detail, it is indeed implied in his analysis on the rhetorical roles of 'even though', especially in relation to the role he calls "*justification*". Here in this section I would like to probe into such a possibility, and to demonstrate that it could substantiate the on-balance premise in a better way on the basis of his linguistic insights about "even though".

As is discussed in section 4, by extending Adler's analysis of "even" to "even though", Hansen has explained in a comprehensive way the semantic and rhetorical meanings of 'even though'. Among them, the most important insights are about the different rhetorical roles played by "even though" in argumentative contexts. According to Hansen, there are three different roles to be specified that are corresponding to "three interlocking components" shared by the rhetorical meaning of 'even' and 'even though', and "they have to do with doubts, surprise, and having reasons" (p. 46). For the first, following Adler's observation that the use of 'even p' signals that the speaker acknowledges a recognition of doubt associated with p, Hansen contends that the expression 'p even though q', similarly, indicates "an explicit recognition of the fact that there are reasons, worthy of recognition, to doubt that p is the case; those reasons are represented by q" (p. 46). He takes this to be the first rhetorical role of "even though", and calls it *doubt*.

The second role is termed by Hansen as *unexpectedness*, which is clarified as the effect that "in sentences of the form 'p even though q' an element of surprise is attached to the assertion of p" (p. 47). This insight is also inspired by Adler's remark that, in sentences of "even a has P", "'even' brings our attention to the fact that it is (highly) *contrary-to-expectation* that the term it stresses has the property claimed, and yet it asserts, nevertheless, that it does have that property" (Adler 1992, p. 22, italics original). Accordingly, asserting an even-statement signals that the truth of the statement that follows 'even' is unexpected, and thus surprising. However, notably, unlike Adler, who explains the notion of unexpectedness by means of a pragmatic scale (Adler 1992, pp. 23-24), Hansen prefers to unpack it in terms of *presumption*. In a word, the recognition of some doubt in relation to a statement undermines its presumptive status, hence it would be surprising to see it being asserted. As Hansen has clarified, "our analysis of 'p even though q' sentences will include the hypothesis that the presumption for q creates a presumption for not-p.... So the surprise element accompanying 'p even though q' can be explained by the fact that p is contrary to what we presumed to the case" (pp. 47-48).

The third role, termed *justification*, is simply the consequence of the former two roles. In Hansen's words, "to assert something that we expect others to doubt and find surprising, is to put ourselves in a position of having to defend the claim with reasons" (p. 48). As he explains, "with the assertion of the form 'even a has P' the speaker implies (conversationally) that s/he is able to give a sufficient reason for the claim that 'a has P'" (p. 46). Accordingly, the third role of "even though" refers to the same effect that by making a claim in the form of 'p even though q', the speaker is making an implicit commitment to "having reasons for p" (p. 48), and the speaker also "implies that s/he has a good reason for p" (p. 47). As we have seen in section 4, by relying upon this *justification* role, Hansen has also worked out an account that takes the structure of balance-of-considerations arguments (i.e., 'p because r, even though q') as being created for defending p in a context where "p even though q" is to be claimed. And such an account, in turn, further backs up his novel structure based on an intermediate inference to "even though".

Although Hansen has not talked directly about the issue of the on-balance premise when examining these rhetorical roles, I think he still paves a way for validating its presence by his discussions of the *justification* role. To start with, in order to substantiate the *justification* role of even-though expressions, Hansen has resorted to the claim that there is "a general normative requirement of having to give reasons for p if not-p has presumptive status" (p. 48). However, he does not offer any further specification regarding the norms for the reasons *per se* that are to be given in this context, except for claiming that "by using 'p even though q' ...the speaker implies that s/he has a *good* reason for p" (p. 47, italics added). But, what is meant by "a good reason for p", if we may ask, in such a context where not-p has the presumptive status because of a doubt about p that is caused by q? The answer would seem to be obvious: the reason provided can either undermine the presumption of not-p in this context, or contribute to establish a presumptive status for p that is more plausible than that of not-p. If this is indeed the meaning of "a good reason for p" in Hansen's articulation of the *justification* role of even-though expressions, then it would also be possible to legitimize the presence of an on-balance premise in balance-of-considerations arguments by means of such a normative requirement. To be more specific, if a balance-of-considerations argument is indeed an attempt to defend a claim (p) with a reason (r) in front of an already-expressed counter-consideration (q) which creates doubt for p or a presumption for not-p, then such a reason needs to be *strong enough* to remove that doubt, or to undermine the counter-consideration as a reason for establishing the presumptive status of not-p. In other words, the reason "r" needs to be *stronger* than the counter-consideration "q" in the sense that the former can eliminate the negative support or relevance of the latter in the context of creating a presumption for p. It seems that this interpretation well accords with the idea that is to be captured by the on-balance premise in Hansen's structural model. Hence it is in this way that we could reach Hansen's claim that the argument schema "k even though q, because p" implies that p is stronger than q, and therefore to substantiate the presence of the on-balance premise in any balance-of-considerations arguments. Compared to the other justification by means of the unequal strength in even-though conjunctions discussed in last section, I believe this one is much better and more promising. Basically, the former is grounded on the understanding of the contrastive import of "though", while the latter is rooted in the rhetorical meaning of "even". Hansen has given insights into both respects through his linguistic analysis of the "even-though" relation, however, as we have suggested, these insights are of unequal plausibility, thus have different potential for defending his own structural account of balance-of-considerations arguments.

7. CONCLUSION

In this chapter I examined Hansen's work on the structure of balance-of-considerations arguments. Unlike other scholars who envisage only one conclusion being drawn in a balance-of-considerations argument, Hansen regards it as having a sub-argument structure in which an intermediate conclusion is first drawn by an inference to "even though", and then the final conclusion is inferred from that intermediate claim. Hansen takes such an inference to "even though" as the unique form of reasoning in balance-of-considerations arguments, and then proposes for them a novel structural account. The idea of an inference to "even though" is further grounded on Hansen's particular view of the role of counter-considerations in balance-of-considerations arguments, a view that takes counter-considerations as something that are claimed to be outweighed in an on-balance premise. Accordingly, since the notion of an on-balance premise plays a crucial role in his account, Hansen has tried to further justify its presence from a linguistic perspective. By extending the insights of Ducrot and Adler about the indicators of 'but' and 'even', Hansen has undertaken a systematic analysis of the meaning and function of "even though" in argumentative contexts. Through that analysis, Hansen has offered us a general account for the "even-though" relation, and further defended his own structural view of balance-of-considerations arguments with a linguistic foundation. Nevertheless, by interpreting the concessive meaning of 'even though' in terms of Ducrot's notion of "orientation", Hansen has misconceived the contrastive import of "even though" to be an effect of unequal strength, and in that way he has failed to offer sufficient justification for the presence of the on-balance premise in his novel structure. But, as argued in this paper, Hansen has also pointed out another possible way to justify the on-balance premise when he is elaborating the rhetorical roles of 'even though'. It is based upon the rhetorical meaning of 'even', and it can be developed to validate the presence of on-balance premise by means of presumption.

ACKNOWLEDGEMENT: The work in this paper is supported by the National Social Science Fund of China (18ZDA033).

REFERENCES

Adler, J. E. 2013. Are conductive arguments possible? *Argumentation*, 27(3): 245-257.

Adler, J. E. 1992. Even-arguments, explanatory gaps, and pragmatic scales, *Philosophy and Rhetoric*, 25(1): 22-44.

Blair, J. A. 2016. A defense of conduction: A reply to Adler, *Argumentation*, 30(2): 109-128.

Blair, J. A. 2011. A critical examination and development of Wellman's theory of conductive argument, in Zenker, F. (ed.). *Argumentation: Cognition and Community*, Windsor, ON, (CD ROM), pp.1-15.

Blair, J. A., & Johnson, R. H. (eds.). 2011. *Conductive arguments: An overlooked type of defeasible reasoning*. London: College Publications.

Bermejo-Luque, L. 2019. The Appraisal of Conductions, *Informal Logic*, 39(2): 123-145.

van Eemeren, F. H. *et al.* 2014. *Handbook of Argumentation Theory*, Dordrecht: Springer.

Govier, T. 2011. Conductive arguments: Overview of the symposium. In J.A. Blair & R.H. Johnson (eds.), *Conductive Arguments: An Overlooked Type of Defeasible Reasoning* (pp.262-276), London: College Publications.

Govier, T. 2010. *A Practical Study of Argument*. (7th edition). Belmont CA: Wadsworth, Cengage Learning.

Govier, T. 2005. *A Practical Study of Argument*. (6th edition). Belmont CA: Thomson/Wadsworth.

Govier, T. 1999. Reasoning with pros and cons: conductive arguments revisited. In T. Govier, *The Philosophy of Argument* (pp.155-180). Newport News, VA: Vale Press.

Govier, T. 1987. *Problems in Argument Analysis and Evaluation*. Dordrecht: Foris Publications.

Govier, T. 1979. Carl Wellman's Challenge and Response. *The Informal Logic Newsletter*, 2(2): 10-15.

Hansen, H. V. 2010. The structure of balance-of-consideration arguments. Paper presented at the Association for Informal Logic and Critical Thinking session, American Philosophical Association Central Division meeting, Chicago, February.

Hansen, H.V. 2011. Notes on balance-of-considerations arguments. In J. A. Blair & R. H. Johnson (eds.), *Conductive Arguments: An Overlooked Type of Defeasible Reasoning* (pp.31-51). London: College Publications.

Hitchcock, D. 2013. Appeals to considerations. *Informal Logic* 33(2): 195-237.

Hitchcock, D. 1981. Deduction, induction and conduction. *Informal Logic Newsletter*, 3(2): 7-15.

Jin, R. 2011. The structure of pro and con arguments: a survey of the theories. In J. A. Blair, & R. H. Johnson (eds.). *Conductive arguments: An overlooked type of defeasible reasoning* (pp. 10-30). London: College Publications.

Juthe, A. 2019. Reconstructing Complex Pro/Con Argumentation, *Argumentation*, 33(3): 413-454.

van Laar, J. A. 2014. Arguments that take Counter-considerations into Account, *Informal Logic*, 34(3): 240-275.

Pollock, J. 2008. Defeasible Reasoning, in J. Adler & L. Rips (eds.), *Reasoning: Studies of Human Inference and its Foundations* (pp.451-470), Cambridge University Press.

Possin, K. 2016. Conductive Arguments: Why is This Still a Thing?, *Informal Logic*, 36(4): 563-593.

Possin, K. 2012. The Myth of Conductive Arguments, *Inquiry: Critical Thinking across the disciplines*. 27(3), 29-33.

Rubin, R. & Young, C. M. 1989. *Formal Logic: A Model of English*. Mountain View: Mayfield.

Wohlrapp, W. 2011. Conductive argument: A misleading model for the analysis of pro- and contra- argumentation. In Blair and Johnson (pp. 210-223).

Xie, Y. 2020. On the logical reconstruction of conductive arguments, in Frans. Van Eemeren & B. Garssen (eds.) *From Argument Schemes to Argumentative Relations in the Wild*, Dordrecht: Springer.

Xie, Y. 2017. Conductive argument as a mode of strategic maneuvering, *Informal Logic*, 37(1): 2-22.

Yu, S. & Zenker, F., 2019. A dialectical view on conduction: Reasons, warrants, and normal suasory inclinations, *Informal Logic*, 39(1): 32-69.

ABOUT THE AUTHOR: Yun Xie is an associate professor of philosophy at Sun Yat-sen University, and a full-time researcher in the Institute of Logic and Cognition there. He has published several papers in the field of argumentation theory, and serves as an Editorial Board Member for *Informal Logic* and *Journal of Argumentation in Context*.

xieyun6@mail.sysu.edu.cn

CHAPTER 13.

CHRISTIAN KOCK'S ATTACK ON SUFFICIENCY

J. ANTHONY BLAIR

ABSTRACT: In *Deliberative Rhetoric, Arguing About Doing*, Professor Christian Kock expresses his dissatisfaction with the notion of sufficiency as it used by Johnson and Blair (and others) as a criterion of a logically good argument. In this paper I examine Professor Kock's arguments against our use of that criterion, in order, first, to try to understand them, and second, to assess their merit. I try to answer two questions in this paper: (1) What is Professor Kock's case against "sufficiency"? and (2) Is Professor Kock right about "sufficiency"?[1]

KEYWORDS: ARS, Christian Kock, *Deliberative Rhetoric*, good argument, *Logical Self-Defense*, sufficiency

INTRODUCTION

In our informal logic textbook, *Logical Self-Defense* (1977, 1985, 1993, 1994, 2006) Ralph Johnson and I proposed that to be log-

---

1. This chapter has benefitted from Hans Hansen's comments based on a close reading of an earlier version, for which I thank him. I am of course responsible for the errors that remain. This generosity of insightful constructive comments is typical of Professor Hansen, who has been a friend, colleague and supporter for over 30 years. I dedicate this chapter to him.

ically good a communication offered as an argument will satisfy three criteria. Its offered premises will be acceptable (i.e., worthy of acceptance); they will be relevant (i.e., have probative bearing on the argument's conclusion); and the relevant premises will be sufficient (i.e., provide adequate grounds for accepting the conclusion). In a recent collection of his papers, *Deliberative Rhetoric, Arguing About Doing*, Professor Christian Kock (2017) expresses in several of the essays his dissatisfaction with the notion of sufficiency. In fact, Professor Kock is unhappy with all three purported criteria, or at least with our handling of them, but, in this essay, I take up only his dissatisfaction with sufficiency.

Part I of the essay collects the criticisms that he levels against sufficiency as a criterion of argument merit and offers a formulation of the overall case that he builds, attempting to provide a faithful account of Professor Kock's position and his arguments in support of it. In Part II, I examine these arguments critically, contending that Professor Kock misconstrues the sense of 'sufficiency' used by the informal logicians, so that many of his criticisms miss the mark. I also contend that there are certain contexts for the use of practical arguments for which sufficiency does make sense as a criterion.

PART I: PROFESSOR KOCK'S CASE AGAINST SUFFICIENCY

The index of *Deliberative Rhetoric* lists 19 places in the 20 essays in the book where the terms 'sufficiency' or 'sufficient' occur, although not all bear on Professor Kock's critique. I here examine those that do.

I.1 Either sufficiency is superfluous or else it is a muddled concept

In the Introduction, Professor Kock argues as follows:

> In practical reasoning [as distinct from epistemic reasoning] ... [t]here is no "truth" anywhere about what [for example] the correct

level of taxation and welfare programs might be, and so there is no deductively binding (i.e., "logically valid") reasoning available to tell us which of … two disagreeing groups is right. There is not even such a thing as "cogent" or "sufficient" reasoning to this effect—if the words "cogent" or "sufficient" are to have any discernible meaning. I say this because I admit to being impatient with the use of these terms in discussions of what a "good" argument is. The accepted meanings of these words is that if a piece of reasoning has one of these qualities (which are often taken to be the same) then it deductively entails its conclusion. Then why not say that—if that is what one means? If that is not what one means, then I find the meaning of these words unclear, and I tend to see the use of them as an attempt to, on the one hand, reject deductivism and, on the other hand, to have it too. (3) [Numbers in parentheses are page numbers in *Deliberative Rhetoric*.]

I take Professor Kock's objection to characterizing practical reasoning as "sufficient" (or "cogent") to be that the use of such terminology faces a destructive dilemma. Either 'sufficient' means "deductively valid" and nothing more nor less, in which case it is superfluous or empty; or else its meaning is unclear, and in effect its use is an ill-conceived attempt to reject deductivism—ill-conceived because it has the appearance of rejecting deductivism, but to have any discernible meaning it must mean nothing other than "deductively valid", so that to use the term is to accept deductivism. His essays in the book are focused on practical reasoning (reasoning about what to do), and one of the book's principal theses is that practical reasoning is different in important respects from epistemic reasoning (reasoning about what to believe). It remains to be seen whether his objection in this passage to the use of "sufficiency" applies to its use in epistemic reasoning too, for the argument as expressed above, on the face of it, seems to be an unqualified rejection of sufficiency as a criterion of either or both.

I.2 Sufficiency is not applicable to practical arguments because there can be equally good arguments on both sides of a practical issue.

Later in the Introduction, where he is summarizing each paper, Professor Kock gives a somewhat different argument against sufficiency as a criterion of "good" arguments, but he does so in a context in which he is concerned to focus on deliberative or practical reasoning and arguments.

> Several thinkers in these fields [of moral and political philosophy] help understand the occurrence of what we may call legitimate dissensus: enduring disagreement even between reasonable people arguing reasonably. It inevitably occurs over practical issues, e.g., issues of action rather than truth, because there normally will be legitimate arguments on both sides, and these tend to be incommensurable, i.e., they cannot be objectively weighed against each other. Accordingly, "inference," logical "validity," and "sufficiency" are inapplicable notions. (11)

Here Professor Kock does not linger over the "either superfluous or meaningless" objection. Even if sufficiency can (or could) stand on its own feet as a concept (as distinct from logical validity), it is not (or would not be) an applicable criterion for the assessment of deliberative debate. No argument can be "sufficient" to settle a controversy whether to take an action or adopt a policy, because there can be equally "legitimate" arguments on both sides. In such cases, the argument(s) for neither side can be sufficient to decide the question. Thus, the criterion is not applicable to arguments over practical issues.

I.3 Sufficiency is not applicable to practical arguments because practical arguments come in degrees of strength and sufficiency doesn't, because it is a binary concept.

In Chapter 5, Professor Kock again takes up his dissatisfaction with sufficiency (and with acceptability and relevance) as "criteria to be applied in argument evaluation" (94), which he attributes to informal logic, and to Johnson and Blair in particular, along with others. He does so as part of his case against argumentation theory's "basing argument appraisals in practical reasoning on the recognition of an inference from argument to conclusion" (*ibid.*). Why? Because "in practical argumentation even legitimate arguments legitimate no inference to [a] proposal; instead they provide an impact of a certain strength..." (*ibid.*). He says, "We may speak of these three as the recognized dimensions of argument evaluation" (*ibid.*), and then asks, "If argumentation theory is to conceptualize degrees of strength in arguments, which of these dimensions would it affect, and how?" (95).

> Sufficiency... is by its nature a quantitative, not a qualitative concept; it is about there being enough of something. In argument evaluation it says there is enough acceptable, relevant argumentation to cross a certain threshold. But "sufficiency," like the other concepts in the triad, is a binary criterion. This is how it is used in mathematics, where, e.g., a condition is either sufficient or it is not; there is no such thing as its being "somewhat" sufficient, or "more" sufficient than another condition. However, in practical reasoning arguments differ along the quantitative dimension not just in a binary (on-off) way, but by degrees;... We have just seen the counterintuitive consequences of insisting on a purely binary conception. Yet most philosophical argumentation theory lacks theoretical tools to deal with degrees along the quantitative dimension.

When it comes to appraising practical arguments, the merits or faults of practical arguments come in degrees of strength. The concept of "sufficiency," being binary, cannot be applied.

In summing up his case at the end of Ch. 5, Professor Kock says,

> Theorists have been afraid of opening the door to gradualism in the appraisal of argument strength... Thus newer concepts to substitute traditional "validity" have not managed to (or even sought to) escape binarism; that is equally true whether the criterion suggested is "sufficiency," or, as in Walton's presumptive reasoning, correct use of argument schemes. (102-103)

Here he lumps Johnson and Blair, as advocates of sufficiency as a criterion of argument strength, in with those whom he takes to reject gradualism in argument strength.

I.4 Sufficiency doesn't apply to practical arguments because there can be no "proof" in practical argument and sufficiency presupposes that proof is possible.

In the paper that became Chapter 7 in the book, Professor Kock at one point lists and discusses seven "distinctive features of practical argumentation not captured by models or theories designed for theoretical argumentation" (138). Number three on the list includes the following:

> … in practical argumentation no party can be logically proven to be either right or wrong. This is tantamount to saying that reasons in practical argumentation can never be "valid" in the traditional sense of entailing their conclusion, nor can they be "sufficient" to entail a conclusion. No reasons in practical argumentation entail the proposals for which they argue. No reasons are "sufficient." No matter how many reasons you may muster for your proposal, your opponent is never compelled by those reasons to accept it… (139-140)

In this passage (and in the text surrounding it) Professor Kock makes it clear that his attack on sufficiency here, at least, is limited to, or at least focused on, its use as a criterion for the appraisal of practical arguments. His contention might be expressed this way: in practical reasoning there are no arguments such that it is impossible for their conclusions to be false if their premises are true; or, what he takes to be equivalent, there are no arguments such that if one accepts their premises one has sufficient grounds for accepting their conclusion.

I.5 No proof is possible in practical argument because they are subjective.

In a chapter titled, "Norms of Legitimate Dissensus," Professor Kock invents a realistic dialogue in which a couple discusses a particular armchair that's for sale. The couple, Dick and Jane, "happen to agree on all the advantages and drawbacks of the armchair" (180) but Dick values its comfort so highly he wants to buy it, while Jane finds its ugliness so prohibitive that she will not have it in the house. "The example of the armchair," Kock asserts, "shows that in the practical domain pro and con arguments may be real and relevant simultaneously" (*ibid.*), which "means that in practical argumentation no party can be logically proven to be either right or wrong. In principle, arguments in the practical domain can never be 'valid' in the sense of entailing their conclusion, nor can they be 'sufficient' to entail a conclusion" (181).

Having established to his satisfaction "that practical reasoning is a separate domain of argumentation with particular properties" (*ibid.*), he asks what norms appropriately apply in that domain, and answers:

> First, we may conclude that as criteria in argument evaluation, the notions of validity, inference and sufficiency all have to go; no arguments for or against actions have any of these properties. "Sufficiency" or "adequacy" are no change or improvement on the traditional "validity" requirement. If "sufficiency" is to have a clear meaning, it must mean, as in mathematics, that there is an inference. An inference, in a nutshell, is the negation of choice. (*Ibid.*)

I.6 Another expression of the "subjectivity" argument

In a chapter in which Professor Kock makes the distinction between arguing for a proposition and arguing for a proposal, he draws attention to a

> … distinct property of arguments about proposals: Although they may be perfectly real, relevant, and hence "good," they never are what logicians call "valid," in the sense that if the argument is true, then the truth of the conclusion follows by necessity (i.e., as an inference). Since proposals can be neither true nor false, validity is a misplaced concept in relation to argumentation about proposals. Not only could the "truth" of a proposal not follow from anything, but neither does the adoption of the proposal "follow" by any kind

of necessity or inference from any number of "good" arguments. The proposed action may have n undeniable advantages speaking in its favor, which hence earn the status of "good" arguments, yet they are not valid in the traditional sense, nor are they even "sufficient," neither singly nor in conjunction. (192)

Defending these assertions, he notes that proposals have advantages and drawbacks that can be valued differently by different people, since people have different and incompatible values that are incommensurable and subjective (192-195).

I.7 Sufficiency is not applicable to practical argument because it requires comparing the arguments on both sides and that's not possible if both sides are backed by sufficient arguments.

In a discussion of the dialectical obligations of participants in political debate, Professor Kock makes the following remarks:

> No quantity of good arguments on one side is in itself sufficient to decide the matter. Just as attempts at blank rebuttal of counterarguments are often not appropriate, because the counterarguments are in fact perfectly good, so also does a debater not sufficiently honor his dialectical obligation merely by marshaling all the good arguments speaking for his own policy. A comparison of the arguments on the two sides is still called for, and if this is not allowed, the third parties have still not been helped to make their own comparisons. (203)

His argument here is that no matter how strong an argument may be for either side of a dispute about what to do, formulating either argument can never be sufficient to make that side's case because there is a dialectical obligation to take the additional step of comparing the two arguments and trying to show that one's own arguments are stronger than the others'.

I.8 Other statements of the "sufficiency is superfluous or meaningless" argument and of the "sufficiency is binary [whereas grounds in practical arguments come in degrees]" argument.

In the last place in the book where 'sufficiency' or 'sufficient' is indexed, Professor Kock returns to an argument we have already noted. It is that sufficiency is a dichotomous, "On/Off" concept whereas practical argumentation has only relative weight, which comes in degrees. It is worth quoting the entire passage in which he makes this argument, but first it bears noting that earlier in the chapter (213) he had said:

> Building on the work of informal logicians such as Johnson and Blair (2006), Blair (2012), Johnson (2000), and Govier (1987, 2009). I would posit the following three dimensions of argument appraisal in practical reasoning. Arguments should be:
>
> 1. Accurate
>
> 2. Relevant
>
> 3. Weighty

He proceeds to spell out how accuracy and relevance are to be understood, and then comes our passage:

> As you may have noticed, the weight criterion just popped up here. In choosing the term "weight" I deviate from the term most frequently used by informal logicians such as Anthony Blair: "sufficiency." The problem is that sufficiency is dichotomous. A quantity is either sufficient for some purpose or it isn't; it cannot be "rather sufficient." Do I have sufficient time to catch my plane? I cannot catch my plane to some extent. Also, sufficiency is known in mathematics in phrases like "the necessary and sufficient condition." A condition is sufficient for something to be the case if that something necessarily follows; that is, deductive inference obtains. Informal logicians rightly want to abandon deductive inference as a necessary condition of good argumentation; but if they include "sufficiency" in their criteria, either that means that deductive inference

is still required—or it has some other meaning which is fuzzy and idiosyncratic. (216)

In addition to the "On/Off" objection, Professor Kock ends with another version of the "sufficiency is either superfluous or it's meaningless" dilemma. Either 'sufficient' means "deductively entails" (which informal logicians want to reject as a necessary condition of good arguments) or, if it doesn't mean that, it is meaningless ("fuzzy and idiosyncratic").

These passages are the raw material from which we must extract Professor Kock's case against sufficiency. I have tried to be adequately informative in the extent of the quotations I've selected, and fair in my restatements of the arguments.

I.9 My interpretations of Kock's arguments

Sorting through these passages, I find in them one argument against sufficiency as a criterion for argument merit in general, and five arguments against sufficiency as a criterion for practical arguments—that is, arguments about what to do—in particular.

Objection A. The argument against sufficiency as a criterion for argument merit in general runs as follows: It is not clear what the informal logicians have in mind by 'sufficient'. It seems to mean the same as 'valid', but if that is so, it is a superfluous concept. If it means something other than valid, it is not at all clear what it does mean. Either way, it is not a useful criterion for the merit of either kind of argument, epistemic or practical.

The other arguments against sufficiency are reasons why it is not an appropriate criterion for the merit of practical arguments, and they apply even if the more powerful Objection A can be overcome and a case can be made that sufficiency is a coherent concept different from validity. These other arguments apply against validity as well, but I will consider them just insofar as they apply against sufficiency. I sketch them here in no particular order, and letter them only for convenience of reference.

Objection B. In practical reasoning there can be equally good arguments—acknowledged as such by both sides—both for and against a proposal. But if to be a good argument an argument must be sufficient to establish its conclusion, the arguments that make a case both for and against a proposal cannot be good arguments, for none of them, alone or collectively, succeeds in establishing the conclusion they are supporting. Enduring dissensus occurs because there normally tend to be legitimate arguments about practical issues on both sides and these tend to be incommensurable, which is to say they cannot be objectively weighed against one another. It follows that neither side can produce arguments that deductively entail the correctness of its position or that are sufficient to establish the correctness of its position. Hence, sufficiency is inappropriate as a criterion for the merits of practical arguments.

Objection C. Professor Kock also presents a slightly different version of Objection B, which I would reconstruct as follows. Because practical decision-making has a subjective dimension, there can be no "proofs" of practical conclusions. But when grounds can count as sufficient, they establish the truth of their conclusion, that is, they prove them. Thus, sufficiency works as a criterion, if at all, only where "proofs" are possible—not for practical arguments.

Objection D. Arguments for and against policy or action proposals come in degrees of strength. For instance, if it can be shown that a policy stands to benefit all the stakeholders, that is a weightier argument in its favour than showing that it will likely benefit only a small group of them. A criterion for argument merit must allow for differences in the degrees of strength of support. But sufficiency is a binary, On/Off concept. Something is either sufficient or insufficient. So, it cannot recognize degrees of argument merit. Thus, it isn't an appropriate criterion.

Objection E. In the case of many practical disagreements, the parties grant one another's arguments. Dick concedes that the armchair is really ugly, but wants it for its comfort (in this case, he prefers comfort-plus-ugliness to beauty-minus-comfort); Jane concedes that the armchair is really comfortable, but does not want it because it is so ugly (in this case, she prefers beauty to comfort-plus-ugliness). Their incompatible subjective preferences are what have to be negotiated, not any disagreements about the objective properties of the chair. There is no place in such scenarios for judgements of sufficiency or insufficiency. The arguments about objective properties are not sufficient to settle the disagreements, and there is no way for judgements of sufficiency or insufficiency to get a grip on subjective preferences. Sufficiency just isn't an appropriate criterion in the case of such practical arguments.

Objection F. Insofar as sufficiency is equivalent to validity, it precludes choice. A valid argument with true premises imposes its conclusion: having accepted its premises, one has no reasonable choice but to accept it. But practical reasoning aims at presenting one with a reasonable free choice. Hence sufficiency qua validity is not an appropriate criterion for the merit of practical argument.

PART II: IS PROFESSOR KOCK RIGHT ABOUT SUFFICIENCY?

II.1 Sufficiency is not problematic.

Let me begin by discussing the charge that sufficiency is problematic. That contention is a thread running through Professor Kock's critique, and it constitutes objections A (either equivalent to deductive validity or meaningless), D (binary, hence inapplicable to practical reasoning), and F (precludes choice).

Objection A. Either sufficiency is the same as deductive validity (and so is redundant) or it is meaningless. First, it has to be conceded that sufficiency is a potentially ambiguous concept. In *Logical Self-Defense* Johnson and I overlooked this ambiguity. It stems from a second ambiguity, namely the one that lurks in the meanings of 'logic' in the phrase "a logically good argument."

One sense of 'logic' may be found in Aristotle's theory of a logically good argument in the sense of an argument that establishes its conclusion. Classically, such an argument is deductively valid or inductively strong ("proving the universal through the particular's being clear" *Posterior Analytics* 71a8–9), its conclusion is different from its premises, and its premises are either "true and primitive" or are accepted by "everyone, or by the majority or by the wise" (*Topics* 100 a20–101a4). Thus, a logically good argument in this sense cannot have a false conclusion if it is deductively valid or an improbable conclusion if it is inductively strong. Johnson and I introduce a modification of this model in *Logical Self-Defense*, where "acceptable premises" replace "true premises" and "relevant and sufficient" replaces "deductively valid or inductively strong". Modern logic, on the other hand, focuses on the necessary consequences of propositions. From this perspective, a logically good argument is one whose premises deductively entail the conclusion, whether or not its premises are true, or differ from its conclusion. A logically good argument in this sense can have a false conclusion, and is to be distinguished from a sound argument, namely one that is both logically good in this sense and has true premises. I don't think that anyone owns the meaning of 'logically good argument' and one may use the term either in the classical way or the modern way, but it is important to be clear about the difference and to use the label consistently.

The distinction between these two senses of 'logically good' —what I am dubbing the classical and the modern—is important for present purposes because it underlies a distinction between two concepts of sufficiency. Using the concept of sufficiency related to the classical sense of logical goodness, if the relevant premises are acceptable and it would be unreasonable to reject the conclusion, given the premises, the argument is logically good. With such an argument, it would be unreasonable to insist on additional evidence before granting the conclusion—even if more evidence could be imagined, and even if the evidence adduced so far fails to deductively entail the conclusion. The evidence, in such cases, is sufficient in the sense in which Johnson and I were using the term. However, in the modern sense of 'logically good', such an argument could not count as logically good, for its premises fail to deductively entail the conclusion, and logical goodness is reserved for arguments whose relevant premises deductively entail their conclusion. It seems that Professor Kock took us to mean 'logically good' in the modern sense, in which case sufficiency would indeed be equivalent to deductive validity.

A difference between an argument that has sufficient support because it is deductively valid and an argument that has sufficient support although it is deductively invalid is that the former is not defeasible whereas the latter is defeasible. So, not only can there be clear cases of evidential sufficiency due to entailments, but there can also be clear cases of evidential sufficiency although the premises do not logically entail the conclusion. Examples would be statistical arguments about voting preferences, aesthetic arguments about historical artistic influences, moral arguments about obligations owed, and so on and on. There can be clear cases of evidential excess, such as continuing to add evidence for a proposition after a thorough case for it has been made and accepted by all. This can happen frequently enough that rules of order for legislative bodies have been formulated to authorize the chair to cut off timewasting support for or against a motion that has already been decided.[2] And there can be clear cases of insufficiency, such as judgements about a person's character based on their country of birth or the colour of their skin or the religion within which they worship. There are not sharp dividing lines between two vices at the extremes and the virtue in the middle. Whether one's evidence fails to be sufficient, is

2. See, e.g., *Roberts Rules of Order*.

enough, or is more than enough for the purpose at hand can be contested.

So sufficiency is not caught on the "equivalent to deductive validity" horn of the dilemma that Professor Kock alleges, nor is it caught on the "fuzzy and idiosyncratic" horn either. In the case of arguments whose premises deductively entail the conclusion, if those premises are true or otherwise acceptable, their support is sufficient to establish the conclusion. But even if the premises do not deductively entail the conclusion, assuming that they are true or otherwise acceptable, they can supply sufficient support to justify accepting the conclusion. Defeasible argument schemes can have instances in which the premises sufficiently support the conclusion, provided that their associated critical questions are appropriately answered. Argument scheme theory is hardly idiosyncratic or fuzzy.

Our concept of sufficiency is exhibited in the examples of "sufficient" proof of guilt as beyond meaningful doubt in criminal law and "double-blind and independently replicated" studies serving as the gold standard for "enough" evidence in medical research. Even though there are indeed frequently borderline cases in situations when practicality requires decisions in spite of uncertainty, there are also in such matters as these situations in which there are absolutely clear-cut, open and shut cases too. The accused is beyond question guilty as sin; the pharmaceutical company's new drug to treat condition X demonstrably is effective and has benign side effects. When the members of a qualified and well-balanced hiring committee, judging independently, unanimously agree that a particular candidate for a job is not only excellently qualified but also clearly superior to all the other applicants measured in terms of the criteria for the position (agreed-upon as appropriate), and has no disqualifying properties, and these judgments are based on ample reliable evidence—including the "subjective" impressions of well-informed and experienced judges of personnel in that position, then the hiring committee clearly has sufficient evidence to recommend offering her the position. What more do they need?

Objection D. Sufficiency is a binary (On/Off) concept, which doesn't allow for degrees of support. Locked in to seeing sufficiency as equivalent to deductive validity, Professor Kock fails to recognize that sufficiency in the sense used in informal logic is not a binary concept; it's a vague concept. If, by calling it a "fuzzy" concept, he means to make the point that there can be situations in which it is not clear whether the grounds adduced in an argument are sufficient, he is right, but that is no objection. Vague concepts admit of unclear cases. But if he means that it is unintelligible, he is mistaken. Vagueness is a necessary fact of life. Professor Kock identifies the concept of sufficiency used by informal logicians with the concept of sufficiency used in speaking of the logically necessary and sufficient conditions that serve to define or uniquely identify a concept. The latter is an "On/Off" or binary concept, but it is not the one used when your host asks you if you have sufficient water for your whiskey ("I think so. [Sip.] Oh, perhaps a drop more."), or if you wonder if your income is sufficient for you to afford to carry a mortgage on a dwelling ("It's more or less enough. It will mean cutting corners and giving up a few luxuries."). "More or less enough" can be a perfectly reasonable judgment, and it implies that sufficiency can come in degrees.

What counts as a sufficient amount of something depends on the situation, and often what is declared to be sufficient is contestable.[3] Sufficiency's vagueness is due to there being situations

---

3. In a recent article, G.C. Goddu (2019) makes much the same point: "What counts as 'enough' often varies from context to context. For example, in civil litigation, the conclusion of wrongdoing has to be supported by a preponderance of the evidence, i.e., the possibilities in which the defendant did what they are accused of, should be the case in more than 50% of the possibilities in which the provided evidence is true. But in criminal cases, the conclusion of wrongdoing should be supported beyond a reasonable doubt (which, at least if we take the vast majority of judge's views on what that means, is

in which it is open to reasonable disagreement or doubt or question whether support for a claim is sufficient or not; it emphatically does not mean that there are no situations in which it is incontrovertible that there is a sufficient, or an insufficient, or an excessive, support. One instance is usually not be enough to establish a generalization; a thousand instances may be far more than needed.

Sufficiency of evidence, or of other kinds of grounds, is a virtue of at least epistemic arguments. It is a mean between the extremes of insufficiency, at one extreme, and excess, at the other. There are clear cases of insufficient grounds (e.g., jumping to the conclusion that there are lots of fish in a lake based on quickly catching one on your first cast) and clear cases of excessive evidence (e.g., blackflies are a scourge in the Canadian forests and tundra in the month of June). There are also cases in which witnessing one occurrence of a phenomenon is sufficient to justify a generalization (e.g., one test suffices to show that if you touch the red-hot coals of a campfire for a few seconds, you will be badly burned). In between, there can be room for controversy about how much evidence is enough.

When a case is made for an empirical claim, often it's easier to identify insufficient evidence than say what would be sufficient. To predicate a property of all the members of a large but identifiable group, say Central American asylum-seekers at the American border with Mexico, based on the behavior of a handful of them (murderers, rapists), is to draw a conclusion based on insufficient evidence. It has a name: hasty generalization. A causal generalization based solely on a correlation is

above 80%). Statistical significance for supporting various hypotheses in the sciences is often set at 95% or higher. Determining what should count as 'enough' in various contexts is often extremely challenging. At the very least, some of what counts as 'enough' depends on the importance of the outcome. For example, since criminal sanctions are so much higher than civil sanctions, we demand more assurance that the evidence supports the conclusion of wrongdoing in the criminal case than in the civil case."

almost always arguing from insufficient evidence. You need, as well, evidence to rule out alternative hypotheses, such as that there is some third factor causing both correlates. There are standards of sufficiency that tests of a new medicinal drug must meet before it is declared safe and effective enough to be sold to the general public. There are uses of sufficiency as a criterion of arguments in support of both particular causal claims (why an automobile accident occurred) and also general causal claims (what causes lung cancer). All of these are defeasible.

Objection F. Sufficiency precludes choice. Professor Kock is right that if an argument with true premises deductively entails its conclusion, one has no choice about whether to accept the conclusion. However, since, as we have seen, an argument can contain sufficient support without entailing its conclusion, in such cases one has to be open to the possibility that, despite the strength of the evidence, the conclusion might be false. Thus, accepting the conclusion of an invalid argument with sufficient premises requires an element of choice, though it must be conceded that as the evidence becomes more powerful, the option of rejecting the conclusion is increasingly unreasonable.

II.2 Sufficiency cannot be a criterion of practical reasoning or argument

I turn now to the last three arguments in Professor Kock's case against sufficiency, Objections B, C and E.

Objection B is that in practical reasoning there can be equally good arguments on both sides of a question, but there cannot be sufficient arguments on both sides of a question, so sufficiency cannot be a criterion of good practical reasoning. At one time, I shared the view expressed in Objection B. In a commentary on a paper by Jens Kjeldsen, "Virtues of visual argumentation" at the 10th OSSA conference at the University of Windsor in 2013, I made the following remarks.

> Prof. Kjeldsen proposes that there can occur situations in which there can be a valid argument on both sides of an issue. He can't

be meaning good and 'valid' in the logician's sense, according to which an argument is valid just in case, if its premises are true, then its conclusion cannot possibly be false, and good (or "sound") if its premises are also true. For, on that definition, two arguments with true premises and contradictory conclusions cannot possibly both be valid.

Assuredly, reasonable advocates on either side of any of these issues would have to concede that there can be arguments that deserve to be taken seriously on both sides: none of these controversies is a case of all reason on one side and all unreason on the other. Perhaps the point can be expressed by noting that there are truths on both sides of all these issues that deserve to be taken into account when trying to decide what policies are best. If that is what it means to have good and valid arguments on both sides, I agree.

However, that is not equivalent to the claim that two arguments on different sides of an issue can have equal acceptability, relevance and sufficiency (ARS)—assuming with Kjeldsen that these are the criteria of a logically good argument. This claim could be true for the acceptability and relevance of the reasons on both sides, but it cannot be true for their sufficiency. Here is why. In order for the conclusion of any argument (A1) to be sufficiently supported, there cannot be an argument (A2) against its conclusion [that is, against the conclusion of (A1)] that has not been successfully refuted. This requirement follows if one understands a logically cogent argument to be one the relevant reasons of which entitle those entitled to accept them to accept the claim on the basis of those reasons. For one cannot be entitled to accept a claim against which there is a logically cogent argument. So, if there is a logically good argument (A2) for the contradictory of a position on an issue like the ones Prof. Kjeldsen lists, then that (A2) is an argument that the argumentation in support of that position (A1) has failed to refute. In such a case, the first argument (A1) has not satisfied the sufficiency criterion. Therefore, it cannot be true that two arguments on different sides of an issue may have equal acceptability, relevance and sufficiency.

I was here expressing in another way the position Professor Kock is asserting in Objection B. However, I now think that the comment on Professor Kjeldsen's claim concedes too much, that Kjeldsen was right in one respect and in that respect Kock is and Blair was mistaken.

Taking sufficiency to be a criterion of a good argument, if the ground level arguments for and against a proposed action or policy are both good arguments, the result is a stalemate. If that is all one has to go on, one is equally entitled to opt for either proposal and a forced decision can be the outcome of a coin toss. *But* this picture leaves out the complexity of most deliberation about policies. The premises of ground-level arguments are typically the conclusions or meta-level arguments, and these can be both normative and sufficient. (On the ground-level, meta-level distinction, see Finocchiaro 2013.)

Imagine a situation in which a choice has to be made between two acts or policies. Suppose there are two alternatives, do X and do not do X. Suppose further that a case can be made for each alternative. That is, it has been admitted by all deliberators, there are good reasons for doing X and there are good reasons for not doing X. There are benefits and burdens with each option. As pointed out by Professor Kock, there can be good reasons for an action or policy at the same that there are good reasons against it. Suppose, further, that in coming to the judgement that something, call it A, is a good reason to do X, an argument was made (and accepted as a good argument by all the deliberators) for the conclusion that A is a good reason for doing X . The conclusion is not, "Do X"; it is "A is a good reason for doing X." Suppose the deliberators had judged that A is a good reason for doing X (perhaps it will save millions of dollars, or perhaps it can be done quickly, in time to meet an urgent need, and so on) *because*, among other things, the premises of A together are sufficient, in the informal logician's sense, to support that conclusion. It has not been concluded that X should be done, but only that A is a good reason for doing X. Still, in that case an argument has been accepted by all the deliberators as sufficient to establish its conclusion. And its conclusion is a normative claim. If the suppositions I have listed are acceptable (and I think it is realistic to expect that to be possible in some situations) it follows that sufficiency can serve as a criterion of good meta-level arguments in arguments about what to do.

Objection C: When grounds can count as sufficient, they establish the truth of their conclusion, that is, they prove them. Thus, sufficiency works as a criterion, if at all, only where "proofs" are possible. But there can be no "proofs" of practical conclusions. So, sufficiency cannot be a criterion of good arguments with practical conclusions. The reply to this objection is implicit in what I have argued already. Judgments of sufficiency are defeasible. They do not establish the truth of their conclusion for all time and so are not equivalent to formal logical or mathematical proofs. This objection is due to the mistaken identification of sufficiency with deductive validity.

Objection E: In situations like Dick and Jane's disagreement over the ugly, comfortable easy chair, it is the incompatible subjective preferences that have to be negotiated, not any disagreements about the objective properties of the chair. There is no place in such scenarios for judgements of sufficiency or insufficiency. De gustibus, non disputandum est. *Sufficiency just isn't an appropriate criterion in the case of such practical arguments.* On this last point I agree with Professor Kock that sufficiency doesn't apply in such cases, but the reason it doesn't apply is that *arguments* cannot resolve subjective differences, so *no* criteria of argument merit *of any kind* belong there. It remains to be seen whether there always is a subjective element in practical judgments, and even if there is, whether disagreements over what to do are always due to differences of subjective preferences.

PART III: SUMMARY OF OBJECTIONS & REPLIES

In this essay I have argued that Professor Kock's attack on sufficiency goes too far. By focusing on one kind of sufficiency—deductive entailment—as the meaning of the term, he has overlooked another concept of sufficiency that does useful work in argument analysis and evaluation. I conclude with summaries of Professor Kock's objections to sufficiency and my replies to them.

Objection A: Sufficiency is redundant or meaningless.

Reply: Sufficiency is distinguishable from deductive validity, so it is not redundant; and there are many examples of its application, so it is not meaningless.

Objection B: Sufficiency cannot be a criterion of a good practical argument when, as is usually the case, there are good arguments on both sides of a practical issue, for in that case if one side's arguments were good, those on the other side could not be good.

Reply: This objection assumes that, like deductively valid arguments, arguments with sufficient support are not defeasible, whereas in fact they are.

Objection C: Sufficiency requires that "proof" is possible, but in practical arguments subjective factors are relevant but cannot be proved.

Reply: Subjective factors may tip the balance in "all things considered" judgements, but they do not thereby invalidate the interim conclusions that there are good arguments on both sides of a practical issue.

Objection D: Arguments for and against practical conclusions come in degrees of strength, but sufficiency is a binary or On/Off concept not admitting of degrees.

Reply: This objection is based on the mistaken view that the concept of sufficiency used as a criterion of argument merit is the same as that used in mathematics, or in "necessary and sufficient conditions".

Objection E: The presence of subjective factors bearing on practical decisions rules out sufficiency.

Reply: First, subjective factors are not always at issue or in conflict in practical decisions. Second, when subjective factors decide the matter, that can be a case in which otherwise sufficient considerations are defeated.

Objection F: Practical reasoning properly understood leaves agents with the opportunity to make a free choice, but the criterion of sufficiency precludes choice.

Reply: The defeasibility of sufficiency allows for choice. One may choose to have subjective preferences trump a good argument to the contrary.[4]

REFERENCES

Blair, J. Anthony. 2013. Commentary on "Virtues of visual argumentation" by Jens Kjeldsen. Proceedings of the 10th OSSA conference at the University of Windsor. https://scholar.uwindsor.ca/ossaarchive/OSSA10/

Finocchiaro, Maurice A. 2013. *Meta-argumentation, An Approach to Logic and Argumentation Theory.* London: College Publications.

Goddu, G. C. 2019. "Logic and critical thinking". In J. Anthony Blair (ed.), *Studies in Critical Thinking,* Ch. 19. Windsor, ON: Windsor Studies in Argumentation, Vol. 8.

Johnson, Ralph H. and Blair, J. Anthony. 2006. *Logical Self-Defense.* New York: IDEA Press. (Reprint of the US edition, the 4th, 1994 New York: McGraw-Hill, Inc.) 1st ed. (1977), 2nd ed. (1983), 3rd ed. (1993) Toronto: McGraw-Hill Ryerson.

Kjeldsen, Jens. 2013. "Virtues of visual argumentation" *Proceedings of the 10th OSSA conference at the University of Windsor.* https://scholar.uwindsor.ca/ossaarchive/OSSA10/

Kock, Christian. 2017. *Deliberative Rhetoric: Arguing About Doing.* Hans V. Hansen (ed.). Windsor, ON: Windsor Studies in Argumentation, Vol. 5.

---

4. I wish to thank Christopher Tindale for comments on earlier drafts of this essay.

ABOUT THE AUTHOR: Anthony Blair is a Professor of Philosophy Emeritus at the University of Windsor, a Senior Fellow at the Windsor Centre for Research in Reasoning, Argumentation and Rhetoric, a founder and co-editor of *Informal Logic*, author (with Ralph Johnson) of *Logical Self-Defense.* He has published extensively in informal logic, argumentation theory and critical thinking and is a recipient of the International Society for the Study of Argumentation Distinguished Scholarship Award for lifetime achievement.

CHAPTER 14.

TOOLS FOR TEACHING AND LEARNING BASIC ARGUMENTATION SKILLS

DOUGLAS WALTON

ABSTRACT: This paper explains five argumentation tools that are especially applicable to the teaching and learning of informal logic in educational settings. Three of them are argumentation schemes, argument diagrams, and use of presumptive reasoning in argument diagramming to elicit implicit premises and conclusions. The fourth tool is a dialectical model of argumentation that takes the context into account by using formal models of dialogue. The fifth is a dialectical model of explanation suitable for use in educational settings.

KEYWORDS: argumentation, education, critical thinking, presumptions, informal logic, dialogue models, argument diagramming, dialectical explanation

1. INTRODUCTION

This paper explains some argumentation tools that are proving to be useful for teaching argumentation skills in educational settings: argumentation schemes, argument mapping (diagramming) tools, formal dialogue models and a dialectical model of explanation. First, it explains argumentation schemes that identify patterns of reasoning linking premises to a conclusion with defeasible assumptions that can be challenged by raising critical questions. Schemes have been applied to collaborative argumentation in examples of arguing to learn (Nussbaum 2008; Nussbaum and Edwards 2011; Macagno and Konstantinidou 2013).

Second, it applies argument mapping tools for making argument diagrams that are useful to represent arguments visually. Such argument mapping tools are now widely used to structure educational interactions (Andriessen and Schwartz 2009). They are designed to help a user visualize the premises and conclusions of arguments and display a sequence of connected arguments chained together to support an ultimate conclusion. Empirical research has shown that argument mapping is a useful learning and teaching methodology (Dwyer, Hogan and Stewart 2013). More than fifty computational argument mapping tools are described by Scheuer *et al.* (2009), and each of them has different features and main applications to different tasks. Three such tools are illustrated in this paper, the Rationale system (van Gelder 2015), the argument visualization diagram tool used by Nussbaum and Edwards (2011), and the argument mapping tool of the Carneades Argumentation System (Gordon 2010; Walton and Gordon 2019).

Third, the paper explains how everyday argumentation from the simplest to the most complex examples is based on the ability to fill in missing propositions and the inferences drawn from them using plausible reasoning of a kind that is based on common knowledge of the way things are standardly done in circumstances familiar to agents putting forward or responding to arguments. An argument diagram is used to illustrate how presumptions necessary to understand the argumentation in a natural language text can be found as implicit premises or conclusions.

Fourth, it is explained how formal dialogue models in argumentation systems can be applied to help users analyse and critically evaluate arguments based on plausible reasoning of the kind found in everyday conversational discourse. Formal models of dialogue take an argument to be an interaction between two or more intelligent rational agents and that represent different conversational settings of an argument. It is now well recognized that argumentative interactions play an important role in computer-supported collaborative learning (Baker 2003, 47; Nussbaum 2011). The dialectical model is shown to be a framework for presumptive reasoning (Hansen 2003; Hansen *et al.* 2019). Since the schemes most important for use in educational settings are defeasible, the conclusion of an argument can be tentatively accepted as a presumption in a dialogue, even though it is vulnerable to later defeat.

Fifth, the paper outlines the dialectical approach to explanation that has now achieved such wide acceptance in cognitive science and artificial intelligence (Miller 2019). Much of what a teacher does in any field can better be described as "explanation" rather than "argument". This paper introduces a dialectical concept of explanation that is suitable for use in teaching and learning in conjunction with the argumentation tools described in the prior parts of the paper.

2. ARGUMENTATION SCHEMES

The standard example of an argumentation scheme is the one for argument from expert opinion. This type of argument is not well modeled by deductive logic, because doing so would imply that if a source is an expert in a domain of knowledge then whatever that source says has to be right. This approach implies that experts are never wrong, but recent research (Freedman 2010) offers a substantial body of evidence suggesting that experts (including scientists, financial experts, physicians, consultants, health officials and experts offering advice on personal relationships), are typically and even characteristically fallible. There are many reasons for this fallibility. One of them is that scientific evidence-based reasoning, in order to qualify properly as being scientific reasoning, has to be falsifiable, meaning its result has to be given up should stronger evidence be gathered showing that the hypothesis question is not supported. In general, especially when it comes to taking the advice of experts in complex domains such as health or finance, it needs to be realized that such recommendations are defeasible, meaning that they are vulnerable to defeat as new information comes in. For this reason, the argumentation scheme for argument from expert opinion is configured as inherently defeasible form of argument.

Major Premise: *E* is an expert.
Minor Premise: *E* asserts that *A* is true (false).
Conclusion: *A* is true (false).

Because this form of argument is defeasible, it is subject to critical questioning, and it needs to be treated as a defeasible type of argument rather than as a conclusive one.

Any defeasible argumentation scheme is evaluated by using a set of basic critical questions matching the scheme. The critical questions function as avenues for exploring potential weaknesses in the argument.

There are six basic critical questions matching this scheme for argument from expert opinion (Walton, Reed and Macagno 2008, 310):

CQ1: Expertise Question. How knowledgeable is *E* as an expert source?
CQ2: Field Question. Is *E* an expert in the field that *A* is in?
CQ3: Opinion Question. What did *E* assert that implies *A*?
CQ4: Trustworthiness Question. Is *E* personally reliable as a source?
CQ5: Consistency Question. Is *A* consistent with other experts' opinions?
CQ6: Backup Evidence Question. Is *E*'s assertion based on evidence?

CQ1 relates to the expert's level of mastery of the field F. CQ4 relates to the expert's personal reliability and trustworthiness. For example, if it comes to be known that the expert has something to lose or gain by saying A is true or false, such evidence can be taken to imply that the expert may not be reliable about judgments pertaining to A. The asking of a critical question suspends the argument temporarily until it has been answered successfully. Nussbaum and Edwards (2011) explore critical questions as refutational argument strategies that are useful for teaching argumentation skills to students to help increase their abilities to generate and critique arguments. Their work has shown how tools developed by argumentation theory can usefully be applied to classroom-based instruction.

Argument from Witness Testimony	Argument from Verbal Classification	Argument from Rule
Argument from Expert Opinion	Argument from Appearances (Perception)	Argument from Threat
Argument from Analogy	Argument from Positive Consequences	Argument from Popular Opinion
Argument from Precedent	Argument from Negative Consequences	Direct Ad Hominem Argument (Personal Attack)
Practical (Goal-Directed) Reasoning	Circumstantial Ad Hominem Argument	Argument from Correlation to Cause
Argument from Evidence to a Hypothesis	Abductive Reasoning	Argument from Commitment
Argument from Negative Evidence	Argument from Sunk Costs	Slippery Slope Argument

Table 1: List of Typical Argumentation Schemes

A list of some of some commonly used argumentation schemes is presented in Table 1. The names of the schemes give the reader an idea of what each scheme is about, but these schemes along with their matching critical questions can be found in (Walton, Reed and Macagno 2008).

Nussbaum (2011, 89-90) has also presented a useful list of twenty argumentation schemes along with critical questions that match each scheme.

Deductively Valid Argument	Inductively Strong Argument	Plausible Argument
Every person who does a good job should get regular pay that reflects the value of his or her work. Alice is a person who does a good job. Therefore, Alice should get regular pay that reflects the value of her work.	Most people who do a good job should get regular pay that reflects the value of their work. Alice is a person who does a good job. Therefore, Alice should get regular pay that reflects the value of her work.	It is widely accepted that people who do a good job should get regular pay that reflects the value of their work. Alice is a person who does a good job. Therefore, Alice should get regular pay that reflects the value of her work.

Table 2: Three Types of Arguments

According to Nussbaum (2011, 90) a proposition is said to be plausible if it is reasonable to accept it. Plausibility can often be equated with the source of a proposition. For example an instance of witness testimony, a news account or personal observation can be a source of evidence used to claim that a proposition is plausible.

It is possible to treat deductively valid forms of argument such as strict *modus ponens* (If *p* then *q*; *p*; therefore *q*), and inductively strong forms of reasoning, such as reasoning from a sample to a population, as argumentation schemes. However the schemes mentioned in Table 1 do not fit into either category. The examples in Table 2 illustrates the difference between plausible arguments of the kind associated with the schemes shown in Table 1 and the two other types of arguments. The plausible type of argument shown at the right in Table 2 is presumptive and defeasible in nature.

Defeasible arguments are heuristics that are necessary in law, science and everyday life, although they are also risky, as they are associated with fallacies. The best way to approach them is to see them as warranting a kind of tentative acceptance that is subject to critical questioning. They are often weak as arguments, merely conjectures or guesses, but can be strengthened through the asking and getting answers to the critical questions if the pro evidence outweighs the contra evidence.

3. ARGUMENT MAPPING TOOLS

Rationale (http://rationale.austhink.com/) is probably the easiest very helpful argument mapping tool for students to learn to use without much training. It can easily be applied to examples of arguments to help students get a better grasp of good essay writing structure, to learn skills of working with reasoning and evidence generally, and to prepare for debates (Davies *et al.* 2019).

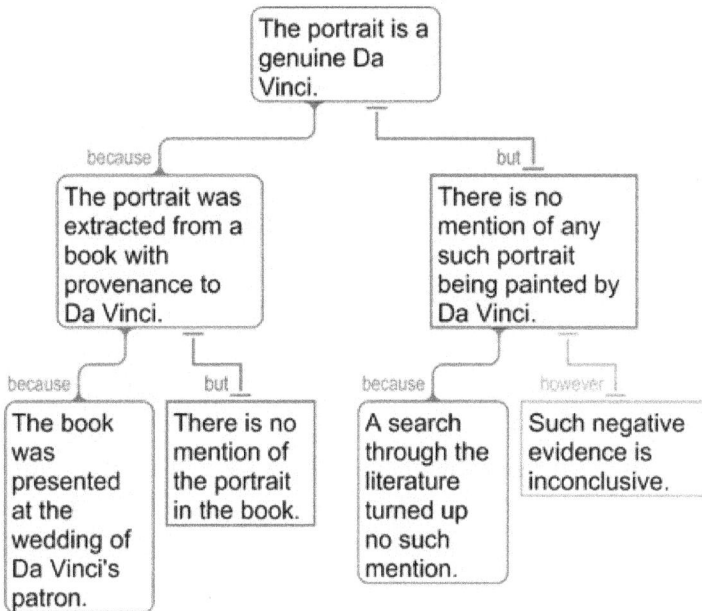

Figure 1: A Rationale Argument Map

Of the three systems mentioned here, it is certainly the easiest for a beginner to start using. A Rationale argument map is drawn in the form of a tree structure is shown in Figure 1.

The proposition shown in the text box at the top is called the contention. It represents the main issue or topic under consideration. The contention represents the ultimate claim to be proved by the argumentation that appears below it. The proposition just under it on the left side, stating that the portrait was extracted from a book with provenance to da Vinci, offers a reason (indicated by the word 'because'); it gives evidence that supports the contention. The proposition under the contention on the right side (indicated by the word 'but') attacks the contention. This proposition is called an objection. It conveys evidence that goes against the contention.

The proposition at the bottom right, indicated by the word 'however' and stating that such negative evidence is inconclusive, is the premise of an argument suggesting that we should have reservations about the proposition just above it. This argument is one that is often called the argument from negative evidence, also sometimes called the argument from ignorance.

The argument map in Figure 1 illustrates a typical argumentation sequence that examines the pro arguments as well as the con arguments relevant to proving or disproving the ultimate claim at issue. One can see such an argument map as a way of representing and extending an integrative argument of the kind defined by Nussbaum and Edwards (2011). An integrative argument is one that provides reasons for one side but is at the same time open to acknowledging and replying to counterarguments put forward by the other side. The tool advocated by Nussbaum and Edwards (2011, 448) as a means of visually modeling an integrative argument is called the argument visualization diagram (AVD). It is a graphic organizer that a participant in argumentation uses to write a display representing opposed arguments on each side of an issue also formulated on the diagram. The AVD enables participants in argumentation not only to maintain arguments and counter- arguments in working memory, but also to organize their thoughts in approaching the problem of how to evaluate the arguments. Rationale extends this capability by providing a visual representation of how a chain of connected arguments on each side of an issue, pro and contra, are connected together and anchored to the ultimate issue. By this means we can extend the notion of an argument further by seeing it as an organized sequence of premises and conclusions interacting with an opposed argument that is also a connected sequence of premises and conclusions.

There are also some powerful artificial intelligence argumentation systems that can be used to make argument diagrams and that use such graphic structures not only to identify and analyse arguments, but also to evaluate them and to use the tool to invent new arguments to prove a claim (Walton and Gordon 2019). The Carneades argumentation system is a formal and mathematical model of argumentation that has a user interface that can be used to visualize an argument as an argument map (diagram) showing the premises and the conclusion, and linking arguments together in sequences.[1] An argument map is displayed as a bipartite directed graph, consisting of statement nodes and argument nodes connected by edges, or arrows representing inferences from statements to other statements (Gordon 2010). See the example diagram in Figure 2. Carneades incorporates argumentation schemes, and it can be used to construct arguments as well as to evaluate them (Walton and Gordon 2019). It has an automated argument assistant that enables a search to find arguments in a knowledge base to support or attack a claim.

However, you don't need any of these automated tools to make a helpful argument diagram. You can use a pencil and paper, and this method can often be a useful first step before using one of

1. The Carneades Argumentation System along with a manual, can be accessed at http://carneades.github.com.

these systems to make a more refined and pleasing version of the diagram. Or you can use a drawing tool such as Mocrosoft Visio (available in Microsoft Office), or yEd (free to download)[2] to draw the text boxes and arrows. Still, these automated systems can produce a professional-looking diagram that sums up and analyzes an argument in a way that is easier for an audience to understand and remember. Also, the tools that can be applied using them, such as argumentation schemes and critical questions, make it possible to probe into the structure of the argument in depth, to find objections to it, and to analyze it to find missing premises.

4. PRESUMPTIONS IN PLAUSIBLE REASONING

Argumentation of the kind we consider in natural language discourse, such as in everyday conversations and legal reasoning, is typically presumptive in nature, and depends on implicit premises and conclusions based on common knowledge about the way things standardly happen in situations that parties to the argumentation are familiar with. Walton, Tindale and Gordon (2014, 114) set out eleven defining characteristics of plausible reasoning.

1. Plausible reasoning goes from more plausible premises to a less plausible conclusion.

2. Something is found plausible when hearers have examples in their own minds.

3. Plausible reasoning is based on common knowledge.

4. Plausible reasoning is defeasible.

5. Plausible reasoning is based on the way things generally go in familiar situations.

6. Plausible reasoning can be used to fill in implicit premises

2. http://www.yworks.com/en/products_yed_download.html

in incomplete arguments.

7. Plausible reasoning is commonly based on appearances from perception.

8. Stability is an important characteristic of plausible reasoning.

9. Plausible reasoning can be tested, and by this means, confirmed or refuted.

10. Probing into plausible reasoning by questioning it is a way of testing it.

11. Plausible reasoning admits of degrees of strength.

Plausible reasoning is defeasible, meaning that it is vulnerable to retraction as new evidence enters a situation. A proposition that appears true to one observer may appear to be false to another. Thus it is possible to have two arguments from the same evidence, each of which is plausible in its own right, but that lead to opposite conclusions. The Sophists of ancient Greek philosophy and rhetoric provided the classical example, as recorded by Aristotle (*Rhetoric* 1401^{b}17).

> The *Art* of Corax is composed of this topic. For if a man is not likely to be guilty of what he is accused of, for instance if, being weak, he is accused of assault and battery, his defence will be that the crime is not probable [*eikos*]; but if he is likely to be guilty, for instance, if he is strong, it may be argued again that the crime is not probable [*eikos*], for the very reason that it was bound to appear probable [*eikos*]. (Aristotle 1926, 335; modified translation of Kraus, 2010, 362).

The example is one where the question of whether, in a contested case, the one man or the other committed the assault. There are arguments on both sides. The defence of the weaker man will be that it is not plausible that he committed the assault, for obvious reasons. But turning this argument on its head, the stronger man could argue that it is not plausible that he committed the assault either, because it is common knowledge that if the case went to trial, it would be bound to appear to a tribunal, such as a jury, that the stronger man would be unlikely to have committed the crime because he knew very well that it would look bad for him in court. This would give him a reason not to attack the smaller man. Essentially, the argument of the stronger man in any future tribunal would be that it is not plausible that he would have committed the assault, because people would think it plausible that he did, given the uncertainty about which man assaulted the other.

Following along the lines of the research of Walton, Tindale and Gordon (2014), the argumentation in the example can be analysed by means of an argument diagram, showing how the implicit premises and conclusions are brought to the surface (Figure 2). Eleven of the fourteen premises are marked as implicit presumptions, indicated by the dashed borders of the rectangles in which they appear. The round nodes (circles) represent the arguments connecting the propositions that are the premises and conclusions together. A pro argument is indicated by a plus sign, while a con argument is indicated by a minus sign. The pair of opposed conclusions are shown at the far left. Each of these is attacked by a network of connected argumentation.

When the argument was put forward that, for these reasons, the weaker man was not likely to assault the stronger one, that move might win the case, on balance, provided the stronger man has put forward no counterargument. The weaker man's argument shifts a weight of presumption to the other side. But what happens when the stronger man's argument, shown as argument -a2 in Figure 2, is put forward? This move is enough to raise some doubts about whether the weaker man's argument is convincing enough to lead to a finding that the stronger man committed the assault. Hence the presumption shifts back to the other side.

How strong the argument on either side needs to be in order to win depends on the standard of proof operative in the case. In the modern system of common law the standard of proof applicable in a criminal case is for the argumentation to meet the "beyond reasonable doubt" standard of proof. We do not need to go into the question of which, if any, standard of proof would have been used in a Greek tribunal of this kind. The example is interesting enough in that it illustrates that we can use argumentation and argument diagram to show how the argumentation on both sides depends on presumptions that are implicit in the wording of the case we are given.

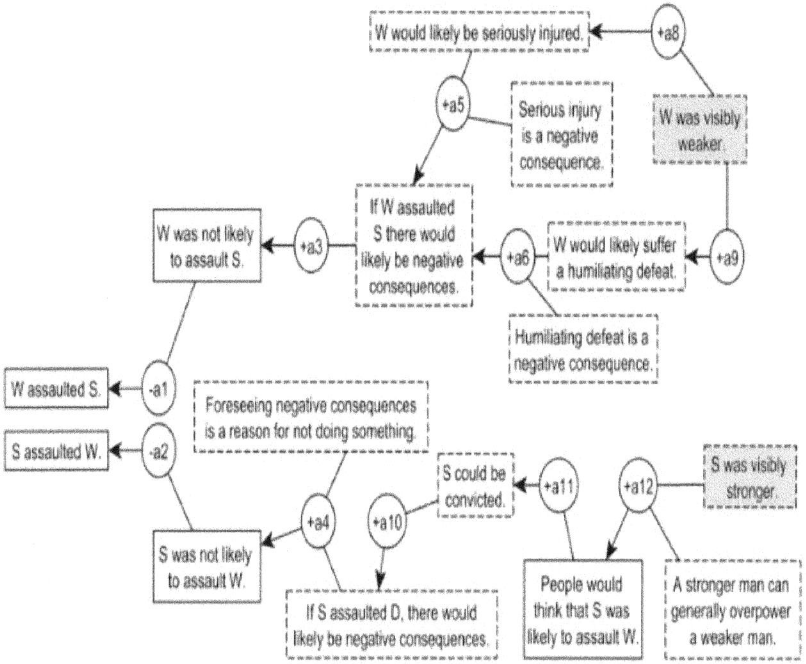

Figure 2: Argument Diagram of the Stronger and Weaker Man Example

The interpretation of the argumentation in the example visually displayed in Figure 2 is only a plausible interpretation that can be argued against by constructing alternative argument diagrams that represent other supposedly plausible interpretation of the same text Greek text translated into English. Indeed, the interpretation shown in Figure 2 is different, not in general outline, but in specific details from the argument diagram given by Walton, Tindale and Gordon (2014, 95) to represent the sequence of argumentation in the example. Walton (2019) offers three different interpretations of this same example using three argument diagrams and four argumentation schemes. Readers can argue at a metalevel about which of these interpretations is the most plausible one based on the textual evidence.

But there are also some differences in the tools used. The interpretation of Walton, Tindale and Gordon used argumentation schemes to help build the diagram, such as the scheme for argument from negative consequences, whereas the interpretation of Figure 2 did not. The main reasons it did not was limitations of space. But anyway, readers can look at the comparable diagram of Walton, Tindale and Gordon to see how schemes are used in interpreting the argumentation in the example.

5. FORMAL MODELS OF DIALOGUE

As defined by Nussbaum and Edwards (2011, 448), an integrative argument represented by an AVD is a visual representation of an argument that displays pro arguments for one side and also con arguments that the other side can put forward. This model suggests that argumentation can take the form of a dialogue between a proponent and an opponent. On this model, argumentation schemes and argument maps are not sufficient by themselves to provide an adequate method for analyzing and evaluating argumentation in a natural language text discourse. It is also important to take into account the communicative setting in which an argument was used for some purpose. The standard way of doing this in argumentation studies is to use a dialogue model to distinguish between different types of dialogue that represent such communicative settings. The dialogue provides a normative model that can be applied to offer evidence to show whether an argument is correct or incorrect when used for some conversational purpose, such as to resolve a conflict of opinions or make a decision on what to do.

The dialogue models described in this paper arose from the practical task of assisting users to analyze and critically evaluate arguments of the kind found in everyday conversational discourse and in other contexts like legal and scientific argumentation. Such a model is normative because it sets standards for logical inference based on argumentation schemes and procedural standards that give requirements for how to take part collaboratively in a dialogue with a speech partner. These standards are structured in formal models of dialogue. The model of argumentation it is built on reaches a decision on whether to accept a claim or not based on the arguments both for and against the claim, and therefore on this view, an argument always has two sides, the pro and contra (Walton 2013). They take turns making moves that contain speech acts. Speech acts are performed by each participant at each move in the dialogue, and the structure of the dialogue is defined by rules (protocols) that set preconditions and post-conditions regulating how the speech acts used as permissible moves in that type of dialogue.

A dialogue is defined in Carneades as an ordered 3-tuple $\{O, A, C\}$ where O is the opening stage, A is the argumentation stage, and C is the closing stage. Dialogue rules define what types of moves are allowed (Gordon 2010). At the opening stage, the participants agree to take part in some type of dialogue that has a collective goal. Each party also has an individual goal but the dialogue itself has a collective goal, that is a goal shared by all the participants. The initial situation is framed at the opening stage, and the dialogue moves through the opening stage toward the closing stage.

In Table 1, the type of dialogue is identified in the left column and its main properties are identified in the three matching columns on the right. The critical discussion type of dialogue of van Eemeren (2010) has the collective goal of resolving a conflict of opinions that represents the ultimate issue to be decided. In the dialogue classification system of Walton (2013), it is taken to be a species of persuasion dialogue. Not all instances of persuasion dialogue are instances of a critical discussion for the reason that in some instances, the two sides have a valuable discussion that gives each of them (and the audience) deeper insights into the reasons supporting or rebutting the positions of both sides.

TYPE OF DIALOGUE	INITIAL SITUATION	PARTICIPANT'S GOAL	GOAL OF DIALOGUE
Persuasion	Conflict of Opinions	Persuade Other Party	Resolve Issue
Inquiry	Need to Have Proof	Verify Evidence	Prove Hypothesis
Discovery	Need an Explanation	Find a Hypothesis	Support Hypothesis
Negotiation	Conflict of Interests	Get What You Want	Settle Issue
Information	Need Information	Acquire Information	Exchange Information
Deliberation	Practical Choice	Fit Goals and Actions	Decide What to Do
Eristic	Personal Conflict	Hit Out at Opponent	Reveal Deep Conflict

Table 3: Seven Basic Types of Dialogue

In every dialogue there is a commitment store (Hamblin 1970; 1971) consisting of a set of statements. As each move is made, a rule governing the speech act determines which statements need to be added to or removed from the commitment store. For example, asserting that a statement is true commits one to defend the statement unless one withdraws the commitment. The traditional theory of rational cognition in the social sciences as well as in analytical philosophy has taken a BDI (belief-desire-intention approach). Belief is a psychological construct that is hard to determine when evaluating argumentation, whereas commitments are more stable and observable (Nussbaum 2011, 88). On the commitment model of argumentation, a successful argument of the proponent in a dialogue must be based on premises that are commitments of the respondent. This requirement has important implications for how the model supports collaborative learning

There can be dialectical shifts from one type of dialogue to another during the same sequence of argumentation. For example, suppose a contractor and homeowner are negotiating on the price of a foundation repair, and they shift to the issue of whether it would be a good idea to install an additional inch of concrete wall. This would be a shift from negotiation to deliberation, and then there might be a shift to information-seeking dialogue as they look into the building code requirements for thickness of concrete walls in a house basement. Or to give another example, during a divorce dispute, a couple are negotiating who should look after the children, but the mediator shifts the discussion to a persuasion dialogue on the issue of which party is in the best position to undertake the task of looking after the children. Each side must give reasons, and this shift could be beneficial because it makes the dialogue less eristic.

Educational discourse can involve all seven types of dialogue, but is most closely related to discovery, inquiry and information-seeking. Educational dialogue centrally involves a transfer of knowledge from one party to another. It also involves the typical situation where one party tries to explain something to another (sometimes successfully). A special type of dialogue called examination dialogue is defined as a species of information-seeking dialogue. In collaborative learning, two parties are trying to share knowledge, but in the typical pedagogical situation found in all schools and universities, there is an asymmetry. One party is supposed to lack some specific knowledge and the other (the teacher) is supposed to impart that knowledge to the first party (the student). To build this model, we have to have some basic idea of what knowledge is supposed to be. The theory takes a dialogue approach to knowledge and explanation that is different from the traditional theories of knowledge and explanation in analytical philosophy.

6. A DIALECTICAL MODEL OF EXPLANATION

What is the difference between argument and explanation? The difference arises from the purpose of the dialogue the two parties are supposedly taking part in. When requesting an argument to support a claim, the questioner is asking for evidence to back up the claim, because she has doubts about whether the claim holds. When requesting an explanation, the questioner is asking for the respondent to bring her to understand something that she is presently unable to understand. The purpose of an explanation, in other words, is to convey understanding from one party to another in a dialogue. The purpose of an argument is to prove something that there is doubt about. An argument is here understood as a claim put forward by one party in a dialogue together with premises to support that claim as a conclusion that can be derived from premises. A good argument, therefore, should always be based on evidence that supports its claim and gives the person to whom it was directed a reason to accept the proposition that is claimed to be true. But on asking for an explanation of a particular proposition or state of affairs, the questioner is not thereby expressing doubt that this proposition is true. She is merely indicating that she does not understand it, and she is requesting that the other party do something to give her the required understanding. The essential difference between the two speech acts is that the proposition queried in the case of an explanation is not doubted. For example if you ask me for an explanation of the Challenger spacecraft explosion, you are not asking me to prove that the spacecraft exploded by giving evidence to support that claim. You are asking me for some sequence of reasoning that can enable you to understand how or why the spacecraft exploded. This might be the recounting of a sequence of events showing how the intense heat of the rocket motor melted the O-rings, producing a fire.

The new dialectical theory (Walton 2011) models an explanation as a dialogue between two agents in which one agent is presumed by a second agent to understand something, and the second agent asks a question meant to enable him to come to understand it as well. An explanation is not only a deduction from general laws, or only a message delivered by one party to the other, but the result of joint attempts in a dialogue for the parties to reach mutual understand (Dillenbourg *et al.* 1996, 205). In the dialogue model of explanation, a successful explanation has been achieved when there has been a transfer of understanding from the party giving the explanation to the party asking for it. The dialogue model articulates the view of Scriven (2002, 49): "Explanation is literally and logically the process of filling in gaps in understanding, and to do this we must start out with some understanding of something." The required type of dialogue has an opening stage, an explanation stage and a closing stage. The notion of understanding employed is based on scripts (stories) of a kind employed in artificial intelligence research (Schank 1986). Whether a transfer of understanding has taken place in an explanation is tested by a shift to an examination dialogue.

How can understanding be transferred from one party to another? This transfer process works by the explainer helping the explainee to make sense of something by using common knowledge to fill gaps in a script that initially seems to be an anomaly. A script is a connected sequence of events or actions that both parties understand in virtue of their common knowledge about the ways things can be generally expected to happen in situations both are familiar with. In the famous restaurant script (Schank 1986), a man enters a restaurant goes to a table, picks up a menu, orders soup, eats the soup when it arrives, pays the bill when it arrives, gets up and leaves the restaurant. Suppose that part way through this script, he unexpectedly gets up from his chair and pulls his pants down. That would be an anomaly, suggesting the need for an explanation. But then suppose we are told that he spilled hot soup on his legs. Now we understand what happened, or at least we can, once some further gaps in the sequence are filled in.

Education typically involves the situation where a teacher has the task of trying to explain something to a student, where the student can be expected to know some things but not others. In argumentation, an argument always needs to be based on the commitments of the respondent in order be successful, for example in a persuasion dialogue. Similarly in a successful explanation, the explainer has to base her explanation of what has appeared to be an anomaly to the explainee on what the explainee already understands, or thinks he does at any rate.

7. SUMMARY OF THE GENERAL APPROACH

The tools explained above suggest a general approach to collaborative argumentation-based learning of critical thinking skills that has ten general characteristics.

1. It analyzes and evaluates argumentation for a claim on a balance of evidence where there is evidence for it as well as against it, using standards of proof.

2. It views rational argumentation as a dialogue procedure, implying that two heads are better than one when assessing claims about what to accept based on evidence.

3. It uses critical questioning as a way of finding weak points in an argument, and it can represent critical questions as special types of premises in an argument map.

4. It views argumentation as procedural, meaning that prov-

ing something is taken to be a sequence with a start point, and an end point as represented on an argument map.

5. It is commitment-based. It uses a database of commonly accepted knowledge that includes previous arguments and commitments expressed in them.

6. It is dynamic, meaning that it continually updates its database as new information comes in that is relevant to an argument being considered.

7. It is defeasible, meaning that an argument being considered is subject to defeat if new relevant evidence comes in that refutes the argument.

8. It is presumptive, meaning that in the absence of evidence sufficient to defeat it, a claim that is the conclusion of an argument can be tentatively accepted as a presumption, even though it may be subject to later defeat.

9. It does not aim to prove something is true as knowledge that must be accepted beyond all doubt, but recognizes bounds of human rationality. It includes the study of error and fallacy.

10. It comprises the study of explanations as well as arguments, and because of its dialogue format, enables a systematic distinction to be drawn between them.

REFERENCES

Andriessen J. and Schwarz, B. 2009. Argumentative design. In M. Muller Mirza and A. Perret Clermont, *Argumentation and Education* (Eds.), pp.145-174. Dordrecht: Springer.

Baker, M. 2003. Computer-mediated Argumentative Interactions for the Co-elaboration of Scientific Notions, Arguing to Learn. Dordrecht: Kluwer, 47-78.

Davies, M., Barnett, A. and van Gelder, T. 2019. Using computer-aided argument mapping to teach reasoning. In J. A. Blair (Ed.),

Studies in Critical Thinking, pp. 131–175. Windsor, ON: Windsor Studies in Argumentation.

Dillenbourg, P., Baker, M., Blaye, M. and O'Malley, C. (1996). The evolution of research on collaborative learning. In E. Spada and P. Reiman (Eds), *Learning in Humans and Learning in Humans and Machine: Towards an Interdisciplinary Learning Science*, pp. 189-211. Oxford: Elsevier.

Dwyer, C. P., Hogan, M.J. and Stewart, I. 2013. An examination of the effects of argument mapping on students' memory and comprehension performance, *Thinking Skills and Creativity*, 8, 11-24.

Eemeren, F. H. van. 2010. *Strategic Maneuvering in Argumentative Discourse*. Amsterdam: Benjamins.

Freedman, D. H. 2010. *Wrong: Why Experts Keep Failing Us – and How to Know When Not to Trust Them*. New York, Little Brown and Company.

Gelder, T. J. van. 2015. Using argument mapping to improve critical thinking skills. In M. Davies and R. Barnett (Eds.), The Palgrave Handbook of Critical Thinking in Higher Education, pp. 183–192. Basingstoke U.K.: Palgrave Macmillan.

Gordon, T.F. 2010. An overview of the Carneades argumentation support system. In C.W. Tindale and C. Reed (Eds.), *Dialectics, Dialogue and Argumentation. An Examination of Douglas Walton's Theories of Reasoning*, pp. 145-156. London: College Publications.

Hamblin, C. L. 1970. *Fallacies*. London: Methuen.

Hamblin, C. L. 1971. Mathematical models of dialogue, *Theoria*, 37, 130-155.

Hansen, H. V. 2003. Theories of presumptions and burdens of proof. In: J. Anthony Blair *et al.* (Eds.), *Informal Logic at 25: Proceedings of the Windsor Conference*. CDROM. Windsor, Ontario: Ontario Society for the Study of Argumentation.

Hansen, H. V., Kauffeld, F. J., Freeman, J. B. and Bermejo-Luque L, (Eds.). 2019. *Presumptions and Burdens of Proof: An Anthology of Argumentation and the Law*. Tuscaloosa, University of Alabama Press.

Kraus, M. 2010. Perelman's interpretation of reverse probability arguments as a dialectical *mise en abyme, Philosophy and Rhetoric*, 43(4), 362-382.

Macagno, F. and Konstantinidou, A. 2013. What students' arguments can tell us: Using argumentation schemes in science education, *Argumentation* DOI 10.1007/s10503-012-9284

Miller, T. 2019. Explanation in artificial intelligence: Insights from the social sciences, *Artificial Intelligence*, 267 (Feb.), 1-38.

Nussbaum, E. M. 2008. Collaborative discourse, argumentation, and learning: Preface and literature review. *Contemporary Educational Psychology*, 33, 345-359.

Nussbaum, E. M. 2011. Argumentation, dialogue theory, and probability modeling: Alternative frameworks for argumentation research in education, *Educational Psychologist*, 46: 2, 84-106.

Nussbaum, E. M. and Edwards, O. V. 2011. Argumentation, critical questions and integrative stratagems, *Journal of the Learning Sciences*, 20, 433-488.

Schank, R. C. 1986. *Explanation Patterns: Understanding Mechanically and Creatively*. Hillsdale, New Jersey: Erlbaum.

Scheuer, O., Loll, F., Pinkwart, N. and McLaren, B. M. 2009. Computer-supported argumentation: A review of the state of the art. *International Journal of Computer-Supported Collaborative Learning*, 5(1), 1-67.

Walton, D. 2013. *Methods of Argumentation*. Cambridge: Cambridge University Press.

Walton, D. 2019. Plausible argumentation in eikotic arguments: The ancient weak versus strong man example, *Argumentation*, 33(1), 45-74.

Walton, D. and Krabbe, E. C. W. 1995. *Commitment in Dialogue*. Albany: State University of New York Press.

Walton, D. and Gordon, T. F. 2019. How computational tools can help rhetoric and informal logic with argument invention, *Argumentation*, 33(2), 2019, 269-295.

Walton, D., Reed, C. and Macagno, F. 2008. *Argumentation Schemes*. Cambridge: Cambridge University Press.

Walton, D., Tindale, C. W. and Gordon, T. F. 2014. Applying recent argumentation methods to some ancient examples of plausible reasoning, *Argumentation*, 28(1), 85-119.

ABOUT THE AUTHOR: Douglas Walton (1942-2020) received his PhD from the University of Toronto in 1972. He was the Distinguished Research Fellow of the Centre for Research in Reasoning, Argumentation and Rhetoric and held the Assumption Chair of Argumentation Studies at the University of Windsor from 2008-2013. He had been Visiting Professor at Northwestern University, the University of Arizona, and the University of Lugano (Switzerland). In 2009 he was given the Faculty of Arts and Social Sciences Dean's Special Recognition Award of the University of Windsor, in recognition of excellence in research, scholarship and creative activity. In the area of argumentation studies he published 50 books, as well as 350+ refereed papers, and had over 20,000 citations of his writings. He was the keynote speaker in 2019 for the Munich Winter School "Scientific Reasoning and Argumentation" hosted by the International Doctoral School at the Ludwig-Maximilians University in Munich.

CHAPTER 15.

MILL'S DEFENSE OF A RAWLSIAN CONCEPTION OF SOCIAL JUSTICE

BRUCE RUSSELL

ABSTRACT: Briefly, this is what I'll discuss in this essay: first, Mill's conception of happiness, intrinsic good, and morality; then a presentation of Rawls's conception of social justice; then evidence that Mill supported a similar conception but on utilitarian grounds. Finally, I offer a metaethical reason in favor of a non-utilitarian defense of this conception.[1]

KEYWORDS: Mill's Greatest Happiness Principle, Rawls on social justice, Mill on social justice, intrinsic value, competent judges, life prospects, basic structure of society, normative epistemology, act utilitarianism, rule utilitarianism.

1. This paper comes out of my dissertation, *Rawls and Utilitarianism: A Comparison and Critique*, which was directed by Fred Berger. He died suddenly at too young an age a few years after I completed my dissertation with him. I would like to dedicate this paper to him in gratitude for all the help and encouragement he provided.

1. MILL'S CONCEPTION OF HAPPINESS AND MORALITY

For Mill, a person's happiness consists in all those things that the person desires for their own sakes that produce *the feeling of happiness* = pleasure in that person. Here is what Mill says in *Utilitarianism.*

> What was once desired as an instrument for the attainment of happiness has come to be desired for its own sake. *In being desired for its own sake it is, however, desired as part of happiness.* The person is made, or thinks he would be made, [to feel] happy by its mere possession; and is made [to feel] unhappy by failure to obtain it. The desire of it is not a different thing from the desire of happiness any more than the love of music or the desire of health. They are included in happiness. They are some of the elements of which the desire of happiness is made up. (CW, X, 236; U, Ch. IV, parag. 6. My emphasis on the entire sentence, Mill's on "part" in that sentence; my words in brackets. See, also, the preceding and succeeding paragraphs in U).[2]

Mill's use of the word "happiness" is ambiguous: sometimes it means the feeling of happiness, sometimes happiness itself. For a given person, happiness itself consists of everything that person desires for its own sake that will produce *the feeling of happiness* (that Mill often refers to as "pleasure"; see *U*, Ch. II, parag. 2) in that person when the desire for that thing is fulfilled.

Of course, it is not my conception of happiness, nor yours, nor anyone else's conception of happiness that is the standard of morality. That standard is given by what competent judges would desire for its own sake and take pleasure in, that is, by peo-

---

2. References to Mill's writings will be to the *Collected Works of John Stuart Mill* (Toronto: University of Toronto Press, 1963-91), ed. J. M. Robson, and indicated by "CW" followed by the volume number and then the relevant page numbers. In the case of Mill's *Utilitarianism*, I will refer to passages by "U" followed by the relevant chapter and paragraph number in the chapter.

ple who have experienced all different sorts of pleasure.[3] Here's what Mill says about the standard of morality:

> According to the greatest happiness principle, as above explained, the ultimate end, with reference to and for the sake of which all other things are desirable – whether we are considering our own good or that of other people – is an existence exempt as far as possible from pain, and as rich as possible in enjoyments, both in point of quantity and quality; the test of quality and the rule for measuring it against quantity being the preference felt by those who, in their opportunity of experience, to which must be added their habits of self-consciousness and self-observation, are best furnished with the means of comparison. This, being, according to the utilitarian opinion, the end of human action, is necessarily also the standard of morality, which may accordingly be defined "the rules and precepts for human conduct," by the observance of which an existence such as has been described might be, to the greatest extent possible, *secured to all mankind*; and not to them only, but, so far as the nature of things admits, to the whole sentient creation. (*CW*, X, 214; *U*, Ch. 2, parag. 10. See, also, parag. 12. My italics) [4]

3. Rawls recognizes that the preferences of competent judges is Mill's criterion of intrinsic value, adding only that it is what the competent judges prefer "under conditions of liberty" that determines intrinsic value (ATOJ, 209). He credits G. A. Paul with making him aware of this interpretation of Mill's criterion of value (ATOJ, 209, note 7). In *Happiness, Justice, & Freedom* (1984), Fred Berger says of Mill, "Ultimately, however, in decisions concerning intrinsic goods, the final evidence is what is preferred by persons who are experienced and knowledgeable," (p. 50) what Mill called "competent judges." See, also, Berger, pp. 49, 51, 287, 288. Berger argues that Mill thought that over history these competent judges have preferred certain things like freedom (autonomy), security, a sense of dignity, the exercise of our distinctively human faculties, etc. This creates what Berger calls a "meshing" or weighting problem that pluralistic intuitionists face, but that Mill hoped to solve, insofar as the happiness that is to determine what is right and wrong consists of various ingredients that might be weighed in different ways (say, security more heavily than freedom or vice versa). See Berger, pp. 50, 286.

4. Note that Rawls says, "The common good I think of as certain general conditions that are in an appropriate sense *equally to everyone's advantage*" (ATOJ, 246; my emphasis). I believe that what Mill means by "the General Happiness" is close to what Rawls here means by "the common good".

How does this standard of morality relate to Mill's views about our moral obligations? Here is what he says about wrongness,

> We do not call anything wrong unless we mean to imply that a person ought to be punished in some way or other for doing it – if not by law, by the opinion of his fellow creatures – if not by opinion, by the reproaches of his own conscience (*CW*, X, 246; *U*, Ch. V, parag. 14).

I take it that here Mill is offering *an analysis* of *the concept* "wrong." (Berger (1984, 108) cites David Lyons as holding this view too). It's something that utilitarians and non-utilitarians alike should accept. They will differ in their *conceptions* of wrongness because they will have different standards for determining whether "a person *ought* to be punished in some way or other" for his actions.

On my interpretation of Mill, his view is not a maximizing view but a means-end view. The end is given by what he calls "the ultimate end" or "the end of human action," which is to be "secured to all mankind," and so far as possible to "the whole sentient creation." There is no room here for making trade-offs that might justify a majority in oppressing a minority in order to maximize happiness. The end of morality is for *everyone* to enjoy the kind of life described in Mill's statement of the standard of morality.

The "art" of morality determines the relevant end and Mill thought that any art,

> ...proposes to itself an end to be attained, defines the end, and hands it over to the science...The only one of the premises, therefore, which Art supplies, is the original major premise, which asserts that the attainment of the given end is desirable (from Mill's *Logic*, *CW* VIII, 944-45).

Mill thought that social science must provide grounds for adopting secondary rules which if followed will likely lead to the desirable end. These secondary rules comprise "the rules and precepts for human conduct," as they are referred to in the above passage about the standard of morality. He calls one part of social science "which inquires into the laws of succession of social states," "social dynamics," and the other part, "social statics," "which inquires into the laws of coexistence of various aspects of any given state of society."[5] Suppose the ultimate end, E, is a society of the sort described in Mill's statement of the standard of morality, but one society is in state A and another in state B, both short of E. Social dynamics will provide evidence to determine the best rules for the first society to get from A to E and the second from B to E. These need not be the same sets of rules. And social statics will provide evidence to determine what the best set of rules is for approaching as close as possible to the ultimate end for a given society at a given time.

Mill's reference to the "rules and precepts of human conduct" as defining the standard of morality has led people to see him as a Rule Utilitarian (RU). Also, in Ch.II of *Utilitarianism*, Mill says the following about an action "whose consequences in the particular case might be beneficial":

> ...it would be unworthy of an intelligent agent not to be consciously aware that the action *is of a class* which, *if practiced generally*, would be generally injurious, and that *this is the ground of the obligation* to abstain from it. (CW, X, 220; U, Ch. II, parag. 19 (end); my italics)

Mill also wrote that,

> The creed which accepts as the foundation of morals, Utility, or the Greatest Happiness Principle, holds that actions are right in pro-

5. See Mill's *Logic, Collected Works, VIII*, Chpt. 10, secs. 5 and 6 for his discussion of social statics and dynamics. This passage is from pp. 944-45. See, also, his *Logic, Collected Works, VIII*, pp. 873-74 where he discusses the science of ethology which studies the ways to produce qualities in human beings that are desirable. Ethology can deduce middle (intermediate or secondary) principles from the general laws of human nature and, in the case of morality, they will found secondary principles of morality which should be used to guide human conduct except in cases where secondary principles conflict.

portion as they *tend to promote happiness*, wrong as they *tend to produce the reverse*. (CW, X: 210; U, Ch. II, parag. 2; my italics)

Berger notes that J. O. Urmson thinks that, "it makes sense only to speak of the tendency of a *class* of acts, not of an individual act, and this would commit Mill to a rule-consequence position" (Berger, 68). But Berger goes on to argue that it also makes sense to talk about the tendencies of individual acts (see, Berger, 68, 74, and various places at 73-120). So the above quoted passage does not settle the question of whether Mill was a rule- or act-utilitarian.

The penultimate quotation from Mill says that the generally injurious consequences of general performance of a type of act are the *ground* of our obligation to abstain from performing a particular act of that type. Berger (p. 94) interprets this to mean that those consequences are good *evidence* (*epistemic grounds*) of the *tendency* of the *particular act*, and for Mill this tendency is what actually determines whether the act is wrong, not the general consequences of general performance of acts of this type. But the bad consequences of a general practice of lying is, at best, very weak evidence that my lying *on a particular occasion*, say, to benefit my child, will tend to have bad consequences. And there may be stronger contrary evidence that it will not have such consequences. So Mill could not conclude, as it seems he would, that I would have an obligation to abstain from lying on this occasion. It seems that Mill's answer to the question of whether I am obligated to tell the truth on this particular occasion is that I should stick to the rule because the general consequences of the general practice of acting according to the rule of veracity *actually determine* the moral status of the action and do not merely provide evidence of the tendency of the particular action, contrary to Berger's interpretation of Mill.

In the passage about exceptions to moral rules, Mill sounds like some sort of Rule Utilitarian, but in other places he sounds like an Act Utilitarian.[6] My interpretation of Mill that reconciles these apparently contradictory views of moral obligation is the following: the secondary rules that the Greatest Happiness Principle (GHP) supports determine the rightness and wrongness of actions *unless they conflict*. If they do, then what the (GHP) itself requires determines the rightness and wrongness of actions. On this interpretation, when Mill sounds like an Act Utilitarian, it is because he is assuming that there is a conflict between secondary rules or because he is arguing that there can be exceptions to those rules.

Berger (p. 54) rightly points out that the following passage from Mill does not entail that the rightness and wrongness of actions is determined by the (GHP) *only when* there is a conflict between secondary rules, but it does show that Mill thought one of its roles is to do that. So I am not basing my interpretation of Mill on the following passage, but I believe it makes the best sense of the totality of the evidence provided by Mill's writings, both the passage that makes him sound like a Rule Utilitarian and those that make him sound like an Act Utilitarian.

> We must remember that *only in these cases of conflict* between secondary principles *is it requisite* that first principles should be appealed to (CW, X, 226; my italics; U, Ch. II, last paragraph in the chapter. Mill makes a similar point in his "Remarks on Bentham's Philosophy," CW, X: 110-111).

6. For instance, when he compares intermediate generalizations or secondary rules to landmarks and direction-posts on a traveler's way, and the traveler's destination to the general happiness (U, Chpt. II, next to last parag.) See, also, his *A System of Logic* in *The Collected Works of John Stuart Mill* (Toronto: University of Toronto Press, 1974), VIII, 944, where he compares someone who goes by the rules instead of the reasons that found them to a physician who allows his patients to die because he follows the (general) rules for treating patients and ignores the particular situation. Other places that make Mill sound like an act utilitarian who treats secondary rules as heuristics include: a letter to John Venn (1872) in *CW*, XVII (Letter 1717A); "Thornton on Labor and Its Claims," *CW*, V, 659; "Taylor's Statesmen," *CW*, XIX, 638-41.

The view I am attributing to Mill is not standard Act Utilitarianism because according to my interpretation insofar as the secondary rules do not conflict a person really should act in accordance with them *even when that person knows that doing that conflicts with what the (GHP) requires*. Act Utilitarianism (AU) would see the secondary rules as heuristics, or even strategy rules as Berger calls them (pp. 72-73) that can *practically* require strict adherence in certain circumstances even when that involves doing what is wrong (though not what is *known* to be wrong) according to the (GHP). Act Utilitarianism says that a person is really obligated to do what (AU) says even if there is no conflict within the secondary rules and they imply that you ought to act contrary to (AU).

The view is also not a species of standard Rule Utillitarianism because (RU) would have no implications about what a person is obligated to do if the secondary rules conflict in a given case, unless the rules also included a non-utilitarian higher-order rule for adjudicating such conflicts. But on my interpretation of Mill, the (GHP) is *the utilitarian higher-order rule* for adjudicating such conflicts. So on my interpretation, Mill's version of utilitarianism will have implications about what a person should do in the case of conflicts between secondary rules, and those implications can be different from the implications of standard (RU) if it has any.

For Mill, duties of justice are a special sub-class of duties; they are perfect duties that are owed to particular persons, not imperfect duties that, as Kant says, allow "leeway in the interest of inclination" (See, CW, X, 246; U, Ch. V, parag. 15). If I owe you money, then I have a duty of justice to repay you. However, if I have a duty to bring aid to the suffering, I can choose to fulfill this duty by helping the sick or the starving, etc. So the duty to bring aid is not a duty of justice.

But duties of justice that individuals have are different from what social justice requires.

2. SOCIAL JUSTICE

2.1 Rawls

For Rawls, social justice concerns,

> ...the basic structure of society, or more exactly, the way in which the major social institutions distribute fundamental rights and duties and determine the division of advantages from social cooperation. By major institutions I understand the political constitution and the principal economic and social arrangements. Thus the legal protection of freedom of thought and liberty of conscience, the competitive markets, private property in the means of production, and the monogamous family are examples of major social institutions. Taken together as one scheme, the major institutions define men's rights and duties and influence their *life prospects*, what they can expect to be and how well they can hope to do. The basic structure is the primary subject of justice because its effects are so profound and present from the start. (ATOJ, 7; my emphasis; cf., 54, 96 where Rawls again says that the primary subject of justice is the basic structure of society)

As most moral philosophers know, Rawls argues for three principles, a first principle governing liberty and a second one with two parts governing life prospects. These three principles which are to govern the basic structure of society are: the Greatest Equal Liberty Principle (GELP); the principle of Fair Equality of Opportunity (FEOP); and the Difference Principle (DP). The (GELP) requires the greatest extent of basic liberties compatible with like liberties for all. The basic liberties include political liberties, such as the right to vote and to freedom of speech, and personal liberties, such as liberty of conscience and freedom of thought, the right to hold private property, freedom of association, and freedom from arbitrary arrest and seizure (cf., ATOJ, 61).

Rawls acknowledges that Mill has "forceful arguments" that "under some circumstances anyway...might justify many if not most of the equal liberties." But he thinks that Mill's "contentions" will not "justify an equal liberty for all" without "standard utilitarian assumptions" (ATOJ, 210). According to Rawls, these assumptions are,

> ...a certain similarity among individuals, say their equal capacity for the activities and interests of men as progressive beings, and in addition a principle of the diminishing marginal value of the basic rights assigned to individuals. (ATOJ, 210; cf. 159)

I do not believe that Mill's arguments do rest on these "standard utilitarian assumptions." Instead, they rest on assumptions about what competent judges would desire, and I believe that Mill would say that they would desire a society where the basic liberties are protected *for everyone*. As the above quote indicates, the utilitarian standard requires that "an existence such as has been described might be, to the greatest extent possible, *secured to all mankind*" (see, also, U, Ch. V, three parags. from the end). So the Greatest Happiness principle would require the most extensive basic liberties compatible with like liberties *for all*, that is, would require the (GELP). Perhaps, contra Mill, the competent judges would not desire a society where the basic liberties are secured, or would desire that the presumption of equality built into the (GHP) would be overridden, but I do not believe that Mill would think that the (GELP) is recommended because it is *instrumentally good* that it be recognized and enforced. Rather, I think he would say that everyone's having the greatest extent of equal basic liberties is intrinsically good and that the (GELP) can be overridden only if that is needed to obtain other intrinsic goods.

Despite acknowledging that Mill's criterion of intrinsic value are the preferences of competent judges (see note 2, above), when he criticizes Mill's utilitarianism, Rawls interprets Mill as having a satisfaction theory of the good (ATOJ, 26, 449) and so imagines that if a majority of society "has an abhorrence for certain religious or sexual practices, and regards them as an abomination," that would justify limiting the liberty of the minorities to engage in these practices, even if they were kept from public view (ATOJ, 450; also, 210-11). But on my interpretation of Mill, it is only the desires of the competent judges that count from the standpoint of the Greatest Happiness Principle, and Mill has a means-end conception of morality, not a maximizing one. The secondary rules are justified because adhering to them is the best means to eventually achieve the ultimate end where everyone has equal basic liberties and everyone is so altruistic that they care as much about the happiness of others as about their own happiness. (See U, Ch. II, parag. 18 where Mill links utilitarianism to the golden rule and the last few pages of U, Ch. III where Mill argues for the promotion and expansion of a natural feeling of unity with others.)

Rawls believes that in favorable conditions the (GELP) takes precedence over the other two principles but in less favorable conditions what he calls the General Conception of social justice applies, which allows trade-offs between liberty and opportunity, income and wealth, and the bases of self-respect (ATOJ, 303). Mill might agree for he says,

> After the means of subsistence are assured, the next in strength of the personal wants of human beings is liberty...The perfection both of social arrangements and of practical morality would be, to secure *to all persons* complete independence and freedom of action, *subject to no restriction but that of not doing injury to others.* [7]

For Rawls, once the (GELP) has been satisfied, a just society must satisfy two other principles. The principle of Fair Equality of Opportunity (FEOP) says:

> ...those with similar abilities and skills should have similar life chances. More specifically, assuming that there is a distribution of natural assets, those who are at the same level of talent and ability, and have the same willingness to use them, should have *the same*

7. *Principles of Political Economy, Collected Works II,* pp. 208-09; my italics. I take this quote to indicate that Mill would support Rawls's (GELP) and its priority to his other two principle in what Mill would call "favorable conditions."

prospects of success regardless of their initial place in the social system, that is, irrespective of the income class into which they are born. (ATOJ, 73; my emphasis)

The FEOP basically says that holding natural endowments constant, everyone should have the same life prospects regardless of what social class they have been born into. Currently, children born into families of unskilled laborers often have worse life prospects than children born into families of entrepreneurs even though the children have similar native endowments and aspirations (cf., ATOJ, 78). The (FEOP) is supposed to address those inequalities by disallowing differences in the social class into which persons are born to affect their life prospects.

However, even if inequalities in life prospects due to the social class into which a person is born are removed, inequalities in life prospects due to differences in native endowments can remain. In contemporary American society, people born with an aptitude for math and science have better prospects than those who do not. The FEOP disallows such differences when the differences in life prospects are due to social and economic starting places. Still, it allows difference in life prospects due to differences in native endowments: it allows the race to go to the swiftest, the strongest, and the brightest even if inequalities in life prospects due to class differences have been eliminated. As a first approximation, the Difference Principle prohibits differences in life prospects that depend on differences in native endowments. Ultimately, it allows them if and only if they will improve the life prospects of those in the group that have the lowest such prospects.

Together the FEOP and DP govern life prospects due to starting points based on socio-economic considerations and native endowments, respectively. When it comes to allowing inequalities in life prospects, both considerations are relevant. Rawls says,

...even if it [the principle of fair equality of opportunity] works to perfection in eliminating the influence of social contingencies, it still permits the distribution of wealth and income to be determined by the natural distribution of abilities and talents...There is no more reason to permit the distribution of income and wealth to be settled by the distribution of natural assets than by historical and social fortune...For once we are troubled by the influence of either social contingencies or natural chance on the distribution of shares, we are bound, on reflection, to be bothered by the influence of the other (ATOJ, 73-75).

Also,

The pervasive and continuous influence of our *initial place in society* and or our *native endowments*, and of the fact that the social order is one system, is what characterizes the problem of justice in the first place (ATOJ, 171; my emphases).

Some people have interpreted the DP to govern inequalities in income and wealth, period, but it's clear that Rawls is interested in these inequalities only insofar as they affect the life prospects of even those born into the same socio-economic class. He is interested in the "distribution of shares" of income and wealth, and in general of the prospects of success, that people *can look forward to* given their *starting places*.

To re-emphasize, Rawls says that the subject of social justice is the basic structure of society because,

...its effects are so profound and pervasive, *and present from birth*. This structure favors some *starting places* over others in the division of the benefits of social cooperation. It is these inequalities which the two principles are to regulate. Once these principles are satisfied, other inequalities are allowed to arise from men's voluntary actions in accordance with the principle of free association. (ATOJ, 96; my emphasis. See the start of this section for another quote about the basic structure from ATOJ, 7.)

Rawls says that he has a pure procedural notion of social justice when it comes to the basic structure of society (ATOJ, 85-88,

274-75).[8] That means that he does not believe that there is some independent standard to determine what is the just distribution of the benefits and burdens of social cooperation for which we must design procedures that guarantee (as with perfect procedural justice) or make likely (as with imperfect procedural justice) that such a standard will be met (see ATOJ, 85-86 for Rawls's distinction between perfect, imperfect, and pure procedural justice). He thinks that when it comes to pure procedural justice, if the procedure is just, then whatever distribution that results will be just, as happens in fair gambling situations. Rawls believes that if the basic structure of society is just, that is, if there is what he calls "background justice," then the resulting distribution of income, wealth, power, opportunity, the bases of self-respect, and the value of the basic liberties will be just, whatever it happens to be (ATOJ, 274-75; cf., 304)

Rawls' second principle does not prohibit LeBron James and Steph Curry from making a lot of money as a result of many people paying to watch them play basketball. It only prohibits "bumps" in the social fabric that result from many such exchanges when and only when they create obstacles to those born less fortunate.[9]

---

8. Rawls says that for utilitarianism "the basic structure is a case of imperfect procedural justice" (ATOJ, 89), for the end to be achieved is the General Happiness and the basic structure should be constituted in the way that best achieves that end. For Mill, adherence to the secondary rules founded on evidence from the social sciences are the means by which that end is achieved. Presumably, Rawls would agree with the libertarians that the actual holdings of individuals are just *only if* exchanges between parties are not due to force, fraud, or manipulation.

9. Rawls does not think that inequalities in income and wealth are unjust in themselves and so by their nature demand attention from the standpoint of justice. He says that unequal inheritance of wealth and intelligence are not inherently unjust but both "should satisfy the difference principle" (ATOJ, 278).

2.2 Mill

Mill says many things that indicate that he would also accept Rawls's second principle, both parts of which are concerned with life prospects based on starting points (both natural and socio-economic) over which no one has control. In several places he remarks how being born rich or poor has an enormous impact on one's lot in life. In an essay in which he discusses the proper use and constraints on endowments made for public benefit, he says,

> The real hardship of social inequalities to the poor, as the reasonable among them can be brought to see, is not that men *are* unequal, but *that they are born so*; not that those who are born poor do not obtain the great objects of human desire unearned, but that *the circumstances of their birth* preclude their earning them; that the higher positions in life, including all which confer power or dignity, can not only be obtained by the rich without taking the trouble to be qualified for them, but that even were this corrected...none, as a rule, except the rich, have it in their power to make themselves qualified.[10]

In another essay, after remarking that "few are born to riches and many to penury," Mill says,

> No longer enslaved or made dependent by force of law, the great majority are so by force of poverty; they are still chained to place, to an occupation, and to conformity with the will of an employer, and debarred *by the accident of birth* both from the enjoyments, and from the mental and moral advantages, which others inherit without exertion and independently of desert. [11]

A few pages later in the same essay, he writes,

> The most powerful of all the determining circumstances [of the lot of individuals] is birth. Some are born rich without work, others are

10. In "Endowments," *Collected Works* V, 627-28. Mill's emphasis on "are," mine on the rest.
11. From Mill's "Chapters on Socialism," *Collected Works* V, 710; my italics.

born to a position in which they can become rich *by* work, the great majority are born to hard work and poverty throughout life, numbers to indigence. Next to birth the chief cause of success in life is accident and opportunity.[12]

Mill is opposed to the huge influence birth and luck have on the life prospects of people. He certainly would support Rawls's principle of Fair Equality of Opportunity whose aim is to eliminate inequalities in life prospects that stem from different socio-economic starting points. But would he also endorse Rawls's Difference Principle that concerns inequalities based on differences in native endowments?

In a review of M. Dupont-White's writings on centralization, Mill criticizes the "English thinkers" who ignore the effects of "natural inequalities" in "the race of life" for desirable positions.

> …for in racing for a prize, the stimulus to exertion on the part of the competitors is only at its highest when all start fair, that is, when natural inequalities are compensated by artificial weights; and the complaint is, that in the race of life all do not start fair; and unless the State does something to strengthen the weaker side, the unfairness becomes utterly crushing and dispiriting.[13]

Mill, like Rawls, thinks that inequalities in life prospects based on differences in either socio-economic or natural starting points are unfair. Would he, like Rawls, endorse allowing some such inequalities if doing that could improve the life prospects of those with the poorest prospects? In the sentences before those just quoted, Mill indicates that those who think "the strong should be allowed to reap the full advantage of their strength" are mistaken but that they are right in thinking they should be allowed *some* advantages as an incentive to "exert their strength" from which all can benefit.

---

12. "Chapters on Socialism," p. 714; my parenthetical addition.

13. In Mill's "Centralisation," *Collected Works* XIX, 591.

It appears that Mill would accept both parts of Rawls's second principle, that is, both the principle of Fair Equality of Opportunity and the Difference Principle, though, of course, on utilitarian, not contractarian, grounds, as well as Rawls's principle of Greatest Equal Liberty and its priority. In other words, Mill would accept Rawls's conception of social justice given "favorable conditions" where liberty has priority.

3. NORMATIVE EPISTEMOLOGY

In a nutshell, Rawls's view is that a theory of social justice is epistemically justified just in case "it fits our considered judgments [of justice] in reflective equilibrium" (ATOJ, 111; cf., 579). Considered judgments will be non-inferential judgments that we make in circumstances where we are not influenced by self-interest nor biased by religious or personal convictions. "Our" refers to competent judges who are reasonably intelligent and understand well what it is that they are judging. The process of reflective equilibrium requires us to seek consistency between our more specific and more general considered judgments.

More recently T. M. Scanlon has defended a similar normative epistemology in *Being Realistic About Reasons* (2014). By a person's considered judgment he means,

> ...what *seems* clearly true to her after she has been unable to discover any "implausible implications or presuppositions" of the proposition that is the object of that "seeming." (p. 84; cf. pp. 82-83 and 85)

In my, "A Defense of Moral Intuitionism," I define an intuitions as:

...the psychological state people are in when some proposition seems true to them solely on the basis of their understanding that proposition.[14]

People have objected that no proposition seems true to people *solely* on the basis of their understanding it, not even "All bachelors are unmarried males" or "2 is the only even prime." The objection is that other psychological states or conditions are partly the cause of why we believe these propositions. In light of this objection, I modify my account of intuition as follows: a person has an intuition that P if and only if P seems true to her primarily on the basis of her understanding P and would still seem true to her on that basis if whatever other actual causes of its seeming true to her were absent. This seems to capture a relevant epistemological difference between the propositions I just gave about bachelors and the number two and the propositions that "All crows are black" and that "There are more than 2 people in this room."

Scanlon thinks that we can have considered judgments about general principles as well as about specific cases. I think the same about intuitions and that reflective equilibrium seeks consistency between our intuitive judgments (which are based on our intuitions) at all levels of generality. We share the view that standards of justification vary from domain to domain and that reflective equilibrium is the proper standard for the normative domain. Where we differ is that on Scanlon's account of considered judgments, they can be empirically based. I am trying to give an account of *a priori* intuitions that can serve as the foundation of non-empirical, philosophical justification.

I want to conclude by discussing two quotes from Rawls: one about the scope of fundamental moral principles and the other about the reliance on empirical considerations as a means of rec-

14. Bruce Russell, "A Defense of Moral Intuitionism," in *Does Anything Really Matter? Essays on Parfit on Objectivity* (Oxford: Oxford University Press, 2017) Peter Singer (ed.), p. 232.

onciling fundamental principles with more specific considered moral judgments. The first quote is this:

> Some philosophers have thought that ethical first principles should be independent of all contingent assumptions, that they should take for granted no truths except those of logic and others that follow from these by an analysis of concepts. Moral conceptions should hold for all possible worlds. (ATOJ, 159)

Rawls rejects this approach that seeks moral conceptions that hold for all possible worlds. However, that does not mean that moral philosophy should not seek necessary truths about, say, what justice requires in such-and-such circumstances. It might be necessarily true that: if conditions *ABC* obtain, then justice requires *XYZ*, even though it is not necessarily true that justice requires *XYZ*, for it may not require that where conditions *ABC* do not obtain.

Rawls recognizes that utilitarianism can offer reasons for adhering to secondary rules that have implications that accord well with our considered judgments of justice (ATOJ 26, 28, 159-61, 207, 209-11, 450). But he says the following about his own view in contrast to utilitarianism:

> Justice as fairness, by contrast [to utilitarianism], embeds the ideals of justice, as ordinarily understood, more directly into first principles. This conception relies less on general facts in reaching a match with our judgments of justice. It insures this fit over a wider range of possible cases. (ATOJ, 160; cf., 32, 161, 210-11)

Rawls calls *some* considered judgments "provisional fixed points" because they represent our "firmest convictions." Among those are the following: (i) religious intolerance and racial discrimination are unjust (ATOJ, 19-20); (ii) no one deserves his place in the distribution of native endowments, any more than one deserves one's initial starting point in society (ATOJ 104; cf., 311); (iii) everyone ought to have equal liberty of conscience (ATOJ, 206); and (iv) each person possesses an inviolability founded on justice that even the welfare of society as a whole cannot override (ATOJ, 3; cf., 4, 28, 586). Though this last example is not explicitly claimed to be a "provisional fixed point" by Rawls, he often appeals to it in criticisms of utilitarianism.

He also thinks that utilitarianism can avoid conflict with at least some of these considered judgments only by making empirical assumptions that prevent it from implying contrary judgments. I agree, including, in the case of Mill, empirical assumptions about what the competent judges would desire. I argued above that for Mill what is intrinsically good is what competent judges would prefer when choosing among things that would give them pleasure, not the satisfaction of *de facto* desires. Still, it is questionable that even in "favorable conditions" most of them would prefer greater basic liberties over well-being, prefer that all be treated as equals, and, in general, care about the happiness of others as much as their own. Many may prefer "plenty and a chain to liberty and a bone," [15] and favor their own interests and the interests of friends and loved ones over strangers.

There seem to be even more radical counterexamples to Mill's "choice criterion of value." Suppose it turned out that Mill's competent judges preferred the pleasure of child molesting to the pleasures of the intellect, contrary to what Mill believes. That would not make it true that it is better to molest children than to read a book, listen to music, visit a museum, watch a movie, or view a television series. Mill's choice criterion of value seems vulnerable to counterexample and must rely on general empirical facts to reach a match with our judgments of value. [16]

15. From Aesop's tales.

16. In *On What Matters*, Derek Parfit offers five examples that I will call *Agony, Anorexia, Burning Hotel, Early Death,* and *Revenge,* at least some of which seem to be clear counterexamples to what he calls Subjectivism. *Anorexia, Early Death, and Revenge* seem to involve giving up a lot for at most a little: *Anorexia,* a healthy life for a slim figure; *Early Death,* years of happiness and accomplishments for some trivial reason; *Revenge,* years of freedom and happiness

I think it would be an epistemic disadvantage for Mill's utilitarianism even if it could be shown empirically that competent judges would prefer what Mill calls "the higher pleasures" to the lower ones and what are intuitively moral pleasures to immoral ones. As Rawls says, that a "conception relies less on general facts in reaching a match with our judgments of justice [and that] It insures this fit over a wider range of possible cases" is an advantage (ATOJ, 160). As in science, so in philosophy, scope matters: other things being equal, a theory with greater scope and fewer auxiliary hypotheses is better than a theory with narrower scope and more auxiliary hypotheses. So even if Mill can defend a conception of social justice similar to Rawls's, Rawls's defense is superior.

I think the goal of moral philosophy should be to find necessarily true conditionals whose antecedents are as wide as possible consistent with the conditional's being necessarily true. In philosophy in general, I think the goal of theories is maximum scope with minimal reliance on empirical assumptions to accommodate *a priori* intuitions. Because Rawls's conception of social justice can meet that requirement better than Mill's, Rawls's defense is superior to Mill's.

REFERENCES

Berger, Fred R. 1984. *Happiness, Justice, and Freedom: The Moral and Political Philosophy of John Stuart Mill*. Berkeley: University of California Press.

Lyons, David. 1977. "Human Rights and the General Welfare." *Philosophy and Public Affairs* 6 (Winter), 113-29.

Lyons, David. 1976. "Mill's Theory of Morality." *Nous* 10 (May), 101-120.

to get back at someone for a trivial reason. There is no reason in principle why Mill's competent judges could not want what those in these examples are assumed to want.

Rawls, John. 1971. *A Theory of Justice*. Cambridge, MA: Harvard University Press.

Robson, John M. (ed.). 1963-1991. *The Collected Works of John Stuart Mill*. Toronto: University of Toronto Press.

Russell, Bruce. 1978. *Rawls and Utilitarianism: A Comparison and Critique*. Ph.D Dissertation: University of California at Davis.

Russell, Bruce. 2017. "A defense of moral intuitionism." In Peter Singer (Ed.) *Does Anything Really Matter: Essays on Parfit on Objectivity*, pp. 231-58. Oxford: Oxford University Press.

Urmson, J. O. 1953. "The interpretation of the moral philosophy of J. S. Mill." *The Philosophical Quarterly* 3 (January), 33-39.

ABOUT THE AUTHOR: Bruce Russell is a professor of philosophy at Wayne State University. He has essays on a wide variety of topics including: epistemology, ethics and meta-ethics, philosophy of religion (the problem of evil), and philosophy of film (on the philosophical limits of film). He is the author of the entry on *a priori* justification and knowledge in the *Stanford Encyclopedia of Philosophy*. He raises goats in California and has a winery there whose motto is: think deeply and play like a kid.
bruce.russell@wayne.edu

CHAPTER 16.

RHETORICAL ANALYSIS OF AESTHETIC POWER – IN MUSIC AND ORATORY

CHRISTIAN KOCK

ABSTRACT: The article attempts to make non-trivial statements about properties of great music that help make it "great." The examples are two movements by J.S. Bach. The approach is "rhetorical" in that it not only involves close scrutiny of the music itself, but also consideration of the impact that properties of the music may have on listeners. Phenomena like expectation, fulfilment, deferral, frustration and surprise are crucial here – all generated by the ways specific properties of the music may interact with an attentive listener. My analysis, I suggest, parallels St. Augustine's analyses of how selected biblical passages achieve great rhetorical impact.

KEYWORDS: Johann Sebastian Bach cello suites, music, rhetoric, form, Kenneth Burke, Leonard B. Meyer, anticipation, fulfilment, Augustine *De doctrina christiana*, Roman Jakobson

Kenneth Burke says in his first book, *Counter-Statement*, that "form is the creation of an appetite in the mind of the auditor, and the adequate satisfying of that appetite" (Burke 1931, 31).

For "appetite," say "desire" or "expectation." *Music* is particularly apt to raise such expectations because its interest to the audience depends less than that of literature on whatever content is conveyed, and correspondingly more on form. Burke says: "Music, then, fitted less than any other art for imparting information, deals minutely in frustrations and fulfilments of desire" (1931, 36).

The philosopher, musicologist and composer Leonard B. Meyer wrote about expectations, frustrations and fulfilments in his *Emotion and Meaning in Music* (1956). He was inspired by Dewey's *Art as Experience*, in particular the idea that emotion is generated when a tendency, an "urge," is inhibited. In a later article he explicitly connects these mechanisms for the creation of emotion and meaning in music with value. "Value," says Meyer, "has something to do with the activation of a musical impulse having tendencies toward a more or less definite goal and with the temporary resistance or inhibition of these tendencies" (1959, 489).

Burke would agree, but has more to say. In *Counter-Statement*, he cites the scene in *Hamlet* where Hamlet, Horatio and Marcellus meet at midnight, expecting Hamlet's father's ghost. It doesn't come. Instead they hear the trumpets as the King "keeps wassail" inside the castle, and they drift into other topics, such as the excessive drinking habits of Danes. *Then* the ghost arrives. Burke: "all this time we had been waiting for the ghost, and it comes at the one moment which was not pointing toward it. The ghost, so assiduously prepared for, is yet a surprise." Not only does the delay make for increased satisfaction; what also contributes is the fact that the resolution comes at an unexpected moment. Moreover, note that the ghost's arrival is simultaneously two opposite things: fully expected *and* surprising.

All this contributes to what Burke calls "eloquence." He further claims that eloquence, thus defined, "is simply the end of art, and is thus its essence" (1931, 41).

BACH'S CELLO SUITES, RHETORICALLY ANALYZED

I will try to show how such eloquence is also embodied in music by Johann Sebastian Bach. My examples are drawn from his suites for solo cello. Musicians call these suites "the cellists' Holy Grail." To understand why they have earned this exalted status – that of instantiating musical genius in pure form – I will approach them with a rhetorical ear and eye.

In Bach's day composers were told to study rhetoric; this helps explain why, for example, Bach called some of his keyboard works "Inventions," alluding to the rhetorical term. However, rhetorical terms, as they have mostly been applied to classical music in later times, refer to lesser, more local items: standard "figures" that are supposed to conventionally signify certain affects. But I suggest that if an analysis is to approach Bach's inventive genius, it must be rhetorical in a fuller sense. That implies going beyond figures based on conventional semiotic codes (such as "a falling semitone means a sigh") and integrating the *listener's involvement with the unfolding music*.

Rhetoric as I will understand it is about how human artifacts impact audiences. In musical rhetoric, *expectation* is central, especially expectation generated by relations between segments of the unfolding music – and, as we shall see, by relations between relations.

It is central to remember that listening to a piece of music is not like surveying a map – that is to say, a material, motionless object which, while it may have all sorts of interesting structural and semiotic properties, lacks the temporal-processual dimension. Listening is a *mental* and *temporal* phenomenon: to listen is to be part of an unfolding process, where the listener is aware of what has gone before, but unaware of what is to come. (Even in the case of texts that one has read before, or music that one knows well, a qualitative difference will persist between what was perceived before the present moment and what comes after, even if both are well-known. The nature of that difference will be a topic for another, rather complex discussion. It is worth noting, however, that neglecting that difference and treating, for example, a literary text as if everything in it were present to the interpreter's all-seeing eye simultaneously and in the same way is a fallacy that academics are particularly prone to.)

So, like all rhetoric, musical rhetoric must take into account that we deal with *temporal* artifacts in this sense; and we cannot take that into account without considering the artifact as something perceived, moment by moment, by a human perceiver – a listener.

The kind of rhetoric I speak for is one that tries to capture some of the sources of the aesthetic impact made by works of art, such as, e.g., these suites by Bach. Such rhetoric ventures to point to some of the features that allegedly makes this music especially "great"; it asks what makes certain works of music more aesthetically powerful than so much comparable music that, while respectable in its workmanship and deserving to be played, never attains anything like the same level of aesthetic merit.

In a sense, asking this sort of question is similar to doing what ancient rhetoricians did when they asked what makes, e.g., the rhetoric of Demosthenes much more powerful than that of other orators – or what make various passages and poems in diverse genres "sublime." The latter question was asked by the unknown rhetorician Longinus about the time of Christ when he wrote the famous treatise on the "sublime," *Peri hypsous*; among those who asked the former question was a writer like Hermogenes of Tarsus (of the second Century A.D.), who wrote, among other things, a treatise on *deinotēs* – the all-conquering power that words may wield over audiences. (*Deinos* is the word for "powerful" that is part of the compound "dinosaurus.")

In the world of music, what is this power, and what specifically is the difference between music that has it and music that does not? For example, a contemporary of Bach such as Georg Philipp Telemann had an output that was very much larger than even the massive production of Bach. Its craftsmanship is considered impeccable, and much of it is charming and certainly has value; Bach clearly respected his slightly older colleague. Yet there is general agreement that in nothing by Telemann do we reach the same level as with the best works of Bach.

It is not a new and alien idea that a rhetorical approach should help identify that in Bach which makes much of his music greater than anything by, for example, Telemann, or even than most of the works of Handel. But we do not often get analysis that uses rhetoric to do a close reading of the sources of aesthetic greatness; often the claims of analyzing greatness tend to be based on terms in which greatness is already implied, which gives them a question-begging or circular character. An example is this:

> We hear a great deal about the neglected minor masters; the one thing that separates them irrevocably and discretely from the great composers is that shattering force of imagination that produces music at the same time utterly original and quintessential, unprecedented and yet magnificently right. There is such works as the *Suscepit Israel* of the *Magnificat*, the opening pages of the B-minor Mass, the *Confiteor*, the *Dona nobis pacem*. They speak as unmistakably in terms of rhetoric as they operate within the sublime mathematics of Bach's technique. (Kerman 1949, 110)

In such a statement, despite its use of terms like "rhetoric" and "mathematics," much of what it says remains effusive and hard to pin down to the specific features of the notes Bach wrote. Terms like "shattering force," "utterly original," "magnificently right" or "sublime mathematics" make one ask: What more exactly constitutes this shattering, magnificent, sublime rhetoric in the music of Bach, and what is mathematical about it? Could we have pointed out to us in the scores where some of that greatness is, and what it is made of?

In all fairness, the article just quoted does proceed to make statements about the works mentioned that approach more specific, identifiable properties. Yet they still do not amount to actual close readings, pointing to notes on the page. Meyer tried to do that. In his 1959 article about "value and greatness in music," he looks closely at two composers' treatment of fugue subjects: one by Geminiani, another Bach, and he tries to show identifiable properties in Bach's treatment that make it aesthetically more powerful than Geminiani's.

Kenneth Burke had also been writing about similar questions for a couple of decades at that time, primarily in regard to literature, even though he was very knowledgeable about music too. He says, for example, that an "eloquent" work "bristles with disclosures, contrasts, restatements with a difference, ellipses, images, aphorism, volume, sound-values, in short all that complex wealth of minutiae which in their line-for-line aspect we call style and in their broader outlines call form" (1931, 37-38).

Bach's music bristles with "restatements with a difference." This is just one type of a relation between segments; one subtype of it is that a segment may be restated in a longer form. This may generate an expectation that an even longer version will follow. The notion of expectation makes further phenomena relevant: expectations may be fulfilled – *as* we expect and *when* we expect; or they may be fulfilled in a different way than expected, or at another point in time, or both; or it may be frustrated or diverted, and surprise may follow. Some phenomena pertain, not to relations between segments, but to *relations between relations* – and so forth. A complex play of phenomena ensues between the unfolding music and the listener, where, I suggest, an impression of aesthetic power or "greatness" may arise in listeners from a feeling that the music is always "one step ahead" in a reflective guessing game: the composer seems to have known and taken into account what we think he will be doing.

THE SIXTH SARABANDE

Let us first hear and consider the *sarabande* from cello suite #6. This suite, the last of the set of six, is by far the most complex of them, surely the most impressive and also the most technically demanding for the modern cellist, partly owing to the fact that it clearly was written for an instrument, unknown today, with five strings instead of four. A look at any edition shows a wealth of big chords and double stops far exceeding what we have in the other suites, to say nothing of some hair-rising rhythmical intricacies.

We will mainly look at linear aspects of the music, which are easier to follow by looking at the score. It will be a good idea for the reader to listen to a performance first. The Internet has dozens of them on YouTube and various streaming services, some audio, some video. If I may suggest a performance of the sarabande that I listen to with particular pleasure, it may be heard at the website julietandrupkock.com, under the heading "Media." (The performing cellist happens to be my daughter.)

The phenomena you will see and hear include parallelisms and *gradatio* patterns, either realized or merely expected; also, there will be surprises caused by unexpected turns, partial repetitions, and by an unpredictable alternation between patterns; in addition, on more than one level, we will find a pattern I call *climactic tricolon* – a pattern that helps create the inhibition Meyer talks about of the urge towards an anticipated resolution.

We may begin with a small-scale climactic tricolon. In one essay by Burke (reprinted in *Philosophy of Literary Form*) he lets Mark Antony of *Julius Caesar* address the audience on the work's "processes of appeal." Burke notes: "Friends, Romans, countrymen . . . one – two – three syllables: hence, in this progression, a magic formula."

The sarabande opens with a related formula: a gradual increment (a *gradatio*, as ancient rhetoricians would say) regarding the number of notes per measure: Measure 1 has three notes, measures 2 and 3 have four notes each, measure 4 has five notes. (A double stop counts as one note.) But the next four measures discreetly defy any expectation we may have at the present point of a repetition of this pattern: measure 5 does have three notes, and measure 6 has four, but measure 7 has six notes. However, if this makes us expect a quicker rise in the number of syllables (because we not only perceive relations between segments, but also relations between relations), then we find, surprisingly, that measure 8 only has three notes. In the excerpt below (Figure 1) the number of notes in each measure (an objective fact) is given in ordinary type; expectations that may be generated by these facts are given in italics.

Figure 1: The first part of the sarabande

After the first part of the movement (the above excerpt) has been repeated, the second part begins in measure 9 with the same rhythm as in measure 1 and measure 5, so we might expect the pattern to continue in measure 10 with the rhythm that we know from measure 2 and 6. That does not happen. On the other hand, measure 11 brings an unexpected repetition of the rhythm from measure 10. Will we then get more repetitions of it? No, but measure 12 unexpectedly brings us the same rhythm as we had in measures 2 and 6 – a rhythm that we may have expected in measure 10, but then we didn't get it.

Figure 2: The first 12 measures

Another of the bristling minutiae that make this piece come to life is its use of contrasting patterns. We have "jagged" bits with big leaps and dotted notes (as in measure 6), alternating with even, stepwise passages that make for a smooth motion (as in measure 7). Also, we have a constant but unpredictable change between measures with an emphatic second beat ("agogic accents" characteristic of sarabandes), and measures without them; in Figure 3 (below), measures with agogic accents are marked in one color (or dark shading) and those without them in another (or light shading). Further, glimpses of minor (measures 10-12 and 28-29) offset the prevailing major tonality.

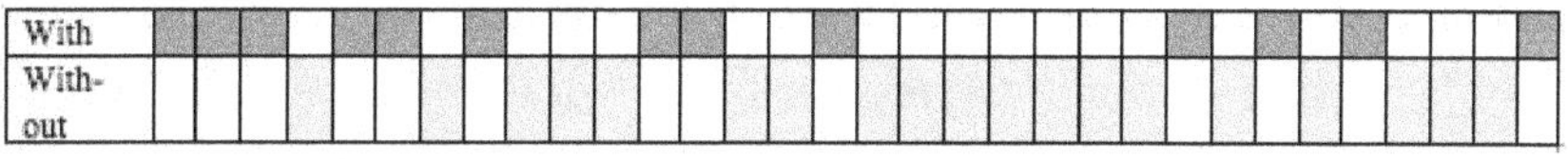

Figure 3: Measures with and without characteristic sarabande rhythm
(emphasis on second beat)

Furthermore, familiar rhythms alternate with new ones in a pattern that is irregular and unpredictable. Measure 13 and measure 14 give us two rhythmical patterns we have not heard before, but measure 15 repeats the rhythm of measure 7, and measure 16 repeats that of measures 2, 6 and 12. The measures that repeat rhythms heard earlier (illustrated in Figure 2 by the thin arrows that point backward in the music) help create a (probably subliminal) feeling of cohesion in the movement – a "web" of restatements with differences that tie it together, while at the same time creating a feeling of organic diversity. It is an effect reminiscent of many phenomena in nature.

A CULMINATING CLIMACTIC TRICOLON

A pattern involving larger units is the use of *tricolon*, more specifically tricolon with an expanded or otherwise more important third element; a term for this might be a *climactic tricolon*. This feature is a version of the "law of the number three," which the Danish folklorist Axel Olrik (1969 [1908]) considered to be one of the "epic laws" of folk narrative. It is at least as important in music. We may hear the whole sarabande as a climactic tricolon: the repeated first part constitutes the first two elements; the second part, which begins in a manner parallel with the first, but turns out to be three times as long, is the third, expanded element.

Also, measures 17-18, 19-20 and 21-24 constitute a climactic tricolon, as will be clear from a look at the score of the entire movement (Figure 4, below; as before, objective facts about the music are given in ordinary type, whereas expectations and other likely responses by a listener are given in italics). The three segments in this climactic tricolon form what musicologists call a sequence: the first segment (measures 17-18) is paralleled one step lower by the second (measures 19-20), and the third (measures 21-24) appears at first to restate the pattern yet another step lower; however, it continues and turns out to have four measures, while the first two elements had only two each.

After this sequence comes what appears to be a similar sequence: a new climactic tricolon that parallels the first seems to be under way. Measures 25-26 constitute the first element, while measure 27 appears to be the beginning of the second element. The expectation that the second climactic tricolon will be completed in a manner similar to the first is likely to be strong here; however, in measure 28 that expectation is abruptly thwarted by the eighth notes.

PATTERNS THAT GET BROKEN

At the same time, another expectation that may have formed subliminally in the listener up until now is also thwarted: so far, everything has been "divisible by four," i.e., the movement so far has consisted of four-measure units. This is a structure well known from most types of folk music used for dance; sarabandes also used to accompany a certain dance (one that churchmen originally considered vulgar and lewd). The expected third element of the second climactic tricolon would have been a four-measure unit. Instead, we get only three measures of that: in measure 28 we abruptly get a new beginning of something that turns out to be a five-measure ending.

Two small rhythmical surprises further contribute to the disruption that occurs here: in measure 28 we get the first eighth notes in the piece, but immediately after – in measure 29 – that effect is topped by another "first": two sixteenth notes, the latter of which is even part of a syncopation (also the first in the piece), creating a momentary "hobbling" effect.

All these "eloquent" local effects contribute to the overall effect of delaying the expected ending, inhibiting our desire for the goal we have foreseen all along. In the last measure the final tonic chord is delayed for a moment, one last time, by the C# on the first eighth note – an "appoggiatura," i.e., a preparatory note on the downbeat that does not belong to the following tonic chord.

Figure 4: The entire movement

EXPECTATION, PAINFULLY DEFERRED,
TRIUMPHANTLY FULFILLED

My second example is drawn from the Prelude of suite # 1. This is probably the most famous movement from the six suites and the one most frequently played and used in feature films, TV series and documentaries, etc. One memorable example is Peter Weir's 2003 period epic *Master and Commander*, in which the beginning of this movement accompanies the approach of Russell Crowe's English man-of-war to the unexplored Galapagos Islands.

The example is chosen to illustrate a singularly effective use of the delay technique also found on a smaller scale in the sarabande and used by Bach in innumerable pieces: creating an expectation, keeping it alive and intensifying it while delaying its fulfilment. In the words of Burke, Bach here executes "the creation of an appetite in the mind of the auditor, and the adequate satisfying of that appetite."

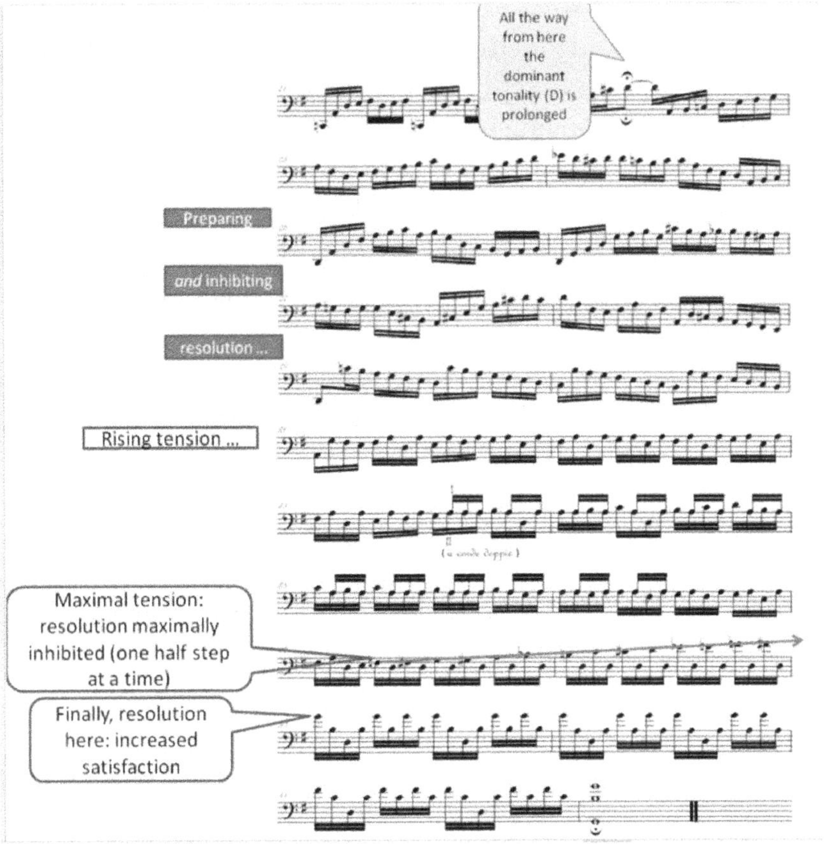

Figure 5: The last half of the Prelude from Suite no. 1

It is the principle that Leonard Meyer chose to focus on in his demonstration of what makes an excerpt from Bach aesthetically superior to one from Geminiani (1959). Meyer was a pioneer in the way he integrated the temporal unfolding of the music and the concurrent responses of the alert listener in his approach, on the background of a musicology dominated by a purely architectonic, *a*temporal conception of musical form. One of the few musicologists who also emphasized music as a temporal experience was Edward T. Cone (e.g., 1977; 2009). In philosophical aesthetics, Jerrold Levinson has argued compellingly, in *Music in the Moment* (1997) and elsewhere, that a musical work is an elapsing process, not an architectonic object. The ways in which musical aesthetics is thoroughly based on expectation are illuminated in David Huron's monograph *Sweet Anticipation* (2006).

The first cello prelude is a case in point to exemplify all these insights. Along with many other eloquent features, it exemplifies a unique degree of resistance to the desire for a resolution and, by the same token, it intensifies that desire in the listener. A verbal parallel that rhetorical scholars might remember is a passage in Martin Luther King's *Letter from Birmingham Jail*, as analyzed by Leff and Utley (2004): a 331-word sentence that delays the short, climactic main clause until the very end by enumerating the trials of segregation undergone by black Americans, thus iconically conveying their rising impatience by working up impatience in the readers. The first prelude is suited to metaphorically suggest an adventurous outgoing journey, followed by a long desired, long delayed triumphant homecoming – precisely the kind of story that the *Odyssey* narrates. One might think of the plot structure of countless folktales, or of Tolkien's *The Hobbit* – subtitled *There and Back Again*.

Figure 5 (above) shows the last half of the movement. Of the 42 measures, no less than 17 (measures 22-38) constitute one long prolongation of the tonality of the dominant, D major. This constantly heightens the desire for the expected resolution on the tonic (G major) – at the same time as it resists and defers that resolution. When it finally comes, the feeling of release and gratification is correspondingly great – we might say triumphant. The inserted comments point out key features.

Again, it is advisable to hear the a performance of the entire movement. (And again, the website julietandrupkock.com offers one, under the heading "Media.")

THE TRANSCENDENT APPEAL OF NUMBER

It may seem odd to suggest such a purely formal or "formalistic" analysis. But that is precisely the kind of analysis that Augustine offers in his attempt to demonstrate Paul's mastery of rhetoric – a part of his larger argument that Christianity should adopt and use the resources of rhetoric because the biblical writers themselves did. Throughout the analysis, Augustine points only to purely *numerical* and *grammatical* properties. There is no word in his commentary on Paul's theology or his religious exhortations to the Corinthian congregation. Instead, Augustine seems to focus exclusively on properties of the kind that arouse expectations, and on the extent to which expectations are either fulfilled or thwarted. All these phenomena are analogous to the phenomena I pointed out above in Bach's music.

In particular Augustine's analysis points out parallel patterns and *gradatio* patterns. A repeated property makes us expect that property to continue; a relation between units (e.g., an augmentation, where, for example, units in a series grow incrementally longer) makes us expect that relation to continue. For both, it is unpredictable how long the text will continue to fulfil our expectations by continuing these patterns, and to what extent it will thwart those expectations. An expectation thwarted surprises us and invites us to form new expectations. A pattern may be broken fully – or broken in some respect and continued it another, thereby fulfilling and thwarting our expectations at the same time.

The fact that Augustine's focus is so firmly on *formal* relations, especially those that may be expressed in *numbers*, might seem odd in such a great a theologian and philosopher as Augustine; but precisely in him, it is in fact not so odd.

Augustine himself was not only a formidable orator and a great rhetorical theorist; he was also deeply affected by music and wrote a large (but unfinished) treatise on it. He had been susceptible to aesthetic pleasure all his life, and his first work (written before his conversion, now lost) was a treatise on beauty, *De pulchro et apto*. In the *Confessions*, he writes about how deeply he was moved by the church music he heard at Milan, in particular Ambrose's hymn *Deus creator omnium*. As a Christian, he revised his earlier aesthetic theory, now seeing aesthetic pleasure as a step on the way to an understanding of the eternal truth of God's universe. As Brennan has it, "number was for Augustine the unifying principle in the movements of the stars, in geometry and in music" (1988, 270).

This was in essence the theory that he expounded in the highly complex and sophisticated treatise *De musica* (written 387-391). Its central idea is that numbers, the simple integers, explain the capacity music has to engross us – and also that they may open our minds to the divine constitution of the universe. Similarly, in his analysis of powerful biblical rhetoric, Augustine seems to have seen simple numerical relations as crucial to the capacity of the highest rhetoric to captivate us, just as they were crucial to music's aesthetic power and to an understanding of the deepest nature of the universe.

UNDERSTANDING THE POWER OF PAUL'S ORATORY

To start from the beginning of the passage that Augustine has analyzed from Paul's Second Epistle to the Corinthians, we note that he simply describes segment #1 as a *circuitus* with two *membra*. These are grammatical terms that do not exactly fit the ones used by grammarians nowadays in analyzing modern languages, but they have to do with the size and hierarchical status of the units in question. A *circuitus* (plural *circuitūs*) is broadly speaking the counterpart of a complete sentence – a fully "rounded" unit (hence *circuitus*). A *membrum*, as that term suggests, is a part of a sentence that is one step lower hierarchically – loosely corresponding to what we would call a "clause." Finally, there is a *caesum*, derived from *caedo*, to cut or sever – in other words, a unit lower than a clause, corresponding to our "phrase."

As the table (Figure 6) shows, the first three segments constitute a series with three *circuitūs* consisting of two, three and four *membra*, respectively, in that order. The second segment is grammatically similar to the first in being a *circuitus* made of *membra*, but on this background there is a difference: it has three *membra* rather than two. This, I suggest, will create a (secondary) expectation in a listener/reader that the relation between the first two units (we may call it an augmentation) will be followed up by a further augmentation from segment 2 to segment 3. And this expectation, as the table shows, is fulfilled. In rhetorical terms, we now seem to have a *gradatio* – a figure that one might well expect, perhaps more strongly than before, to continue with a further augmentation in the following unit(s). That expectation, however, is thwarted: segment 4 only has two *membra*.

The listener/reader – if he or she is at all attuned to expecting oratory of some power – may now assume or expect that a new series or pattern is under way. The augmentation series seems to have been discontinued, but a series of *circuitūs* that all have two *membra* might be a possibility. If this new expectation has in fact been created in the listener, segment 5 confirms it; if it has not been created yet, segment 5 creates it by being formally similar to segment 4: a *circuitus* with two *membra*. Thus, it is now very natural for the reader/listener to expect a continuation of this similarity series, and that in fact happens: segment 6 too is a *circuitus* with two *membra*. Will this series continue? No, segment 7 is short, consisting of just three *caesa*. Now what? The reader/listener who remembers what has gone before might now be expecting a new kind of inter-segment relation on a higher level: first, there was an augmentation series of three segments; then came a similarity series, also of three segments—so a natural expectation will be that somehow segments will continue to come in sets of three.

The table goes on for a few more verses to indicate how Augustine's analytical comments seem consistently to concern formal (grammatical) features that may cause "the creation of an appetite in the mind of the auditor, and the adequate satisfying of that appetite," to quote Burke; Augustine's analysis goes on for good deal longer, but throughout it he concentrates on how Paul has deployed his building blocks "with tasteful variety" (*cum decentissima varietate*), expressed in terms of grammatical concepts and numbers.

Note that to apply Burke's "adequate satisfying" formula to what Bach does in his music and Paul in his epistolary oratory (as analyzed by Augustine), we must take these words in a wide sense: they cannot just refer to expectations fulfilled in exactly the way the "auditor" expects them to be. Burke, in another of the quotes we began with, talks about both "frustrations and fulfilments of desire," and in the scene from *Hamlet* he notes that although the ghost appears just *as* Hamlet, his companions and the audience expect it will, it doesn't appear *when* they expect it.

Great music and great oratory have in common, among other things, that they raise expectations which they sometimes fulfil, sometimes defy, perhaps in a surprising way, thereby perhaps raising new and different expectations. Sometimes these expectations are deferred but kept alive, which increases their intensity and makes the fulfilment so much more satisfying when it eventually comes; sometimes the fulfilment of the expectation comes not only at an unexpected moment, but in an unexpected way.

A fascinating commentary on the whole of *Hamlet*, presented by the great psychologist L.S. Vygotsky in his early work, *The Psychology of Art* (completed as a PhD dissertation in 1925, English translation 1971), argues that the curve of the entire play depends on the satisfying of an appetite (for revenge of Hamlet's father's murder)—an appetite almost endlessly deferred and

Segment N[0]	Latin	English	Augustine's analysis	Listener/reader experience
1	iterum dico, ne quis me existimet insipientem esse;	I repeat, let nobody take me for a fool;	circuitus with 2 membra	
2	alioquin velut insipientem suscipite me, ut et ego modicum quid glorier.	Or if you do, then accept me as a fool, so that I too may have my little boast.	circiutus with 3 membra	The sentence is one clause longer. *Expectation:* a gradatio with even more clauses in the sentence
3	Quod loquor non loquor secundum deum, sed quasi in stuititia, in hac substantia gloriae.	What I am saying I am saying not with the Lord's authority, but as a fool, in this boastful confidence.	circuitus with 4 membra	Expectation fulfilled. *Expectation:* gradatio to continue
4	Quonian quidem multi gloriantur secundum carnem, et ego gloriabor.	Since many people boast of worldly things, I will boast too.	circuitus with 2 membra	Expectation thwarted. *Expectation:* bipartite structure to continue?
5	Libenter enim sustinetis insipientes, cum sitis sapientes.	For although wise yourselves, you gladly tolerate fools.	circuitus with 2 membra	Expectation fulfilled. *Expectation:* bipartite structure to continue
6	Toleratis enim, si quis vos in servitutem redigit,	You put up with it if someone makes slaves of you,	circuitus with 2 membra	Expectation fulfilled. *Expectation:* bipartite structure to continue
7	si quis devorat, si quis accipit, si quis extollitur,	if someone preys on you, if someone takes advantage of you, or puts on airs,	3 caesa	Expectation thwarted. Surprise: the previous sentence continues with a string of three short clauses *Expectation:* tripartite structure to continue?
8	si quis in faciem vos caedit. Secundum ignobilitatem dico, quasi nos infirmati sumus.	or if someone slaps you in the face. I speak in terms of embarrassment, as though I was made to look weak.	3 membra	Expectation fulfilled. *Expectations:* tripartite structure to continue; gradatio (from caesa to membra) underway?
9	In quo autem quis audet (in insipientia dico), audeo et ego.	But whatever anyone dares to boast of (I am speaking as a fool), I dare to boast of it too.	3 membra	Expectation fulfilled: tripartite structure repeated; expectation thwarted: gradatio not under way. *Expectation:* tripartite structure to continue
10	Hebraei sunt? et ego. Israelitae sunt? et ego.	Are they Hebrews? I am too. Are they Israelites? I am too. Are they the	3 question-caesa with 3 answer-caesa	Expectation fulfilled: tripartite structure repeated. Surprise: gradatio is now

Figure 6: Augustine's analysis of Corinthians II, 11, 16-30 in De Docrina Christiana IV, 7

forgotten, and then suddenly fulfilled, in an unexpected way and at an unexpected moment. Vygotsky's idea in this work, that the "psychology of art" is the psychology of the *audience*, not the author, is paralleled verbatim by ideas developed by Burke at the same time and put forth in *Counter-Statement*. All these phenomena, we should remember, are involved in the "adequate satisfying" of our appetites and expectations, that is to say, in the way a musical or verbal artifact creates them and handles them.

THE LISTENER'S ROLE

It should be emphasized that in the kind of rhetorical analysis I have attempted above, and in the way I read Augustine's analysis of biblical rhetoric, there is a key factor that (still) gets little systematic attention in academic analyses of, for example, great music: the unfolding experience of the listener (the audience). As soon as one talks about "appetites" or "expectations," one involves some construction of the listener. If one does not want to talk about the listener's experience because it is felt to be too unwieldy, variable and subjective, then all notions of expectations and the phenomena that go along with it – such as memory, fulfilment, frustration, surprise, suspense, and several others – are excluded from one's analysis, and that analysis will, I suggest, be correspondingly barren and oblivious of most of the factors that matter most in aesthetic experience.

This is where rhetoric – always mindful of audience – ought to do a better job. As I have noted, there have been thinkers in antiquity as well as in modern times who have felt a need to integrate the audience perspective to be able to talk about what is great – whether in oratory, literature, or music. One more pioneering scholar should also be mentioned: Roman Jakobson. Although he was one of the founders of modern structuralism, he was also, unlike many structuralists, keenly aware of the audience perspective. However, he tended to express that awareness in objectifying, purely structural terms. For example, one of his most quoted pronouncements regarding what he calls "the poetic function of language" says, in italics: *The poetic function projects the principle of equivalence from the axis of selection into the axis of combination* (1960, 358). What this means is essentially that in the poetic function of language, there is a focus on noticing and comparing units along the unfolding sequence of a text (what Jakobson calls the *syntagmatic* dimension of the text) – units that are either similar or different, or both in some combination. In the above analyses, precisely that kind of comparison was constantly at the center. But who performs the noticing and comparing – and all the other mental operations that depend on them? No one but the reader – the audience – the listener. Doing that means to be activating the poetic function; the poetic function is a transaction between artifact and perceiver. Jakobson, in another famous dictum, says: "The set (*Einstellung*) toward the message as such, focus on the message for its own sake, is the poetic function of language" (1960, 356). Here it is quite clear that this "set" exists nowhere but in the reader/audience/listener.

Likewise, being the audience for great rhetoric or literature or music means to be "set" or *eingestellt* or attuned to the sort of phenomena that Augustine's analysis of Paul's text looks at, and which my analyses of Bach's music similarly attempt to explore. The greatness of Bach's music, I suggest, lies in its structurally based capacity to initiate an interaction between artifact and listener that the listener experiences as great.

REFERENCES

Augustine. 1996. *De Doctrina Christiana*. Edited and translated by R.P.H. Green. Oxford: Oxford University Press.

Brennan, B. 1988. Augustine's "De musica." *Vigiliae Christianae*, 42(3), 267-281.

Burke, Kenneth. 1931. *Counter-Statement*. Berkeley: The University of California Press.

Burke, Kenneth. 1967. Antony on behalf of the play. In *The Philosophy of Literary Form: Studies in Symbolic Action*, 2nd ed., pp. 329–343. Baton Rouge, LA: Louisiana State University Press. Orig. in Southern Review 1935.

Cone, E. T. 1977. Three ways of reading a detective story OR a Brahms Intermezzo. *The Georgia Review* 31(3): 554-574.

Cone, E. T. 2009. *Hearing and Knowing Music: The Unpublished Essays of Edward T. Cone.* Princeton University Press.

Dewey, John. 1934. *Art as Experience.* New York: Minton, Balch & Company.

Huron, David. 2006. *Sweet Anticipation. Music and the Psychology of Expectation.* Cambridge, MA: MIT Press.

Jakobson, Roman. 1960. *Linguistics and Poetics. In Style in Language.* Cambridge, MA: MIT Press, 350-377. Repr. in *Selected Writings III (Poetry of Grammar and Grammar of Poetry).* The Hague: Mouton, 18-51.

Kerman, J. 1949. Rhetoric and technique in J.S. Bach. *The Hudson Review*, 2(1): 105-112.

Leff, M. C., & Utley, E. A. 2004. Instrumental and constitutive rhetoric in Martin Luther King Jr.'s "Letter from Birmingham Jail." *Rhetoric & Public Affairs*, 7(1), 37-51.

Levinson, Jerrold. 1997. *Music in the Moment.* Ithaca: Cornell University Press.

Longinus. 2014. *On the Sublime.* Translated by Benjamin Jowett. Scotts Valley, CA: CreateSpace.

Meyer, Leonard B. 1956. *Emotion and Meaning in Music.* Chicago: University of Chicago Press.

Meyer, Leonard B. 1959. Some remarks on value and greatness in music. *The Journal of Aesthetics and Art Criticism* 17(4): 486-500.

Olrik, Axel. 1908. Episke love i folkedigtningen. *Danske Studier* 5: 69-89. Translation: The epic laws of folk narrative." English translation in A. Dundes, (Ed.), *The Study of Folklore*, pp. 131–141. Englewood Cliffs, NJ: Prentice-Hall 1965.

Vygotsky, Lev Semenovich, and V. V. Ivanov. 1971. *The Psychology of Art.* Translated by Scripta Technica. Cambridge, MA: MIT Press.

Wooten, Cyril W. 1987. *Hermogenes on Types of Style.* Chapel Hill: University of North Carolina Press.

ABOUT THE AUTHOR: Christian Kock is Emeritus Professor of Rhetoric at the University of Copenhagen. He has done research on political argumentation and debate, the history of rhetoric, rhetorical citizenship, credibility, journalism, literary studies, aesthetics, linguistics and writing pedagogy. He is author, editor, co-author or co-editor of c. 20 books in Danish and English, most recently *Rhetorical Deliberation: Arguing about Doing* (Windsor Studies in Argumentation) and numerous articles for scholarly as well general audiences. He is a frequent commentator in the media on rhetoric and political debate. His main non-academic interest is music; he has played in, chaired or served on the board of various ensembles and organizations in classical music.

HANS V. HANSEN PUBLICATIONS

SELECTED PUBLICATIONS OF HANS VILHELM HANSEN

Books Edited:

Hansen, Hans V., Fred J. Kauffeld, James B. Freeman & Lilian Bermejo-Luque (Eds.). (2018). *Presumptions and Burdens of Proof, An Anthology of Argumentation and the Law.* Tuscaloosa, AB: University of Alabama Press. Pp. x, 1-305.

Hansen, Hans V. (Ed.). (2017). Christian Kock, *Deliberative Rhetoric: Arguing About Doing.* Windsor, ON: Windsor Studies in Argumentation. Pp. x, 1-366.

Hansen, Hans V. (Ed.). (2014). *Riel's Defence: Perspectives on his Speeches.* Montreal: McGill Queen's University Press, Pp. viii. 1-331. [Also the author of the Introduction (pp. 1-18) and the Preface (pp. 19-24).]

Hansen, Hans V. & Pinto, Robert C. (Eds.). (2007). *Reason Reclaimed: Essays in Honor of J.A. Blair and R.H. Johnson.* Newport News, VA: Vale Press. Pp. xiv, 1-313.

Hansen, Hans V. & Walton, Douglas (Eds.). (2006). *Fundamentals of Critical Argumentation, Vol. 1.* Critical Reasoning and Argumentation. Cambridge: Cambridge University Press.

Hansen, Hans V. & Pinto, Robert C. (Eds.). (1995). *Fallacies: Classical and Contemporary Readings.* University Park, PA: Pennsylvania State University Press. Pp. xii,1-356. [Also the author of the Introductions to Part I (pp. 3-18) and to Part IV (pp. 315-317).]

Chapters in Books:

Hansen, Hans V. (2019). In search of a workable auxiliary condition for authority arguments. In F.H. van Eemeren (ed.), *Argument Schemes to Argumentative Relations in the Wild*, pp. 25-40. Cham, CH: Springer.

Hansen, Hans V. (Ed.) (2014). Louis Riel's address to the jury. In H.V., Hansen (ed.), *Riel's Defence, Perspectives on His Speeches*, pp. 35-44. Montréal: McGill-Queen's University Press.

Hansen, Hans V. (Ed.) (2014). Louis Riel's address to the court. In H.V., Hansen (ed.), *Riel's Defence, Perspectives on His Speeches*, pp. 45-71. Montréal: McGill-Queen's University Press.

Hansen, Hans V. (2014). Narrative and logical order in Louis Riel's address to the jury. In H.V. Hansen (ed.), *Riel's Defence. Perspectives on His Speeches*, pp. 135-165. Montréal: McGill-Queen's University Press.

Hansen., Hans V. (2014). Mill, Informal logic, and argumentation. In Anton Loizides (ed.), *John Stuart Mill's A System of Logic: Critical Appraisals*, pp.192-217. London: Routledge.

Hansen, Hans V. (2012). An enquiry into the methods of informal logic. In Henrique Jales Ribeiro (ed.), *Inside Arguments: Logic and the Study of Argumentation*, pp. 101-16. Newcastle upon Tyne: Cambridge Scholars Publishing.

Hansen, Hans V. (2011). Notes on balance-of-consideration arguments. In J.A. Blair & R.H. Johnson (eds.), *Conductive Arguments: An Overlooked Type of Defeasible Reasoning*, pp. 31-51. London: College Hans V., (2006) Mill and Pragma-Dialectics. In P. Houtlosser & A. van Rees (eds.), *Considering Pragma-Dialectics*, pp. 97-107. Mahwah NJ: Lawrence Erlbaum.

McLeod, Jane A. and Hansen, Hans V. (2005). Argument density and argument diversity in the license applications of French provincial printers, 1669-1781. In F.H. van Eemeren & P. Houtlosser (eds.), *Argumentation in Practice*, pp. 321-336. Philadelphia: John Benjamins

Hansen, Hans V. (2003). The rabbit in the hat: The internal relations of the Pragma-Dialectical rules? In F.H. van Eemeren, J.A. Blair, C.A, Willard & A.F. Snoeck Henkemans, (eds), *Anyone Who Has a View*, pp. 55-68. Dordrecht: Kluwer.

Hansen, Hans V. (1997). Mill on inference and fallacies. In D.N. Walton & A. Brinton (eds.), *Historical Foundations of Informal Logic*, pp. 125-143. Aldershot: Ashgate.

Articles in Refereed/Peer Reviewed Journals:

Hansen, Hans V. (2019). Fallacies, *Stanford Encyclopedia of Philosophy* (19000 words). 4-year update and revision of 2015.

Hansen, Hans V. (2016). Studying argumentative behaviour, *Cogito*, 7, 29-46. Invited.

Hansen, Hans V. & Fioret, Cameron (2016). A searchable bibliography of fallacies, *Informal Logic*, 36, 432-472.

Hansen, Hans V. (2015). Whately on kinds of arguments, *Cogency*, 7, 81-108.

Hansen, Hans V. (2015). Fallacies, *Stanford Encyclopedia of Philosophy* (Invited.)

Hansen, Hans V. & Walton, Douglas (2013). Argument kinds and argument roles in the Ontario provincial election, *Journal of Argumentation in Context*, 2, 226-258.

Walton, Douglas & Hansen, H.V. (2013). Arguments from fairness and misplaced priorities in political argumentation, *Journal of Politics and Law*, 6, 78-94.

Hansen, Hans V. & McLeod, Jane (2012). Petitioning the king: The case of provincial printers in eighteenth-century France, *Argumentation*, 26, 161-70.

Hansen, Hans V. (2002). Whately on arguments involving authority, *Informal Logic*, 26, 319-340.

Hansen, Hans V. (2002) An exploration of Johnson's sense of 'argument', *Argumentation*, 16(3), 263-276.

Hansen, Hans V. (2002). The straw thing of fallacy theory: The standard definition of 'fallacy', *Argumentation*, 16(2), 133-155.

Woods, John & Hansen, Hans V. (2001). The subtleties of Aristotle on non-cause, *Logique et Analyse*, 44(176): 395-415.

Hansen, Hans V. (2000). Logic and misery: Walton's "Appeal to Pity", Critical Study. *Informal Logic*, 20, 169-184.

Hansen, Hans V. (1998). Locke and Whately on the argumenation *ad ignorantiam*, *Philosophy & Rhetoric*, 31, 55-63.

Woods, John & Hansen, Hans V. (1997). Hintikka on Aristotle's fallacies, *Synthese*, 113, 217-239.

Hansen, Hans V. (1996). Whately on the ad hominem: A liberal exegesis, *Philosophy & Rhetoric*, 24, 400-415.

Hansen, H. Vilhelm (1994). Reductio without assumptions? *Logique et Analyse*, 37(147-148), 329-337.

Hansen, Hans V. (1990), An informal logic bibliography, *Informal Logic*, 12, 155-184.

Articles in Refereed/Peer-Reviewed Conference, Symposia. Roundtable, Proceedings and Publications:

Hansen, Hans V. (2016). Studying argumentative behaviour, *Dialogues in Argumentation*. In Ron von Burg (ed.), Windsor Studies in Argumentation, Venice Conference.

Hansen, Hans V. (2012). Are there methods of informal logic? In Frank Zenker (ed.), *Argumentation: Cognition and Commu-*

nity, Proceedings of OSSA 9 conference, 2011. Windsor, ON: OSSA, CD Rom.

Hansen, Hans V. (2012). Commentary on "Whose Toulmin and which Logic?". In Frank Zenker (ed.), *Argumentation: Cognition and Community* , Proceedings of OSSA 9 conference 2011. Windsor, ON: OSSA, CD Rom.

Hansen, Hans.V., Godden, David; Groarke, Leo (2012)., Informal logic and argumentation: An Alta conversation. In R.C. Rowland (ed.), *Reasoned Argument and Social Change*—Proceedings of the 2011 Alta Conference. NCA, 48-62.

Hansen, Hans V. (2012). Political discourse and argumentation profiles. In *Proceedings of 2012 Croatia Rhetoric Conference*. Windsor, ON: Windsor Studies in Argumentation.

Hansen, Hans V. (2011). Using argument schemes as a method of informal logic. In F.H. van Eemeren, B. Garssen, D. Godden and G. Mitchell (eds.), *Proceedings of 7th ISSA conference* (2010), pp. 738-749. Amsterdam: SicSat (CD Rom).

Hansen, HansV. (2009) Commentary on Mohammed's "Ad hominem as a derailment of confrontational stage manoeuvring. In J. Ritola (ed.), *Argument Cultures* (Proceedings of OSSA 8). Windsor, ON: OSSA, CD Rom.

Hansen, Hans V. (2007). Feteris on teleological evaluative argumentation. In H.V. Hansen, C.W.Tindale. J.A. Blair & R.H. Johnson (eds.), *Dissensus & Search for Common Ground* (Proceedings of OSSA 7). Windsor ON: OSSA CD-Rom.

Hansen, Hans V. (2007). Mill on Argumentation, *Proceedings of the 6th conference on the International Society for the Study of Argumentation*, pp. 571-581. Amsterdam, SicSat.

Hansen, Hans V. (2005). Did Mill have a theory of argumentation? Abstract. In D. Hitchcock (ed.), *The Uses of Argument*, Proceedings of the OSSA Conference at McMaster University, p. 189. Hamilton, ON: McMaster University.

Hansen, Hans V. (2003). Commentary on James Freeman's "Progress without regress on the dialectical tier". In J.A. Blair,

D. Farr, H.V. Hansen, R.H. Johnson & C.W. Tindale (eds.), *Informal Logic @ 25*, Proceedings of the Windsor conference of OSSA, 2003. Windsor, ON: OSSA CD-ROM.

Hansen, Hans V. (2003) Theories of presumption and burden of proof In J.A. Blair, D. Farr, H.V. Hansen, R.H. Johnson & C.W. Tindale (eds.), *Informal Logic @ 25*, Proceedings of the Windsor conference of OSSA, 2003. Windsor, ON: OSSA CD-ROM.

Hansen, Hans V. & McLeod, Jane A. (2002). Argumentation Theory as a Tool of Historical Analysis: Arguments used to obtain printer licences in eighteenth-century France, pp. 753-758. In F.H. van Eemeren, J.A. Blair & C.A. Willard (eds.), *Proceedings of the 5th ISSA Conference.* Amsterdam: Sic Sat.

Hansen, Hans V. (2002). The rabbit in the hat. In F.H. van Eemeren, J.A. Blair & C.A. Willard (eds.), *Proceedings of the 5th ISSA Conference*, pp. 433-436. Amsterdam: Sic Sat.

Hansen, Hans V. (2002). Professor Krabbe's wider sense of 'dialectic'. In H.V. Hansen, C.W.Tindale. J.A. Blair, R.H. Johnson & R.C. Pinto (eds.), *Argumentation and its Applications*, Proceedings of the OSSA 2001 conference. Windsor, ON: CD-Rom

Hansen, Hans V., (2000). Commentary on Zagars's "What about the context?" In C.W. Tindale, H.V. Hansen & E. Sveda, *Argumentation at the Century's Turn*, Proceedings of OSSA 1999. St. Catharines, ON: OSSA, CD-Rom.

Hansen, Hans V. (1999). Argumental deduction: A program for informal logic. In F.H. van Eemeren, R. Grootendorst, J.A, Blair & C.A. Willard (eds.), *Proceedings of the 4th Conference of the International Society for the Study of Argumentation*, pp. 311-316. Amsterdam, Sic Sat.

Hansen, Hans V. (1998). Commentary on Dale Jacquette, In H.V. Hansen, C.W. Tindale & A.W. Colman (eds.), *Argumentation and Rhetoric*, Proceedings of OSSA 1997 at Brock University. St. Catharines, ON: OSSA, CD-Rom.

Hansen, Hans V.(1996). Aristotle, Whately, and the taxonomy of fallacies. In D.M. Gabbay & H.J. Ohlbach, *Practical Reasoning:*

International Conference on Formal and Applied Practical Reasoning, pp. 318-330. Berlin, Springer.

Conference Proceedings Edited:

Hansen, H.V., Tindale, C.W., Blair, J.A. & Johnson, R.H. (Eds.) (2007) *Dissensus & the Search for Common Ground*. Proceedings of the 7th OSSA conference. Windsor, ON: OSSA, CD Rom.

Tindale C.W., Hansen, H.V., Blair, J.A., Johnson, R.H. & Pinto, R.C. (Eds.). (2004). *Informal Logic @ 25*, Proceedings of the 2003 OSSA conference. Windsor, ON: OSSA/University of Windsor, CD-Rom.

Hansen, H.V., Tindale, C.W., Blair, J.A. & Johnson, R.H. (Eds.). (2003). *Argumentation and its Applications*. Proceedings of the 2001 OSSA conference. Windsor, ON: OSSA/SSHRC, CD-Rom.

Tindale, C.W., Hansen, H.V. & Sveda, E. (Eds.). (1999). *Argumentation at the Century's Turn*, Proceedings of the 1999 OSSA conference. St. Catharines, ON: OSSA, CD-Rom.

Hansen, H.V., Tindale, C.W. & Colman, A.V. (Eds.). (1998). *Argumentation and Rhetoric*, Proceedings of the 1997 OSSA conference. St. Catharines, ON: OSSA & SSHRC, CD-Rom.

Tindale, C.W. & Hansen, H.V. (Eds.). (1998). Rhetorical *Considerations in the Study of Argumentation*. Selected papers from the 1997 OSSA conference, Brock University. *Argumentation* 12(2), 141-340.

Hansen, H.V. & Tindale, C.W. (Eds.). (1995). *Argumentation and Education*. Selected papers from the 1995 OSSA conference, Brock University. *Informal Logic*, 17(2), 123-324.

Book Reviews of . . .

Gensler, Harry J. (2005). *Historical Dictionary of Logic*. In *Informal Logic*. Pp. 185-188.

Freeman, James, B., (2005). *Acceptable premises: An Epistemic approach to an informal logic problem*. In *Notre Dame Philosophical Reviews*.

Eemeren, F.H. van, Grootendorst, R., Blair, J.A. and Willard, C.A. (eds.) (1998). *Fundamentals of Argumentation Theory*. In *Philosophy & Rhetoric*, 31. Pp. 71-74.

William Hughes, *Critical Thinking: An Introduction to the Basic Skills*. (1994). In *Informal Logic*, 16, pp. 141-145.

Paul Teller (1992). *A Modern Formal Logic Primer, i and ii*. In *Teaching Philosophy*, 15, pp. 378-380.

Ruchlis, Hy (1991). *Clear Thinking*. In *Teaching Philosophy*, 14, pp. 85-88.

Walton, Douglas N. (1991). *Practical Reasoning*. In *Argumentation*, 5(4), pp. 449-453.

Workshops Presented:

Hansen, Hans V. New directions in argumentation scholarship, *Rhetorical Society of Americas Biennial Institute*, Kent State University, Kent, Ohio, 2005.

www.ingramcontent.com/pod-product-compliance
Lightning Source LLC
Chambersburg PA
CBHW030013110426

42741CB00033B/846